Accession no.
01143236

D1685605

Irish Studies

LIBRARY

Tel: 01244 375444   Ext: 3301

This book is to be returned on or before the
last date stamped below. Overdue charges
will be incurred by the late return of books.

UNIVERSITY COLLEGE
CHESTER

CANCELLED
CANCELLED

1 5 MAR 2006

Other titles in *The Essential Glossary* series

Forthcoming

Irish Studies
The Essential Glossary

Editor: John Goodby

Authors: Alex Davis
John Goodby
Andrew Hadfield
Eve Patten

LIBRARY

ACC. No.   DEPT.
01143236

CLASS No.

**UNIVERSITY
COLLEGE CHESTER**

·1675096

ARNOLD

A member of the Hodder Headline Group
LONDON
Distributed in the United States of America by
Oxford University Press Inc., New York

First published in Great Britain in 2003 by
Arnold, a member of the Hodder Headline Group,
338 Euston Road, London NW1 3BH

http://www.arnoldpublishers.com

Distributed in the United States of America by
Oxford University Press Inc.,
198 Madison Avenue, New York, NY10016

© 2003 Arnold

All rights reserved. No part of this publication may be reproduced or
transmitted in any form or by any means, electronically or mechanically,
including photocopying, recording or any information storage or retrieval
system, without either prior permission in writing from the publisher or a
licence permitting restricted copying. In the United Kingdom such licences
are issued by the Copyright Licensing Agency: 90 Tottenham Court Road,
London W1T 4LP.

The advice and information in this book are believed to be true and
accurate at the date of going to press, but neither the authors nor the publisher
can accept any legal responsibility or liability for any errors or omissions.

British Library Cataloguing in Publication Data
A catalogue record for this book is available from the British Library

Library of Congress Cataloging-in-Publication Data
A catalog record for this book is available from the Library of Congress

ISBN 0 340 80740 7 (hb)
ISBN 0 340 80741 5 (pb)

1 2 3 4 5 6 7 8 9 10

Typeset in 10/13pt Minion by Phoenix Photosetting, Chatham, Kent
Printed and bound in Great Britain by MPG Books Ltd, Bodmin, Cornwall

What do you think about this book? Or any other Arnold title?
Please send your comments to feedback.arnold@hodder.co.uk

Contents

Preface

Ireland is a favourite subject of study and discussion, both in the English-speaking world and further afield. There are many reasons for this. Standing as it does as the main marker of the 'Celtic', Ireland boasts a rich cultural heritage, one distinguished above all by its outstanding literary achievement. Its history is a complex, often traumatic one, which offers many parallels with those of contemporary emergent nations, while its continuing divisions are reminders of the consequences of empire – metropolitan and ex-colonial, industrialized (even post-industrialized). Yet, still perceived in terms of rural stereotypes, Ireland in both the Republic and Northern Ireland illustrates many of the problems attaching to that much-questioned concept, 'the nation'. Complicating things still further is the fact that, although it is a small country, with a tiny population, Ireland has had an influence on the world out of all proportion to its size and wealth, through emigration and the acquisition and mastery of an international lingua franca, English. In all of these various ways, it remains one of the most striking examples we have of supposedly ex-centric, marginal cultures shaping those presumed to be dominant.

Irish Studies, as opposed to Irish history, or the study of Irish literature, is a new discipline. It has developed over the last 20 or so years from a fruitful, if occasionally confusing, convergence of several subjects, history, economics, literature, music, cultural studies, colonial and postcolonial theory, and migration studies among them. It has emerged, above all, from an understanding of the rich anomalousness of Ireland, of the pluralism and variety of Irish experiences. Thus, it is often at variance with the desire for some essential 'Irishness', sensing as it does that such a desire often says more about non-Irish expectations than any local requirement for authenticity. Irish Studies comprehends, that is, the extent to which Irish experience involves an often contradictory, even paradoxical combination of the 'backward look' and breakneck modernization, from the time of the first colonial plantations to the decade of the peace process and the 'Celtic Tiger'. Nowhere is this more apparent than in the rise of 'Irish Studies' itself, which originated not only in Ireland but also in the Irish diaspora – a diaspora marked by the very combination of ruthless modernity and fierce nostalgia which was the subject of its concern. Yet if the size of Ireland is belied by its contribution to the world, this nevertheless makes it more graspable than many other cultures. As a result, a glossary such as this can offer to cover a wide range of topics with a fair degree of comprehensiveness. And, while the main focus has been on the twentieth century, the amount of material dealing with earlier periods – roughly half – is generous enough to allow the reader to understand in some depth the forces which have shaped the Ireland of today.

There are around 400 entries, all written by the four authors listed on the dustjacket, each of whom is an expert in his or her period. The small number of contributors ensures that there is consistency in the standard, style and tone of the entries. Andrew Hadfield is responsible for the pre-1800 entries, Eve Patten for those on the nineteenth century, while the twentieth century has been split, with Alex Davis taking the first half and myself the second. As editor, of course, I have sought to ensure the accuracy of all the material included; final responsibility for any faults, flaws and omissions is mine alone. Each entry in the glossary seeks to convey the essentials of the subject, but we have necessarily been selective. We hope, however, that readers will follow up cross-references and Index entries as appropriate, and will wish to pursue our suggestions for further reading.

As this implies, the glossary can be used in a number of ways. In straight reference mode, the reader may simply look up relevant entries in their alphabetical place, ranging from the Abbey Theatre to W. B. Yeats. In a more exploratory mode, the reader may follow the cross-references between entries. All words in small capitals within the text are also headwords (or close cognates) for other entries. In this way, readers will be able to map out their own paths of discovery, building up a larger picture of the subject and its contexts. In thematic mode, a reader may wish to read a group of entries covering a series of related events or topics. These are given in the list of themes which follows. Many of these deal with specific historical events; we have tried to write these in a way which allows a continuous narrative to be constructed by the reader who seeks to follow a chronological trail. In a more haphazard, but potentially equally rewarding, way, the reader is encouraged to use the Index to follow up lines of enquiry which are not specified by the glossary entries. The comprehensive nature of the Index will allow more fugitive links and connections to be made, permitting the reader to read athwart or against the grain of orthodox narratives and canonical listings. Finally, readers may take up the suggestion to consult the further reading recommendations; the full form of these references is given in the Bibliography.

Themes

Historical topics

Historical periods or moments

In rough chronological order: archaeology, Tara, Celts, Vikings, Norman Invasion, Reformation, Counter-Reformation, Williamite Wars, Penal Laws, Catholic Emancipation, World War I, World War II, neutrality, economic expansion, the Troubles, 'Celtic Tiger'.

Significant events

Norman Invasion, Nine Years War, Battle of Kinsale, Flight of the Earls, Rebellion of 1641, Battle of the Boyne, Act of Union, Famine, Dublin Lockout, Easter Rising, Anglo-Irish War, Civil War, Boundary Commission, Constitution, Republic, economic expansion, internment, Bloody Sunday, Anglo-Irish Agreement (1985), Downing Street Declaration (1993), Smythe Case, Good Friday Agreement (1998).

Colonialism and relations with Britain to 1968

Laudabiliter, colonization and plantation, The Pale, Munster Plantation, Ulster Plantation, New English, Old English, Oliver Cromwell, Penal Laws, United Irishmen, absenteeism, Phoenix Park Murders, Anglo-Irish War (Black and Tans), Stormont, Economic War, Republic of Ireland.

Troubles and peace process

Troubles, New Ireland Forum, internment, Bloody Sunday, power sharing, direct rule, Anglo-Irish Agreement (1985), Downing Street Declaration (1993), Good Friday Agreement (1998).

Themes

Social and political topics

Political parties

Cumann na nGhaeleadh, Fianna Fáil, Fine Gael, (Irish) Labour Party, Northern Ireland Labour Party (NILP), Irish Parliamentary Party, Sinn Féin, Social Democratic and Labour Party (SDLP), (Ulster) Unionist Party and Democratic Unionist Party (see unionism).

Political groups and movements

boycott, Catholic Committee, Northern Ireland Civil Rights Association (NICRA), Defenders, Irish Volunteers, Irish Citizen Army (ICA), Land League, Orange Order, Ulster Defence Association (UDA), Ulster Volunteer Force (UVF), Volunteers, Whiteboys, Young Ireland.

Cultural institutions

Abbey Theatre, Aosdána, Gate Theatre, National Gallery of Ireland and Municipal Gallery, Royal Irish Academy.

Religion

Catholism, Catholic Emancipation, Catholicism, Church, Irish, Druids, Penal Laws, Presbyterianism, Church of Ireland, Reformation and Counter-Reformation, inquiries and tribunals, souperism.

Economy

agriculture, 'Celtic Tiger', Economic War, economy, economic expansion, emigration, laissez-faire, population.

Law

Brehon Law, parliaments, Poyning's Law, Statutes of Kilkenny, Land Acts, Home Rule, Stormont, Dáil, Constitution, Coercion Acts.

Education and welfare

hedge schools, Literacy, Maynooth, medicine, Poor Law, Queen's Colleges, Trinity College Dublin (TCD).

Gender issues

abortion, Constitution, contraception, divorce, women (social position of), sexuality, 'X' Case.

Ideas and movements in culture

Genres

architecture, art (painting and sculpture), bardic poetry, 'Big House', drama, film, music (classical), rock and pop music traditional and folk music, showbands, statues (Dublin), television and radio.

Cultural movements and leisure

antiquarianism, cultural nationalism, Young Ireland, Literary Revival, Gaelic League, Irish-Ireland, Belfast Group, Gaelic Athletic Association (GAA), tourism.

Publishing, press and media

censorship, journals, newspapers, *The Nation*, *The Bell*, *Dublin University Magazine*, Dolmen Press, film, radio and television.

Legend and myth

Cú Chulainn, mythology, *Lebor Gabála Érenn*, Literary Revival, *Táin Bó Cuailnge*.

Theoretical debates

authenticity, hybridity, modernization, modernization theory, revisionism, colonialism and postcolonialism, women (social position of).

Notes on authors

John Goodby is Senior Lecturer in English at the University of Wales, Swansea. He has published widely on Irish and British poetry and is the author of *Irish Poetry since 1950: From Stillness into History* (2000). He edited the twentieth-century Irish poetry section of the online *Annotated Bibliography for English Studies* (1998), *Colonies of Belief: Ireland's Modernists* (1999) (with Maurice Scully) and the New Casebook title *Dylan Thomas* (2001) (with Chris Wigginton). He was a member of the ESRC's Transnational Communities programme Axial Writing project (1998–2002), investigating contemporary representations of Irishness in England.

Alex Davis is Senior Lecturer in English at University College Cork. He has written widely on English, Irish and American literature and is the author of *A Broken Line: Denis Devlin and Irish Poetic Modernism* (2000), and editor of *Modernism and Ireland: The Poetry of the 1930s* (1995) (with Patricia Coughlan), and *The Locations of Literary Modernism* (2000) (with Lee Jenkins). He founded, and has been chief organizer of, the regular series of UCC conferences on new and experimental Irish poetry.

Andrew Hadfield is Professor of English at the University of Wales, Aberystwyth. He has published extensively on Irish history and culture, and is the author of *Spenser's Irish Experience: Wilde Fruit and Salvage Soyle* (1997). He edited *Representing Ireland: Literature and the Origins of Conflict, 1534–1660* (1993), with Willy Maley and Brendan Bradshaw and *Strangers to that Land: British Perceptions of Ireland from the Reformation to the Famine* (1994), with John McVeagh. He is the co-editor of vol. III of *The History of the Irish Book* (with Raymond Gillespie) and is a regular reviewer for the *Times Literary Supplement*.

Eve Patten is Lecturer in English at Trinity College Dublin. She held a two-year Junior Fellowship at the Institute of Irish Studies in Queen's University Belfast before spending three years with the British Council in Eastern Europe, and has published widely on nineteenth- and twentieth-century Irish writing (recent articles deal with the ideology of Irish science, W. B. Yeats, Emily Lawless, the Northern Irish novel, contemporary Irish fiction and Irish-English literary relations). She is editor of the Irish Cultural Studies section of the online *Annotated Bibliography for English Studies* (1998) and is a contributor to Blackwell's *Companion to Irish Culture*. She is currently completing a book on civic culture in Victorian Ireland and is a regular reviewer for the *Irish Times*.

Acknowledgements

I should like to thank my fellow contributors, Eve Patten, Andrew Hadfield and Alex Davis, for their time, tolerance of the vagaries of email editing, and ability to condense complex issues within the constraints set by the glossary format. I would also like to thank Ronan Kelly, who acted as Eve Patten's Research Assistant, for his valuable contribution to the book. From all of them I learnt much about Ireland, and even more about the limits of my own knowledge.

As the editor, I am grateful personally to many friends and colleagues for the invaluable support they gave when I was working on the glossary and writing my share of contributions to it. Along with the other contributors, these include Marcella Edwards, Caroline and Mike Franklin, Ann Heilmann, Rob and Caroline Penhallurick, Neil Reeve, Steve Vine, Chris Wigginton, and Tom and Marie Cheesman. I would also like to register my debt to the courteous and efficient staff of the Inter-Library Loans section at the Library of University of Wales, Swansea, and to our first editor at Arnold, Elena Seymenliyskaya, as well as her successor, Eva Martinez. A prolonged bout of illness interrupted my labours on the glossary in the summer of 2001, and it would be remiss of me not to express my deep gratitude to staff at the Singleton NHS Trust Hospital, particularly those attached to Ward 11 and the hydrotherapy and physiotherapy units, for their care, skill and patience in nursing me back to health.

Finally, I realize that while we were working on the book it was – as always – those closest to the four of us who had to put up with most. From all of us, then, it is to our long-suffering families that this glossary is dedicated.

John Goodby
Swansea
November 2002

Abbey Theatre The Irish Literary Theatre (ILT), subsequently Irish National Theatre, known as the Abbey Theatre, was the brainchild in 1897 of W. B. YEATS, Augusta, Lady GREGORY and Edward Martyn. The Irish Literary Theatre's opening productions, in 1899, were Yeats's *The Countess Cathleen* and Martyn's *The Heather Field*. Opposition greeted Yeats's play, which had been accused of anti-CATHOLIC and anti-Irish sentiments; nevertheless, the first season was generally well received.

In 1900 the ILT staged Martyn's *Maeve*, Alice Milligan's *The Last Feast of the Fianna*, and George MOORE's *The Bending of the Bough*. 1901 saw a double-bill of Moore and Yeats's *Diarmuid and Gráinne* and Douglas HYDES's *Casadh an tSúgáin* (*The Twisting of the Rope*), directed by William Fay.

The ILT folded in 1901; but Fay's Irish National Dramatic Company, which included Fay's brother, Frank, effectively continued it in 1902 with Yeats's *Cathleen Ni Houlihan*, featuring Maud GONNE in the title role, and George Russell's *Deirdre*. In 1903, the National Theatre Society was formed, with Yeats as president and Fay as stage-manager. The Irish National Theatre's productions in 1903 included Yeats's *The Pot of Broth* and Lady Gregory's first play, *Twenty-Five*. In October of that year, J. M. SYNGE's *In the Shadow of the Glen* was staged, with Fay in the role of the tramp. It was attacked by Arthur GRIFFITH, but with Synge the theatre had found a major dramatist, and his *Riders to the Sea* followed in 1904.

In 1904 the society found a permanent home in Abbey Street, thanks to the patronage of Annie Horniman, a wealthy admirer of Yeats, who gave the theatre an annual grant until 1910. Yeats now placed himself, Synge and Gregory in firm control of the Abbey's repertoire, and in 1910 Lennox Robinson became manager and, later, fellow director with Yeats and Gregory. New plays by Yeats, Gregory and Padraic Colum in 1905–6 were followed by the production of Synge's *The Playboy of the Western World* on 27 February 1907, which was broken up by protests, and outraged nationalist and Gaelic circles owing to its apparently demeaning depiction of the Irish peasantry. In 1909 the Abbey staged George Bernard SHAW's *The Shewing-up of Blanco Posnet*, banned in England; it was the first of several Shaw productions, including *Arms and the Man* (1916) and *Man and Superman* (1917). Notable productions during the 1920s were Sean O'CASEY's *The Shadow of a Gunman* (1923), *Juno and the Paycock* (1924) and *The Plough and the Stars* (1926). In 1924, the Abbey became state-subsidized, and a government appointee joined the directors.

From the 1930s through the 1960s, the Abbey's production values flagged, and many of the new plays it staged were of doubtful merit, though there were exceptions, such as M. J. Molloy's *The King of Friday's Men* (1948). In 1951, it burnt down; the new theatre opened in 1966, though plays were performed at other venues in the intervening years.

Much of the major work of leading Irish dramatists, including Brian FRIEL, Tom MURPHY, John B. Keane, Thomas Kilroy, Frank McGuinness and Tom McIntyre, has been performed since the 1960s at the Abbey.

Further reading

Fermor (1954). Frazier (1990). Gregory (1913). Welch (2003).

abortion   Abortion became a major issue in Irish politics in the 1980s. Following the legalization of abortion in the UK in 1967, Irish women went there for terminations (the number is now estimated to be 6,000 per annum). Public opinion in the Republic followed the teaching of the CATHOLIC CHURCH in condemning abortion, but silently allowed it to be dealt with abroad. In the wake of the success of the McGee case on CONTRACEPTION, however, conservative groups such as Society for the Protection of the Unborn Child (SPUC) formed the Pro-Life Amendment Campaign. Their aim was to pre-emptively amend the CONSTITUTION to prevent abortion ever being carried out in Ireland. In 1983 they persuaded the government to call a referendum to guarantee the right to life of the foetus, which they won: 35 per cent of the electorate voted in favour of an eighth amendment, Article 40.3; the majority of 'yes' to 'no' votes was 425,096 out of a total electorate of 2,358,651.

To date, the Irish legislature has not enacted any statute to implement the amendment, although it did allow SPUC to seek injunctions to stop abortion counselling and the giving of information which would help women obtain abortions in Britain. The difficulty of using a constitutional prohibition to deal with such a complex moral and social question was highlighted when a High Court ban on an under-age rape victim travelling abroad to obtain an abortion (the 'X' CASE) was overturned by the Supreme Court in 1992. Following this, a second referendum, held later that year, amended the Constitution to take into account the right to travel and for freedom of access to information. While women may now receive 'non-directive counselling' on abortion, they cannot be informed as to where a termination of a pregnancy may be obtained. Books with information on the subject have been censored, as have magazines with articles on abortion or counselling services.

The 1967 Abortion Act has still not been extended to Northern Ireland, and it is estimated that 40 women a day travel from there to the UK for abortions. The anti-abortion campaigns south of the border forged unusual alliances in the north, with fundamentalist Protestant churches there supporting the Catholic Church in its backing of the 1983 amendment, while many northern Catholics supported the CHURCH OF IRELAND, PRESBYTERIAN and other churches in the Republic, which questioned the right of the state to legislate in such areas. Abortion remains a highly contentious issue; in March 2002, Pro-Life groups forced a referendum to outlaw the advances made by reformers in the 'X' case, but the vote confirmed the earlier ruling. In the Republic in particular the depth of passions aroused shows that the abortion debate touches a raw nerve of national self-identity, and fears concerning MODERNIZATION, the changing role of the family, and the increasing independence of women.

Further reading

Garvin (1988). McWilliams in Hughes (ed.) (1991). http://struggle.ws/wsm/abortion.html

absenteeism The practice whereby Irish landlords resided in England, leaving the management of their Irish estate to agents or 'middlemen'. Their absence was widely resented, as it often led to a lack of investment in and poor administration of their Irish land. Absentee landlords came to stand as a symbol of English indifference to Irish needs, and were frequently caricatured in the writing of the period: see Maria EDGEWORTH's novel *The Absentee* (1812).

Act of Union The measure which effectively abolished the Irish PARLIAMENT and instituted the LORD LIEUTENANCY and Dublin Castle as the seat of government in Ireland, with MPs from 100 Irish constituencies transferred, along with 32 peers, to Westminster. The concept was grounded in British fears of what separation might lead to, particularly in the wake of the UNITED IRISHMEN-led rebellion of 1798 and continued peasant agitation. It was also encouraged by the vision of the British Isles as a complete economic partnership and trading unit, with Ireland expected to contribute to UK expenses at a ratio of two to fifteen (though the Irish Exchequer remained separate until 1816, and Britain continued to impose a tariff on Irish grain imports).

The Union was highly controversial, and opposed by many on both sides of the religious divide. The leader of Ireland's last independent parliament, Henry GRATTAN, led a vociferous campaign against the move, stressing its intrinsic religious discrimination – CATHOLICS were still excluded from parliamentary and state office – and its perceived economic and representational inequity. Others were inevitably in favour of the protection and imperial consolidation the Act was seen to offer. The bill, which was initially narrowly defeated in January 1799, eventually passed through both parliaments during the following year, and came into force in January 1801.

The Union marked a watershed in British and Irish relations, with historians subsequently divided over the extent to which it exacerbated Irish economic decline, particularly when war with France increased the financial demands placed on both countries. The post-Union decades were to see continued agitation for REPEAL of the Union in a series of popular and political agitations, including the national campaign led by Daniel O'CONNELL. Meanwhile, representations of the country depicted pre-Union Ireland as a glorious epoch of Irish cultural and political independence, set against the degradations of the nineteenth century. Maria EDGEWORTH's 1800 novel *Castle Rackrent* is frequently cited (somewhat anachronistically) as symbolizing the eclipse of a pre-Union Ascendancy. In twentieth-century writing, Seamus HEANEY's poem 'Act of Union' (*North*, 1975), translates the event into the image of a forced coupling between a masculine, imperial England and a feminine, subjected Ireland.

Further reading

Foster (1988).

Adams, Gerry (1948–)   Militant republican, politician, author. Born West Belfast and President of Sɪɴɴ Féɪɴ since 1983, Adams sided with the Provisional IRA in the split of 1969–70. He was one of the IRA leaders who met the British government for talks in 1972, and while imprisoned in the Maze Prison (H-Blocks) began to formulate, with Danny Morrison and Martin McGuinness, the strategy of a simultaneous armed and democratic struggle which emerged from the ʜᴜɴɢᴇʀ sᴛʀɪᴋᴇs of 1980–81. He became MP for West Belfast in 1983. An astute and forceful leader, Adams is the first to have aligned the military and political wings of ʀᴇᴘᴜʙʟɪᴄᴀɴɪsᴍ since Partition. He is the author of *The Politics of Irish Freedom* (1986), which takes a view of Irish history as straightforwardly ᴘᴏsᴛᴄᴏʟᴏɴɪᴀʟ, and of a bestselling autobiography, *Before the Dawn* (1996).

Further Reading

Adams (1986, 1996). Coogan (1996).

'AE' (Russell, George William) (1867–1935)   Poet, painter, visionary and economist. Born in Co. Armagh, Russell moved to Dᴜʙʟɪɴ in 1878 where, at the Metropolitan School of Art, he met W. B. Yᴇᴀᴛs. His spiritualist preoccupations, reinforced by Yeats, led him to join the Theosophical Society in 1886, write for *The Irish Theosophist*, co-edit the Theosophical *The Internationalist* and, in 1898, establish the Hermetic Society, the latter devoted to the study of the ideas of Madame Blavatsky. Russell's Cᴇʟᴛɪᴄ mysticism conjoined a pragmatic social vision for Ireland. In 1897 he began working for Sir Horace Pʟᴜɴᴋᴇᴛᴛ's co-operative venture, the Irish Agricultural Organization Society, and he edited the society's journal, *The Irish Homestead*, from 1905 to 1923, and its successor, *The Irish Statesman*, from 1923 to 1930 (see ʟɪᴛᴇʀᴀʀʏ ᴀɴᴅ ᴄᴜʟᴛᴜʀᴀʟ ᴊᴏᴜʀɴᴀʟs). As editor, Russell tirelessly promoted the work of many younger Irish poets, including Padraic Colum, Susan Mitchell and Seamus O'Sullivan. He included their work in the important anthology, *New Songs*, a volume which broke with the introspective verse and wavering cadences of the Celtic Twilight in favour of more robust folkloric forms. However, Russell's own poetry, from *Homeward: Songs by the Way* (1894) up until the *Collected Poems* (1913), remained mystical and conventionally symbolist. Of his prose works, *The Candle of Vision* (1918) explores Russell's mystic life, and its concentration on the relationship between inner and national life was continued in *The Inner and the Outer Ireland* (1921).

Russell refused a nomination to the Irish Senate in 1922. Increasingly disillusioned with the Irish Free State, he emigrated to England in 1933, where he died.

Further reading

Allen (2003).

agriculture and agrarianism   Throughout its history Ireland has been identified as a predominantly agricultural economy, its land – though prone to problems of poor drainage – fertile and rich in resources. Its earliest economic system was pasturage. Though there was some supplementary grain tillage, cattle farming dominated the culture and cattle were prized as currency – hence the frequency of cattle raids, such as that described in the Gaelic epic, the Táin bó Cuailnge. In the sixteenth century, Plantation would alter farming patterns slightly, with the introduction of orchards and fenced enclosures on the larger estates, but, overall, farming methods remained primitive despite the beginnings of a countrywide road system. As the population expanded, grain harvesting increased with bread becoming a mainstay of the diet. The potato also made its appearance, and by the late eighteenth century had become a staple, as a generally reliable crop easily grown on remaindered land and providing some degree of nutrition. Over-reliance on the 'lumper' potato, however, grown widely across the country by the nineteenth century, would lead to devastation during the Famine.

The majority of the rural Irish held no land of their own, but leased and farmed what they could afford on estates run by middlemen, in the frequent absence of the landlords (see ABSENTEEISM). Many labourers or cottiers simply worked where they could for pay, often travelling huge distances. But small farms were not economical and many landlords and large lease-holding farmers were keen to move towards larger, demesne-sized units. In the long wake of the Famine, as families struggled and failed to pay rents, evictions and clearances became an increasingly common occurrence in rural life, as vividly depicted by novelists such as William Carleton and Charles Kickham. Tensions over land continued to rise, particularly as profits fell. In the late 1870s, a combination of bad harvests and falling grain prices led to crisis, with 1879, when the potato crop suffered widespread blight, a disastrous year for Irish agriculture. These pressures on the system combined with persistent claims for tenant rights and land acquisition, leading ultimately to the formation of the Land League and the agrarian outrages of the Land War (1879–82). Prime minister Gladstone's first Land Act of 1881 did little to alleviate long-term problems, and the agrarian disturbances and campaigns of rent resistance continued into the late 1880s. By the turn of the century, many landlords were keen to sell up. The Wyndham Land Act of 1903, which facilitated tenant purchase of the land, was therefore a major step towards a complete overhaul of the Irish land economy. But difficulties would persist into the twentieth century, with labour-intensive farming, lack of investment, and continued patterns of high EMIGRATION contributing to the underdevelopment of Irish agriculture as a whole.

Those who worked on the land played a major part in shaping Irish society after

Independence, since the Land Acts had created a relatively stable and conservative small farmer class. The co-operative movement was a new development from the 1890s, which united and helped small farmers, and had a particular success in dairy processing where eventually 100 per cent of the industry came under farmer control (see Sir Horace PLUNKETT). But in general agricultural improvement was very slow; small, uneconomic, marginal farms in the West persisted, while wealthy graziers increased elsewhere. Moreover, international market conditions kept Irish farming locked into this framework, and the cost of the ECONOMIC WAR with Britain in the 1930s was largely borne by small farmers.

One problem was the preponderance of small uneconomic farms in the West; the government attempted to deal with this by setting up the Congested Districts Board in 1891 by BALFOUR. This had purchased and redistributed over 2,000,000 acres by 1923; renamed the Land Commission, it allocated a further 2,800,000 acres to about 140,000 families before being wound up in the 1980s (although by that time the subsistence groups in rural society had largely been squeezed out). Even so, the harshness of life on the land drove many to leave it during the 1940s and 1950s. The gap between the reality and government ideal is best illustrated in Éamon DE VALERA's PATRICK'S DAY BROADCAST of 1943 (and rural electrification, for example, was not completed until the 1970s). The small farmer economy collapsed in the late 1950s as the output from larger farms drew level with it, and important small farm enterprises, such as pig and poultry rearing, became industrialized. Although Irish membership of the Common Market after 1973 helped maintain farming's importance through subsidies from the European Common Agricultural Fund, it was eclipsed during the 'CELTIC TIGER' decade of the 1990s, when the industrial and services sectors were transformed. As a result agriculture today accounts for only 7 per cent of total employment and 5 per cent of exports.

Further reading

Brody (1973). Crotty (1966). Drudy (ed.) (1982).

alcohol   The Irish traditionally drink more alcohol than other Europeans. Indulgence was encouraged by the association of alcohol with social events such as wakes, weddings and festivals. During the eighteenth century, whiskey (*usquebaugh*) became the most widely consumed drink, along with poteen (*poitín*), a spirit illegally brewed from potatoes. In the nineteenth century, the national movement for temperance gained widespread support and, by the 1840s, the production of whiskey in Ireland had almost halved (see FATHER MATHEW). Historians have also suggested that the stereotype of the drunken Irishman was largely an English myth, fabricated to support the concept of a nation unfit to govern itself.

Further reading

Malcolm (1986).

Allingham, William (1824–1889)   Poet, editor and diarist. Born in Ballyshannon, Co. Donegal, William Allingham worked as a customs officer and, later, as editor of *Fraser's Magazine*. A friend of English poets Alfred Tennyson and Robert Browning, and of writer and political prophet Thomas Carlyle, he was also close to members of the Pre-Raphaelite artistic brotherhood, with Dante Gabriel Rossetti providing illustrations for Allingham's *Day and Night Songs* (1854) and *Flower Pieces and Other Poems* (1888). Allingham is usually noted for his journal, published as *A Diary* (1907), which, along with his extensive correspondence, provides lively material on the leading Irish and British literary figures of the day. Politically, he was known as a sympathizer with the Irish peasantry, and his long poem, 'Lawrence Bloomfield in Ireland' (1864), which includes evocative scenes of peasant evictions, promotes a policy of liberal paternalism among Ireland's landlord classes. Generally his poetry is regarded as minor and sentimental, though interesting for its descriptions of Irish rural life and scenery, and W. B. YEATS would later applaud him as 'the poet of Ballyshannon'. A keen folklorist, he is remembered for his much anthologized poem 'The Fairies'.

Anglo-Irish   A term used to describe the English-speaking Protestant aristocracy which dominated Irish government from the eighteenth century onwards. The term 'ascendancy' is also frequently used. The Protestant landed class came to dominate Irish life after the end of the WILLIAMITE WARS and the defeat of the Catholics resulting in the confiscation of their land. Anglo-Irish literature refers to Irish writing in English but is rarely used now partly because of the association with the Anglo-Irish ascendancy in the eighteenth century and partly because it homogenizes a whole series of different types of writing. This in turn makes it seem as if all the varieties of writing in English produced in Ireland – much of which does not describe Ireland and some of which is indifferent or hostile to Ireland and the Irish – belong to the same tradition.

Further reading

Beckett (1976).

Anglo-Irish Agreement (1938)   This was a fundamental revision of the 1921 treaty with Britain, and marked the end of the ECONOMIC WAR. It followed the redefinition of the Irish relationship with Britain contained in the 1937 CONSTITUTION. By it, Ireland recovered the naval facilities the British had kept at Berehaven, Cobh and Lough Swilly. Britain waived its claim on £100m in annuities for a lump sum of £10m. Ireland assured Britain that these ports would not be used against her in case of war. The importance of the Agreement was that Ireland could declare itself neutral in future, since none of its territory was being used by another power.

Further reading

Lee (1993).

Anglo-Irish Agreement (Hillsborough Accord) (1985)   The British and Irish governments had established links as early as 1980 on cross-border security, sharing power supplies and trade agreements, initiating a process which would lead to the 1985 treaty. 1980 also saw them establish an Anglo-Irish Intergovernmental Council to continue co-operation on what were significantly defined, for the first time, as 'the totality of relationships within these islands'. Even as it met, however, relations between the two governments soured over the HUNGER STRIKES of 1980–81 and the Falklands War (1982), during which Charles HAUGHEY's FIANNA FÁIL government called for a UN-negotiated settlement, angering the British. On the other side, the British attempt to evolve a purely internal settlement by setting up an Assembly for Northern Ireland in 1982, without consulting Dublin, annoyed both the nationalist parties there and in Northern Ireland. The SDLP and SINN FÉIN stood in elections to the Assembly in that year, but refused to take their seats by way of protest.

Nevertheless, a momentum was maintained on the long-term effort to find solutions. The NEW IRELAND FORUM, which met in 1983 to explore solutions within an Anglo-Irish framework, was one way in which this was done. A new urgency was injected into the broader process with Sinn Féin's successful embrace of electoral politics. In the 1982 Assembly elections they did well; subsequently they threatened to supplant the SDLP as the main nationalist party in the province (by 1985, for example, Sinn Féin were winning seven seats on BELFAST city council to the SDLP's six). Both British and Irish governments were forced to support the SDLP in order to demonstrate to the CATHOLIC population that its constitutional NATIONALISM could benefit them more than Sinn Féin's 'ballot box and armalite' strategy. This could only be done by broadening the context of any solution beyond the Britain–Northern Ireland axis. Talks between Margaret Thatcher, the British Prime Minister, and the two Taoisachs, Haughey and Garrett FITZGERALD, continued, despite Thatcher's rejection of the recommendations of the NEW IRELAND FORUM in November 1984.

What finally emerged from the negotiations was the ANGLO-IRELAND AGREEMENT of 15 November. This created a joint ministerial conference of British and Irish ministers, backed by a joint secretariat of civil servants at Mayfield in Northern Ireland to monitor political, legal and other issues of interest to nationalists. It also stated that the British government's aim was devolution of power to a body having 'widespread acceptance' – in other words, not one which permitted the dictatorship by a majority, as had been the case with STORMONT. But the emotive phrase 'POWER SHARING' was not used, and these concessions to nationalists were matched by the Agreement's confirmation of the constitutional status quo of Northern Ireland, by which the government of the Republic officially accepted that unification could not occur without the approval of the majority of the population there.

Despite this acceptance, unionists were furious both with the content of the Agreement and with the fact that their political parties had not been consulted, although the SDLP clearly had. The trauma of this moment was best captured in a speech by the UUP MP Harold McCusker in the House of Commons, when he described how on 15 November he had stood outside Hillsborough Castle in the rain 'like a dog and asked the Government to put in my hand the document that sold my birthright' (a graphic image captured in Tom PAULIN's poem 'An Ulster Unionist Walks the Streets of London'). Among other things, one effect was to sever the long-standing links between the British Conservative Party and the UUP.

On 23 November James Molyneaux, leader of the Unionist Party, and Ian PAISLEY of the DUP, addressed up to 200,000 unionists outside Belfast City Hall and launched a protest and a campaign of 'passive resistance' to the agreement. But there was no repeat of the overthrow of the power-sharing executive of 1974, since there was no devolved structure for loyalists to destroy. The 13 Unionist MPs resigned their seats and forced by-elections in January 1986, allowing the unionist population to express its opposition to the Agreement. But overall unionist support fell 80,000 votes short of the 500,000 target the unionist parties had set themselves. On the other hand, Sinn Féin's share of the nationalist vote dropped from 42 per cent to 35 per cent. This suggested to the British and Irish governments that their strategy was working and should not be changed.

Further reading

Arthur (2000).

Anglo-Irish Treaty (1921) Constitutional provision for Partition having been passed at Westminster in December 1920, public and political opinion, and army demoralization, forced the British government to agree a truce in the ANGLO-IRISH WAR in July 1921. DE VALERA sent a delegation to London which included Michael COLLINS, Arthur GRIFFITH, George Gavan Duffy and Erskine Childers; the British delegation was headed by the British Prime Minister, Lloyd George. Britain had already rejected De Valera's proposal of a form of 'external association' between Britain and Ireland, with Ireland having reciprocal citizenship and republican status within the Commonwealth (that is, within the group of Dominion status nations – Canada, Australia, New Zealand, South Africa). The Irish rejected British offers of Imperial Dominion status because it would involve Ireland too deeply in the British Empire. Britain then offered a special, less compromising form of the Oath of Allegiance (retitled 'Fidelity') to the Crown. The treaty provided for complete independence in domestic affairs, full fiscal autonomy, and an almost free hand in external affairs, and accepted, on the Irish side, the British strategic need to continue to occupy their naval bases in Ireland. The real sticking-point lay in recognition of the Crown, however qualified; technically, it meant that the 26-county state recognized by the treaty could not be called a 'Republic'. Faced with resistance, Lloyd George threatened the immediate resumption of hostilities; but he also offered the inducement of a BOUNDARY COMMISSION to fix the borders of Northern Ireland. The implication was that at least two of the six counties claimed by

UNIONISTS would be given to the Free State, and that the remaining statelet would prove to be unviable, and would have to throw in its lot with the Free State. Under duress, the delegation signed the treaty. Although the Supreme Council of the IRB passed the treaty by eleven votes to four, the DÁIL only ratified the treaty by a tiny majority of seven, on 7 January 1922, with De Valera opposing it. As divisions hardened between treatyites and anti-treatyites, CIVIL WAR loomed.

Further reading

Foster (1988). Lee (1993).

Anglo-Irish War (War of Independence) (1919–1921) Following SINN FÉIN's victory in the December 1918 elections, divisions swiftly developed between those REPUBLICANS who felt a negotiated independence was possible and those who felt that only force of arms would achieve this aim. It was to advance this latter position that on 29 January 1919 Tipperary IRISH VOLUNTEERS (soon to be known as the IRISH REPUBLICAN ARMY, or IRA) killed two members of the Royal Irish Constabulary (RIC). A pattern of arms raids on barracks and killings of policemen developed through the year. From mid-1919, as leader of the IRISH REPUBLICAN BROTHERHOOD and the IRA, Michael COLLINS used his intelligence network to coordinate a guerrilla war which, in his words, was not so much intended to defeat Britain militarily as to '[force] the fighting … creating a general state of disorder through the country'.

By the end of 1919 the RIC, which suffered most of the war's casualties, suffered from low morale, losing numbers, and being forced to abandon outlying barracks. To counter this the British government recruited reinforcements from ex-servicemen, known as the Black and Tans and Auxiliaries. These arrived in Ireland between March and August and fought the IRA with counter-terror methods, escalating the brutality on both sides. One Black and Tan atrocity, at Gort in Co. Galway, was memorialized by W. B. YEATS in 'Nineteen Hundred and Nineteen', which refers to 'dragon-ridden' days and nights that 'sweat with terror', and of how 'a drunken soldier/Can leave a mother, murdered at her door,/To crawl in her own blood, and go scot-free'. The IRA campaign was backed by other forms of action: hunger strikes, efficient propaganda and a dock and railway strike in May 1920. By summer that year the civil authority in many rural areas was effectively in Sinn Féin hands. The climax of the violence is taken to be 21 November 1920 (called 'BLOODY SUNDAY') when, following the killing of 11 British officers (the so-called 'Cairo Gang') by the IRA in DUBLIN, Black and Tans fired into a football crowd at Croke Park, Dublin, killing 12 civilians.

The government countered destabilization with the Restoration of Order Act in August 1920, which introduced military courts of inquiry, and eventually martial law, but they were unable to extinguish the IRA campaign. By June 1921, the IRA numbered 3–5,000 active members, pitted against 40,000 troops, 12,500 RIC men, and 1,500 Auxiliaries. While they could not hope to win a military victory, their stubbornness and the pressure of public opinion, in Britain and abroad, convinced Lloyd George that a settlement would have to be found. In July 1921 a truce was agreed, and peace negotiations began in October.

The war, while localized and small-scale by contemporary European standards, was traumatic enough. 700 people were killed and 1,200 injured. A large part of CORK city centre was burnt down by the Black and Tans, while the IRA fired the Customs House in Dublin as well as many large private houses. As longer-term legacies, the war led directly to the CIVIL WAR, while IRA incursions into the North were used to justify repressive measures there, and permanently soured relations between the two new states.

Further reading

Hopkinson (2002).

Annals of the Four Masters   There are numerous annals of Irish history dating from the late middle ages, all of which are important sources of Irish history. These include the *Annals of Connacht*, written in the fifteenth or sixteenth century, which record events from 1224 to 1544; the *Annals of Inisfallen*, the main early source for the history of medieval Munster, which record events up to 1326; the *Annals of Loch Cé*, which were written in the late sixteenth century and record events in Roscommon up to 1590; and the *Annals of Ulster*, which are a major source for the history of the O'NEILL FAMILY and were also probably written in the late sixteenth century. The annals contain lists of significant facts and dates listing battles, the births and deaths of kings, marriages, and the founding and progress of monasteries and other religious foundations. Some contain extensive commentary but most simply record information for the relevant year.

The most celebrated book of annals is that written (1632–36) by the Four Masters, Mícheál Ó Clérigh, Cúchoigíche Ó Clérigh, Fearfeasa Ó Maoilchonaire, and Cúchoigríche Ó Duibhgeannáin, four Franciscan friars resident in Bundrowse, Co. Donegal. The work, which carefully designed with the help of other monasteries in Europe, was commissioned to collect and collate all available material on Ireland and so counter the myth that Ireland was a rude, uncivilized country, as the work of many English writers had claimed. The *Annals* circulated widely in manuscript and have become a key source for modern historians.

Further reading

O'Donavan (ed.) (1848–51).

antiquarianism   Antiquarianism flourished throughout Europe in the eighteenth and early nineteenth centuries. It is characterized by an interest in all aspects and artefacts of the past, especially architectural, artistic, linguistic, literary and religious elements. While this often had a political dimension, nowhere was this more pronounced than in Ireland. The most celebrated Irish antiquary was Charles Vallancey, who held that the earliest inhabitants of Ireland were highly civilized and came from the eastern Mediterranean. This model quickly gained currency, as it was implicitly anti-English to posit a pre-Norman golden age. It was only with the advent of modern scholarly practices, encouraged by the establishment of the ROYAL IRISH ACADEMY, that even the most extreme theories about Irish as the language of the Garden of Eden or the use of round towers for fire worshipping could finally be laid to rest. Nonetheless, the antiquarian impulse can be discerned in the work of Thomas MOORE, Lady MORGAN, Samuel FERGUSON and even in the name of the FENIANS, in which the past was mined for its validation of contemporary identity politics.

Aosdána   'Aosdána' derives from the Irish *áes dána*, meaning 'men of art'. It was established by An Comhairle Ealaíon (the Irish Arts Council) in 1983, with the purpose of honouring those who had made an outstanding contribution to the arts in Ireland, in any medium. Membership is limited to 150 places and vacancies are filled by election among Aosdána members themselves. Crucially, members are eligible to receive an annuity, the Cnuas, to free them for full-time pursuit of artistic work. Aosdána meets in general assembly at least annually to discuss issues relevant to it, or concerning the broader status of the arts in society. Especially significant achievement is recognized by the election of members as Saoi (derived from the Irish word *saoi*, meaning 'master', or 'expert'). To date these have included Samuel BECKETT, Louis LE BROCQUY, Sean O'FAOLAIN and Francis STUART.

archaeology   Ireland has an impressive archaeological legacy and contains many well-preserved and important sites from the New Stone Age (Neolithic period) to the later Middle Ages. The earliest settlements recorded in Ireland date from *c.*6000 BC and are situated near the coast in Cos. Antrim, Down and Louth, and along the River Bann. A series of barrows and various forms of tombs survive, as do artefacts such as pottery, axe-heads and flint arrows. The two main forms of tomb surviving in Ireland are the portal tomb, which consist of two upright stones forming the entrance to an earth barrow (now eroded so that the remains seem to be standing stones); and the court tomb, in which a passage leading to the burial chamber becomes an open space itself. Striking portal and court tombs survive in Mayo, Sligo and Donegal.

More spectacular are the large passage tombs, subterranean burial chambers in a circular mound, reached by long stone-lined passages. The most significant of these is the one at New Grange, situated on the River Bann in Co. Meath, which is one of the finest prehistoric sites in Europe, and part of a series of passage tombs which include those at Knowth and Dowth. New Grange is probably pre-Celtic, dating from *c.*3300–2900 BC, and has a gap in the roof that enables the sun's rays to shine into the passage during the winter solstice. The tomb has a number of decorated stones. In early Irish literature it is frequently referred to as the otherworldly dwelling of some of the gods. Ireland also contains a number of wedge tombs, named because the burial chamber forms a point at the back. Most of these are situated in Munster; the main sites are at Derry, Tyrone and Moytirra, Co. Sligo, dating from the early Bronze Age (*c*.2000 BC). The characteristically Irish lake dwelling, the *crannóg*, a wooden platform extending into the lake built for protection from enemies, also dates from the Bronze Age.

The arrival of the CELTS in Ireland coincided with the advent of the Iron Age (*c*.300 BC). Their main contribution to Irish building is the ring fort, many of which survive. These consisted of a circular ditch and bank built around a dwelling. They survived well into the Middle Ages in many parts of Ireland and some were still used as sites in the seventeenth century. The Celts also built hill forts which were more complex structures on higher ground, used mainly for military purposes. The most important site is that at TARA, and there is also a fine example at Grianán Ailigh on the Derry/Donegal border. A great number of forts have survived in Ireland, partly because it was thought to bring bad luck if sites were disturbed. There are also a vast number of standing stones or dolmens, which served as gravestones and to mark boundaries, as well as stone circles, surviving mainly in Ulster and south-west Munster. Such archaeological remains have had an impact on numerous literary works. John Montague's lyric, 'Like Dolmens Round My Childhood, the Old People', works through using the conceit that the dead become enshrined in a landscape that is replete with reminders of the past.

Ireland also contains VIKING remains, excavated in the Dublin Quays area during the 1970s, and a large archaeological heritage from the Norman occupation, since the Normans built a large number of forts and small castles. These were often occupied or used by later settlers. Edmund SPENSER lived in a Norman Castle at Kilcolman, Co. Cork, when he settled on the MUNSTER PLANTATION.

Further reading

Harbison, Potterton and Sheehy (1976). Waddell (1998).

architecture   The earliest surviving architectural forms in Ireland are the remains of ring forts (see ARCHAEOLOGY), a good example of which is Dun Conor, Inishmaan, Aran Islands, which also shows how the fort would have been surrounded by carefully divided fields and plots of land where the local population would have lived.

The Medieval Period: The advent of Christianity led to the establishment of monasteries, the early examples of which were fairly basic stone buildings such as the one reconstructed at MacDara's Island, Co. Galway. The advent of the NORMANS led to the establishment of the Romanesque style, illustrated well in the square forms and semicircular arches of St Mary's, Glendalough, and the impressively decorated West door with a round arch of Killeshin, Co. Leix. The Normans also brought the Cistercian order to Ireland, which spread rapidly and extensively throughout the country (see Church, Irish). The Cistercians introduced a Gothic style of architecture illustrated in the grand remains of the monasteries at Mellifont, Co. Louth, and Jerpoint, Co. Wicklow. St Patrick's Cathedral, Dublin, built in the thirteenth century, bears a close resemblance to its English Gothic counterparts and has an impressive nave.

Most Irish castles also date from the Norman period when every family and settlement constructed a fortified dwelling to protect them from the hostile native Irish. Like those constructed in England, such castles had a square keep surrounded by a high outer wall with a series of towers at key points and a fortified portcullis gate. Most Norman castles served as grand dwellings for local magnates long after their strategic importance had disappeared. There are also a large number of smaller square towers dotted throughout Ireland, especially in Munster.

The early modern period: Little remains of the few towns constructed in Ireland in the early Middle Ages because so many of the buildings were made out of wood or other materials which have not survived. Only in the sixteenth and seventeenth centuries were many small fortified settlements made out of stone, such as the walled town of Fethard, Co. Tipperary. Many of the grand country houses, such as Burntcourt, Co. Tipperary, and Mallow Castle, Co. Cork, also date from the seventeenth century. Like the Norman towers, these were also often square in design, imitating the earlier fortified buildings. In Dublin the houses of more middle-class citizens may have survived, although it is difficult to date anything with certainty before 1725 and it is hard to argue that such buildings differ significantly from those produced in England at the same time.

The eighteenth century: Many of Dublin's public buildings owe a great deal to the Palladian style which was a fashionable architectural style in the British Isles in the early eighteenth century, a good example being the Provost's House, Trinity College. Similar in style are the Upper Castle Yard and ostentatious pillar-fronted Parliament House in College Green, designed by Irish MP Edward Lovett Pearce (?1699–1733), and later completed by James Gandon (1743–1823). The latter became synonymous with Georgian Dublin's elegant classical façades, when, under the patronage of Lord John Beresford, he designed the Four Courts, the Customs House, and the King's Inns, all to classical precepts of construction. Such buildings helped to give Dublin its Georgian style as, under the Ascendancy in the mid-eighteenth century, wealthy landowners consolidated their country estates and commissioned fashionable townhouses in Dublin.

Irish country houses, such as Castletown, Co. Kildare, designed by Pearce and Alesandro Galilei (*c.*1720–30), and Summerhill, Co. Meath, are often similar in execution and bear a close resemblance to such English country estates as Stowe. In the second half of the eighteenth century a more full-blown classical style came into vogue, as demonstrated in the Royal Exchange and rotunda complex, both in Dublin. In the last years of the century there was also a taste for wild and romantic country estates such as Downhill, Co. Derry, built on the orders of Lord Hervey, Bishop of Derry. Unfortunately this proved rather too rough for the refined tastes of its owner who spent most of his time elsewhere.

The nineteenth century: In the early nineteenth century, Gandon's legacy passed to Francis Johnston (1760–1829), who retained a classical sensibility in his remodelling of the Houses of Parliament, but other styles now began to emerge. A Gothic note was introduced by the collaborating Irish architects Thomas Deane (1792–1871) and Benjamin Woodward, who, influenced by the English Gothic revivalist John Ruskin, produced ornate designs for the Engineering Building at Trinity College (completed in 1857) and the Kildare Street Club. Gothic style also featured in the new QUEEN'S COLLEGES, while buildings at MAYNOOTH college were designed by Augustus Pugin. An Englishman, Pugin was the main force behind the mid-century boom in Gothic revival architecture in Ireland, influencing the Irish-born ecclesiastical architect J. J. McCarthy (1817–82), whose medievalist designs for parish churches throughout the country provided a powerful symbol of a reaffirmed CATHOLIC identity.

However, modern industrial building methods, using steel and glass, also appeared; examples include the Palm House (1839–52) in the Botanic Gardens, BELFAST, by Richard Turner (1798–1881). In a related development, the growth of railways led to the spread of suburbs and satellite towns, such as at Bray in the 1850s and 1860s. Little of this, however, apart from the odd landlord-designed village, reached the Irish countryside.

The twentieth century: The beginning of the twentieth century witnessed an Edwardian architecture even more grandiose than that of the Victorians in buildings such as Belfast City Hall (1906) and the Government Buildings in Upper Merrion Street, Dublin (begun 1904), an attempt to conjure up Dublin's Georgian past on a mammoth scale. In church building, there was a reaction against the highly ornate forms of Gothic; reflecting the LITERARY REVIVAL in literature and culture generally, one fashion was for Hiberno-Romanesque designs, as in the church at Spiddal, Co. Galway, by W. A. Scott (1871–1921), dedicated in 1907. Even so, the churches in Ireland were slow to patronize modern architecture. The Church of Christ the King at Turner's Cross, in CORK (1927–31), designed by the American Francis Barry Byrne, a student of Frank Lloyd Wright, was deemed so shocking that it remained an isolated case until the 1960s.

Elsewhere, however, architectural styles gradually changed under the influence of twentieth-century functionalism. The Irish version of the 1920s modernist house style was the 'Sunshine' houses designed by Robinson and O'Keefe (*c.*1932), while cinemas reflected the 'streamlined' English style. Other examples of the use of modern style were the Dublin Airport Terminal Building by Desmond FitzGerald (1941) and the Busárus (Bus Station) (1953) in Dublin, by Michael Scott.

A mixture of aesthetic and environmental conservatism and sluggish economic development has prevailed in Irish cities and the tower blocks of other countries are not to be found in Ireland (although this has not prevented philistine redevelopment, particularly in Dublin). Thus, while the influence of Mies van der Rohe is apparent in the 15-storey Liberty Hall in Dublin (1965), or the County Hall in Cork (1968), it is significant that the corporation successfully demanded that the former have its two upper storeys removed after being completed. More indicative of later twentieth-century modern architecture in Ireland is the smaller-scale New Library at TCD (1961–67) by Ahrends Burton and Paul Koralek. Generally, a new acceptance of modernity is now combined with an awareness that much of Ireland's architectural heritage has survived, and the provisions of the National Monuments legislation of 1952–54 have recently been extended.

Further reading

Craig (1982). Harbison, Potterton and Sheehy (1978).

Arnold, Matthew (1822–1888) English poet and essayist, whose essay *On the Study of Celtic Literature* (1859) is seen as a seminal document in the development of CELTICISM. Borrowing heavily from the French enthnologist Ernest Renan, Arnold effectively argues that the quintessential characteristics of the Celtic personality, including sentimentality, vivid imagination and a tendency to rebel against 'the despotism of fact', render it unsuitable for self-government.

art Irish visual and fine art has often been overlooked, and it is still sometimes asserted that Ireland is more important for its literature than its fine arts. However, there is a rich treasury of Irish art from the pre-Christian period onwards which can be divided up into a series of historical categories; the Celtic era; the Medieval period; the Renaissance; the eighteenth century; the nineteenth century; the modern period; and the contemporary period.

The Celtic era: The earliest art works that survive in Ireland are objects decorated with abstract patterns, often spirals or simple geometric patterns such as those inscribed on the kerb stone at the entrance to the burial chamber at NEW GRANGE. The Bronze Age and the Iron Age produced numerous decorative objects made from gold and other precious metals which were similarly inscribed, such as the Broighter Collar, found in a hoard dating from the first century AD. Later artefacts of note include the famous Tara Brooch and the Ardagh Chalice (both eighth century). Art was able to flourish when Christianity arrived in Ireland because the network of monasteries and other religious institutions provided a means of supporting artists and skilled craftsmen. Ireland contains numerous decorated crosses from the pre-Norman period, such as the high cross at Durrow, Co. Offaly. There are also a large number of illuminated manuscripts with richly adorned Celtic patterns as well as abstract humans and animal figures, including the Book of Durrow (seventh century) and the BOOK OF KELLS.

The Medieval period: The VIKING invasion in the ninth century had a disastrous effect on Irish art because so much was looted from monasteries and so many religious institutions were destroyed. Nevertheless religious art continued as it had before, with more stone crosses decorated with religious subjects, impressive gold jewellery, and elaborate shrines being produced. The NORMAN INVASION provided the impetus for more glamorous objects, financed in part by the wealthy dynasties who moved to Ireland. Perhaps the most outstanding object dating from this period is the Cross of Cong (*c.*1123), part of a shrine which was said to contain a shard from the true cross and produced by order of the High King. The Normans also built a series of abbeys and castles (see ARCHITECTURE). By the twelfth century Celtic art had been super-seded by a more European Gothic style of art and architecture.

The later Middle Ages and the Renaissance: The most important development in this period was the advent of painting as a more widespread phenomenon. It is also worth noting that some of the finest woodcuts produced in sixteenth-century Britain, those contained in John Derricke's *The Image of Irelande* (1581), are of Irish subjects. Ireland did not have enough wealthy subjects to make portraiture the dominant art form that it was elsewhere in Europe, although two major painters, James Gandy (1619–89) and Thomas Pooley (1646–1723), were attracted to Ireland by patrons, the latter by the Duke of ORMOND. Ormond was also responsible for the visit of Francis Place (1647–1728) who painted a series of landscapes of DUBLIN and other areas.

The eighteenth century: Portraiture now developed into one of the dominant art forms. The most important early eighteenth-century painter was Charles Jervais (1675–1739), best known for his portrait of Jonathan SWIFT. Other major painters include James Latham (1696–1747), who painted George BERKELEY, and Thomas Frye (1710–62). Later painters include Nathaniel Hone (1718–84), Hugh Douglas Hamilton (1739–1808) and Thomas Hickey (1741–1824). Landscape painting also assumed a greater significance, especially towards the end of the century when a taste for wild and uncultivated scenery became fashionable. Windswept and rugged scenes of the Irish coast, such as the Giant's Causeway, were frequently produced, starting with those of Susanna Drury, whose work was honoured by the Dublin Society. The cult of the sublime, given impetus by Edmund BURKE's essay *A Philosophical Enquiry into the Sublime and Beautiful* (1757), assumed a central role in Irish art, notably in the work of George Barrett (1732–84), who produced romantic and sublime views of the Irish countryside, very much in the manner of the French artist Claude Lorraine. It also included James Barry (1741–1806), whose most celebrated work is *King Lear Weeping over the Dead Body of Cordelia*. Cork-born and Dublin-trained, and sponsored by Edmund BURKE early in his career, Barry was also a controversial figure. A friend of William Blake, he began as a neo-classical painter but, having discovered REPUBLICANISM, turned his skills to highly political and allegorical scenes. Among the most famous of these is *Ulysses and a Companion*, which depicts Burke with a finger to his lips, attempting to silence Barry on his dangerous political views.

Sculpture began to develop in Ireland in the second half of the eighteenth century when John Van Nost (*d.*1787) came to Dublin from London (*c.*1750); those who followed included Simon Vierpyl (1725–1810), Patrick Cunningham (*c.*1774) and Edward Smyth (1749–1812). In the nineteenth century this tradition would be extended by Patrick MacDowell (1799–1870) and John Henry Foley (1818–74), both of whom enjoyed success in London, working on the Albert Memorial together. While nothing by MacDowell now survives in Ireland, Foley's statues of GOLDSMITH (1861), Burke (1868) and GRATTAN (1876) in College Green are among his very best works. (See STATUES (DUBLIN).)

The nineteenth century: The tradition of the sublime and landscape continued in nineteenth-century Ireland, as represented by Francis Danby (1793–1861), who specialized in landscapes but also painted biblical and historical scenes. Danby studied with James Arthur O'Connor (1792–1841), one of the most prolific Irish landscape painters of the period, and George PETRIE. Many nineteenth-century painters also worked as topographical illustrators for the numerous guidebooks to Ireland which began to flood the country following advances in engraving and printing techniques and the rise of domestic TOURISM in the period. In 1823 the Royal Hibernian Academy was established, which formalized the teaching and exhibition of Irish art, and enabled Irish painters to compete for commissions with their English counterparts. It succeeded so well that the best-known Irish artists of the Victorian era were those who worked in England; they included William Mulready (1786–1863), Daniel Maclise (1806–70) and Frederick Burton (1816–1900).

Modern and modernist art: Probably the first modern Irish painter was Nathaniel Hone the Younger, who studied in Paris with Couture (Manet's teacher). At his best, as in *Old Woman Gathering Sticks* (*c.*1872), he approaches the social critique of Millet and Courbet. Walter Osborne (1859–1903) lacks Hone's breadth and sweep, but his work is more varied and lyrical and includes Dublin scenes, such as the empathetic study of a poor family, *In the Phoenix Park: Light and Shade* (*c.*1885). By this period, Irish artists were tending to study and work in Europe as well as, or in preference to, England. A good example was Roderic O'Connor (1860–1940), who worked with Gaugin and produced the first Irish post-Impressionist paintings, although Stanhope Forbes (1857–1947) became the central figure in the Newlyn School in England.

The BELFAST-born Sir John Lavery (1856–1941) was a leading Irish painter of the 1880s and 1890s, famed both as a landscapist and as a sensitive portraitist of women and children. Lavery became interested in Irish politics, and one of his best later works is *Requiem Mass for Michael Collins, Pro-Cathedral, Dublin 1922*. His contemporary, Sarah Purser (1848–1943), was the first of a series of women painter-organizers who have been central to Irish artistic life since 1900. She helped found An Túr Gloine/The Glass Tower Studio (1903), inaugurating a stained-glass movement which included Evie Hone (1894–1955) and Harry Clarke (1889–1931). Clarke's work was indebted to Beardsley and Art Nouveau, as evidenced in his *Eve of St Agnes* windows, and he was also a superb book-illustrator.

Earlier, in the work of Frank O'Meara (1853–88), the spirit of the Literary Revival entered Irish painting. Most obviously, John B. Yeats (1839–1922) left an unrivalled portrait gallery of the Revival's leaders, including the fine *George Moore* (1902). More influentially, Yeats's son Jack B. Yeats (1871–1957) adopted Revival subjects, as in his illustrations to Synge's *The Aran Islands* (1907). In terms of official and society painting, however, early twentieth-century Irish art was dominated by Lavery and Sir William Orpen (1878–1931). Orpen, a youthful prodigy, blended Manet-like brushwork with polished academy technique, and achieved an international reputation as a recorder of the glamour of Edwardian society. Like Lavery he was made an official war artist in WWI and painted the official portrait of the heads of state gathered to sign the Versailles Treaty in 1919.

Orpen's unionism meant he had had no use for the concept of 'Irish' art; but the trend of painting in Ireland was largely in this direction after Independence. However, while Jack B. Yeats was able to develop his personal form of expressionism, for many artists the Free State led to a somewhat burdensome self-consciousness about what being Irish meant, as in the work of Sean Keating (1889–1977) and Paul Henry (1876–1958). Keating, Orpen's leading pupil, opposed avant-garde 'anarchy' as President of the Royal Hibernian Academy in 1948–62; he developed academicism in a social-realist direction in paintings such as *Men of the West* (1916) and *The Race of the Gael* (c.1939). Henry, with his wife the artist Grace Henry (1868–1953), moved to Achill in 1910, founding a distinct Irish landscape school. At its best, as in *Dawn, Killary Bay*, this can be masterly; but in lesser hands the West as a subject often dwindled to merely formulaic depictions. Two of the finest artists of this generation, W. J. Leech (1881–1968) and Mary Swanzy (1982–1978), exemplify the unevenness, eclectic style and occasional high achievement of many Irish artists of the time.

The two greatest innovators in modern Irish painting were Evie Hone and her friend and co-worker, Manie Jellett (1896–1943), the first Irish Cubist. Both had studied with Lhote and Gleizes in Paris, returning to exhibit in Dublin in 1924. There had been significant previous exhibitions of modern painting, notably by Hugh Lane, a nephew of Lady Gregory, in 1904 (see National Gallery of Ireland). However, the Hone-Jellett exhibition was the first by Irish artists with a desire to establish advanced modernist practice in Ireland itself. 'AE' described Jellett's work as 'artistic malaria', and she and Hone also faced opposition from the traditionalist RHA. As in other media, artists suffered from post-revolutionary puritanism, and art in the Free State tended to polarize between academic and modernist painters. Remarkably, however, women artists were not marginalized in Ireland as much as elsewhere and other women painters, such as Nano Reid (1905–81), played a leading role.

During WWII, Basil Rákóczi and Kenneth Hall moved to Dublin from London where they organized the White Stag Group, exhibiting in 1940. Their work mixed surrealism, expressionism and abstraction, and galvanized Jellett, Hone and Louis Le Brocquy into forming the Irish Exhibition of Living Art (IELA) in 1943, a vital force in

Irish painting until around 1960. The mid-century also saw the flourishing of two of Ireland's leading twentieth-century sculptors, F. E. McWilliam (1909–92) and Oisin Kelly (1915–81). McWilliam was heavily influenced by surrealism, and responded to the TROUBLES with a memorable series of bronzes entitled *Women of Belfast*, while Kelly was an artist at his best working on a smaller scale, although his sculptures of James LARKIN and Austin CLARKE are outstanding; a successor generation included Alexandra Wejchert (1921–), Hilary Heron (1923–73), Imogen Stuart (1927–) and Gerda Fromel (1931–75). The 1940s also saw the founding of the CEMA gallery in Belfast and the emergence of a gifted generation of artists, notably Colin Middleton (1910–83), William Scott (1913–90), Gerard Dillon (1916–71) and Daniel O'Neill (1920–74), helping to lay the basis for a thriving contemporary artistic scene in Northern Ireland.

Contemporary art: As elsewhere in the postwar world, modernism has been co-opted by officialdom. In Ireland, this process accompanied the modernization of the 1960s. However, it was complicated by a strong resistance to internationalist abstraction from the Romantic modernist strain in Irish art. In this sense, the search in the 1960s for a successor to Jack B. Yeats is revealing; it centred on Patrick Collins (1911–94), whose Revivalist melancholy found expression in the flat surfaces and restricted palette of paintings such as *Tinker's Moon* (1967). The Independent Artists Group was founded in 1960 to represent a figurative and semi-abstract aesthetic; its members, such as Nancy Wynne-Jones (1922–) often treated the perennial Irish subject of landscape as a source of lasting value and AUTHENTICITY, while Louis le Brocquy's portraiture supplemented and extended a neo-Celticist visual language. However, by 1970 an abstract international modernism, antagonistic to 'Celticist' traditions, and embodied in the work of the leading IELA painters, such as Patrick Scott (1921–), was being touted as the hegemonic Irish artistic style in accord with the self-consciously modernizing ethos of the Arts Council of Ireland. This was also reflected in the Rosc exhibition, a large four-yearly event launched in 1967 to put Ireland on the international exhibition circuit.

The 1980s witnessed a figurative neo-expressionism emerging in reaction against both trends. This led to the advancement of the neglected Patrick Graham (1938–), who had designed posters for the CIVIL RIGHTS movement, and whose artworks used collage, torn canvases, and painterly treatments of sexual and religious subjects, often incorporating enigmatic captions. This group's 1983 show, *A New Spirit in Painting*, was criticized for its strongly masculinist bias. Nevertheless, a new sense of history and politics was developing. *Circa*, set up by the Artists' Collective of Northern Ireland in 1981, criticized the valorization of landscape in Ireland. Their political concerns had been heralded in the work of Jack Pakenham (1938–), whose 1970s *Allegories for Ulster* paintings use blindfolds, scenes of torture, ventriloquists' dummies and broken dolls. Victor Sloan, the best-known Irish photo-artist, subjected images of loyalist PARADES to distortion and palimpsestic overworking, while Dermot Seymour (1956–) fused Troubles, media discourse and landscape traditions, using motifs such as British Army border posts and helicopters. In the Republic, political themes also feature in the hyper-naturalistic painting of Robert Ballagh (1943–), an active supporter of republican causes, and Micheal Farrell (1940–2000), whose *Madonna Irlanda or 'The Very First Real Irish Political Picture'* (1977) reworks Boucher's *Blonde Odalisque* (1752).

The sexual politics both of colonial relationships, and of male attempts to reinscribe them, bear upon the themes of landscape and of surveillance from feminist perspectives; these are reflected in work by women artists which questions the gender neutrality of landscape and the male gaze, such as that by the sculptor Kathy Prendergast (1958–) (in works such as the installation *Land* (1990), shown at the Liverpool Tate). Elsewhere, the outstanding tradition of women working in the visual arts is reflected in the careers of Maud Cotter, Pauline Cummins and Dorothy Cross.

In 1989 institutional provision for modern art was notably improved by the conversion of the Royal Hospital at Kilmainham, Dublin, to house the Irish Museum of Modern Art.

Further reading

Arnold (1969, 1991). Fallon (1994). Harbison, Potterton and Sheehy (1978). Kennedy (1991). Lucas (1973). McAvera (1989).

Ascendancy (Protestant)   Refers to the supremacy in Ireland of a Protestant elite, usually defined in terms of land ownership and affiliation to the CHURCH OF IRELAND. Ascendancy families were generally of Anglo-Irish stock, descended from Norman, Old English or CROMWELLIAN lineage, but included many from a Gaelic background. They rose to pre-eminence in the eighteenth century, maintaining power over the Catholic population through the mechanism of the PENAL LAWS, and dominating the Irish parliament. Not all the Ascendancy was of the nobility or landed classes: many of its members were professional or clerical men, educated at TRINITY COLLEGE and constituting the *haute bourgeoisie* of the capital, where they lived stylishly in the elegant townhouses of DUBLIN'S Georgian squares.

In the mid- to late eighteenth century the Protestant Ascendancy was keen to stamp its identity on Ireland through the expansion and redesign of houses and landed estates in the countryside, and the commission of great classical public buildings in Dublin (see ARCHITECTURE). It exercised its influence, too, through various organizations and institutions. Trinity College was seen as a bastion of Protestant Ascendancy privilege and exclusivity, while the Royal Dublin Society, established in 1731 for the promotion of agriculture and the useful arts, and the ROYAL IRISH ACADEMY, home of many eminent Ascendancy scientists and antiquarians, were similarly identified with Ascendancy patronage and interests. Ascendancy culture, meanwhile, was seen as one of civility and scholarship, of the literature of SWIFT, GOLDSMITH and SHERIDAN, or the philosophy of BURKE and BERKELEY.

The high-point of the Protestant Ascendancy coincided with the last independent Irish parliament in the late eighteenth century. After the ACT OF UNION, its already troubled relationship with England, to which it looked for protection, deteriorated considerably, while the gains of a Catholic population through EMANCIPATION, land agitation and municipal reform further undermined Ascendancy authority and privilege. The image of the Ascendancy remained evocative, however, in the literature of later nineteenth- and twentieth-century Irish writers, who frequently expressed nostalgia for this seeming golden age. In poems such as 'The Fisherman' and plays such as *Purgatory*, W. B. YEATS drew on the elite society of eighteenth-century Ireland as a touchstone of aristocratic leadership, cultivation and love of country, while novelists such as SOMERVILLE AND ROSS and Elizabeth BOWEN charted in fiction the demise of this former ruling caste (see 'BIG HOUSE').

astronomy   During the nineteenth century Irish astronomy developed significantly, following the establishment of a major observatory at Dunsink, outside Dublin, in 1783. Henry Ussher, the first Professor of Astronomical Science at TRINITY COLLEGE, was responsible for the appointment, in 1827, of the brilliant young William Rowan HAMILTON, as Astronomer Royal at Dunsink, where he would remain for the rest of his life. A second observatory was built at Armagh in 1790 under the auspices of Archbishop Richard Robinson, to be headed by the renowned astronomer Thomas Romney Robinson. Many amateur enthusiasts also participated in astronomical observation, most notably William Parsons, third Earl of Rosse, who built the largest reflector telescope in the world – nicknamed 'the Leviathan of Parsonstown' – at his home, Birr Castle in Co. Offaly. The 'Leviathan' was built partly in order to clarify the substance of *nebulae* or cloudy patches of light in the night sky: those nebulae correctly identified by Rosse as tightly knit star clusters are still known as 'The Rosse Spirals'. Several women, finally, were keen amateur astronomers, including Agnes Clerke, author of *A Popular History of Astronomy during the Nineteenth Century* (1885).

authenticity   The idea of authenticity has featured prominently in debates about Ireland, from the earliest times. The category has consistently been appealed to in debates, such as those concerning the IRISH CHURCH in the Middle Ages; this was felt to be more authentic than Roman CATHOLICISM by the indigenous church, but seen as degenerate, and hence inauthentic, by visitors such as GERALD OF WALES. Likewise, it informed the debates of eighteenth-century ANTIQUARIANS concerning the Irish and the IRISH LANGUAGE, and was central to the LITERARY REVIVAL, particularly as it saw the West as a repository of essential Irishness (see CORKERY). All forms of politically mobilized NATIONALISM and REPUBLICANISM have appealed to the authentic as a category to validate their activities. Conversely, the charge of inauthenticity, or un-Irishness, has been levelled at cultural products as various as the poems of Thomas MOORE, James JOYCE's *Ulysses* and the *Father Ted* TELEVISION series; often this charge results from viewing HYBRIDITY as a form of impurity, rather than as creative.

Contemporary debates, often drawing on the writings of critical theorists such as Theodor Adorno, attempt to show how authenticity always eludes the moment in which it seems to be captured or defined. The concept is central to current discussions of Ireland's COLONIAL and POSTCOLONIAL status. Critics using the work of Homi Bhabha, for example, argue that the colonizer finds inauthenticity in colonial societies (or, better, misrecognizes the 'other' culture as less than fully human); for Bhabha, postcolonial writing is not the kind that simply inverts the categories of this colonial recognition (dirt as purity, barbarity as refinement, sloth as wise passivity, etc.), but the kind which undermines it by mimicry and HYBRIDITY (with Joyce often cited as exemplary in this regard). For Adorno, the notion of authenticity is embedded in power relations; nevertheless, some critics have claimed that in the postcolonial context authenticity (or 'strategic essentialism') may legitimately be deployed against globalizing, neo-imperialistic discourses which aim at flattening national and regional differences. However, Luke GIBBONS's demonstration of the way 'regressive modernization' makes a similarly selective use of authenticity reveals the dangers inherent in such a strategy.

Further reading

Bhabha (1994). Graham and Kirkland (1999).

Auxiliaries see **Anglo-Irish War (War of Independence)**

B

Balfour, Arthur (1848–1930) Conservative Prime Minister 1902–05, and Chief Secretary for Ireland, 1887–91, known as 'Bloody Balfour'; introduced coercive legislation for Ireland (Criminal Law and Procedure Act, 1887) in response to growing agrarian violence and protest. Also associated with policies of CONSTRUCTIVE UNIONISM during the 1890s, which sought to alleviate demands for HOME RULE by facilitating tenant land purchase, increasing the powers of local government, and expanding access to university education in Ireland. His brother Gerald was Chief Secretary for Ireland in 1895, and was responsible for passing the 1896 LAND ACT. (See also Sir Horace PLUNKETT.)

Banim, John (1798–1842) and **Banim, Michael** (1796–1874)   The Banim brothers were Kilkenny-born Catholic novelists who collaborated on a series of picturesque tales and historical novels aimed at presenting a sympathetic version of Ireland to an external readership. Heavily influenced by their admired mentor, Walter Scott, and writing under the pseudonym of the O'Hara brothers, they published their first series of *Tales of the O'Hara Family* in 1825. Their emphasis on realistic depiction of Irish peasant or 'cabin' life, against the grain of popular literary caricature, is evident in works such as *The Nowlans* (1826) and *The Mayor of Wind Gap* (1835), but they were most successful in their contribution to the early development of Irish historical fiction. In *The Boyne Water* (1826), *The Croppy* (1828) and *The Denounced* (1830), they offer an embryonic analysis of the history of Ireland from the Williamite Wars to the 1798 Rising. John Banim is usually identified as the major creative force in the partnership, but both brothers are seen as formative influences on a fictional tradition faithful to the details of ordinary Irish life and speech.

Banville, John (1945–)   Novelist and journalist. Born in Wexford, Banville is widely regarded as the most stylish and inventive Irish novelist of his generation. His first book was *Long Lankin* (1970), a collection of short stories, which was followed by a novel, *Nightspawn* (1971) set in Greece on the eve of the military coup of 1967. The existential unease generated there is used to different but equally compelling effect in *Birchwood* (1973), a Gothic-fantastic variation on the traditional 'Big House' theme (a theme which recurs in later novels). Banville's most ambitious project to date has been the quartet comprising *Doctor Copernicus* (1976), *Kepler* (1981), *The Newton Letter* (1982) and *Mefisto* (1986). These explore the inner lives of real and imagined scientists of genius. Drawing on the ideas of Thomas Kuhn and Arthur Koestler, Banville's account of the tangled roots of the modern scientific worldview conflates science and imagination, central Europe and Ireland, to work against the anti-scientific and romantic-organicist grain of standard Irish self-representations. *The Book of Evidence* (1989) is a confessional murder tale, while *Ghosts* (1992), its sequel, shares the same central character and theme of guilt, but also investigates the issue of Authenticity, falsity, and art-as-delusion. Later novels include *Athena* (1995), *The Untouchable* (1996), *Eclipse* (2000) and *Shroud* (2002). Banville is a stylish and ironically playful writer, fully at home in the contemporary Postmodern climate, who self-consciously draws on, in order to extend, the experimental legacy of Joyce, O'Brien and Beckett.

Further reading

McCarthy (2000). McMinn (1991).

bardic poetry   Also referred to as classical Irish poetry. Bardic poetry is syllabic verse, invariably rhymed, composed in Irish by professional poets. It has an ancient, pre-

Christian ancestry but died out in the seventeenth century when the English finally achieved domination over Ireland. Bards were trained in schools and went on to serve a particular clan or master and their purpose was to recite verse on specific public occasions, often with a musical accompaniment. Bardic poetry tended to deal with subjects appropriate for such occasions: the celebration of a great victory, praise of a lord or mythical hero or the lament of the death of a great king. The verse often shows signs that it is composed for oral delivery – the repetition of key motifs and phrases, rhymes, structures that allow the poet to make last-minute changes or allow for minor memory lapses – but is always ornate and complicated in style, illustrating the formal skill such highly trained poets possessed. There were strict rules dictating which forms of rhyme, assonance and alliteration, and forms of grammatical construction could be used in places within specific types of poetry.

The levels and roles played by the bards were carefully and strictly organized, as was expected of all professions in traditional Irish society. Poets were divided into two types: the more important *fili*, who were responsible for preserving knowledge, law, mythology and language, and who were often linked to religious offices; and bards, who, strictly speaking, were less important and less gifted poets whose job was simply to compose verse. Poets were trained in a series of schools established throughout Ireland, many dating from the twelfth century. A bardic family ran each school, so that certain literary dynasties were associated with different areas of Ireland, examples being the Mac an Bhairds in Donegal, the Ó Dálaighs in Cork, and the Ó hUiginns in Sligo. The bards enjoyed enormous prestige and had a powerful presence within Irish society. New English settlers such as Edmund Spenser noted with considerable envy how respected Irish poets were, as did Sir Philip Sidney, son of the Lord Deputy, Sir Henry Sidney, who commented that in 'Ireland, where learning goeth very bare, yet are their poets held in a devout reverence'. He also repeated the often-made comment that poets could rhyme their enemies to death. Incurring the wrath of a bard was a source of great shame, frequently leading to a painful humiliation.

A large corpus of bardic poetry survives from the late Middle Ages and Renaissance – some 1800–2000 poems, many of them dating from the sixteenth and seventeenth centuries. The most important poets are Dáibhí Ó Bruadair and Aogán Ó Rathaile. The bards tended to be nostalgic and deeply conservative, as are most privileged people who feel their position under threat. Many poems attack bards who were seen to have prostituted their art by working for vulgar English landowners. Ó Bruadair composed a lament for the declining world of the bards, 'The High Poets are gone', which links their decline to the 'world's waning', and laments 'their books in corners greying into nothing/and their sons without one syllable of their secret treasure'.

Further reading

Knott (1960). Ó Tuama and Kinsella (eds) (1981).

Barrington, Sir Jonah (1760–1834)   Writer and politician, famous for his memoirs of life amidst the aristocracy of eighteenth and early nineteenth century Ireland: see his *Personal Sketches of my Own Time*, 3 volumes (London, 1827–32).

Beckett, Samuel (1906–1989)   Novelist, playwright and poet. Beckett was born in Foxrock, Dublin. He studied modern languages at Trinity College, Dublin, graduating in 1927. In 1929, he took up a position as *lecteur* at the École Normale Supérieure, in Paris, and formed a close friendship with the Irish poet and critic, Thomas MacGreevy. Through MacGreevy, Beckett met James Joyce, whose 'work in progress', subsequently *Finnegans Wake*, he would defend and praise in his contribution to the essay collection, *Our Exagmination Round His Factification for Incamination of Work in Progress* (1929). In 1931, Beckett's short monograph, *Proust*, appeared in the Dolphin Books series published by Chatto and Windus (further critical prose can be found in *Disjecta* (1983)), while his own creative work began with the poem *Whoroscope* (1930), the collection of short stories centring on the figure of Belacqua, *More Pricks than Kicks* (1934), and the novel *Murphy* (1938).

Beckett spent WWII in France, during which he became a member of the Parisian Resistance, fleeing to Roussillon subsequent to his cell's betrayal. In the Vaucluse he wrote *Watt*, published in 1953. After the war, Beckett began to compose in French, in an effort to strip his writing of superfluities; the first fruit of which was *Mercier et Camier*, finished in 1946. His major prose work is a trilogy of texts, translated into English as *Molloy* (1951–54), *Malone Dies* (1953–58) and *The Unnameable* (1953–58). The Trilogy investigates, among other topics, human existence within time and the mind's problematic relationship with external reality through a series of comic-grotesque stories, each of which increasingly dismantles narrative conventions. Beckett's deconstruction of the novel in this work is at one with the dramatic experi-mentalism of *Waiting for Godot*, a play written in the late 1940s. *Godot*'s denuded landscape is the setting for the fruitless expectations of two vagrants, whose dialogue mixes metaphysics and the patter of the musical hall stage.

Beckett's dark humour is equally present in other major plays: *Endgame* (1957), *Krapp's Last Tape* (1958), and *Happy Days* (1961). Later dramatic works are yet more minimalist than these already spartan dramas, as Beckett pares down action and character still further. The enigmatic, insistent tone of Becket's last extended prose narra-tive, *How It Is* (1961–64), prefigures that of the later prose, which follows the short plays or 'dramaticules' in its radical concision, as in *Imagination Dead Imagine* (1965), *Ping* (1966) and the final trilogy, *No How On* (1989).

Further reading

Fletcher (1970). Kenner (1969). Pilling (ed.) (1993). Ricks (1993).

Behan, Brendan (Breandán Ó Beacháin) (1923–1964)   Playwright, poet and novelist, Behan was born in Dublin into a working-class republican family. He became a member of Fianna Éireann, the IRA youth organization, and composed political poems for various nationalist newspapers and magazines. In 1939 he was involved in the IRA's bombing campaign in Britain, and was convicted in 1940 for the possession of explosives and sentenced to three years, the majority of which was spent in a borstal in Suffolk. While in prison, Behan learnt the IRISH LANGUAGE, and offered the ABBEY two Irish plays, one, *The Landlady*, a translation of an English-language original; both plays were rejected. After his release, under a general amnesty for political prisoners, he wrote a number of poems in Irish, but gave up Irish verse by the early 1950s.

At this date, he became known in DUBLIN for his wit, while he also wrote radio drama for Radio Éireann and various short stories, and worked on his autobiographical *Borstal Boy* (1958), a comic masterpiece, and a play, *The Quare Fellow*, rejected by the Abbey and the GATE, but staged by the Pike Theatre in 1954, and revived to great acclaim in London by Joan Littlewood in 1956.

Behan followed up this theatrical success with *The Hostage* (1958), a thorough reworking of his Irish-language play *An Giall* (1958) which exploits with great and daring success the techniques of Littlewood's Theatre Workshop. The play's riotous assemblage of song, dance and satire contrasts with the more sombre humour of *The Quare Fellow*.

The latter stages of Behan's career were overshadowed by his alcoholism. *Confessions of an Irish Rebel* is an indifferent sequel to *Borstal Boy*; *Brendan Behan's Island* (1962) and *Brendan Behan's New York* (1964) are amusing but largely anecdotal compositions, generated with the aid of the tape recorder; while, at his death, he left an unfinished play, *Richard's Cork Leg*, and a portion of a novel, *The Catacombs*.

Further reading

Cronin (1976). De Búrca (1993). Kearney (1977).

Belfast   Taking its name from the Irish Béal Féirste, or 'the mouth of the ford', Belfast was founded in 1603 by Arthur Chichester as a base for English and Scottish settlers. During the eighteenth century, Belfast began to develop as a trading and commercial centre, building on the weaving and linen production of the surrounding region. It also gained a reputation for political radicalism driven largely by disaffected Presbyterians, many of whom were engaged in the UNITED IRISHMEN rebellion of 1798. After the ACT OF UNION, Belfast maintained some of its connections to radical and liberal traditions but with the expansion of its industrial capacity, through linen, distilling, and later in the century engineering and shipbuilding, it increasingly identified its prosperity with the Union. The population grew considerably during this century, from 25,000 in 1808 to almost 350,000 in 1901. In 1888 Belfast was granted 'city' status. By the close of the nineteenth century, it had also become defined as a bastion of ORANGEISM and of a conservative UNIONIST ideology derived in part from the long-term influence of Henry Cooke (see PRESBYTERIANISM); it was here that the Solemn League and Covenant was signed in 1912.

CATHOLICS, meanwhile, remained in the minority, and incidents of sectarian violence began to occur on a regular basis. During the HOME RULE crisis of 1911–14, and again after WWI, large-scale violence occurred. Unionists feared that Belfast's successful industries would suffer from tariffs which they thought a Dublin government would impose. By this time, Harland and Wolff was the greatest shipbuilding firm in the world, launching the *Olympic*, the *Mauretania*, and the ill-fated *TITANIC*, while Belfast now had a City Hall built to reflect its civic pride (see ARCHITECTURE). It had also the stirrings of a cultural life, with Forest Reid becoming the first Belfast novelist to achieve an international reputation, and the Ulster Literary Society (inspired by the Celtic Revival in the South), established in 1904.

However, after the war decline set in as staple industries – linen, shipbuilding and engineering – began to decline. This situation was confirmed by the Depression; unemployment in shipbuilding was 65 per cent in 1932, the same year in which the STORMONT parliament building was opened. Sectarianism was reinforced by the IRA's military campaign against Partition between 1920 and 1922, when Catholic areas were attacked, families displaced, and 11,000 Catholics and Protestant socialists driven from the shipyards and factories. As the new capital of Northern Ireland, Belfast was subject to some new initiatives, such as the first UK municipal airport in 1924, but housing was neglected, education became further sectarianized, and the brief unity of Catholic and Protestant workers in protests against cuts in Outdoor Relief payments in 1932 soon faded. Despite this, cultural life improved; John Lavery became the first Belfast artist to win a major reputation, and John HEWITT was a significant presence. However, it has been claimed that it took WWII to save the city, bringing as it did Short Brothers, the aircraft manufacturers, and generally boosting employment and spreading wealth. This was just as well, because German bombing found the city woefully unprepared; two heavy raids, in April and May 1941, killed 800 and injured at least 1,700, destroying 1,600 homes and damaging 28,000. In a rare gesture of cross-border co-operation, Southern fire crews drove north to help put out fires caused by the raids.

After 1945, Belfast faced the usual problems of modernization of many other British cities. Its traditional industries continued to decline – the replacement of passenger liners by air travel meant that the launch of the *Canberra* in 1960 was the end of an era – but were replaced by new ones, such as artificial fibres. New artists emerged – writers associated with the BELFAST GROUP, such as Seamus HEANEY, Stewart PARKER and Michael LONGLEY, and novelists such as Sam Hanna BELL, Michael McLaverty and Brian MOORE, whose downtrodden characters constituted a powerful criticism of the unforgiving aspects of the city. Belfast also made a major contribution to 1960s rock and pop music in the form of VAN MORRISON, and to football in the shape of George Best.

The determining factor of the last 30 years in Belfast has, unavoidably, been the Troubles, which have increased the usual problems of decline and regeneration; between 1969 and 1975, 25,000 homes were destroyed or damaged by explosions. In addition, continuing redevelopment – such as the Westway and the Divis Flats (1972) – has broken up the traditional communities of Sandy Row, the Falls and the Shankill. The Troubles also saw the erection of 'Peace Lines' barriers between different communities, and increased ethnic polarization as well as senseless and heartbreaking tragedies, including the murderous activities of the 'Shankill Butchers', and the death of three children which led to the Peace People movement (whose founders were awarded a Nobel Peace Prize in 1976). An attempt to turn the city around began in the 1980s with campaigns such as the council's 'Belfast Smiles Better'; despite the sentimentality of the we-can-take-anything attitude, regeneration has occurred. This was helped by the fact that Thatcherite cuts in housing and education expenditure did not bite as deeply as elsewhere in Britain. Belfast has benefited greatly from peace, and the Waterside Arts Centre is a major new development which puts something of a seal on recovery. Long-term problems – of housing and employment – are, however, still being tackled. Despite its forbidding reputation, Belfast is the location for some of the best modern Irish writing, by Derek Mahon, Ciaran Carson and Glenn Patterson.

Further reading

Bardon (1982, 1992). Bardon and Burnett (1996). Bardon and Coulin (1985). Beckett (1983).

Belfast Group A literary discussion group and workshop founded by Philip Hobsbaum in 1963, commonly regarded as the cradle of the Northern Irish poetry renaissance of the 1960s, which included fiction writers, painters, translators, dramatists, and critics, as well as poets.

Further reading

Brown, T. (1975). Kirkland (1996). Longley, E. (1994). Longley, M. (1994).

Bell, Sam Hanna (1909–1990) Fiction writer and broadcaster. Born in Scotland to an Ulster Scots family; brought up in Belfast where he attended the Belfast College of Art. Bell began writing documentary scripts for the BBC and, supported by Louis MacNeice, served as their features producer. He was a mainstay of intellectual life in Northern Ireland for many years, founding *Lagan* with John Boyd and Bob Davison in 1943, the year he published his the short stories of *Summer Loanen* and, later, supporting *Fortnight* (see JOURNALS). Bell's first novel, and arguably his best work, is *December Bride* (1951), the story of his mother's family, which he had been encouraged to write by Sean O'Faolain. It tells the story of a servant girl who lives with two brothers, having sexual relations with both, and who refuses to name the father of her child to the local Presbyterian minister. Finally, in order that her daughter can marry, she has to choose to marry one of the brothers. The novel was successfully filmed by Thaddeus O'Sullivan in 1990. *The Hollow Ball* (1961), set in 1930s Belfast, reflects Bell's socialist opposition to the UNIONIST establishment, as did his support for Sam THOMPSON in the struggle to stage and broadcast *Over the Bridge.*

Further reading

Foster (1974).

Bell, The (1940–1954)   The most important journal of post-Independence Ireland, *The Bell* was a monthly founded and edited in its first series by Sean O'FAOLAIN, and later by Peadar O'Donnell and Anthony CRONIN). It carried articles of social analysis and description as well as literary work, ranging from housing conditions and EMIGRATION to policy on the IRISH LANGUAGE and horse racing. It published Patrick KAVANAGH's *The Great Hunger,* and other contributors included Brendan BEHAN, Elizabeth BOWEN, Flann O'BRIEN and Liam O'FLAHERTY. The journal was a conduit for international awareness and a focus for national self-analysis at a time of CENSORSHIP, isolation, and a generally philistine social consensus. It encouraged new writers (as in the 'Young Writers Symposium' of 1951), and forged links with Northern Irish writers such as John HEWITT. Although O'Faolain's final editorial complained that he had been trying to 'harvest thistles', *The Bell* nevertheless anticipated the more accommodating climate of the 1960s.

Further reading

Cairns and Richards (1988). Smyth (1998).

Berkeley, George (1685–1753)   Philosopher and Bishop of Cloyne. Berkeley was born at Dysart Castle, Co. Kilkenny, and educated at TCD, where he became a fellow (1707). He published *An Essay Towards a New Theory of Vision* in 1709, which argues that we see light and colours rather than real objects, prefiguring the more sustained arguments of his idealist philosophy which appeared soon after. In 1710 he published *The Principles of Human Knowledge,* his major work. Berkeley argues that things only exist when we see them, a principle enshrined in his often-quoted Latin maxim, *esse est percipi* ('to be is to be perceived'). In attempting to refute a materialist theory of knowledge which he regarded as inevitably leading to atheism, Berkeley claims that God exists as an infinite form of mind which can be known by men and women. Objects as such do not exist: rather, God's universe is made up of minds which know and ideas which are known. Berkeley's philosophy made little initial impact until he published a more accessible statement of his ideas in *Three Dialogues between Hylas and Philonus* (1713). At this point he was in London, where he became friendly with a number of major literary and intellectual figures, including Alexander Pope, Joseph Addison and Sir Richard STEELE. Berkeley returned to Ireland in 1721, having travelled in Europe and written essays criticizing recent scientific developments.

Berkeley became Dean of DERRY in 1724 and in 1729 was involved in a project, which ultimately proved unsuccessful, to establish a mission in Bermuda for the benefit of both colonists and natives. Following this he published an attack on free-thinking and atheism, *Alcphron, or the Minute Philosopher* (1732), a defence of his idea of perception, *Theory of Vision Vindicated* (1733), and a work on mathematics, *The Analyst* (1734). In the same year he became Bishop of Cloyne and moved to Co. Cork. While he appears to have taken little interest in his clerical duties in Derry, Berkeley became a conscientious pastor in Cloyne and acquired a reputation as a champion of the poor. He turned his attention to questions of political economy and published numerous queries in *The Querist* (1735, 1736 and 1736). This collection tackles many problems including the causes of poverty, education, fashion, and banking. Berkeley's last three significant works were: *Siris: A Chain of Philosophical Reflections and Inquiries concerning the Virtues of Tar-Water* (1744), which argued that tar-water was a panacea for most ailments; *Words to the Wise* (1749), an appeal to the CATHOLIC CHURCH to help deal with poverty in Ireland; and *Maxims Concerning Patriotism* (1750).

Berkeley is one of the most significant philosophers to have written in English and a pivotal figure in eighteenth-century thought. He had an important impact on later Irish literature, his ideas being employed in a variety of ways by James JOYCE, Flann O'BRIEN and Samuel BECKETT.

Further reading

Pitcher (1977).

'Big House'   Refers to the historical and literary concept of the Irish great house and surrounding estate, usually occupied by a member of the Protestant ASCENDANCY. With close links to the Gothic tradition, 'Big House' novels frequently describe the decline of Protestant authority through the symbol of the decay or destruction of the house itself. Maria EDGEWORTH's *Castle Rackrent* (1800), which describes the dissipation of an aristocratic family and the eventual transfer of their property to their Catholic steward, is frequently cited as one of the earliest treatments of the theme. It became a staple trope of nineteenth-century Irish fiction, with high points in Sheridan LE FANU's *Uncle Silas* (1864) and SOMERVILLE AND ROSS's *The Real Charlotte* (1894). In twentieth-century writing, notable 'Big House' novels include Elizabeth BOWEN's *The Last September* (1929) and Molly Keane's *Good Behaviour* (1981), while variants on the tradition include Aidan HIGGIN's *Langrishe, Go Down* (1966) and John BANVILLE's *Birchwood* (1973). W. B. YEATS's poems on the subject of Coole Park, home of his friend Lady GREGORY, and his play *Purgatory* (1939) are part of the same tradition, and convey a nostalgia for a noble aristocratic age threatened by the encroachment of a modern, democratic Ireland.

Further reading

Rauchbauer (ed.) (1992).

Bloody Sunday   This phrase was applied to the brutal attacks by police on crowds on 31 August 1913, during the Dublin Lockout, and also to one of the bloodiest days of the Anglo-Irish War. However, it now almost invariably refers to a notorious incident of the 1968–1994 Troubles. This occurred when a banned Civil Rights march in Derry, called to protest against Internment on Sunday 30 January 1972, was fired upon by soldiers of the First Battalion of the Parachute Regiment. Thirteen demonstrators, all unarmed, were killed (another later died in hospital). The incident sealed the alienation of nationalists from the army and the British state in Northern Ireland. Three days later protesters burnt down the British Embassy in Dublin. The impact on domestic and international opinion was profound and provoked a fundamental change in British policy, with Stormont prorogued (suspended) on 24 March 1972 in favour of direct rule. However, the subsequent Tribunal of Inquiry into the shootings, chaired by Lord Widgery, the Lord Chief Justice, exonerated the soldiers involved and suggested that the demonstrators were armed. Seamus Heaney's 'Triptych' and 'Casualty', are literary responses, and the Widgery Report is savaged in Thomas Kinsella's 'A Butcher's Dozen' (1972). Bloody Sunday has been commemorated annually since 1972, and an inquiry is currently shedding new light on the event.

Further reading

Walsh (2000).

Boland, Eavan (1944–)   Poet. Born in Dublin, and educated at TCD, Boland's *New Territory* (1967) and *The War Horse* (1975) marked the emergence of a powerful women's voice in contemporary Irish poetry. *In Her Own Image* (1980) confronts the hitherto taboo subjects of women's sexuality and issues arising from it, using short-line stanza forms derived from Sylvia Plath. *Night Feed* (1982), by contrast, celebrates the virtues of Boland's own domestic existence. The difference between the two books may be taken to highlight the distinction between her own middle-class feminism and more radical versions which began to emerge from the Irish women's movement at this time. *The Journey and Other Poems* (1986) extends Boland's interest into the unwritten history of Irish women, and the relation of women to the female stereotypes of national literary tradition, an issue addressed in the prose pamphlet *A Kind of Scar* (1989). *Outside History* (1990), as its title suggests, attempts to get beyond the restrictions of such stereotypes. In *Object Lessons: The Life of the Woman and the Poet in Our Time* (1996), the autobiographical sources of the poetry are discussed at some length. She was a co-founder in 1980 of the Irish feminist press Arlen House. A prolific writer, Boland's celebration of the ordinary, the suburban, and the lives of women, both reflected and anticipated major changes in Irish society, going against the Romantic, masculine grain of existing poetry and helping to redefine it in the process.

Further reading

Boland (1996). Haberstroh (1996).

Book of Leinster An important twelfth-century manuscript collection of 187 vellum folios, compiled at the court of Dairmuid Mac Murchada (more famous as the king of Leinster who precipitated the way for the NORMAN INVASION by asking the Normans to help him fight his dynastic struggles with other Irish rulers). The work was probably compiled by a number of scribes. It contains manuscripts of the LEBOR GABÁLA and the TÁIN BÓ CUAILNGE, as well as works of genealogy and other literary works including a list of some 350 tales that a poet should know.

Other key Irish manuscript collections are the *Book of Lecan*, compiled in the late fourteenth or early fifteenth century, which also contains a version of the *Lebor Gabála*, and an inaugural poem to an Irish chieftain; the long *Book of Lismore* (198 folios), compiled in the fourteenth century for the MacCarthy family, which contains a translation of Marco Polo's travels, alongside various saints' lives, poems, sagas and other tales; the *Book of the Dun Cow*, written down in the late eleventh century, which contains a version of the *Táin Bó Cuailnge* and other works from the Ulster Cycle as well as a poem in praise of St Columba; and the *Book of the O'Conor Don*, a seventeenth-century manuscript of bardic poetry of some 422 folios containing 385 poems.

Boru (Bóroime), Brian (941–1014) One of the most successful of early Irish kings. He became King of Munster in 976 and soon consolidated his power within the province. He then embarked on a programme of expansion, attacking the VIKINGS at Limerick, before turning against other ruling dynasties in Leinster. By 996 he was ruler of the southern half of Ireland, although he was forced to come to terms with his main rival, Máel Sechnaill II (Malachy), the high king who ruled most of the north. They united to defeat the Vikings in Dublin at the battle of Glenn Máma (999), before their alliance broke down. Brian Boru then defeated Malachy and forced him to acknowledge that he was the high king of Ireland, demonstrating that the high kingship was not simply a possession of the O'NEILLS.

Brian's control over Ireland was never complete and he had to deal with various rivals. In 1012 Leinster and Dublin attempted to challenge his power. Brian fought a successful campaign in Leinster but was killed after a bloody victory against the Vikings and their allies at Clontarf in 1014. He was buried in Armagh and later became a celebrated hero of folklore and literature, seen as a crusading Christian hero defending Ireland from the pagan Viking hordes.

Further reading

Ó Corráin (1972).

Boucicault, Dion (1820–1890) Theatrical manager and author of some 140 plays, notably *The Colleen Bawn* (1860) and the popular comedy *The Shaughraun* (1874). His work is seen as having fostered a stereotype of Irish sentimentality and charm.

Boundary Commission (1925)   Established by the Anglo-Irish Treaty of 1921, by the time the Commission met expectations were low on both sides. The Free State no longer believed it could bring about unity, although it did hope for the transfer of high concentrations of nationalists from Northern Ireland. But Sir James Craig had already received assurances from sympathizers in the British government that the Commission would make only minor readjustments. In the event, it judged that the onus of proof for changing the 1920 arrangements lay with those requesting them. In this sense, and given its small territorial adjustments in favour of Northern Ireland, the Commission acted more in unionist than nationalist interests. Northern nationalists, in particular, felt bitter and abandoned. The final agreement also effectively removed the functions theoretically exercised by the Council of Ireland, a consultative body established in 1921, deepening the isolation of the two states.

Bowen, Elizabeth (1899–1973)   Novelist and short story writer. Born in Dublin to an Anglo-Irish family, raised in Bowen's Court in Co. Cork, she records memories of her upbringing and its location in *Seven Winters* (1943) and *Bowen's Court* (1942) respectively. Bowen's first novels, which draw on experience of an early, dissolved, engagement, and a life spent mainly in southern England, include *The Last September* (1929) and *To the North* (1932). In 1923, she published the first of six short story collections, *Encounters*; a *Collected Stories* appeared in 1980. Bowen was a master of this form which she felt, more than any other, allowed for extremes of human experience. Many of her novels also deal with extremes. Thus, in *The House in Paris* (1935) and *The Death of the Heart* (1938), the effects of a disrupted childhood are explored, while *The Heat of the Day* (1949) draws on Bowen's experience of life in London during WWII, during which she reported on the situation in Ireland to the Ministry of Information. Like the stories in *The Demon Lover* (1945) this novel summons up the city's wartime atmosphere of treason, secrecy and alluring phantasmal beauty. The best of her later novels are *A World of Love* (1955) and *Eva Trout* (1969), and she published two volumes of essays, *Collected Impressions* (1950) and *Afterthought* (1962).

   Bowen has become increasingly valued since her death. Her fictions are haunted in several senses – peopled with threatening figures, often older women, rootless adults, and orphaned or isolated children seeking surrogate parents, they focus on psychological states and nuances of sensibility, identifying whatever is grotesque and disruptive under a cool surface. Although only two of her novels are set wholly in Ireland, the mixture of poise and impermanence links her writing to that of many more obviously Irish writers.

Further reading

Glendinning (1977). Lee (1981). Lessner (1989).

boycott This term for the strategic ostracism of an individual was inspired by the events of 1880 when tenants on Lord Erne's Co. Mayo estate, angered by his refusal to lower rents, isolated and blacklisted his land agent, Charles Cunningham Boycott. A film, *Captain Boycott*, was made in 1947.

Boyne, Battle of 1 July 1690 (12 July new style) the most famous battle of the WILLIAMITE WAR which occupies a central place in the LOYALIST calendar. The JACOBITE army (25,000), led by JAMES II, confronted WILLIAM III's army (36,000) on the River Boyne at Oldbridge, three miles north of their garrison at Drogheda, in order to halt their opponents' march towards Dublin. When a decoy force misled the Jacobite forces into thinking that a concerted attack was being launched from the West, James moved most of his troops to block their advance but was unable to attack because of the terrain. The main Williamite army advanced and the Jacobites were forced to retreat for fear of being surrounded. Losses were not heavy: only about 500 Williamites and 1,000 Jacobites were killed.

Although not the most strategically important battle of the war, the Boyne entered folklore mainly because of the behaviour of the two kings. While William fought bravely at the centre of his army, James fled before his troops were defeated and has been cast as the figure of the cowardly king ever since. The anniversary of the battle was celebrated throughout the eighteenth century but assumed a greater importance in the 1790s as the main celebration of the ORANGE ORDER, reminding Catholics of Protestant superiority in the North of Ireland. Violence occurred regularly when the marches to commemorate the battle took place especially in Belfast.

Brehon Law The term applied to English interpretations of Irish law after the Tudor invasion of the sixteenth century. Irish law was frequently attacked by English commentators because it was thought to be excessively lenient towards serious offences which were punished by a fine rather than a harsher penalty. This was principally because Irish society was based on the importance of kinship groups. Hence killing and murder were often punished by the demand for a fine (*ériac*) to be paid to the victim's relations rather than a centrally administered punishment. The same went for injuries caused and theft. Fines were worked out according to the rank of the victim involved, social stratification being a key principle in Irish society. English commentators were also scandalized by the fact that men were permitted to have more than one wife and criticized the Irish legal system for failing to stamp out such perceived violation of the natural order. They also disapproved of the legally sanctioned practice of children being looked after by foster parents, who often played a more important role in their lives than their natural parents did.

Irish law was probably codified in the seventh and eighth centuries but most surviving manuscripts date from the fourteenth to sixteenth centuries.

Brendan the Navigator, St *fl*.580.   Founder of monasteries and explorer. Brendan was born in Tralee, Co. Kerry, and educated as a monk. He founded a monastery at Clonfert, Co. Kerry, which developed into an important training centre for mission-aries until the sixteenth century. Brendan travelled extensively in the British Isles, encountering St Columba in Argyll, and probably also spending some time in Wales, one of the key centres of monastic reform in the seventh century. Brendan is reputed to have died at his sister's convent in Annaghdown, Co. Galway. Numerous places in southern Ireland have been named after Brendan who also seems to have inspired a cult in Brittany, Wales and Scotland.

Brendan is also celebrated for his mythical voyage to the north-west, narrated in the tenth- or eleventh-century Latin prose tale, *Navigato Sancti Brendani Abbatis* (*The Voyage of St Brendan*), which became one of the most important works of the Middle Ages and survives in over 100 manuscripts. Brendan is told of a mythical Land of the Promise of the Saints and sets off to discover it for himself, sailing in a coracle with a few companions. They travel for seven years and have a number of adventures before finally reaching their goal. Brendan returns to Ireland and just has time to narrate all the marvellous things he has seen before he dies. St Brendan's Island appeared on medieval maps and it is possible that Brendan – or another medieval traveller – reached the Americas before Columbus. An expedition led by Tim Severin in 1976–77 managed to reach Newfoundland in a hide-covered coracle, similar to the one Brendan is said to have used in the tale, providing evidence for this supposition. However, it is dangerous to assume that a tale which belongs to the well-known religious genre of the saint's voyage, an allegory of the life of the Christian on earth, can be read as fact. St Brendan's story has often been represented in literary and artistic works.

Further reading

D'Angeli and O'Meara (1994).

Brigid, St (*fl*.fifth century)   Nun and founder of the first convent in Ireland, often referred to as 'Mary of the Irish', Brigid has been a patron saint of Ireland since 1962. Brigid's life, even more than those of many early saints, is steeped in folklore and later embellishments, and it is hard to separate fact from fiction. Brigid was supposedly born into a peasant family near Dundalk, and her parents were baptized by St Patrick himself. She became a nun, and her main achievement was to found the first convent in Ireland in Kildare. She became its abbess until her death. Her relics were buried alongside those of St Patrick at Downpatrick. She is reputed to have performed numerous miracles, and was famous for her kindness and charity. She acquired the name 'Mary of the Gael' when Bishop Ibor was blessed with a vision of her a day after he had seen the Virgin Mary and declared that the two women were identical.

Brooke, Sir Basil (1st Viscount Brookeborough) (1888–1973)   Politician. After serving in WWI, Brooke was elected to the Senate of the first Northern Ireland parliament (1921). He resigned the following year to lead the Ulster special constabulary against the IRA's border raids in Fermanagh. Re-elected (1929) as a UNIONIST member of STORMONT, he served as Minister of Agriculture (1933–41), Minister of Commerce (1941–45), and Prime Minister (1943–63). More sectarian than his predecessor Sir James CRAIG, Brooke was a staunch advocate of Protestant dominance in Ulster and remained opposed to any rapprochement with the REPUBLIC. His inflexibility made him unable to face the challenges of modernization which threatened unionism. He was made Viscount Brookeborough in 1952 and continued to sit at Stormont until 1968. A paternalist figure, Brooke is notorious for his claims that CATHOLICS were inherently untrustworthy, and that he did not have a single one in his personal employ.

Brunswick Clubs   Loyalist, anti-Catholic and pro-Tory societies launched in 1828 partly to replace the ORANGE ORDER which had been declared unlawful. Their numbers increased dramatically in response to the electoral successes of Daniel O'CONNELL: by the close of that year there were at least 200 clubs throughout Ireland.

Burke, Edmund (1729–1797)   Born in DUBLIN, Burke was educated at a HEDGE SCHOOL and TCD. Moving to London, he left law for literature early in his career; by the 1760s he was a valued friend of Garrick, Reynolds and Dr Johnson. The title of his first publication, *A Vindication of Natural Society* (1756), anticipates the rest of his writings, which were concerned to defend organic and evolved features of society and its institutions as opposed to abstract and imposed ones. *A Philosophical Enquiry into the Sublime and the Beautiful* (1757) was a major contribution to a crucial aesthetic field, and not only established Burke's reputation with his contemporaries, but made him a significant influence on writers of the Romantic period. Entering politics, he became private secretary to Lord Hamilton, Secretary for Ireland, in 1759, and then to the Marquis of Rockingham, then the Prime Minister, from 1765. He was elected MP for Wendover in 1764, and Bristol in 1774. Outstanding oratorical and intellectual abilities gained Burke influence in the Whig party, though he did not hold office with them until 1783, and then only briefly.

A conflicting mixture of JACOBITE sympathies and Whig principles made Burke a radical on certain issues – Catholic Emancipation, the rights of the American colonists to Independence, and Irish trade. As a consequence, from 1774 he became a friend and ally of the reforming Whig leader Charles James Fox. But his background also made him a reactionary in other ways, and this was signalled forcefully in his most famous work, *Reflections on the Revolution in France* (1790). Perhaps the most eloquent of all defences of the *ancien régime*, and a deeply felt warning against political terror, *Reflections* was extensively translated and provoked some notable responses, including Thomas Paine's *The Rights of Man* (1791). Burke was isolated in later years, and his opposition to the revolution led to a breach with Fox in 1791; however his accurate prediction of the violence in France enhanced his reputation as a political thinker. In the words of Conor Cruise O'Brien, Burke's divided Irish inheritance was the source of his originality, since it ensured that 'the forces of revolution and counter-revolution exist[ed] not only in the world at large but also within himself'.

Further reading

Gibbons (2003). McCormack (1994). O'Brien (1992).

Butt, Isaac (1813–1879)   Born in Donegal of a Church of Ireland family, Butt was a precocious TRINITY COLLEGE student who became a prominent barrister, professor of Political Economy, and in later life, a leader of the HOME RULE movement. One of the co-founders of the *DUBLIN UNIVERSITY MAGAZINE*, which he edited from 1834 to 1938, he produced a number of literary works including *Irish Life in the Castle, the Courts and the Country* (1840), a story of political rapprochement between a Protestant barrister and a nationalist leader. In 1848 he published a historical novel, *The Gap of Barnesmore* (1848), and in 1863 *Chapters of College Romance*, a collection of tales originally published in the *Dublin University Magazine* under the name of Edward J. O'Brien, detailing the lurid events of undergraduate life.

Butt was initially an avid UNIONIST and an opponent of Daniel O'CONNELL in the 1840 debates on REPEAL, but following the FAMINE his attitudes changed, as evidenced by his complaints against English indifference in *A Voice for Ireland: The Famine in the Land* (1847). He defended William Smith O'BRIEN in the trials of 1848, and became an advocate for land reform, penning economic tracts such as *The Irish People and the Irish Land* (1867), and *Land Tenure in Ireland: A Plea for the Celtic Race* (1866). In 1870, he founded the Home Government Association, which became the Home Rule League in 1873. However, he was seen as too cautious in his approach to constitutional reform and was displaced as the leader of the Irish Party at Westminster by Charles Stewart PARNELL in 1879.

Further reading

McCormack, in Brady (ed.) (1989). Thornley (1964a).

Campaign For Social Justice (CSJ) see **Civil Rights Association (Northern Ireland)**

Carleton, William (1794–1869)   Novelist and short-story writer. Born in Co. Tyrone in 1794 to a Catholic tenant farmer, Carleton's only formal education was in the local HEDGE SCHOOL. After the family's eviction in 1813 he took to the roads as a 'poor scholar', before joining the Ribbonmen (see WHITEBOYS) for a spell, studying for the priesthood, and finally marrying and converting to Protestantism. Thereafter he began writing for the *Christian Examiner*, an anti-Catholic journal edited by Ceasar Otway (1780–1842), publishing the sketches of Irish country life that would be collected as *Traits and Stories of the Irish Peasantry* (in 1830 and 1833). Carleton's writing transcends the crude propaganda of the *Examiner*, and was highly praised for its narrative style and fidelity to detail. Perhaps his greatest triumph was in rendering Irish peasant speech – English words grafted on to Irish syntax – in prose, an achievement long pre-dating J. M. SYNGE. This was also a great influence on W. B. YEATS, who edited a selection of *Stories from Carleton* (1889). Carleton wrote numerous novels, the best of which is *The Black Prophet: A Tale of Irish Famine* (1847), both a record of the suffering of the starving poor and an indictment of those deemed complicit in the disaster (the book is ironically and accusingly dedicated to Lord John Russell, Prime Minister during the Famine). Carleton's later work was more sentimental and less successful. He spent the last years of his life working on his unfinished *Autobiography*, which was edited and published almost a century later by Patrick KAVANAGH. His reputation is secure as the chronicler of the pre-Famine Catholic peasant experience.

Further reading

Kiely (1972).

Carson, Ciaran (1948–)   Poet. Carson was born in BELFAST to a Catholic IRISH LANGUAGE-speaking family. After studying at QUB, he published *The New Estate* (1976). Despite being well received, Carson was dissatisfied with its standard lyric forms and themes, a feeling implicit in a 1975 review of *North* in which he attacked what he saw as Seamus HEANEY's aestheticization of violence. In the radically different style of *The Irish for No* (1987), an alternative to these dominant poetic styles was launched to much acclaim. Carson's new poems owed something to the doubled-back line of the American poet C. K. Williams and the oral style of the detective fiction of George V. Higgins, but even more to TRADITIONAL AND FOLK MUSIC (of which Carson is a practitioner) and the artfully digressive narratives of the Irish seanachie, or storyteller.

The same style of Belfast urban material, hauntingly interspersed with haiku and prose pieces, was deployed in the follow-up volume, *Belfast Confetti* (1989). Like its predecessor, it weaves seemingly arbitrary personal associations with an unmappable inner city world of after-hours bars, redevelopment zones, high-tech surveillance and paramilitary menace. With the 1990s, Carson turned to an exploration of new forms, investigating language, translation, and hallucinogenic and/or metamorphic states. *First Language* (1993), which won the T. S. Eliot Prize, uses rhyme with parodic virtuosity, as does *Opera et Cetera* (1996). *The Alexandrine Plan* (1998) consists of versions of sonnets by Baudelaire, Rimbaud and Mallarmé, while *The Twelfth of Never* (1998) is made up of 77 sonnets with titles from traditional music. In the 1990s Carson also wrote four prose works: *Last Night's Fun* (1996) is a personal meditation on the lore surrounding traditional music; *The Star Factory* (1997) meshes childhood memories with the decline of Belfast; *Fishing for Amber* (1999) includes a history of amber and the Dutch Golden Age; and *Shamrock Tea* (2001) features Jan van Eyck's *The Arnolfini Portrait* among much else.

Further reading

McCracken (1995).

Carson, Edward (1854–1935)   Lawyer and unionist politician. Educated at TCD, Carson was called to the Irish bar in 1877 and proved a highly successful barrister, becoming Solicitor General of Ireland in 1892. Famous for his cross-examination in the trial of Oscar WILDE, he was elected leader of the Irish Unionist Party in 1910, and helped to establish the ULSTER VOLUNTEER FORCE. He died in England but is buried in BELFAST, and his statue stands in front of the Government Buildings at STORMONT.

Cary, Joyce (1888–1957)   Novelist. Born in Co. Londonderry into an ANGLO-IRISH family whose fortunes vanished with the LAND ACT of 1881, Cary grew up in London, holidaying with his grandmother on the Inishowen peninsula. In 1913 he became a civil servant in the Nigerian Colonial Service. He enlisted in the British Army at the beginning of WWI, returning to Nigeria in 1918 and moving to Oxford in 1920. *Aissa Saved* (1932), *The African Witch* (1936), *Castle Corner* (1938) and *Mister Johnson* (1939) all derive wholly or in part from Cary's African experience, and, through their treatment of imperialism, explore the machinations of power and the delicate but essential significance of civilization. Cary's enlightened attitude towards the colonies and belief in their need for self-government is shown in *The Case for African Freedom* (1941). *Castle Corner* also draws on Cary's childhood trips to Inishowen, which provides the setting for the novel *A House of Children* (1941). His exploration of adolescence in the latter is the main preoccupation of *Charley is My Darling* (1940).

Cary's 'Gulley Jimson' trilogy, *Herself Surprised* (1941), *To Be a Pilgrim* (1942) and *The Horse's Mouth* (1944), meditates on the adaptability of adulthood to life's challenges and, like *Castle Corner*, dwells on the often-baleful effects of MODERNIZATION. The darkening political climate of Europe provides the backdrop to *A Fearful Joy* (1949), while in his second trilogy, *Prisoner of Grace* (1952), *Except the Land* (1953) and *Not Honour More* (1955), Cary continues to examine European power politics, its baseness and ruthlessness.

Further reading

Christian (1988).

Casement, Sir Roger (1864–1916)   Born in Sandymount, DUBLIN, and brought up in Ulster, Casement joined the diplomatic service in 1892. He used his position to report on and denounce, to great effect, appalling human rights abuses in the Belgian Congo and among rubber plantation workers of Putumayo in Brazil. He was knighted for his services to the Crown in 1911 and retired. An Irish NATIONALIST, Casement had joined the GAELIC LEAGUE in 1904, and joined the IRISH VOLUNTEERS in 1913. On the outbreak of WWI he went to Germany to secure aid for an insurrection and to try to raise an Irish Brigade from Irish prisoners of war. Returning to Ireland to deter the EASTER RISING, which he thought foolhardy, he was captured on 21 April 1916. After being sentenced to death, the British government allowed Casement's 'Black Diaries', revealing his homosexuality, to be circulated, to turn public opinion against him and besmirch his character in the eyes of puritanical Irish nationalists.

Further reading

Inglis (1973).

Catholic Committee   A pressure group working for the reform of the harsh legislation passed against Catholics in the eighteenth century (the PENAL LAWS). The Catholic Committee grew out of the first Catholic Association established in 1756 to protect and develop Catholic commercial interests. The Catholic Committee was established in 1760 by Charles O'Conor (1710–91), a notable antiquarian, and John Curry (*c.*1710–1780), a historian and writer whose work attempted to exonerate Catholics from charges of brutality, treason and murder during the REBELLION of 1641 and other key events in Irish history. The committee split in 1791 when a more radical and aggressive faction led by John Keogh (1740–1817), a UNITED IRISHMAN who wanted to lead the Committee towards their more revolutionary path, seized control. This new Committee organized the Catholic Convention in 1792, which was held 3–8 December 1792, with the aim of producing a petition from the delegates against the remaining penal laws. These consisted of various businessmen and men of property, some of whom, such as Wolfe TONE, were members of the United Irishmen. This petition was sent to the king, showing contempt for the LORD LIEUTENANT's government in Ireland. It showed that Catholics could organize effectively and efficiently and paved the way for more significant action in the nineteenth century. When the

Catholic Relief Act of 1793, partly brought about by the petition, allowed Catholics to vote and serve in the army and navy, the new Committee formally disbanded. The Committee briefly reformed in 1795 and then again in 1809, agitating for Catholic Emancipation, but was suppressed in 1811.

Catholic Emancipation   Catholic Emancipation was the central issue in Anglo-Irish relations in the first third of the nineteenth century. The Test and Corporation Acts forbade government ministers from taking sacraments anywhere other than in the Church of England. Catholics were specifically banned from entering parliament, voting, or serving in the armed forces. In the late eighteenth century a series of Catholic Relief Acts slightly lessened restrictions. It was generally believed that emancipation would follow the Act of Union, but George III strenuously objected. When the issue was pressed again in 1807 he forced the government to resign, effectively silencing further calls. When the future George IV became Prince Regent in 1811 Catholic hopes were high – the prince had been famously close to Catholic sympathizers – but he quickly adopted his father's policies. By the 1820s even former opponents began to see the probity of the measure, and with the advent of Daniel O'Connell and the Catholic Association (founded 1823) the campaign accelerated. In 1828 O'Connell was elected MP for Clare despite being technically disqualified. Faced with these extraordinary developments and anxious that O'Connell's popularity should not result in civil unrest, the Tory government led by the Duke of Wellington passed the Roman Catholic Relief Act, which became law on 13 April 1829. In practical terms the Act changed little, but its symbolic importance was enormous, as Catholic Ireland felt that it had at last found its voice – and with it, political power.

Catholicism   Catholicism became the main religious belief for most of the Irish population in the sixteenth and seventeenth centuries, so much so that Irish identity and Catholicism have ever since been intertwined. The main impetus behind the spread of Catholicism was the success of the Counter Reformation and the failure of the Protestant Reformation to take hold in Ireland, principally because it was promulgated by the English conquerors and so became seen as an alien form of religion imposed on the Irish. Ireland developed as a country where Catholicism was the popular religion and Protestantism a minority faith imposed by the state (the exception being the north-east where Presbyterianism held sway). Many Catholics supported the claims of the Jacobite pretenders throughout the eighteenth century and hoped for the overthrow of Protestant English rule.

Catholicism in Ireland developed as a humble and impoverished form of religion, lacking the spectacular art and culture of state-sponsored forms elsewhere in Europe. Heavy emphasis was placed on festivals, pilgrimages and other forms of popular worship. The failure of Jacobite revolts in the eighteenth century, and the decision of the papacy to refuse to recognize the Jacobite succession in 1766, meant that the state did not try to suppress Catholicism as vigorously as it had done, and it was tacitly tolerated at a local level while Catholics were kept out of public life by the PENAL LAWS. Catholics in turn were not forced to choose between loyalty to church or state and could exist as disadvantaged but not actively persecuted subjects. This balance started to change at the end of the eighteenth century as Catholics, alongside radical Protestants and republicans, pushed for far-reaching reform (see UNITED IRISHMEN, Wolfe TONE).

From the late eighteenth century onwards, Catholicism in Ireland benefited from a major reorganization of church practices and the formalization of Catholic ritual, which lent consistency to the faith within the country. By the 1820s, the emergence of a Catholic middle class and the continuing presence of a small but significant Catholic gentry added to pressures from the population in general for political reform, leading to the rise of Daniel O'CONNELL. Following CATHOLIC EMANCIPATION in 1829, a middle-class Catholic ascendancy became increasingly visible despite a continued Protestant monopoly in most areas of public life. From the 1840s on, the Church consolidated its grip on the country with a rise in the number of domestic vocations, and a major increase in church attendance, a phenomenon which became known as the post-Famine 'devotional revolution'. During the 1850s, a proliferation of religious societies and an increase in community-based devotional practices such as pilgrimages and the recitation of the rosary or veneration of Sacred Heart combined with a wave of church building to reinforce the centrality of the faith in Irish life. Catholicism came to be closely identified with the objectives of NATIONALISM, and self-government recognized as an essentially Catholic demand. This process was encouraged by the increasing alliance between Catholic clergy and nationalist political leaders in the country, a relationship which added to Protestant fears of the interference of Rome in Irish political and legislative affairs (see HOME RULE). Paul Cullen (1803–78), Archbishop of Dublin from 1852–78, and the first Irishman to be made a Cardinal (1866), was a powerful symbol of these changes. He summoned the first synod of the Irish clergy to be held since the twelfth century, at Thurles in 1850, and opposed the FENIANS while supporting nationalism through the National Association, which he founded in 1864. Despite overall population decline, the number of priests rose by 150 per cent between 1861 and 1911.

The Church's attitude to the EASTER RISING was initially negative, like its response to the FENIANS. But its nationalist links meant it could endorse SINN FÉIN and support the Free State by reining in revolutionary energies and excommunicating anti-treatyites during the CIVIL WAR. As a result the Church found its moral teaching given legal force in the new state, exercising powerful sway through CENSORSHIP and its central role in education, health and welfare provision. Beyond this, its pronouncements on obedience to superior power, on the sanctity of the FAMILY, and on the position of WOMEN and SEXUALITY were all-pervasive. Ireland's new place within world Catholicism was confirmed by its hosting of the International Eucharistic Congress in 1932, and the Church's 'special position' in the life of the nation was recognized in the Constitution of 1937.

The most powerful figure in the mid-century Church, John Charles McQuaid (1895–1973), was, like Cullen a century before, an ultra-conservative Archbishop of Dublin. McQuaid promulgated the total segregation of sexes in education, ended dialogue with other churches, and set a major building programme in motion to match urban growth; between 1940 and 1965, 34 churches were built in Dublin and 26 new parishes formed. Levels of popular devotion were very high; as late as the early 1970s, 91 per cent of adult Catholics in the Republic attended Church once a week. In Northern Ireland, orthodoxy and devotion were even greater than in the south. In the 1940s and 1950s, there were also more than 20,000 members of religious orders. The confidence and energy of the Church was shown in the extent of its foreign missions, often undertaken by the orders; in 1950, the number of priests attached to missions abroad equalled the number in Ireland itself.

The Church generally exercised its sway in the public arena discreetly but effectively; it was accommodating towards minority faiths, backed by the state's support for the *ne temere* decree of 1907, by which children of a mixed Protestant and Catholic marriages had to be brought up as Catholics. When it intervened overtly to modify legislation, as over the Mother and Child Bill in 1951, its effect was decisive, but it risked appearing meddlesome (see MEDICINE). Some attitudes changed in the 1960s, under pressure from internal campaigners and the reforms of the Second Vatican Council (1962–65), established by the liberal pontiff Pope John XXIII. The effects of the latter have probably been over-estimated; even so, many older religious forms traditional in Irish Catholicism were abolished at this time.

Although the Church tried to adapt to secularization and change in the 1960s and 1970s, it encountered serious difficulties. Some of the debates are dramatized in Brian Moore's novel *Catholics* (1972), which pits modernizers against traditionalists, and suggests that the Church may compromise itself out of existence. The development of Knock as a place of pilgrimage and the reception of Pope John Paul II in 1979 testified to the strength of allegiance, and the Church was able to successfully oppose social liberalization in the 1980s, but it continued to lose credibility, particularly among the urban young (see ABORTION, CONTRACEPTION and DIVORCE). Vocations to the priesthood and religious life fell from 1,409 in 1966 to just 92 in 1998. One result has been a loss of morale, compounded by the decline in religious devotion; weekly attendance at Mass has dropped from 77 per cent in 1994 to 55 per cent in 1998. This has occurred against a background of revelations of extensive child abuse and sexual scandals in the 1990s, such as the SMYTH CASE. As a result, the Church has today lost the high level of support it once commanded, and is no longer synonymous with the Irish state and people.

'Celtic Tiger'   The term was formed (somewhat patronizingly) by analogy with the 'Asian Tiger' economies of the Pacific Rim. It was coined as a label for the ECONOMY of the Republic by the Morgan Stanley investment bank in August 1994 at the start of the unprecedented boom which was to last throughout the 1990s; thus, in the seven years from 1995 to 2001 annual average real GDP growth was 9.4 per cent compared with a 2.6 per cent average for the EU, according to government statistics. Within this figure was concealed the even higher rate of growth for the industrial sector, which expanded at an annual rate of 15 per cent. Growth had begun in the late 1980s, halted between 1991 and 1993, and then leapt to the point where per capita GDP surpassed that of Britain in 1997. Unemployment dropped to 4 per cent (against an EU average of 8 per cent) as Ireland transformed itself from a largely AGRICULTURE-based economy to one based on industry and services at the turn of the millennium. Indeed, with over 70 per cent of its GDP now exported, Ireland is the third largest world exporter on a per capita basis (after Singapore and Belgium/Luxembourg). EMIGRATION was not only halted but reversed, as Irish returned from overseas and the country even suffered a skills shortage and advertised for workers abroad.

There were many reasons for this dramatic reversal, which was clearly based on Ireland's ability to attract investment by multinational corporations (MNCs). These include; economic openness since the late 1950s; the fiscal retrenchment introduced by FIANNA FÁIL in 1987; agreements between government, trades unions, farmers and corporations, giving a stable economic environment; a young, educated and flexible, but cheap, labour force; low levels of bureaucracy and easy accessibility to officials and politicians; cheaper transport and electronic communications revolutions to offset geographical marginality. The fact that Ireland is English-speaking and has ethnic links with the USA has also been important for US MNCs. However, the two crucial factors are probably Ireland's membership of the EU and its corporation tax which, at 10 per cent, is the lowest in Europe. Investment has come from MNCs needing to produce within the new European Single Market. Many of these are computing, computer software, drinks concentrates, chemical and pharmaceuticals manu-facturers, and most of their products are exported on to destinations within the EU.

Critics of the 'Celtic Tiger' have pointed out that the boom is vulnerable, based as it is on a handful of foreign firms in a small number of economic sectors. They also argue that the massive discrepancy between Irish workers for MNCs and those in Irish-based firms (the former are nine times more productive than the latter) can only be explained through 'transfer pricing', an accounting practice which allows general corporate pro-ductivity to be attributed to Irish workers in order to qualify it for the Republic's low taxes. They point to the fact that inequalities have increased during the boom, and that little of the Irish treasury's tax windfall has been ploughed back into health services, schools, roads or other areas of the infrastructure (20 per cent of the population still live below the poverty line). Average real earnings have not risen in line with the increase in GDP, but prices – particularly of private housing – have soared.

The 'Celtic Tiger' phenomenon results from the conjunction of globalization with the wholehearted Europeanization of the Irish economy, and represents a historical

LIBRARY, UNIVERSITY COLLEGE CHESTER

reversal of economic sluggishness. While it cannot last indefinitely, it has already had a profound impact on Irish society and self-perceptions. Nevertheless, it must be remembered that the term belongs to government-sponsored attempts to forge a new national identity (the day on which it was first used publicly was also that of the 1994 IRA ceasefire), and that it can be seen as a form of the double-edged 'regressive MODERNIZATION' some of its critics have identified. (See Luke GIBBONS.)

Further reading

Allen (2000). http://www.ntma.ie

Celts derives from the word 'Keltoi' which the Greeks used to define the 'barbarian' people in the north. The Celts probably first became established as a distinct people in *c.*12,000 BC when they became the largest group in Central and Western Europe. The subsequent advance of the Roman Empire and the Germanic tribes in the first century BC forced them to retreat to the West. They became the dominant culture in Ireland in the following centuries, although exactly how and when will probably always be hard to determine. ARCHAEOLOGICAL evidence indicates that their advance was gradual rather than invasive as was once assumed. The Celts were renowned as a martial people, although they never established a coherent empire. Aristotle comments on their prowess and bravery in battle, as does the Greek historian Polybius. Celtic society was also noted for the value it placed on bards and DRUIDS. Celtic religion was based on the worship of the natural world – the oak was their sacred tree – and they were reputed to practise human sacrifice.

Further reading

Chadwick (1970).

censorship The Free State government moved swiftly to restrict freedom of speech in the Censorship of FILMS Act (1923) and the Censorship of Publications Act (1929). Such legislation was not uncommon in the 1920s following the Geneva Convention for the Suppression of Obscene Publications of 1923, and a general climate of censorship and prohibition internationally. In Ireland, however, the Censorship Board was appointed by, and answerable only to, the Minister for Justice. After 1922, revolutionary puritanism, sectarian suspicion and religious reaction against the energies released by conflict all combined for maximum repressive effect. Despite protests from many writers and artists at the time, including George RUSSELL ('AE'), W. B. YEATS and George Bernard SHAW, virtually all modern writing of note, especially fiction, was banned. This was part of a repressive moral climate in which jazz music was prohibited on Radio Éireann (see TELEVISION AND RADIO), and modern dance and women's fashions were frowned upon.

The power of the Censorship Board was multiplied by the activities of members of organizations such as the Catholic Truth Society who vetted material on an individual vigilante basis. Booksellers were intimidated and libraries were purged of 'offensive' material, since any book which contained a reference to sexual activity could be banned despite the Act's requirement to take account of the 'literary, artistic, scientific or historic merit of a book'. A tiny sample of those condemned would include Proust, Faulkner, Hemingway, Sartre, Dylan Thomas, Sholokov, Isherwood, and even an anthropologist such as Margaret Mead. Despite criticism, largely in Sean O'FAOLAIN's THE BELL, Irish writers were routinely denied access to an Irish public, from the banning of Liam O'FLAHERTY's *The House of Gold* (1930) to Lee Dunne's *The Cabfather* (1976). Others, such as Brinsley MacNamara and John McGAHERN, had their books burnt in public, lost their jobs, or were otherwise persecuted and humiliated. As a result, many writers and artists left Ireland to live abroad.

Censorship was the moral and intellectual equivalent of the economic self-sufficiency of the DE VALERA era, its rationale being the desire to distinguish CATHOLIC Irish society from secular British society as sharply as possible. As such it was popular and viewed as a wholesome expression of national identity. It shaped Irish writing by reaction, since writers tended to adopt lyric, inward and realistic styles rather than experimental ones, given isolation and the desire to expose a society which refused to examine itself too closely. Censorship was frequently indiscriminate; a classic, such as Boccaccio's *The Decameron*, could be banned together with pulp fiction titles like *She Died Without Nylons*. So obtuse and swingeing were the Board's activities that it became a badge of honour for Irish writers to produce at least one banned work. Yet, as critics have claimed, even more pernicious than book banning was the infantiliza-tion of Irish society and the celebration of philistinism which censorship endorsed. Ironically, given the xenophobia of the censors, many libraries were reduced to stocks chiefly of imported westerns, romances and crime fiction. Virtually an entire genera-tion of Irish writing is still missing from many Irish libraries.

An Appeal Board was set up in 1946, and censorship was weakened in 1967 when the period of time for which books could be prohibited as 'obscene' was reduced to 12 years, freeing over 5,000 titles. Censorship is now exercised in a more flexible and rational manner than before. Nevertheless, some serious works of fiction and non-fiction – by Angela Carter and Georges Bataille, for example – remain banned. It is important to remember that censorship has applied to other media than print, and that it was widely applied during the TROUBLES by both the British and Irish governments.

Further reading

Brown (1985b). Carlson (1990). Fallon (1998).

Church of Ireland   The Church of Ireland refers to the main Protestant denomina-tion in Ireland. After the Act of Supremacy in 1537, through which the English monarch became Head of the Church, the Church of Ireland effectively took over from the pre-Reformation church in Ireland. However, its power within the country was always out of proportion, given that it catered mainly for English and Scottish settlers and their descendants, while most of the population remained Roman Catholic. Following the Act of Union, the Churches of Ireland and England were declared to have been united 'for ever', and in the early decades of the nineteenth century the Protestant church attempted to consolidate its influence through evangelicalism, philanthropy, and conversions. But its state-supported position was tenuous, and the obligatory payment of Church tithes created enormous resentment among the Catholic and Dissenting population. During the 1830s the Whig government carried out a series of reforms (notably the Church Temporalities Act, 1833) aimed at reducing the authority of the archbishops and rationalizing the income gained from rented church land. This marked the beginning of a process eroding the self-governing status of the Church of Ireland, which increasingly saw itself as besieged and abandoned, particularly against a backdrop of heightened Catholic self-assertion in the 1850s. By the time of the 1861 census, it was revealed that only 11.9 per cent of the Irish population were affiliated to the Church of Ireland, and towards the end of that decade the British Prime Minister Gladstone set in motion the Irish Church Bill, which was eventually passed in 1869. This came into effect in January of 1871, when the Church of Ireland was officially dis-endowed and separated from the Church of England, a process referred to as Disestablishment.

Disestablishment marked the beginning of a long decline, numerically and in terms of its authority, for the Church. Following Partition, Northern Ireland became a majority Protestant state, within which Presbyterians were in a majority over members of the Church of Ireland; in the Free State, Protestants were a small minority (7.4 per cent of the population in the 1926 census), although among them the Church of Ireland was the largest denomination. The Protestant population was fragmented, largely constituted as it was of two groups – landowning gentry, and members of the urban middle class – with very different interests. Without political representation, it was the general synod of the Church of Ireland which ascertained the position of Protestants within the new state by dispatching a delegation to Michael Collins on 12 May 1922. Collins gave assurances that Protestants would be protected.

By and large, Protestants in the southern state were fairly treated and suffered little direct interference from either the state or the Catholic Church. Although divorce was banned and the *ne temere* decree enforced, Protestants and the Church of Ireland were reconciled and adapted themselves to a process of inexorable numerical and social decline through intermarriage and emigration. From the 1920s on, the Church had been at the forefront of ecumenism, a movement to bring the different churches in Ireland together, but for 40 years the Roman Catholic Church stood outside this process. Such processes were given new urgency by the Troubles in Northern Ireland after 1968–69, in which the Church of Ireland tried to play a reconciliatory role between the more combative faiths, and between warring factions. During the 1980s it also found the courage to protest against the CONSTITUTIONAL amendment on ABORTION in the Republic. While judging the practice evil, they nevertheless felt the attempt to legislate on an issue of personal moral judgement was divisive and invasive. In addition, the Church still maintains missions, having in 1992 some 14 member bodies of associate missionary societies, with a total of 65 workers mainly in East Africa and Nepal.

Since World War II several distinguished figures have forcefully made the case for the potentially vital and constructive role of the Church of Ireland in the Republic, and for the need for all the churches to concentrate on the core Christian teaching of brotherly love in Northern Ireland, among them the distinguished essayist Hubert Butler in his *Escape from the Anthill* (1986).

Further reading

Brown (1985b).

Church, Irish   Records suggest that Christianity was first established in Ireland in the fifth century, mainly in the East and South-east of the country as missionaries from Britain, the most famous of these being St PATRICK, started to make an impact. The spread of Christianity in the next few centuries was steady rather than spectacular. By the seventh century the church was well established and had started to absorb and adapt much of the local mythology into its teachings and calendar. Ireland became well known for the number and importance of its monastic centres. Ireland also became famous as a centre of Christian learning and scholarship, notable also for the high quality of the illuminated manuscripts produced such as the *BOOK OF KELLS*. Irish monks travelled to the continent and influenced religious life and theological doctrine.

Irish ecclesiastical pre-eminence was threatened by the VIKING INVASION at the end of the eighth century, although how great the impact was has been disputed by modern historians. Eventually the Vikings started to become absorbed into the local culture and became Christians, and in the early eleventh century the Viking centre at Dublin appointed a bishop. A reform movement in the twelfth century resulted in the establishment of the rigorous and austere Cistercian order in Ireland, led by St Malachy (*d.*1148). The order reached its peak in the thirteenth century (in 1228 there were 34 Cistercian monasteries in Ireland), but then fell into decline.

The NORMAN INVASION also transformed the organization and structure of the Irish church. The ostensible justification for the invasion was the need to bring the Irish church under tighter papal control (see LAUDABILITER) and from the end of the twelfth century the Archbishop of Dublin was effectively subordinate to his counterpart in Canterbury. More English and Anglicized bishops controlled the Irish church and there were disputes among the Irish and Anglo-Irish in the monastic orders. The state of the Irish church before the REFORMATION is a matter of dispute among historians. Some see the church as a corrupt and moribund institution, seriously weakened by the conflict between Irish and Anglo-Irish ecclesiastics. Others point to the rise of the Observant orders (wandering friars who took vows of extreme poverty as a means of combating what they saw as the greed and complacency of the established orders) as a sign that the church was undergoing a period of revitalization which was curtailed by the impact of Protestantism.

After the Reformation, the established church in Ireland was the Church of Ireland which was under the suzerainty of the English king, who was also king of Ireland. The influence of the Church was confined to Anglicized areas, specifically the Pale around Dublin. Elsewhere, CATHOLICISM dominated Gaelic Ireland as the COUNTER REFORMATION spread. And even within the areas it nominally controlled the Church was limited by the adherence of many ANGLO-IRISH to the Catholic faith. The Church of Ireland debated its theological position carefully and painfully but failed to make significant impact on the wider population. In Ulster Presbyterianism was the dominant religion among the settlers, many of whom were of Scottish origin. While it has played an important part in Irish life since the sixteenth century, and helped to form the character of the Anglo-Irish Ascendancy in the eighteenth century, the Church of Ireland has only ever had significant impact in urban areas and has had to play second fiddle to the Catholic Church and, in Ulster, the Presbyterian churches.

Further reading

Corish (ed.) (1985). Ford, Maguire and Milne (eds) (1995).

Civil Rights Association (Northern Ireland)   Taking its cue from the Civil Rights campaign in the USA, and the Campaign for Social Justice (CSJ) established in Dungannon in 1964, the Northern Ireland Civil Rights Association (NICRA) was formed in January 1967 to advance the civil rights of the Catholic minority. The 1944 Education Act and 1960s liberalism had seen the emergence of a generation of educated Catholics and liberal Protestants capable of creating a coalition of groups, including nationalists, socialists, republicans and reform-minded unionists, and following the CSJ it demanded an end to electoral GERRYMANDERING, sectarian bias in public housing and job allocation, and the repeal of the Special Powers Act of 1922. Before this time, the Catholic population had taken only limited interest in the democratic process in Northern Ireland, with Nationalist Party MPs refraining from taking their Westminster, and sometimes STORMONT, seats. Demoralization and political disengagement had produced a fatalistic, conservative politics fixated on the Republic; the Civil Rights Association was the first real attempt to demand the nominal democratic rights on offer to Catholics as UK citizens.

NICRA used the tactics of the international youth protest movement – sit-downs, occupations – and, from mid-1968 onwards, a campaign of MARCHES. These threatened the ancient symbolic beating of boundaries which defined Protestant self-identity in particular. Viewing it as a republican and communist front organization, the response of LOYALISTS (including attacks by the B-SPECIALS and the Royal Ulster Constabulary) was extreme. Following Westminster pressure, Terence O'NEILL announced concessions on almost every demand in November 1968. However, a radical splinter group, People's Democracy, was determined to push for further demands and in January 1969 their BELFAST to DERRY march was savagely ambushed at Burntollet Bridge by supporters of Ian PAISLEY. This triggered the 'Battle of the Bogside' in DERRY in August, loyalist assaults on Catholic areas of Belfast, and the arrival of British troops. The TELEVISING of such events provided a new ingredient and galvanized public opinion in the UK and worldwide in favour of reform. Arguably, the very success of NICRA's tactics meant that marches substituted for other political forms of action, and made it easier to derail the movement along sectarian lines; nevertheless, by November 1968 the movement had acquired a momentum and was unwilling to limit itself to single issues. It was finally wound up following the killings of BLOODY SUNDAY in January 1972.

Further reading

Purdie (1990).

Civil War (1922–1923)   The ostensible cause of the Civil War was the split of SINN FÉIN and the IRA between supporters and opponents of the ANGLO-IRISH TREATY. DE VALERA's suspicion of the IRB, which directed the GAELIC LEAGUE, and in turn directed the IRISH VOLUNTEERS, and which was used by Michael COLLINS to gain acceptance of the treaty, was another factor. Anti-treatyites like Liam Mellowes and Rory O'Connor repudiated the result of the election in June 1922, which gave the pro-treatyites, supported by the LABOUR PARTY, a majority. But technically hostilities began when the pro-treaty Free State forces attempted to expel the dissident anti-treaty garrison from its base in the Four Courts in DUBLIN on 28 June 1922.

Soon completely driven out of Dublin, the anti-treaty 'Irregulars' regrouped in the heartland of the anti-British struggle, in the South and West. After unsuccessful peace moves in September, the Irregulars were denounced by the CATHOLIC CHURCH in October (W. B. YEATS's 'Meditations in Time of Civil War' has the poet encountering both sides, and feeling 'caught/In the cold snows of a dream'). Military casualties alone were between 4,000 and 5,000, and included the assassination of the leader of the Free State, Michael COLLINS, on 22 August, as well as other leading figures on both sides, such as Rory O'Connor, Liam Mellowes, Harry Boland, Erskine Childers, Cathal Brugha and Liam Lynch. Material and financial costs were also high. Many more Irish NATIONALISTS were killed by fellow Irish nationalists in the Civil War than had been killed by the British between 1916 and 1921. The psychological damage of the war's 'poisonous legacy' is more difficult to assess, but there is no doubt that Irish politics were shaped by it for well over half a century, with FINE GAEL and FIANNA FÁIL effectively the parliamentary expression of the two sides. Anti-treatyites had been crushed by force of arms rather than being won over, and when their leader, Frank Aiken, called for a ceasefire on 24 May 1923 he ordered that arms be dumped rather than being surrendered. Armed republicanism survived, in an underground form, as the IRA. Only after 1969, as violence in Northern Ireland made the continued fixation on civil war divisions seem irresponsible, did their importance in politics in the Republic begin to diminish.

Further reading

Hopkinson (1988).

Clarke, Austin (1896–1974)   Poet, novelist and dramatist. A student of Irish and English at UCD (where his MA supervisor was Thomas MacDonagh), Clarke's work was shaped by the events which gave birth to independent Ireland. Progressing from verse epics in the manner of Samuel Ferguson and the early W. B. Yeats, such as *The Vengeance of Fionn* (1917), Clarke showed himself, in *The Cattledrive at Cooley* (1925) and *Pilgrimage* (1929), to be unique in his successful application of the 'Irish Mode' to the lyric. More than merely antiquarian, the Celto-Romanesque setting of many of these, as of his three novels (*The Bright Temptation* (1932), *The Singing Men at Cashel* (1936) and *The Sun Dances at Easter* (1952)), offers an implicit criticism by contrast to growing repressiveness in the Free State. After an unconsummated marriage in 1920, he was deprived of a lectureship at UCD (because the marriage had been solemnized in a registry office, not a church) and driven to make a living in England from 1922. Although he returned to Ireland in 1937, the banning of his novels and exclusion from Yeats's 1936 *Oxford Anthology of English Verse* inform the collection *Night and Morning* (1938), an anguished expression of the paralysing struggle between liberal belief and a philistine Catholic Church. Clarke published no more poetry for 17 years, writing for the stage instead and founding The Lyric Theatre Company in 1944. When he did, it was with the verse satires of *Ancient Lights* (1955), *Too Great a Vine* (1958) and *The Horse-Eaters* (1960). Mordant, but witty and often moving lyrics attack the hypocrisies of 'our ill-fare State' and champion the rights of excluded minorities, while longer meditative poems articulate a humane, negative theology, analysing the erosion of the ideals of 1916, as well as the indignities of old age. In the 1960s Clarke's renewal broadened with *Flight to Africa* (1963), his widest-ranging collection, and his masterpiece *Mnemosyne Lay in Dust* (1966), whose 18 sections fuse guilt, fear of sexual incapacity, religious terror and multiple rejection in poetry of great power and inventiveness. Clarke's final flowering appears in a series of sexually explicit reworkings of classical and Irish mythological narratives, often in dazzling hexameters, collected in *Orphide* (1970) and *Tiresias* (1971).

Further reading

Corcoran (1999). Goodby (1999). Harmon (1989).

Coercion Acts A series of temporary Acts, dozens of which were passed in the nineteenth century, which expedited the conviction of suspected political agitators, Defenders, Land League activists and Fenians. They frequently dispensed with the need for juries in trials, created new offences and set the scales of punishment for those offences. They are a prime indicator of the degree to which Ireland cannot be described as a 'normal' component of the UK at this time, and hence as making the case for colonial and/or postcolonial understanding of the Irish experience. One descendant of the Coercion Acts was the system of non-jury Diplock Courts and supergrasses used by the British state in Northern Ireland in the 1970s and 1980s.

Coffey, Brian (1905–1995) Poet and visual artist. Coffey was praised by Samuel Beckett in 1934 for being alive to 'the breakdown of the object, whether current historical or spook', and aware of a 'rupture of the lines of communication' – comments which link his work to early modernism. Beckett also links Coffey with Denis Devlin and Thomas MacGreevy in order to distinguish him from what he views as the conventionality of poets of the Literary Revival. *Poems* (1930), by Coffey and Devlin, was followed by his *Three Poems* (1933), which was derivative of Eliot. However, the lyric sequence, *Third Person* (1938), explores the complexity of human and divine love in a style which is completely Coffey's own, and introduces the ambiguous texture and hypnotic rhythms of his mature work. It also reveals the importance of Thomist philosophy, which he studied in the 1930s in Paris under Jacques Maritain.

Maritain's speculations on the difficulty for the artist in reconciling Catholicism and modernism may have been responsible for a poetic silence which lasted until the 1960s, when *Missouri Sequence* (1962) and a translation of Mallarmé's *Un Coup de dés* (*Dice Thrown Never Will Annul Chance*) (1965) appeared. *Dice Thrown* can be read as much as a Maritain-inspired rejoinder to Mallarmé's atheistical poetic as a straight translation, something it shares with *Missouri Sequence*, whose Christian existentialism leads to musings on the issues of grace and choice and an equation of poetry with truth – beliefs which had been severely tested during Coffey's time as a philosophy lecturer at the University of St Louis (1947–52). Rejecting in *Sequence* the claim that the very uniqueness of poetry's vision obscures universal truths, Coffey counters that 'Poetry becomes humankind' precisely because 'without [it] nothing exact is said'. From his own emigrant experience, he draws the truth of humanity's existential plight, in which 'we face a testing/based on other grounds than nature's'.

Coffey's later work includes *Advent* (1975), which extends reflections on God and love to beauty, ethics, and environmental issues, which are grounded in details of the poet's life (including the death of his mother and one of his sons). *Death of Hektor* (1980), his finest poem, reflects on Homer's treatment of Hector, and on the heroism of war in general, in the light of possible nuclear war. Like *Advent*, it develops its case not through logical argument, but through an association of images and motifs. Both poems use various rhythmic units, in contrast to the conversational tone of *Missouri Sequence*; and, as in *Un coup de dés*, deploy typographical devices which suggest 'concrete poetry'. Other short poems, such as *Leo* (1968), involved collaboration with visual artists.

One of the most restlessly experimental of modern Irish poets, Coffey is perhaps the most unjustly neglected.

Further reading

Moriarty (2000).

Collins, Michael (1890–1922)   Soldier, politician and statesman. Born in Co. Cork to a NATIONALIST farming family, Collins worked as a bank clerk in London from the age of 15; there he joined the GAELIC LEAGUE and the IRB, becoming a leading figure in the IRB before being summoned to Dublin for the 1916 RISING. He fought in the GPO; afterwards, while still in INTERNMENT, he began to assemble a formidable intelligence network. On release, he used it to penetrate the British governmental structure in Ireland, and following SINN FÉIN's electoral victory in 1918, in the first DÁIL, was made Director of Intelligence in the IRA, and Minister of Finance. During the ANGLO-IRISH WAR, Collins was able to direct a devastatingly effective campaign of infiltration and assassination, paralysing the British intelligence network. While DE VALERA raised support for the Free State in the USA in 1919–20, Collins emerged as a powerful political as well as military figure. It was he who was sent by De Valera to negotiate with the British in London. The ANGLO-IRISH TREATY was signed by Collins and the other Irish delegates, although Collins knew many republicans would find its terms repugnant. On signing it, he is said to have observed 'I have signed my death warrant'. Collins now began forming a regular Irish Army from the guerrilla IRA units, and spending the first half of 1922 trying to keep the disintegrating government forces together, while negotiating with the UNIONISTS in Northern Ireland (which he was nevertheless covertly attempting to destabilize by supplying the IRA there). At the same time he was assuring the British that he was keeping the terms of a treaty which he had never been keen on. It was Collins who, fatefully, gave the order for the assault on the Four Courts, as Commander-in-Chief of the Free State Army, and this pre-emptive strike against anti-treatyites triggered the CIVIL WAR. It was while driving to negotiate a possible ceasefire with leaders of the republican forces that he was ambushed and killed at Béal na Bláth, Co. Cork, on 22 August 1922. His youth and promise have made him an iconic, even cult figure ever since, as evidenced in the success of Neil JORDAN's film of 1997. Had he lived, the Free State would have enjoyed more authority than it did, and the political landscape would not have been as polarized; as it was, the mantle of republicanism descended on De Valera, a decade later.

Further reading

Forester (1989).

colonization and plantation   Ireland has been colonized by waves of aggressive immigrants throughout its history. The first recorded colonizers are the CELTS who had occupied Ireland well before the early Christian era, as they had much of mainland Europe. Ireland escaped colonization by the Romans and the Saxons, a fact proudly noted by numerous later historians, but it was then colonized extensively by the NORMANS in the twelfth century. Many of these became effectively Irish, as Geoffrey KEATING recorded, and many became the OLD ENGLISH who administered the lands controlled by the English Crown. Ireland was colonized much more thoroughly in the sixteenth and seventeenth centuries when the island started to assume its modern political, social and geographical character. Once Henry VIII had declared that he was now king rather than lord of Ireland (1541), the Tudors were committed to establishing control over all of Ireland and not leaving it, divided as it had been throughout the Middle Ages, into the 'lands of peace', where English law and administration functioned, and the 'lands of war', where Irish systems of government held sway.

One of the ways in which the Tudors sought to establish control was through plantations, small colonies of English settlers who, it was hoped, would draw the Irish natives to civilized life, obedience and proper agriculture (sowing corn rather than tending cattle). Often plans for colonization would alternate between suggestions that the English and the Irish should mix together, as this was the best way to encourage the Irish to become civilized, and more military-style operations, which involved removing many of the native Irish from the designated areas and establishing military-style garrisons of English to protect the farming land.

The first plans for plantations were small in scale but as the Tudors failed to make sufficient headway they became more ambitious. There were attempts to establish plantations in Leix and Offaly in the 1550s, which did not survive for long. Sir Thomas Smith's attempt to colonize the Ards Peninsula in Ulster in the 1570s was also a disaster and was easily overthrown by the natives. The MUNSTER PLANTATION, established in the 1590s, was more successful, and indicated that plantations would only work if they were large enough to contain a sizeable English population. The ULSTER PLANTATION was the grandest plan of them all and transformed the population of Ireland beyond recognition in the North-east.

It is important when discussing colonization to distinguish between two key senses of the term. There is the technical sense of establishing a colony of people transported from their native land to another, a definition provided by the example of the ancient Greeks from where the term originates. There is also the more general sense of one country occupying and dominating another one, as England has indeed occupied and dominated Ireland for a large section of its history.

Further reading

Canny (2001).

colonialism see **postcolonialism and colonialism**

Columba, St (Colum Cille) (521?–597) A patron saint of Ireland, alongside St PATRICK and St BRIGID. Columba was born in Gartan, Co. Donegal, into the royal family of Niall, and given the name Colum Cille ('dove of the church') by an angel. He was educated in monasteries at Molville and Clonard, where he studied under St FINNIAN. He then joined the monastery at Glasnevin, but this foundation was disbanded when it was struck by the plague. Columba travelled extensively throughout Ireland founding a series of monasteries and churches in Kells, Derry, Swords and Dunrow. He then became involved in a dispute with Finnian over a copy of St Jerome's Psalter, which Columba was accused of borrowing and copying without permission. King Dairmaid, the high king, ruled in favour of Finnian. Columba then led the Uí Néill against Dairmaid, but was defeated in 561 and sentenced to exile in 563. He sailed to Iona and established one of the key monasteries in the British Isles, which became the missionary centre of Celtic Christianity and enjoyed an enormous reputation throughout Europe. Columba is reputed to have converted the Picts after driving a monster from Loch Ness, as well as the Irish king, Aiden of Dalriada. Columba lived in Iona until his death, but frequently revisited Ireland. He attended the Synod of Druim Cetta (*c.*575–80) where he argued that women should not have to undergo military service and that the bards were a key element within Irish life. Columba was buried on Iona. He inspired a series of works soon after his death, including *Amra Choluim Cille* (*The Eulogy of Colum Cille*), the earliest recorded poem in Irish. Our record of his life is based on Adamnán's (627?–704), a later abbot of Iona, *Vita Columbae* (*The Life of St Columba*). Iona later became known as the author of a series of prophecies, and was said to have predicted the VIKING invasions. Owing to his military background, he is frequently invoked by troops going into battle.

Connolly, James (1868–1916) Political leader, theorist and organizer. Born in Edinburgh to a working-class Catholic family, Connolly enlisted in the British Army at 14, encountering socialist and Marxist ideas for the first time in 1889. In 1896 he became an organizer of the Dublin Socialist Club, moved to DUBLIN, and founded the Irish Socialist Republican Party. He and his family endured great hardship, living in one tenement-block room, as his reputation as an organizer and publicist for the socialist cause grew.

Connolly was a key figure in the labour movement of the UK, a friend of Keir Hardie and other of its leaders, although he was critical of the tendency of its English members to overlook the importance of national differences. He emigrated to the USA in 1903, working for the Industrial Workers of the World (IWW) and the Socialist Party, although significantly he fell out with the American Socialist Party leader Daniel de Leon over the latter's attacks on the CATHOLIC CHURCH. In 1910 he returned to Ireland, becoming organizer of the Socialist Party of Ireland, and in BELFAST in 1911, as Ulster organizer of the Irish Transport and General Workers Union (ITGWU), led a mill-girls' strike. After the arrest of James LARKIN, he was the leader of the Dublin Lockout (1913–14), when he formed the IRISH CITIZEN ARMY as a defence force and adopted the Starry Plough as its banner.

The Ulster crisis and the outbreak of World War I in August 1914 cut across the development of socialism and militant trade unionism in Ireland, but Connolly underestimated the determination of Northern UNIONISTS to reject incorporation with the South under Home Rule. Denouncing the war as an imperialist holocaust, he seems to have despaired at the lack of socialist opposition to it, giving his support to the NATIONALIST movement and so effectively committing the Citizen Army and Irish labour movement against the Allies. He was co-opted to the Military Council of the IRB, second, as Military Commander of the Dublin forces, only to Patrick PEARSE in the EASTER RISING. Connolly may have hoped he could win Pearse and other IRB leaders towards a socialist position, but although he inspired the socialistic clauses of the Proclamation of the REPUBLIC, his death meant that the cause of Labour would be sealed in blood as subordinate to that of the nation. DE VALERA's injunction of 1918, 'Labour must wait', was a logical consequence. Sean O'CASEY, who, as Secretary of the Socialist Party, had resigned as Secretary in 1914 over Connolly's tactics, dramatized the events around the Rising in his Trilogy.

Wounded in the defence of the General Post Office (GPO), Connolly was the last of the rebels to be shot, strapped to a chair because he could no longer stand. He had already predicted, with some accuracy, that Partition would be succeeded by a 'carnival of reaction' on both sides of the border. His writings include *Labour in Irish History* (1907), which casts the Labour movement as continuers of the communitarian ethos of Gaeldom. *Labour, Nationality and Religion* (1910) is a reminder that Connolly argued for the compatibility of Catholic faith with socialist revolution.

Further reading

Greaves (1961). Morgan (1988).

Constitution of the Irish Free State (1922) and Constitution of Ireland (Bunreacht na hÉireann) (1937)

The first constitution of the newly independent Ireland was 'a typical liberal-democratic document', suitable for a modern European republic of any religious denomination. It was based on the concept of popular sovereignty, and so was distinct from the formally deferential political culture of Britain, in which the Crown and parliament are sovereign, and the people are defined technically as their 'subjects'. Like other modern constitutions, it also contained a comprehensive bill of rights.

The 1937 constitution which replaced the one of 1922 retained many of these modern characteristics, but reflected the clerical-conservative direction in which the new state had evolved since then. Four aspects of this can be noted here.

First is the marked CATHOLIC ethos of the constitution. Articles 15, 18–19 and 40–45 forbid the right of divorce, recognize the family as 'a moral institution' and acknowledge the 'special position' in the state of the Catholic Church (although other religions are specifically recognized). Thus, the constitution opens with the words 'In the Name of the Most Holy Trinity …'.

Second, the constitution marks a high point of official anti-partitionist rhetoric, since it was the first instance of the irredentist claim to the six counties of Northern Ireland being given legal form. Article 2 asserts that 'The national territory consists of the whole island of Ireland, its islands and the territorial seas', albeit Article 3 pragmatically notes that 'pending the re-integration of the national territory' the constitution applies only to the territory of the existing state. Although DE VALERA saw the constitution as a bridge over which Northern UNIONISTS might cross – he said that 'If the Northern problem were not there in all probability there would be a flat … proclamation of a republic in the Constitution' – his claim illustrates the continuing lack of comprehension by southern nationalists of unionists' rejection of the southern state.

Third, the position of WOMEN was defined wholly in terms of marriage, FAMILY and home-building. By Article 41.2.1 'the State recognizes that by her life in the home, woman gives … a support without which the common good cannot be achieved'. To ensure that support, the state promised to 'endeavour to ensure that mothers shall not be obliged by economic necessity to engage in labour to the neglect of their duties in the home' – an 'endeavour' in which it signally failed. This domestic definition of women paved the way for a marriage bar in employment so that, on marriage, women automatically lost state employment (in teaching, etc.).

Fourth, primacy was given to the IRISH LANGUAGE. Article 8 recognizes English as only the second official language of the state. In any legal dispute, for example, the Irish text would take precedence over the English. It has been argued that De Valera was attempting to use the language as 'an ethnocentric short-cut to dignity', given its actual state and status in the Free State. Certainly, later governments paid little more than lip-service to making Irish the national language in a meaningful sense, and it was seen as a shibboleth by some even at the time.

The Constitution was approved by 57 per cent of the population (on a 76 per cent turnout) in a referendum in July 1937. From this point on, the Free State was to be known as Éire or Ireland, the British monarch was no longer the official head of state (in Irish law) and Ireland no longer regarded itself as a member of the Commonwealth. The Constitution can be changed by referendum; for example, the 'special position' of the Catholic Church was removed in 1972 (see also ABORTION, DIVORCE and GOOD FRIDAY AGREEMENT).

Further reading

Hanafin in Ryan (ed.) (2000).

Constructive Unionism A series of policies implemented by Conservative governments between 1895 and 1905 in an attempt to mitigate pleas for Home Rule; they consisted largely of concessions on land purchase, the increase of local government powers, and the provision of Catholic university education. See Arthur BALFOUR, Horace PLUNKETT.

contraception Section 17 of the Criminal Law Amendment Act of 1935 in the Free State prohibited the importing and sale of contraceptive devices. These were available in Northern Ireland, but the vast majority of Irish couples were denied control of fertility by any method but the 'rhythm method' or abstinence. The teaching of the CATHOLIC CHURCH on birth control was that every 'act of marriage' must stay open to the possibility of human procreation, and it vehemently resisted the legalization of contraception. Such a stand, together with the poor economic performance of the new state, meant surplus population and EMIGRATION for many Irish children (four-fifths of those born in the 1930s emigrated in the 1940s and 1950s).

In 1969 the Fertility Guidance Clinic opened in Dublin, dispensing contraceptives under a legal loophole which allowed clinics to do so. A family-planning rights group was set up soon afterwards, and although the Church continued to oppose contraception public attitudes began to change. In the early 1970s, Mary McGee, who had already suffered four life-threatening pregnancies, took out an action with her family-planning association against the Irish Customs, who had impounded spermicidal jelly which she had attempted to import. This led to a Supreme Court ruling in 1973 declaring that the right to marital privacy included the right to use contraceptives. These did not become legally available until 1979 with the Health (Family Planning) Act, which legalized the sale of contraceptives, on prescription, to married couples. In 1985 the sale of condoms to over-18s, without prescription, was permitted; and in 1992, partly as a result of the fear of AIDS, they were made still more widely available. Long before this stage, however, the majority of Irish couples had been ignoring Church teaching on the subject; the average number of children dropped from 4.6 per family in 1960 to 2.3 in 1990, and is now less than 2.

co-operative movement see **Plunkett, Sir Horace Curzon**

Cork   Ireland's third and the Republic's second city, Cork takes its name from the 'Great Bog of Munster' (Corcaigh Mor Mumhain) on which it stands at the mouth of the River Lee. Located near the monastic settlement reputedly founded by St Finbar in the seventh century, surrounded (and once regularly flooded) by the channels of the river, the town developed under the VIKINGS and Anglo-Normans and received its first charter from Henry II in 1177. Cork was used as a headquarters by Walter Raleigh, and Edmund SPENSER, who famously described how 'the spreading Lee encloseth Cork with its divided flood', was its Sheriff in 1598. By the late seventeenth century, Cork dominated the export of butter, beef and other provisions from its agriculturally rich hinterland, trading with Britain, Europe and the North American colonies. Its population grew from c.6,000 in 1660 to 27,000 in 1719, 71,000 in 1821, to 130,000 at the present day. In the nineteenth century it was embellished by local architects, including the Pains and Deanes, whose achievements include St Anne's, Shandon (the salmon-topped tower of which is celebrated in Father Prout's 'Bells of Shandon', the Cork anthem). Other notable buildings include the South Gate Bridge, the Crawford Art Gallery, the university (one of the QUEEN'S COLLEGES), Atkins's Lunatic Asylum (said to be the longest building in Ireland), the Revival gem of the Honan Chapel, and the impressive CHURCH OF IRELAND cathedral of St Finbar's. Wealthy 'merchant princes' developed residential areas above the estuary in Sunday's Well, Montenotte and St Luke's, although in the later nineteenth century the city failed to capitalize on its industrial development of earlier decades. Cork was a centre of resistance to British rule during the period after 1916, and part of the city centre, along the main St Patrick's Street, was burnt down in a reprisal by Black and Tans in the ANGLO-IRISH WAR. It was rebuilt, under the peace terms, with an elegant 1920s frontage. Little apart from a brutal replacement for the Opera House and undistinguished suburbs have followed, but since the 1980s the trend to gentrify has had beneficial effects, with a renovation of the Butter Exchange and the part-pedestrianization of the city centre.

Culturally, as in much else, Cork is determinedly independent of Dublin, with its own distinctive social and political life. It has an important School of Music, and has produced the writers Daniel CORKERY, Sean O'FAOLÁIN and Frank O'CONNOR.

Further reading

Bielenberg (1991).

Corkery, Daniel (1878–1964)   Critic, writer, dramatist, and lecturer. Born and educated in CORK, Corkery founded the Cork Dramatic Society in 1908 with Terence MacSwiney and other GAELIC LEAGUE members, writing plays for it (and later the ABBEY), such as *King and Hermit* (1909), in the manner of Lady GREGORY and Douglas HYDE. He was a regular contributor to D. P. Moran's IRISH-IRELAND newspaper *The Leader*. Corkery's three collections of short stories contain his best literary work; the first and most influential, *A Munster Twilight* (1916), shows deep familiarity with the West Cork GAELTACHT.

The linkage of land, people and identity it displays is theorized in his best-known works, the seminal studies *The Hidden Ireland* (1924) and *Synge and Anglo-Irish Literature* (1931). The first deals with PENAL LAW era poets such as Aodhagán Ó RATHAILLE, and popular survivals of BARDIC POETRY. It claims the aristocratic bardic system went underground in the eighteenth century, absorbed by, and enriching, Irish folk culture. O'FAOLÁIN in 1936 and Cullen in 1969 showed that Corkery's claims relied more on assertion than historical fact; nevertheless, the strength of the 'Hidden Ireland' concept, endlessly recycled since, cannot be underestimated, resting as it does on Corkery's considerable powers of historical evocation, and national ideological need. In the second study, the Revival writers are dismissed for not being fully Irish, and a litmus test is proposed for judging the value of Irish writing according to its conformity with '(1) the religious consciousness of the people; (2) Irish nationalism; (3) the land'. Presenting what seemed to be an impeccable academic validation for the twentieth-century peasantry as the inheritors of an immemorial 'greatness', Corkery helped sustain the dominance of the countryside over the city, and he remained ambivalent about the value of any Irish writing in English. Moreover, his ideas did materially shape government policy. Yet, despite the essentialism and simplifications, ideas such as those of the divided colonial self, and of the postcolonial nation as a 'quaking sod' under the feet of the writer, would be relevant, decades later, to the decolonizing nations of Africa and Asia.

Further reading

Cairns and Richards (1988). Cullen (1969). Maume (1993).

Cosgrave, William Thomas (1880–1965) Born in DUBLIN, a member of SINN FÉIN from 1905 and the IRISH VOLUNTEERS from 1913, Cosgrave fought in the EASTER RISING. He was Minister for Local Government in the first Dáil, and first President of the Free State in the second, as Chairman of the Provisional Government after the deaths of GRIFFITH and COLLINS. A supporter of the 1921 TREATY, he formed CUMANN NA NGAEDHEAL in 1923, leading it until 1933. When it became FINE GAEL, he served as Joint Vice-President of 1933–35 and leader 1935–44.

Craig, Sir James (1871–1940) Born in BELFAST, Craig fought in the Boer War. He has been described as an 'unimaginative but devout' stockbroker and self-made millionaire (in whiskey) who became the most active member of the Ulster Unionist Council after 1905. But he was the brilliant organizer behind the campaign against the HOME RULE Bill after 1911 which was fronted by Edward CARSON, with whom he is often twinned. In this capacity he was also the chief organizer of the ULSTER VOLUNTEER FORCE. He was Unionist MP for East Down and Mid-Down at Westminster, and Ulster UNIONIST MP for Co. Down in STORMONT 1921–27. Craig was knighted in 1918 and served in the British Cabinet 1919–21. As leader of the Ulster Unionist Party he was Prime Minister of Northern Ireland from 1921 until his death. In 1927 he was made Viscount Craigavon.

Cromwell, Oliver (1600–1658)   General of the New Model Army during its campaign in Ireland as a key part of the War of the Three Kingdoms, which helped to secure Cromwell's position as Lord Protector of England (1653–58). Cromwell is notorious for his brutal suppression of Catholic, royalist opposition to his rule and his name has entered Irish folklore as a by-word for English bigotry and self-righteous hypocrisy.

Cromwell's campaign in Ireland lasted from August 1649 until May 1650 and is chiefly remembered for the sieges of Drogheda (11 September 1649) and Wexford (11 October 1649). Cromwell's army of 20,000 advanced to Drogheda because they were afraid that the Confederate Catholic forces would link up and form a formidable opposition. They besieged Drogheda which was overwhelmed after heavy bombardment after three days. Some 3,500 defenders were slain of whom about 1,000 were civilians, after they had surrendered. Cromwell defended his army's actions on the grounds that the inhabitants had taken part in the massacres after the Rebellion of 1641, and because he needed to prevent other towns from opposing his army to spare further loss of life. In Wexford 2,000 were slaughtered after they had surrendered. Despite the loss of over 1,000 men at an ambush at Clonmel in 1650, the New Model Army soon subdued Dublin, Ulster, Connacht and south Munster. Before he returned to England, Ireland was effectively under Cromwell's control. Victory was followed by a drastic land settlement, forcing 'rebel' landowners to leave their land and proceed west towards Connacht, leaving their estates for the crown to plunder. The resulting land was surveyed before being sold off to adventurers and soldiers in 1653–54. Although Catholic tenants remained and Ireland was not transformed from a Catholic to a Protestant country through the immigration of English settlers, much of Ireland was now owned by Protestants and the country changed more significantly than at any other time in the early modern period.

Cromwell's actions were clearly controversial and were opposed by radical English thinkers such as the Levellers and the Diggers. He was, hardly surprisingly, condemned by Gaelic poets such as Ó Brudair and has been a target for Irish writers ever since, notably in Brendan Kennelly's long poem, *Cromwell* (1983). Cromwell's actions in Ireland have recently been defended as legitimate acts of war by Tom Reilly.

Further reading

Ellis (1975). Reilly (1999).

Cronin, Anthony (1928–)   Poet and writer. Born in Enniscorthy, Cronin was educated at UCD. His literary career began as a poet and as co-editor of The Bell under Peadar O'Donnell, and of the literary journal *Envoy*. Cronin's poetic style blends the Eliot of *Four Quartets*, Auden and Kavanagh; although flat-toned and usually careless of form, it is important for the way it pushes the anti-pastoral of *The Great Hunger* into an urban anti-ruralism rare in Irish poetry. In London in the 1950s, Cronin became literary editor of *Time and Tide* and in 1960 co-founded *X: A literary journal* with the painter Patrick Swift. It was in *X* that his long poem, 'RMS TITANIC' (1960), was published. One of the best treatments of the subject, the poem considers the terrible cost of historical progress in the manner of GOLDSMITH's *The Deserted Village*. Cronin was a columnist for *The Irish Times* and, as cultural advisor to Charles HAUGHEY, was instrumental in founding AOSDÁNA and the Museum of Modern Art at Kilmainham (see ART). An anti-establishment stance is also reflected in his non-poetic writing, which includes the memoir of Brendan BEHAN, Flann O'BRIEN and Patrick KAVANAGH, *Dead as Doornails*; a novel, *The Life of Reilly* (1964); and biographies of O'Brien (*No Laughing Matter*, 1989) and Samuel BECKETT (*The Last Modernist*, 1996).

Cú Chulainn   Mythical hero of the Ulster cycle and, most notably, of the TAÍN BÓ CUAILNGE. Cú Chulainn is famed for his extraordinary deeds of heroic valour, especially those of his youth which are related in the *Taín*. His name means 'the hound of Culann', and this replaced his original name, Sétanta, given to him by his foster-father, Sualtaim. When he was late for a feast at the house of Culann, a smith, Cú Chulainn was attacked by the guard dog which he then killed. When Culann complained about his loss, Sétanta was obliged to take the place of the dog and so acquired his name. He then becomes the champion of the Ulstermen and performs numerous spectacular feats in his short, eventful life, which are told in a variety of tales in the Ulster cycle. He kills the three sons of Nechtan Scéne who attack the Ulstermen and so becomes their first warrior. He woos and wins Emer, despite the fierce opposition of her father, but is later caught between his earthly love for her and that of the goddess, Fand.

Cú Chulainn finally meets his end when his enemies converge on him to avenge the death of Cú Roí, led by the dead man's son, Lugaid. When Cú Chulainn is eventually surrounded and mortally wounded he ties himself to a pillar so that he can fight on to the last. The shape-changing witch, the Morrígan, perches on his shoulder in the guise of a crow. This scene has been frequently represented in Irish art and literature, notably in Oliver Sheppard's (1865–1941) bronze statue in the General Post Office (GPO) in DUBLIN. Cú Chulainn has been the subject of a great deal of subsequent Irish literature and folklore, notably in works by Lady GREGORY and the cycle of plays written by W. B. YEATS.

cultural nationalism   The policy of promoting Irish culture as a basis for national identity, regardless of political and religious affiliations. During the nineteenth century it was fostered by figures such as Samuel FERGUSON, who insisted that Irish Protestants should be educated in the history and literary heritage of Ireland, as a means of proving their commitment to the country and forging relations with their Catholic neighbours. See also YOUNG IRELAND.

Cumann na nGaeldeal   Conservative and ruralist political party founded by William Cosgrave in 1923. In control of the government of the Free State until defeat by Fianna Fáil in 1932, it then merged with the Blueshirts in 1933 to become the United Ireland Party, soon known as Fine Gael.

Curragh Mutiny   The name given to the events of March 1914, in which British Army officers at the Curragh camp outside Dublin were (improperly) given the option by their commander (and opponent of Home Rule) of resigning their commissions rather than 'coercing' Ulster into a united Ireland. Most said they would resign, and this led to the assurance by the War Secretary in Westminster that the army would not be used to enforce Home Rule in Ulster. The capitulation showed that the loyalist confrontation of the government over the Home Rule Bill might well pay off, and that a willingness to challenge parliamentary decisions extended to elements in the British state. Ironically, the effect was to strengthen militant republicanism and weaken constitutional nationalism.

D

Dáil Éireann   At their 'ard-feis' (conference) of 1917 Sinn Féin announced their aim of 'an independent Republic' of Ireland, a strategy which involved withdrawing from Westminster and forming an alternative, Irish equivalent – Dáil Éireann. After crushing John Redmond's Irish Parliamentary Party in the elections in December 1918, this is what Sinn Féin MPs (or TDs) did on 21 January 1919. They were proscribed by the British authorities in October 1919, but after their first meeting the Dáil had made De Valera their *Príomh Aire* (President) and set up ministries in imitation of the existing government, starting the process of gaining recognition abroad.

Numerous members of the Dáil were arrested or went on the run as the Anglo-Irish War intensified. The status of Michael Collins, as Minister of Finance and Commander of the IRA, grew to match that of De Valera, who was in the USA after June 1919 (where he raised $5,000,000 for the new government). Sinn Féin's domination of local politics helped to spread the Dáil's authority nationwide. Alternative institutions, including Dáil courts, were set up; effectively, a situation of dual power existed between the revolutionaries and the British authorities.

After the Anglo-Irish Treaty was signed in July 1921 it was discussed in the Dáil. But already, on 23 December 1920, the Government of Ireland Act – descendant of the Third Home Rule Bill – had been passed at Westminster. Unfortunately, it was designed to solve the 'Irish Problem' as of 1914, not the more radicalized situation of 1920. It provided for two devolved parliaments, one in BELFAST for the six counties of Fermanagh, Antrim, Tyrone, Down, Londonderry and Armagh, and one in DUBLIN for the remaining 26 counties. NATIONALISTS and REPUBLICANS working for a unified, independent Ireland ignored this, and used the subsequent elections to produce another mandate for Sinn Féin and hence for the 'independent Republic'. The British government offered UNIONISTS a nine-county Northern Ireland, anticipating that the religious balance in such a state would favour eventual reunification. But unionists insisted on a six-county state which they could dominate instead, and got their way. On these terms, they then accepted secession from the southern state.

Further reading

Farrell (1971).

Davis, Thomas Osborne (1814–1845)   Poet and patriot. Educated at TCD, Davis surrounded himself with like-minded Protestants disaffected by the Union and committed to raising the cultural profile of the Irish nation. In his speech of 1840, to the members of Trinity's Historical Society, he sought to stir the national conscience of his peers, with an appeal which would become legendary within the REPEAL movement; 'Gentlemen, you have a country…' (*Literary and Historical Essays*, Dublin, 1846).

Davis trained as a barrister and was called to the Irish bar in 1838, but was an unsuccessful lawyer who moved quickly into his preferred fields of literature and politics. In 1841 he joined the ranks of the national Repeal association, led by Daniel O'CONNELL, and became a key figure on several of its operating committees. A year later he collaborated with Charles Gavan DUFFY and John Blake DILLON as one of the founders of the NATION newspaper, in which he would publish a series of persuasive and competent essays voicing his enthusiasm for the nationalist movement. These were later collected as *Letters of a Protestant on Repeal* (Dublin, 1847). He also wrote on music and published a number of poems, including the famous ballad 'A Nation once Again'. Like Duffy, Davis was keen to draw in the Protestant and middle-class sectors of the population who, fearful of a new CATHOLIC ascendancy, had been slow to group behind O'Connell and the mass Repeal movement. He was also concerned that the sectarianism of Ireland's past should not re-emerge in the volatile 1840s, and much of his rhetoric emphasized a policy of racial inclusiveness within the country, promoting an Ireland in which 'the Milesian, the Dane, the Norman, the Welshman, the Scotchman, and the Saxon' might co-exist harmoniously. But this culturalist and pluralist approach put considerable strain on his allegiance with the mass Repeal movement and the separatist, populist policies of O'Connell. The relationship was finally severed when Davis and his YOUNG IRELAND movement agreed to an 1845 Government bill for the establishment and state-funding of the QUEEN'S COLLEGES at Galway, CORK and BELFAST. This proposal, which would introduce broadly non-denominational university education throughout Ireland, was unacceptable to O'Connell and his clerical backers, who regarded it as a defiance of Catholic Church authority.

Davis was an inspirational figure, and a highly charismatic individual who undoubtedly secured the interests of a hesitant middle-class community in the nationalist cause. That he was seen as a figure of such great promise doubtless intensified the shock experienced by his friends and contemporaries when he died suddenly in 1845. Mourned on both sides of the political divide, he attracted a number of tributes, including Samuel FERGUSON's evocative 'Lament for Thomas Davis'. Later, PEARSE acclaimed him as a great patriot forerunner during the build-up to the EASTER RISING, and W. B. YEATS also paid homage in his poem 'To Ireland in the Coming Times', including him with MANGAN and FERGUSON as one of the triumvirate of great nineteenth-century national poets.

Further reading

Davis (1988).

Deane, Seamus (1940–) Critic, scholar, editor and poet. Born in Derry to a working-class family, Deane was educated at St Columb's College, QUB, and Cambridge University. He taught at UCD, moving to Notre Dame University in the USA in 1993. His poetry is collected in *Gradual Wars* (1972), *Rumours* (1977) and *History Lessons* (1983), and reveals a competent technique which can rise to distinction in the intensity of its brooding awareness of the past and the sectarian splintering of society. As a Director of, and the leading presence in, the FIELD DAY COMPANY, Deane published the pamphlets *Civilians and Barbarians* (1983) and *Heroic Styles: The Tradition of an Idea* (1984), in which Irish literature was read in terms of a colonial past and divided present. As elsewhere, a POSTCOLONIAL reading combines in these with a refurbishing of older NATIONALIST critical tradition, although this includes a critique of modernity itself, as experienced in Ireland. Deane's ability to set the ideological terms in which Irish writing was read was reinforced in *Celtic Revivals: Essays in Modern Irish Literature* (1984), *A Short History of Irish Literature* (1986) and *The French Revolution and Enlightenment in England, 1789–1832* (1988). Praised for his work as chief editor of the monumental *Field Day Anthology of Irish Writing 550–1991* (1991), Deane was also attacked for its male bias. His gifts for critical insight and rhetorical urgency are deployed to different effect in the autobiographical novel *Reading in the Dark* (1992), which was shortlisted for the Booker Prize, and the critical book *Strange Country* (1997).

Defenders Catholic secret society, formed to combat the threat of the Protestant Peep of Day Boys. The Peep of Day Boys were formed in Co. Armagh in the 1780s and they terrorized Catholics by raiding their houses at night and wrecking the looms used in the weaving industry. Their aim was to reassert Protestant supremacy, which had been undermined by the repeal of many of the PENAL LAWS in the late eighteenth century, as well as to make sure that they dominated the key local industry. After 1790 groups of Defenders developed in other counties in Ulster, and later into Connacht and Leinster. Their importance as a movement was cemented when they were able to form a loose alliance with the UNITED IRISHMEN in *c.*1796 and some defenders took part in the 1798 rebellion led by Wolfe TONE.

De Valera, Éamon (1882–1975)   Politician and statesman. Born in New York, De Valera grew up in Bruree, Co. Limerick, was educated at Royal University, and became a mathematics teacher in St Patrick's College, MAYNOOTH. He joined the GAELIC LEAGUE in 1908 and the IRISH VOLUNTEERS in 1913, taking part in the Howth gunrunning of 1914. He was the last commandant to surrender after the EASTER RISING, and was sentenced to death; as a US citizen, however, the sentence was commuted and, on release from prison in 1917, he was elected SINN FÉIN MP for East Clare, Sinn Féin President, and leader of the Volunteers. In the anti-conscription agitation he was again arrested, but he escaped, with the help of Michael COLLINS, from Lincoln Jail in February 1919, having been re-elected in the Sinn Féin landslide of 1918. In April 1919 he was elected Príomh Aire (President) of the first DÁIL Éireann. In June 1919 he visited America to gain US and League of Nations recognition and raise financial support for the fledgling Republic. Elected President of the Republic in August 1921, after the conclusion of the ANGLO-IRISH WAR, he resigned on 9 January 1922 in protest against ratification of the ANGLO-IRISH TREATY by the Dáil, and formed the anti-treaty party Cumann na Poblachta. De Valera was Director of Operations of the anti-treaty ('Irregular') IRA during the CIVIL WAR, was arrested and imprisoned by Free State troops from August 1923 to July 1924, and then later in Northern Ireland. In 1926 he resigned the Presidency of Sinn Féin and founded FIANNA FÁIL. Returned at the 1932 election, De Valera led the Free State into an era of isolation during which the aim was for indigenous industries to produce a more self-reliant nation, which would, ultimately, reclaim the northern counties. He also gave the country an international role, playing a significant role in the League of Nations (he was its President in 1932). De Valera's hand was pronounced in the Irish CONSTITUTION of 1937, which removed reference to the British Crown and Governor-General. He also filled the newly created role of Taoiseach (Prime Minister) from 1937–48. During WWII he adeptly maintained Irish NEUTRALITY, which marked a further stage in the evolution of the 'external association' with Britain he had desired in 1921. One defining moment in De Valera's national leadership came in his 1943 PATRICK'S DAY BROADCAST, which famously offers a folksy rural vision although even then it was threatened by poverty and EMIGRATION. He had been the national leader for 16 years when Fianna Fáil were defeated at the 1948 election, and he returned as Taoiseach in 1951–54 and 1957–59, stepping down to Seán LEMASS. From 1959 until 1973, De Valera was President of the Republic. Famous for his incorruptibility and shrewdness, he was the single most influential figure in twentieth-century Irish life; the many attempts to identify his significance include the early poems of Thomas McCarthy, which explore the patriarchal role he adopted. De Valera once even claimed to know the 'hearts' of the Irish people in a near-godlike manner; but his real gift was the ability to present a radical and a warily conservative aspect, often simultaneously.

Further reading

Bowman (1982). Moynihan (1980).

De Vere, Aubrey Thomas (1814–1902) Poet, born on the family estate at Curragh Chase, Co. Limerick, and educated at TCD. In 1851, influenced by his friend Cardinal Henry Newman, he converted to Roman Catholicism. Deeply concerned with the worsening situation in Ireland as the century progressed, de Vere was a model landlord who worked tirelessly during the Famine to care for the afflicted of the region. In 1848 he published *English Misrule and Irish Misdeeds*, a commentary on Anglo-Irish political relations which sought to find a middle ground, particularly on the land question. His poetry, much of which consists of versions of Gaelic legends, remains largely neglected by critics.

Derry Derry's name derives from the 'doire', or oak-wood, beside the site of the monastery founded by St Columba in 546. The town stands on the River Foyle and was attacked by the Vikings, but nevertheless became an important ecclesiastical centre. In 1600 it fell to Sir Henry Docwra in the Nine Years War. Although the British garrison was destroyed by Sir Cahir O'Doherty, in 1608 the city was granted in 1613 to a trading company, the Irish Society of the City of London, and consequently renamed 'Londonderry'. As part of the Ulster Plantation it was planted with Protestant settlers. It achieved its special significance in the Williamite Wars as the result of a heroically resisted siege by the Protestant garrison. However, the nature of Derry was changed by the influx of Catholic settlers from Donegal after the Famine of 1845–49. In the later nineteenth century, shirt-making became the city's basic industry, involving chiefly Catholic women; the growing Catholic population settled in the boglands below the city walls (the 'Bogside' district), and by 1900 formed two-thirds of the population (which is now *c.*60,000). After 1922, unionist manipulation of electoral boundaries, known as gerrymandering, ensured continued Protestant control of the city corporation and discrimination in housing and jobs.

Its border location, isolation and inequalities made Derry a cockpit of the Troubles, which broke out there on 5 October 1968 with the brutal dispersal of a Civil Rights march by police. Similarly, a nationalist attack on the annual Orange march in 1969 led to the declaration of 'Free Derry' and a 'no-go zone' in the Bogside, triggering anti-Catholic violence in Belfast and the arrival of the British Army. The city was also the location of Bloody Sunday in 1972 which ended the Civil Rights campaign and intensified the Provisional IRA's campaign against Protestants and the British presence. Culturally, Derry is significant; apart from the historic city walls and imposing Guildhall, it was the centre for the Field Day Company, and the setting for several plays by Brian Friel. Though now officially known again as 'Derry', the county in which the city stands is 'Londonderry'.

Further reading

McCann (1993).

Devlin (McAliskey), Bernadette Josephine (1947–)   Born in Co. Tyrone, educated at QUB, Devlin was a prominent member of the Civil Rights Association and founder of People's Democracy. She sat as Unity MP for Mid-Ulster 1969–74, and was the youngest woman ever elected to Westminster; in a powerful maiden speech, she attacked the inadequacies of Terence O'Neill's government and Stormont rule. In August 1969 she was sentenced to six months' imprisonment for inciting riot in the 'Battle of the Bogside', in the same year publishing an auto-biography, *The Price of My Soul*. Denouncing the leadership of the SDLP as 'gangsters' she founded the Irish Republican Socialist Party in 1974, but it made little headway. She stood unsuccessfully as an MEP in 1979 and was a spokesperson for the National H-Block Committee in 1980–81, but in 1981 she was severely wounded by loyalist paramilitaries. In her heyday Devlin was an electrifying figure in Irish public life, appearing as she did to symbolize the chance of diverting energies for change into socialist, rather than traditional sectarian, channels.

Devlin, Denis (1908–1959)   Poet and diplomat. Born in Greenock, Scotland, Devlin returned with his family to Ireland when he was 12. He studied English and French at UCD and at the Sorbonne. *Poems* (1930), shared with Brian Coffey, was acclaimed by Samuel Beckett, with whom he shared a disjunctive modernist poetic and a strong aversion to neo-Revival writing. Devlin's next collection, *Intercessions* (1937), both registers the social crisis of the 1930s and seeks religious certainty from a God who appears to have abandoned his creation; use of surrealist techniques is counterpointed by an awareness of contemporary debates on committed writing. Its density and sometimes gnomic quality meant that such poetry was ignored in Ireland and Britain. But in the USA (to which Devlin was posted by the Department of Foreign Affairs during WWII) the religious doubt, sense of isolation, and autonomous forms of his work drew the approving attention of leading New Critics such as Allen Tate and Robert Penn Warren (who edited his *Selected Poems* (1963) after Devlin's tragically early death from leukaemia). Ironically, given his reception at home, US acclaim for *Lough Derg and Other Poems* (1946) made Devlin the only living Irish poet of these years with an international reputation. The late masterpiece, *The Heavenly Foreigner* (1950), uses the French Renaissance poet Maurice Scève and Occitan poetry of *fin'amor*, and centres on memories of a lover in whose finite beauty the speaker hopes to discern the deity of the title. Idealization, however, threatens to dissolve her sentient being, and thus any hope of grasping the essence of the Heavenly Foreigner. 'Memoirs of a Turcoman Diplomat', another late work, reflects on Devlin's profession; while 'The Tomb of Michael Collins' is a reminder that, unlike Beckett or Joyce, Devlin's generation of Catholic modernists was unembarrassed by NATIONALISM.

Further reading

Davis (2000).

diaspora   Diaspora studies recognize the post-Famine Irish as one of the five major historical 'victim diaspora' groups (the others are the Jews, enslaved West Africans, the Armenians and the Palestinians). The Irish diaspora is very large (estimated at anything between 50,000,000 and 70,000,000 globally), and the reservoir of goodwill for Ireland abroad which it represents has recently helped to attract investment and US involvement in the Northern Irish peace process.

An Irish tradition of EMIGRATION meant that a diaspora presence in Britain, the USA and Australia was well established before the Famine of 1845–49. However, the Famine changed its nature, even as it massively augmented it, and in the largest diaspora community, the Irish-American, the 'cult of exile', sense of grievance and anglophobia was strong. The Irish prospered in the US, however, establishing themselves in police departments and other municipal fiefdoms and gradually assimilating. The election of Irish-descended President John F. Kennedy in 1960 broke the unspoken taboo on a CATHOLIC becoming President, and was acclaimed in Catholic Ireland; it has been commonplace for American presidents since to discover 'Irish roots' where possible (Reagan and Clinton are both examples). Many Irish Americans are actually of Ulster Protestant descent; the fact that their distinctiveness has been subsumed by definition of Irishness as Catholic-nationalist shows the defining nature of post-Famine emigration.

In Britain, the Irish are the longest established of all diaspora groups. Their cultural and political situation, which included accommodation with the imperial centre, and with other nationalities (Welsh and Scottish), was necessarily more complex than in the USA. While the Irish contribution to British society was large in the eighteenth century (it includes Farquhar, Swift, Goldsmith and Burke), the ACT OF UNION (1800) and mass emigration caused by the industrial revolution fundamentally changed the nature of the diaspora from ANGLO-IRISH to CATHOLIC. Irish labour was crucial to the industrial revolution, and the numbers of those involved were augmented by Irish poor following the Famine.

The Irish input to British cultural life continued to be substantial, and included painters, composers and writers such as George Bernard Shaw and Oscar Wilde, as well as political activists such as Fergus O'Connor, the Chartist leader. It continued in the twentieth century, extending to new forms such as TELEVISION and ROCK AND POP MUSIC. As in the USA, it is not always obvious where the Irish contribution to the culture of domicile begins and ends; however, a good case could be made for including even figures as seemingly assimilated as James Hanley (in England) or Eugene O'Neill (in the USA). But, however defined, a high price was paid for emigration, exile and assimilation, and the full toll of isolation and loss is only now being fully investigated; the recent nature of this – though now it has been alleviated by better communications and cheaper transport – can be seen in works such as Timothy O'Grady's and Steve Pyke's *I Could Read the Sky* (1997), or Frank McCourt's *Angela's Ashes* (1998). Discrimination against the Irish in Britain was strong until it was partly displaced by anti-black racism, and then renewed by sporadic victimization during the TROUBLES. High rates of ill-health, homelessness and poverty still affect Irish people living in Britain. Nevertheless, vibrant Irish communities have thrived and interacted at all times with the host culture, belying the negative stereotypes, as testified to by the numerous Irish cultural centres, charity organizations and Patrick's Day celebrations which today flourish throughout Britain. Today, the diaspora is more confident, better educated and more self-aware than at any stage in its past.

In Ireland itself there was little by way of official acknowledgement of the Irish abroad until Mary ROBINSON's Presidency. Her gestures to the wider 'family' of the Irish around the world was a major positive step both towards creating a diaspora identity acknowledged by its source, and towards redefining Irish identity in Ireland itself.

Further reading

Coogan (2000a). Hickman (1995). Lloyd (1995). Miller (1971).

Dillon, John Blake (1814–1866)   YOUNG IRELANDER, who joined the Repeal Association in 1841, and collaborated with Charles Gavan DUFFY and Thomas DAVIS in founding the *NATION* newspaper. Escaped to France and then America after the 1848 rising, but eventually returned to Ireland and became MP for Co. Tipperary.

direct rule   Following BLOODY SUNDAY, the ungovernability of Northern Ireland through STORMONT became clear to the British government. On 24 March, it was prorogued, or suspended, by the Conservative government under Edward Heath. Executive power was transferred to a Secretary of State for Northern Ireland (SOSNI), the first of whom was William Whitelaw. He was a member of cabinet at Westminster who would preside over a mini-cabinet of his own junior ministers appointed to administer Northern Ireland government departments. A new Northern Ireland Office (NIO) was created and staffed at the highest levels by British civil servants. From this point on, all Northern Ireland legislation would be dealt with at Westminster, most of it through Orders in Council.

The significance of direct rule is that it marked the end of the British policy of trying to reform Northern Ireland through the UNIONIST government, pursued since 1969. More, it marked the end of the form of devolved government which had been in place since 1921, and hence of the alliance between the British state and Northern Irish Protestants. Intending direct rule to be a temporary measure, however, the British government immediately launched a series of initiatives which might allow them to step back and reconstitute Northern Irish government on a more stable basis, starting with a POWER-SHARING executive.

divorce   Like other aspects of sexual politics in Ireland, divorce is charged with great socio-political significance. In Northern Ireland, the same legislation applies as in the rest of the UK. In the Republic, however, it has been a contentious issue. When the Free State was established in 1921 it seemed that the DÁIL had inherited the Westminster parliament's right to enact divorce legislation. However, the Executive Council declined invoke this power, making divorce a legal impossibility, and drawing a celebrated outburst from W. B. YEATS, then in the Senate, who saw this as a sectarian imposition of Catholic attitudes to divorce upon the Protestant population. Article 41 of the 1937 CONSTITUTION expressly forbade the passing of divorce legislation. This began to be challenged from the 1960s; however, a referendum in 1986 resulted in the substantial defeat of a proposal for divorce legislation. It was not until another referendum in 1995 that the nation voted by a narrow majority of 50.28 per cent in favour of divorce in cases where couples have lived apart for four years.

Further reading

Garvin (1988).

Dolmen Press (1951–1987)   Founded by Liam Miller (1924–1987), Dolmen were the first commercial Irish-based publisher of poetry since 1928. Consciously located in the fine book tradition of W. B. YEATS's Cuala Press, Dolmen under Miller established an international reputation by concentrating on a core group of poets – Austin CLARKE, Thomas KINSELLA and John MONTAGUE – but they expanded their range in the 1960s to cover a wider cultural field. Notable achievements of the press include Kinsella's TÁIN (1969), illustrated by Louis LE BROCQUY, and Montague's *The Rough Field* (1972). Dolmen won many Irish Book Design Awards, and Miller's success encouraged others to establish small presses and publishing houses.

Downing Street Declaration (Joint Declaration) (1993)   This declaration was launched by the Taoiseach, Albert Reynolds and the British Prime Minister, John Major, on 15 December 1993. Deliberately using tortuous syntax, it established the basis for the ceasefires of the following year and a (possibly) comprehensive and lasting peace. These achievements were not apparent at the time because the opacity of the text defied exegesis – it won first prize as the worst piece of official English of 1993.

But the abundant use of coded language allowed for constructive ambiguity (one commentator described it as 'a minor diplomatic masterpiece'), and it set a framework which could make for a constitutional settlement.

The declaration is notable in shelving long-term issues in its bid for an IRA ceasefire. It also invokes Europe, pointing to the need for new approaches in the context of the European Union, and for any new structures or institutions set up in Northern Ireland to take account of newly forged links with Europe. This broader context blurred existing boundaries and had the effect of minimizing the separation of UNIONISM, the REPUBLIC, and Westminster. The Declaration also foregrounded dialogue; it provided for the setting up of a Forum for Peace and Reconciliation in Dublin, charged with making recommendations on how 'trust and agreement' between nationalist and unionist traditions might be promoted. Ten parties and some independent senators were involved when the first session met at Dublin Castle in October 1994, following the republican and LOYALIST ceasefires of earlier that year.

The ceasefires themselves were tentative; the IRA's guarantee pointedly refused to use the word 'permanent', and they were not prepared to decommission weapons as a prelude to all-party talks. Nevertheless, the government began talks with SINN FÉIN three months later. When the IRA claimed that a renunciation of violence was not needed, and that their democratic mandate and the absence of violence were sufficient for all-party talks, the British government stated that there did have to be acceptance of a principle of disarmament, and some decommissioning as an act of good faith. The IRA saw this as a new precondition, and the ceasefire broke down in February 1996. (See GOOD FRIDAY AGREEMENT.)

Further reading

Arthur (2000).

Doyle, Roddy (1958–)   Playwright and novelist. Born in Kilbarack, DUBLIN, Doyle was educated at UCD and taught geography in a local school until the success of his fourth novel, *Paddy Clarke Ha Ha Ha* (1991), which won the Booker Prize, enabled him to devote himself to writing. Doyle's acute observation of Dublin northside working-class lives and keen ear for its speech inform his novels *The Commitments* (1987), *The Snapper* (1990) and *The Van* (1991), collectively known as the 'Barrytown Trilogy'. The first two parts of the trilogy have been filmed by Alan Parker. Despite its popularity, Doyle has attempted to broaden his range; mixed receptions faced the bleak TV series *Family* (RTE and BBC, 1994), but praise was forthcoming for *The Woman Who Walked into Doors* (1996), and *A Star Called Henry* (1999), set around the time of Independence.

Further reading

Smyth (1997).

drama see **Abbey Theatre, Beckett, Corkery, film, Friel, Gate Theatre, Hyde, Literary Revival, O'Casey, Murphy, Shaw, Synge**

Drennan, William (1754–1820)   Poet who was a prominent member of the UNITED IRISHMEN. Drennan was born in Belfast to Presbyterian parents. He studied medicine in Glasgow and Edinburgh, subsequently working in Belfast, Dublin and Newry. His first significant work was a political tract analysing the misrepresentation of the northern counties in the Irish parliament, *An Irish Helot*, published under the pseudonym of 'Orellana' (1784). He was tried for sedition in 1794, but cleared, after he addressed the VOLUNTEERS in 1792. In prison he produced a number of works outlining his radical ideas of the need for political equality between Catholics and Protestants and for Ireland to be independent of England, but ceased to be actively involved in politics after his acquittal. He wrote a ballad, 'The Wake of William Orr', which lamented Orr's execution in 1797 (William Orr (1766–97) was a farmer hanged for initiating two soldiers into the UNITED IRISHMEN). Drennan describes Orr as dying 'for what our Saviour died' in seeking to unite his countrymen, and bemoans his 'Hapless Nation, rent and torn,/Thou wert early taught to mourn;/Warfare of six hundred years!/Epochs marked with blood and tears!' He is also notable for first using the now familiar epithet 'the emerald isle' to describe Ireland in the poem 'When Erin First Rose'. His literary works were published in 1815 and a translation of Sophocles in 1817.

Druids   Class of learned priests in Celtic society who are recorded as existing in France, Britain and Ireland in numerous classical authorities. Druids officiated over religious ceremonies and sacrifices; they were also responsible for interpreting oracles, which gave them great power and influence, akin to wizards, as they were often seen as being able to predict the future. They also served as judges, acting as arbitrators in disputes. Their sacred places were woodland clearings where they met to commune with the Gods. The druids were successfully confronted by St PATRICK and eventually their order was suppressed by the early Christian missionaries, and replaced by Christian priests. Druids often appear in Old Irish literature, especially the wealth of saints' lives, as evil opponents of the Christians, although they are sometimes integrated into a Christian framework.

Further reading

Chadwick (1997).

Drumcree   The Drumcree dispute concerned the right of members of the ORANGE ORDER to MARCH from Drumcree church, outside the town of Portadown in Co. Armagh, down the Garvaghey Road, on 12 July. The road runs through a NATIONALIST housing estate whose inhabitants objected to the passage through their area of what they regard as an intimidatory march by LOYALISTS. They had been campaigning to stop the march for some 10 years before Drumcree made the news in 1995. Orangemen cited past custom as establishing their right to march on this route. For them it was a right, as Ian PAISLEY put it in a speech he made on a platform with David TRIMBLE in 1995, which 'lies at the heart and foundation of our spiritual life … and of the future of our families and of this Province …'. A variety of factors made it important for the Orange Order, the UUP, the DUP, and other loyalist organizations to force the parade through, and in 1995, 1996 and 1997 they succeeded in doing so. On the evening of Saturday 11 July 1998, in Ballymoney Co. Antrim, a pro-Drumcree march protest created the atmosphere in which a Catholic house was petrol-bombed, burning to death Richard, Jason and Mark Quinn, three young brothers. (The poet Tom PAULIN wrote an elegy for their deaths.) Support for forcing the issue at Drumcree that year fell away and the march did not take place. On subsequent occasions, despite the attempts of the Portadown loyalists, the march has been prevented by the police.

Further reading

Bryan (2000).

Dublin   The origins of Dublin's name rest in speculation concerning An Linn Dubh (the black pool); its Irish name, Baile atha Cliath, refers to hurdles anchored to the bed of the river Liffey to provide a fording place. If not established by the VIKINGS, Dublin was given its prominence by them, and it became the Irish capital and centre of the PALE after the NORMAN INVASION in the twelfth century. The office of mayor was created in 1229, and a charter of 1547 gave the city independence from the county sheriff. During this period it was the natural centre for attempts to impose the REFORMATION on Ireland. Its growth in size and importance are marked by a series of events – the founding of TCD in 1592, the publication of a city map in 1610, the laying out of Phoenix Park and Stephen's Green in 1662, and the development of a silk industry in the Liberties area of the city by Huguenot refugees. In 1649, Dublin was the natural point for Oliver CROMWELL's arrival, at Ringsend, as it would be later for James II and WILLIAM OF ORANGE.

The period of Dublin's greatest ARCHITECTURAL splendour was undoubtedly the eighteenth century. An Act of 1757 established the Wide Street Commission, which transformed a city of narrow streets and lanes into the impressive concourses which still structure the city centre. Major thoroughfares, including Rutland Street, Parliament Street, Dame Street, Sackville Street (later O'CONNELL Street), were constructed; squares (Fitzwilliam, Mountjoy, Merrion among them) were laid out; and impressive Georgian terraces built. The Grand Canal was opened in 1779, linking Dublin with its rural hinterland. Among the many impressive public buildings erected, Gandon's Custom House was completed in 1791. Industry also developed; the world-famous GUINNESS brewery was established at St James's Gate in 1759. However, the ACT OF UNION had a disastrous effect on such developments. The removal of the

Dublin-based Irish parliament to Westminster meant that, despite the continuing expansion of the city, many of the ANGLO-IRISH left their townhouses and removed to England. After the FAMINE, impoverished country people moved into some of the deserted Georgian terraces which became slums.

The nineteenth century saw surburban expansion and a shift of power from the ASCENDANCY towards the new middle classes, including Catholics. The place of the gentry in the social elite was gradually taken over by Dublin's professional classes, particularly the doctors and lawyers, whose numbers increased considerably in the Victorian period. City life was also changed by the passing, in 1841, of the Municipal Reform Bill, which dispensed with the largely Protestant authority of the old Dublin guilds and granted voting powers to rate-paying (and increasingly, Catholic) businessmen and traders. Meanwhile, middle-class suburbs served by the new Dublin–Kingstown (later Dun Laoghaire) railway (1834) were springing up to the south of the city. Dublin's role as a port continued to grow, with steady trade in the key areas of distilling, brewing and biscuit making.

By the early twentieth century, Dublin's squalid inner-city slum tenements were a scandalous testimony to official complacency; the 1926 Census showed 22,915 families living in one-room and 39,615 in two-room dwellings. As James CONNOLLY noted, the mortality rates were higher than in Calcutta, with the poor particularly vulnerable to cholera and typhus. The slums were part of the seedy, down-at-heel but intermittently vital Dublin, living off past grandeurs, which is immortalized in the works of James JOYCE, the city's greatest author. In *Dubliners* (1914) and *Portrait of the Artist as a Young Man* (1916) Joyce captures the 'soul of paralysis' of the city *c.*1900, and the struggle to escape it, while his *Ulysses* (1922) makes provincial Dublin of 16 June 1904 the greatest 'metrollops' in modernist literature. Typically, both *Ulysses* and *Finnegans Wake* (1939) stress through their Jewish and Nordic heroes the ethnic diversity of Dublin compared to the rest of Ireland; such celebrations became rarer in the new state, which often acted as though Dublin was an anomaly in the new Ireland. With post-revolutionary fatigue and uncertainty (well-charted in O'CASEY's Dublin Trilogy of plays), despite the need to rebuild the city centre no real action was taken until 1932. Although the suburb of Marino was built in the 1920s, the large-scale relocation of inner-city inhabitants to such new estates as Crumlin and Finglas did not get under way until the 1940s. Even then, central government's ruralist ideology was reflected in the lack of essential social amenities such as transport links, industry, recreation grounds, shops, schools and parks.

The population increased from 394,089 (1926) to 472,935 (1936) to 595,288 (1961), as the city became a modern capital, based on service, finance and administrative sectors rather than the labour-intensive industry of the past. Dublin was the only Irish city to show such growth, as it became a magnet for those constrained or impoverished by rural life, particularly young women. Its 'new jostling spirit' was noted by Sean O'FAOLÁIN as early as the 1940s; by the 1970s, the city had over a million inhabitants and contained a third of the Republic's population. The spirit of alienation and possibility in the 1960s and 1970s can be sensed in the novels of Edna O'BRIEN, just as the voice of the new working-class suburbs was captured by the writers published by Raven Arts Press from the 1970s onwards. However, the 1960s also saw the destruction of much of Dublin's Georgian architecture; other problems followed on from inadequate provision and the high unemployment rates of the 1980s – drugs, crime and vandalism. With more road-building, the city also became increasingly a victim of traffic congestion, while the inner city entered a new spiral of decline. In this light, Dublin's role as European Capital of Culture in 1988 and the Temple Bar project in the city centre were important, showing as they did a recognition that commercial redevelopment was not the only kind possible. Building in the inner city has begun a slow population drift back inwards, helping to revitalize the centre. In the 1990s, reflecting the influx of 'CELTIC TIGER' money and further Europeanization, it was clear that Dublin's problems were being addressed more systematically than in the past, and, in some cases, effectively tackled.

Dublin University Magazine   Founded 1833 by Charles Stuart Stanford and Isaac BUTT (editor until 1838), as the voice of Irish Tory Protestant Unionism. The magazine was closely modelled on *Blackwood's Edinburgh Magazine*, and ran literary reviews, political opinion pieces, profiles, serial fiction and travel writing. While it frequently appeared sectarian in its political perspective, its cultural outlook was inclusive and committed to the elevation of Irish literature and history, and in this respect was greatly enhanced by the presence of cultural nationalist Samuel FERGUSON among its contributors. William CARLETON, James Clarence MANGAN and Sheridan LE FANU (who bought the magazine in 1861) also contributed regularly. Edited by Charles LEVER from 1842, it was seen as becoming increasingly dilettantish in its literary inclusions, and was rivalled by the *NATION*. After several changes of name and ownership, it ceased publication in 1880.

Duffy, Charles Gavan (1816–1903)   Nationalist political leader, journalist and poet. Duffy was born in Co. Monaghan and worked as a journalist on the northern weekly Catholic paper, the *Vindicator*. Committed from an early age in the resurgence of an Irish national culture, he moved to Dublin, where he joined forces with other members of the so-called YOUNG IRELANDERS, Thomas DAVIS and John Blake DILLON, to found, in 1842, the *NATION* newspaper, of which he became editor. Tried for sedition after the failed rising in 1848, Duffy was soon released and in 1849 accompanied his friend, British writer Thomas Carlyle, on his Irish tour. He became MP for New Ross, Wexford, in 1852, but then emigrated to Australia, where he became Prime Minister of Victoria in 1871. He received a knighthood in 1873, and retired to France.

Duffy was perhaps most important as an inspiring and committed literary editor.

In *The Ballad Poetry of Ireland* (1845), he collected pieces by the leading Irish poets of the day as part of a sustained move towards the creation of an accessible Irish literary heritage. Several volumes of memoirs, including *Young Ireland: A Fragment of Irish History, 1840–1850*, and *My Life in Two Hemispheres* (1898) contain valuable insights into the leading personalities and political developments of the period.

Durcan, Paul (1944–)   Poet. Born in DUBLIN, he studied archaeology and medieval history at UCC. With Brian Lynch he published *Endsville* (1967); a first full collection, *O Westport in the Light of Asia Minor,* appeared in 1975. A mesmerizing public performer of his work, Durcan is a genuinely popular poet whose writing blends Patrick KAVANAGH's intuitive lyricism with surrealism, and treads a fine line between prosiness and bardic spellbinding. He consolidated his reputation with *Teresa's Bar* (1976), *Jesus Break His Fall* (1980), *The Berlin Wall Café* (1985) and *Going Home to Russia* (1987). During the 1980s, Irish public opinion caught up with Durcan's social critique, his exploration of marital breakdown, and quasi-feminist ethics. In what is perhaps his best collection, *Daddy, Daddy* (1990), Durcan comically and movingly explores his troubled relationship with his father, a High Court judge, martinet and right-wing FINE GAEL supporter. Later books include *Crazy About Women* (1991), *Give Me Your Hand* (1994), both based on paintings, and *Greetings to Our Friends in Brazil* (1999).

Further reading

Tóibín (ed.) (1996).

Easter Rising (1916)   The ultimate origins of the Rising on the Easter weekend of 1916 may be traced to the rise of militant nationalism following the fall of PARNELL, and the suspension of the Third HOME RULE Bill in the teeth of UNIONIST opposition and with the outbreak of WWI. This disillusioned many nationalists, among them the minority of the IRISH VOLUNTEERS who had followed Eoin MacNeill rather than John REDMOND in the split of 1914. They became the main force for an armed uprising against the British authorities, planned by the FENIAN veteran Thomas Clarke, through the IRB, to take place on Easter Sunday, 23 April. Additional numbers were provided by the IRISH CITIZEN ARMY, led by leader James CONNOLLY, who soon after 1914 came to the conclusion that socialism could only be won within an independent Ireland.

With Sir Roger CASEMENT making their case to the German High Command, the rebels entertained hopes of German support; however the Volunteers' rendezvous on 20 April with the ship bearing them arms, the *Aud*, was missed. The ship was scuttled and Casement captured. Another blow was delivered when MacNeill, who opposed the Rising, countermanded the order issued for mobilization on 23 April. Despite this, and the patchy, isolated action which would inevitably result, the organizers decided to go ahead with the insurrection next day, 24 April, or Easter Monday.

The Proclamation of the Irish Republic was read outside General Post Office (GPO) as it and various other strategic buildings in DUBLIN were occupied. The rebels held out for a week; then, realizing the impossibility of their situation, under heavy artillery fire, and concerned about the numbers of civilian casualties, they surrendered on Friday 29 April. 450 people had been killed and 2,614 wounded. 179 buildings in central Dublin were destroyed at an estimated cost of £3,000,000. There was also widespread disorder and looting in the city centre. In the immediate aftermath, as a result, the Volunteers were highly unpopular with most of the population.

However, the British authorities made the mistake of treating the insurgents harshly. 90 of them, including the leaders, were sentenced to death by court-martial. Thousands more were shipped off to prison camps in England and North Wales. Although the death sentences were commuted for all but 14 of the leaders, the executions began at Kilmainham Jail on 3 May, with PEARSE and MACDONAGH; the last was of CONNOLLY on 12 May. The effect shocked many; it was, according to one commentator, 'Like watching a trickle of blood flow from beneath a locked door'. The revulsion generated led directly to the victory of SINN FÉIN two years later and the ANGLO-IRISH WAR which brought independence. Despite military failure, and the dubiousness of PEARSE's rhetoric of bloodshed to renew the 'right rose tree' (which he compared to CÚ CHULAINN's and Christ's sacrifices), the Rising proved to be an overwhelming symbolic victory. Mythologized since in song, drama (Sean O'CASEY's Dublin Trilogy), film, music (O'RIADA's *Mise Éire* suite) and poetry (YEATS's 'Easter, 1916'), it made the end of British rule in Ireland inevitable.

Further reading

Cairns and Richards (1988).

economic expansion, programmes for   There have been 12 programmes for economic expansion since 1958 in the Republic. The first of these, a five-year plan devised by T. J. Whitaker and implemented by Seán LEMASS, ran to 1962. It envisaged economic growth of 11 per cent for the period 1959–62; actual growth, however, was 23 per cent, with industrial growth far exceeding expectations. Subsequent programmes were less successful, and they fell out of favour as a policy tool. However, they were revived in the late 1980s, and their credibility was restored by the role they appeared to play in bringing about the 'CELTIC TIGER' economy.

Economic War (1932–1938)   The abolition of the Oath of Allegiance to the British Crown, the downgrading of the role of Governor-General, and the withholding of annual payments to Britain agreed under the Anglo-Irish Treaty by the new Fianna Fáil government in 1932 led to a limited 'economic war' with Britain. The British government responded by imposing tariffs on Irish goods, and De Valera retaliated in kind. He said he wanted to 'abolish free trade' as part of the bid for economic self-sufficiency. However, the cattle trade suffered, with exports dropping from 775,000 to below 500,000 head per annum, and a compromise was reached.

economy   Traditionally, the Irish economy has been more underdeveloped and agricultural than that of Great Britain. The industrial revolution led to the establishment of one large industrialized zone of fully-fledged capitalist production in Belfast and the Lagan Valley, first in textiles and then in engineering and shipbuilding, but to only limited and isolated pockets of such concentrated activity elsewhere (attempts to establish a linen industry in Co. Cork in the early nineteenth century, for example, foundered). Under-capitalization meant that the largest industries outside the Belfast areas remained traditional ones, such as brewing (Guinness, founded in the eighteenth century in Dublin, being the chief example).

But this did not mean that Ireland was imperfectly integrated into the capitalist economy of the British Isles; an extensive rail network was developed by 1860, in order to bring Irish agricultural products to the British market. Although relatively well developed economically in comparison with other marginal areas of Europe, the Irish economy was nevertheless asymmetrical. On the one hand much industry was divided along sectarian lines (most concerns in Belfast, where there was the greatest concentration, were Protestant-owned). On the other it was skewed to metropolitan and imperial requirements. Thus, the layout of the railway system shows its major nodal points (such as Limerick Junction) to be either far from the urban centres or located in military garrison towns. It hardly allowed any direct traffic between towns outside Dublin, on which it was almost entirely centred. This served the process of forcing internal trade through the all-consuming capital, in line with the emigration process and English-directed commerce.

Following Partition, the economy of Northern Ireland proved vulnerable to the recession which hit other traditional industrial areas of Great Britain; this decline, staved off by subsidy, new industries (such as aircraft manufacture) and inward investment tax breaks, could not prevent the decline of large-scale heavy industry. By 1990, 68 per cent of GNP came from the services sector, compared to 4 per cent from agriculture and 28 per cent from industrial production. In the Free State, the protectionist policies of Fianna Fáil led by De Valera from 1932 onwards led to the protection of indigenous industry and the attempt to develop import substitution (e.g. peat- rather than coal-fired power stations, run by Bord na Mona). Isolation, however, made for stagnation and a massive increase in emigration in the 1940s and 1950s, which was staunched by the first Programme for Economic Expansion.

Since then, Irish dependency on Britain has lessened (although Britain has remained Ireland's largest single trade partner), while industrialization and economic advance have been sporadic; the break-up and privatization of the semi-state companies in the 1980s, like privatization in the UK, proving a mixed blessing. The reasons for this have been debated in terms of MODERNIZATION THEORY and, indirectly, have been mediated in literature and other cultural media. In both Irelands there has been a 'peace dividend' in the 1990s, particularly for the better off, while the Republic's 'CELTIC TIGER' economy has now outstripped that of the North, and surpasses the UK in per capita GDP. Nevertheless northern and southern states remain peripheral economies on the edge of the EU zone, heavily reliant on transnational corporations for inward investment.

Further reading

Bielenberg (1991). Ó Gráda (1994).

Edgeworth, Maria (1767–1849) Anglo-Irish novelist from an extensive family residing at Edgeworthstown, Co. Longford. Her first major work, *Castle Rackrent* (1800), is regarded as a point of departure for the comic 'BIG HOUSE' novel in Irish literary tradition, and as a satirical comment on the politics surrounding the ACT OF UNION. This was followed by *Ennui* (1809), *The Absentee* (1812), and *Ormonde* (1817). Edgeworth's fiction presents a rather picturesque Ireland of irresponsible landlords and feckless aristocrats, shaped largely for an English readership. Her interests in morals, manners and education also feature in several works, leading to comparisons with Jane Austen, and she is often cited as an influence on her literary acquaintance Sir Walter Scott. Edgeworth was much influenced by the enlightenment views of her father, Richard Lovell Edgeworth, with whom she co-wrote a series of essays on education. She has received significant critical attention from contemporary critics, and is seen as one of the leading writers of an Anglo-Irish literary tradition.

Further reading

Butler (1972).

electrification On of the first requirements of the Free State was to safeguard its own power, in order to lessen dependence on British coal. The prestige Ardnacrusha hydroelectric dam scheme on the River Shannon was one of the key components in the construction of a National Grid in the 1930s; and in 1945 the Rural Electrification Scheme was initiated. There were 400,000 rural dwellings without electricity at the outset; by the end of the scheme, in 1972, some 402,000 had been connected, against the initial target of 200,000. Electrification has often been seen as symbolic of the national will to modernize and achieve self-sufficiency.

Further reading

Shiel (1984).

Emergency, The see **neutrality, World War II**

emigration   High emigration patterns were already evident in Ireland after 1800, before the FAMINE gave rise to a large-scale exodus. In the early decades of the nineteenth century, the numbers migrating to Britain and America began to increase dramatically, with an estimated 1,500,000 leaving Irish shores between 1815 and 1845, driven by the population density (see POPULATION). As Irish-born settlers gained a foothold abroad, they in turn brought out their kinsfolk, and emigration became an established feature of Irish rural life. The numbers were increased by the seasonal migrants who left each year to work on the harvests or in the fisheries (a vivid account of the labour gangs of Donegal children hired for seasonal potato picking in Scotland forms the subject of Patrick MacGill's novel *Children of the Dead End* (1912)). With the decline in hand-weaving farm industry in the north of Ireland in the 1820s, a new and previously economically secure section of the labouring class joined the emigrant trail, to follow the promise of work in Scottish textile factories. Cheaper rates of passage following improvements in transport took effect (and as emigration became a profitable business), adding to the incentives, and to the numbers who seized the chance of economic survival elsewhere.

It was the FAMINE, however, which radically re-drew the demographic map and changed the way emigration was driven. With it, emigration became the only option for several generations of the Irish poor: between 1845 and 1870, approximately 3,000,000 people left Irish shores for the now traditional destinations of America, Canada, Australia and New Zealand, and a swathe of English manufacturing centres. As stories of the passage returned to the homeland, often in the form of the 'emigrant letter', which would be read aloud to the community, a folklore of emigration began to emerge. Horrific details of over-crowding, disease and death on the so-called 'coffin-ships' which carried emigrants across the Atlantic, or of the homesickness and prejudice often experienced by newly arrived immigrants, shaped an enduring and harrowing picture of what it meant to leave home. But, for all its tragic element, the hard mathematics of emigration were impossible to ignore: the fragile nineteenth-century Irish economy simply could not sustain a high level of population, and in rural life in particular the undivided inheritance of a viable FAMILY farm was only possible if some members of the family left to seek their fortune elsewhere (see FAMILISM). Yet, while it was in most cases a necessity, it was an opportunity too, for the thousands of young, unattached Irish men, and – in equal numbers – Irish women, who left the country in this period.

Irish emigration created a DIASPORA which changed the profile of countries across the world; one effect was the influx of CATHOLICISM into the receiving nations, and the Catholic Church itself provided an important conduit for emigration, in its search for new Irish recruits to join religious houses and orders abroad. But the history of emigration has also been one of resentment and prejudice, as the immigrant Irish were used to undercut existing wage levels, and were stereotyped in terms of poverty, stupidity and drunkenness.

Emigration, internally from the land to Irish towns and cities, and externally from Ireland for Britain, the USA and elsewhere, continued to be a way of life in the twentieth century. It was checked somewhat by WWI, the Independence struggle, and the effects of the Depression. But in the early 1940s the outward stream of the 'suitcase brigade' increased again, as people were drawn to war work in Britain, and by the 1950s it had become a flood. Between 1945 and 1961, 500,000 left the southern state, 400,000 of them between 1951 and 1961; 80 per cent of all children born in 1931–41 emigrated during the 1950s. Emigration from Northern Ireland has been less spectacular, but at its height, also in the 1950s, it lost over 90,000 people, or about 6 per cent of the population. A disproportionate number of these were from the Catholic minority; in recent years, however, there have been fears among the Protestant population that emigration is doing more damage to their community.

A 1948 Commission on Emigration found that the commitment to sustaining old rural social patterns was breaking down under the strain of lack of opportunity and the difficulty of forming a FAMILY. The tragic outcome forms the basis of many artistic works of the time, including Brian FRIEL's first major success, the play *Philadelphia, Here I Come!* (1964). Yet official complacency and ambivalence persisted in maintaining that emigration was unavoidable: the country was deemed overpopulated and the exodus a necessary social 'safety valve'. A denial of economic failings went hand in hand with regular moral panics, particularly concerning the high emigration rates of young women (of every 100 girls in Connacht aged 15–19 in 1946, 42 had left by 1951).

Emigration was only slowed with the ECONOMIC EXPANSION PROGRAMME of 1959. However, the new vulnerability of the Republic to world economic forces was revealed in the economically bleak 1980s, when unemployment rose to 20 per cent and the return, as the 'Ryanair generation', of mass emigration. A higher percentage than before of those leaving were the skilled products of the recently overhauled education system; again, this was given a positive spin by officialdom which ascribed emigration now to the naturally adventurous spirit of young professionals seeking experience before returning. As late as 1994, unemployment – the motor of emigration – stood at the mid-1980s level of 300,000. Something of the old fatalism towards emigration still survives. However, inward migration has accounted for almost half the Republic's population increase since 1996, and the country currently advertizes abroad to satisfy its skills shortage.

Further reading

Brown (1985b). Fitzpatrick (1984). Hyland and Sammells (eds) (1991). Mac Laughlin (1994). Miller (1971). O'Toole (1990).

Emmet, Robert (1778–1803)   Member of the United Irishmen who led a failed uprising in 1803. Emmet was a radical student at Trinity College who became one of the new leaders of Irish patriotic opposition to English rule after the failure of Wolfe Tone's attempt to secure French help to defeat the English in Ireland. Like Tone, Emmet went to France for aid after he was expelled from Trinity for his political activities and he remained there from 1800 to 1803, enlisting supporters and assembling an arsenal. Emmet hoped to seize key buildings in Dublin – including Dublin Castle, the city's main fortress which housed the Lord Deputy and much of the civil service – which he thought would inspire a popular uprising throughout Ireland. The uprising was a predictable disaster. It had to be started early when an arms dump exploded on 16 July 1803; the French aid Emmet had relied on did not materialize; and far fewer rebels from Dublin and its surrounding areas were prepared to gamble on victory against overwhelmingly superior forces. The attack on Dublin Castle was abandoned and all the rebels achieved was to kill two significant officials while they controlled parts of the centre of Dublin for two hours. Fifty people died in the uprising and 21 rebels were executed, including Emmet who fled to the Wicklow Mountains. The failure of the rebellion was the last significant revolutionary action of the United Irishmen. Emmet's speeches defending his actions during the subsequent trial have become important testaments of Irish nationalism, although it is hard to verify how much of the surviving text is authentic. Emmet is generally regarded as a romantic revolutionary, impractical and doomed to failure, but a man of principle whose ideas have inspired others to noble aims. His romance with Sarah Curran (1780?–1808), daughter of John Philpot Curran (1750–1817), a prominent Dublin barrister who defended many United Irishmen, also helped to add to his appeal for later writers.

Further reading

Elliott (1982).

Eriugena, John Scotus (c.810–c.877)   The most important Irish philosopher of the Middle Ages, Eriugena taught at the court of Charles the Bald near Laon, France, from c.845. He achieved fame partly as a translator of philosophical works, but more through his own works. He wrote a treatise attacking the doctrine of predestination, but is mainly remembered for *De Divisione Naturae* (*On the Division of Nature*), a treatise which attempts to understand the principles of the nature of the universe. Eriugena divides nature into four categories; nature which can create but is not itself created; nature which was not created and is created; nature which cannot create but is created; and nature which was not created and cannot create. God belongs to the first category and man to the second. Eriugena was heavily influenced by NeoPlatonism, and he was condemned for being a pantheist. Legend has it that he was stabbed to death by the students when visiting Oxford, who used their pens to dispose of him. He had a major influence on later mystical traditions.

European Union (European Economic Community (EEC), European Community (1987–1992), European Union (1992–)) Ireland and the UK joined the then EEC in 1973. While Northern Ireland has generally been suspicious of the organization, in line with Westminster attitudes, figures such as Ian PAISLEY have used the European parliament as a platform, and the EU had an input into the peace processes of the 1990s. By way of contrast, the Republic is one of the organization's most committed member states, albeit for sometimes contradictory reasons. Thus, businessmen and politicians have gained market access and enhanced status; reformers have benefited from liberal legislation, on women's, workers' and other rights; farmers have benefited from the Common Agricultural policy, which has subsidized Irish AGRICULTURE; and infrastructural funds have helped improve the transport network and cultural programmes. Finally, the Republic's membership of the EU and European Monetary Union have attracted investment, fuelling the 'CELTIC TIGER' economy. Despite initially rejecting the Nice Treaty (which proposed the enlargement of the Union by 10 Central and Eastern European nations), the Republic voted in favour of continuing the process of integration in 2002.

F

Faction fights Organized, violent confrontations between rival groups, common during early nineteenth-century Ireland, and vividly depicted by WILLIAM CARLETON in his *Traits and Stories of the Irish Peasantry*.

familism Term coined by the American social anthropologists Arensberg and Kimball in their groundbreaking studies of West Clare rural society of the 1930s, *The Irish Countryman* (1937) and *Family and Community in Ireland* (1940). Familism designates a system of land inheritance which emerged after the Great FAMINE, designed to prevent a recurrence of disaster. This was achieved by preventing a holding being split up among children into ever-smaller holdings, so guarding against vulnerability to crop failure. Only the oldest, or chosen, son inherited, and then only after the death or retirement of his parents. The price to be paid for this was a strict control over the marriage of children, their prolonged dependence upon parents, enforced sexual continence, and the EMIGRATION of 'surplus' members of the FAMILY (see POPULATION). The CATHOLIC CHURCH played a crucial role in the process by defining sin in almost wholly sexual terms. The effects of familism are the subject of much Irish writing up to the 1960s; the most powerful exploration of its devastating effects is Patrick KAVANAGH's *The Great Hunger*.

family   The centrality of the family to the ideology of the Free State was shown by its being enshrined in the 1937 CONSTITUTION, where it is described not in legal terms but as 'a moral institution possessing inalienable and imprescriptible rights, antecedent and superior to all positive law'. However, there has been a convergence with Western family norms since the 1960s, with family sizes falling from 4.6 children in 1960 to 1.9 by 1998 (see CONTRACEPTION and POPULATION, and a trend towards the nuclear family. One reason has been the rise in the numbers of married women in work, up from 5 per cent in 1961 to over 50 per cent in 1999. Moreover, marriage is no longer the only tolerated form of family group; thus, in the early 1960s, less than 3 per cent of births took place outside of marriage, but by 1996 the figure was 25 per cent. By 1992 (the latest year for which statistics are available) 35 per cent of first births (that is, of new family formations) took place outside of wedlock.

Famine   Famine had occurred in Ireland before the Great Famine of 1845–49, notably in 1728–29 and 1741–42, and small-scale regional famines were common in the early nineteenth century. However, the massive social and cultural devastation – immediate and long-term – resulting from the mid-century potato blight (*Phytophthora infestans*), makes it arguably the defining event of modern Irish culture. The factors that led to mass starvation in part of the world's richest political entity are complex, and only recently have they been properly researched and understood. Though the figures are still inexact, it is generally held that, of the pre-Famine population of about 8 million people, at least 1 million died and a further 1 million emigrated when the potato crop failed in three seasons out of four, thereby depriving about one third of the country of its staple diet. The severest effects were felt in the West and South, effectively depopulating many areas. The *laissez-faire* policy of the British government – in effect, a refusal to interfere with the market – meant that relief had to come from local bodies rather than from the state. While some landlords attempted to feed the starving, others took advantage of the calamity and evictions were rife. Significant numbers were killed not by starvation but by diseases such as typhus and cholera. The government eventually introduced soup kitchens in 1847, but only for a period of a few months, and various evangelical and charitable organizations also sought to provide relief (see SOUPERISM).

   After the Famine the population continued to decline, as birth rates were low and EMIGRATION high. Meanwhile the longer-term psychological and political effects began to influence Anglo-Irish relations. The Famine engendered an Anglophobia among many Irish emigrants, many of whom subscribed to John MITCHEL's belief that it was a deliberate policy of genocide, and this pervaded the Irish DIASPORA with a sense of victimhood. These sentiments would feed into the FENIAN movement and beyond. Culturally, too, the Famine has left a long legacy in Irish literature and art, from immediate responses such as William CARLETON's *The Black Prophet* (1847) to contemporary treatments such as Eugene McCabe's *Tales from the Poorhouse* (1999).

It is curiously absent from much LITERARY REVIVAL writing, however, and, although later works such as Liam O'FLAHERTY's novel *Famine* (1937) and Thomas MURPHY's play *Famine* (1968) deal with the subject, it is often for its metaphorical value.

Further reading

Kineally (1994).

Farquhar, George (?1677–1707)   Dramatist. Farquhar achieved a great deal in a short life and helped develop Restoration comedy in England as well as establish a theatrical tradition on the DUBLIN stage. Farquhar, the son of a Church of Ireland vicar, was born and educated in the DERRY area. He attended TCD, briefly acted in Dublin before heading for London with his first play, *Love and a Bottle*, in 1698. He proved to be a success and all nine of his plays were performed in the following decade. The most important of these – *The Recruiting Officer* (1706), the story of a captain enlisting soldiers for the British Army near Shrewsbury who falls in love, and *The Beaux' Stratagem* (1707), the story of two rakes who seek to defraud an heiress by having one of them marry her, only to find that he is really smitten – both had a major influence on subsequent English theatre. Farquhar wrote little that was directly about the Irish or Anglo-Irish, although his first play contains a relatively sympathetic portrait of an Irish character, Roebuck, who has more of a sense of humour and wit than most stage Irishmen who appeared at the time in plays by English dramatists. Elsewhere he portrays untrustworthy Catholics and loyal Irish servants as minor characters.

Further reading

Connely (1949).

Farrell, M. J. see **Keane, Molly**

Fenians and Fenianism   Fenianism is a catch-all term derived from the ancient Irish band of warriors and used to signify those groups that emerged in the 1850s determined to keep alive the militant nationalism that had foundered after the YOUNG IRELAND rising of 1848. To a great extent, its impetus came from the USA, as figures like John O'Mahony (1816–77) shaped immigrant discontents into a coherent force. Support also came from Paris-based exiles such as James Stephens (1824–1901), who founded in DUBLIN in 1858 an organization variously known as 'The Society' or 'The Brotherhood' – the uncertain nomenclature typifying its commitment to secrecy. With the financial support of the American 'Fenian Brotherhood', Stephens's 'Brotherhood' – popularly designated 'Fenians' – rose to prominence throughout Ireland and wherever there were Irish immigrants; by 1865 Stephens claimed there were 80,000 Fenians in Britain and Ireland. Officially, the Catholic Church condemned the movement, though individual priests lent support. With the intention of raising funds for the organization, Stephens founded a newspaper, the *Irish People*, in 1863, causing a split with the American leaders; worse, the breach of secrecy led to a government crackdown resulting in numerous arrests. The weakened Fenian movement staged an insurrection in early 1867, but to little immediate effect. Instead, with the arrests and *cause célèbre* of the MANCHESTER MARTYRS, Fenianism refused to go away, metamorphosing into the IRISH REPUBLICAN BROTHERHOOD (of which the young W. B. YEATS was a member) and exerting considerable influence on PARNELL and the quest for HOME RULE. Today, the term 'Fenian' is often used pejoratively for anyone of either nationalist or republican views, but the continuing importance of Irish-America in Irish domestic politics is perhaps the most significant legacy of the Fenian movement. (See also O'LEARY.)

Ferguson, Samuel (1810–1886)   Poet, antiquarian and key Irish Protestant man-of-letters. Ferguson was born in BELFAST and educated at TRINITY COLLEGE, DUBLIN. A barrister by profession, he developed an early interest in the Irish past, and embarked on his literary career in the early 1830s with a series of picturesque Irish historical tales in the manner of Scott, entitled *A Hibernian Night's Entertainments*. Though initially affiliated to the Scottish journal *Blackwood's Edinburgh Magazine*, he became a leading contributor to the newly launched *DUBLIN UNIVERSITY MAGAZINE*, in which he published, in 1834, a highly critical four-part review of James Hardiman's *Irish Minstrelsy, or Bardic Remains of Ireland*. This review, which forcibly claims for Irish Protestants a right to participate in Ireland's literary heritage, is regarded by critics as a seminal document of nineteenth-century CULTURAL NATIONALISM. Ferguson's passionate engagement with an Irish literary culture would bring him into close contact with Thomas DAVIS, Charles Gavan DUFFY and Thomas Darcy MCGEE, but though he greatly admired the NATION newspaper he never actually became a contributor.

After his 1848 marriage to Mary Catherine GUINNESS, Ferguson retreated from politics, and devoted the remainder of his life to his first love, poetry, publishing his most important collection, *Lays of the Western Gael*, in 1865, and his most memorable Irish epic poem, *Congal*, in 1872. He was also a leading antiquarian, a specialist in the field of Ogham inscriptions (or ancient stone markings). He was appointed as first Deputy Keeper of the Public Records in 1867, led the committee to establish the National Museum of Ireland, and was appointed as President of the ROYAL IRISH ACADEMY in 1882.

An important forerunner to the LITERARY REVIVAL, Ferguson was frequently acclaimed by his successors for his attempts to lay the foundations of a national literature, and YEATS, who lauded him alongside MANGAN and DAVIS in his poem 'To Ireland in the Coming Times', would describe him affectionately as the greatest Irish poet'. He was also an important influence on the twentieth-century Ulster poet JOHN HEWITT, who shared his commitment to the artefacts of local culture and history.

Fianna Fáil The largest and most successful of the southern state's post-Independence political parties, Fianna Fáil was founded by ÉAMON DE VALERA in 1926. It was a populist movement, whose nearest parallels were populist movements in Latin America, such as that of Cardenas in Mexico and Perón in Argentina. Like these, it was based on a pre-industrial bloc of interests which united urban workers, the rural poor, and small capitalists and landowners, in a fight against neo-colonial structures. It began by losing the first election it contested, in 1927, when it was defeated by CUMANN NA NGHAELHEAD; but after the elections of 1932 (when it briefly formed a coalition government with LABOUR) and 1933 (when it won an outright majority), the party governed until 1947, and it managed to dispense with coalition partners until 1989. Though described by one of its future leaders, Seán LEMASS, as a 'slightly constitutional party' in 1928, the peaceful transition from Cumann na nGhaelhead to Fianna Fáil rule confirmed the permanence of Irish parliamentary democracy.

Under De Valera's astute direction, the party saw off threats from left and right of the political spectrum in the 1930s, and the 1937 CONSTITUTION marked a moment of achieved national stability. Similarly, neutrality during what was referred to as 'The Emergency' (WWII) reinforced a sense of national identity. However, the stagnation caused by the party's policy of economic autarky slowly threatened its base of support; by the 1950s, with the state and its founding ideals 'imploding', crisis point was reached. Ideology had to give way to pragmatism, although changing course meant having to persuade the iconic De Valera to give way to the technocrat Seán LEMASS. However, Lemass succeeded in redefining the nationalist project of 1921 in terms of economic openness, and decoupling industrialization from Anglicization. Transition was accomplished relatively smoothly, and Fianna Fáil's second great era in office ran from 1957 to 1973.

After Lemass retired in 1966, Jack Lynch became a popular but undistinguished leader. From 1979 until 1992, however, Fianna Fáil was led by Charles HAUGHEY, the most flamboyant Irish politician of recent times. Under Haughey the party won elections in 1987 and 1989, curbing public spending and thus paving the way, it has been argued, for the 'CELTIC TIGER' economic boom. Haughey resigned, however, in 1992 when he was implicated in a phone-tapping cover-up. In 1993 under Albert Reynolds, Fianna Fáil won again, but in 1994 their coalition government with LABOUR fell when Labour withdrew from the coalition because of Reynolds's role in the SMYTH CASE. Reynolds was replaced by Bertie Aherne. The party lost the 1995 election, but were returned in 1997, in coalition with the Progressive Democrats; this highlights the fact that Fianna Fáil is no longer the natural party of government, but one forced to rely on coalition partners.

Field Day Company The Field Day Theatre Company was founded in 1980 by Brian FRIEL and the actor Stephen Rea, in emulation of the work of the 7:84 Theatre

Company in Scotland, as a way of intervening in the frozen cultural scene of the time. The idea was to commission and produce a new play annually in DERRY, and then tour it throughout Ireland. Behind this there was a recognition of the central role theatre had played in the LITERARY REVIVAL earlier in the century, as site for consciousness raising, and the presumption of a culturally united Ireland. The goal of a politically aware but not agitprop work was perfectly realized in the company's first play, Friel's own *Translations* (1980), which was an instant success and which exemplified their belief in the role played by culture in social change.

After *Translations*, Seamus DEANE, Seamus HEANEY, David Hammond and Tom PAULIN joined Field Day's Board of Directors, and to theatre productions was added an annual pamphlet series. In the first batch of these, it became clearer that Field Day was, in part, a projection onto Ireland of the urge felt specifically by Derry nationalist intellectuals to find a way out of a stale and stalemated condition via 'the idea of a culture which has not yet come to be in political terms', in Deane's words. This notion is identical with that of the 'Fifth Province' (see REPUBLICANISM), and had been adopted from the critical LITERARY JOURNAL *The Crane Bag*. Later batches of pamphlets dealt with Irish identity, the Protestant intellectual tradition, the legal issues posed by violence in the north and literary nationalism. The contributors in this last group were Terry Eagleton, Edward Said and Frederic Jameson, showing an attempt by Field Day to reach beyond Ireland to theories of POSTCOLONIALISM and POSTMODERNISM.

Field Day was by now the most dynamic (and controversial) cultural project in Ireland, but several observers had always suspected its expressed wish to genuinely alter the terms of critical debate. To some degree this arose from a confusion of the polemical pamphlets with the theatrical strand of Field Day's activities to bolster charges of covert nationalist bias. Nevertheless, there were occasions when charges of 'literary provisionalism' seemed justified and Field Day appeared to be the 'martyrs of abstraction' as Edna LONGLEY claimed. Field Day's culminating project, the three-volume *Field Day Anthology of Irish Literature* (1991), with Deane as General Editor, was a major attempt to embody the idealist urge towards unity while representing a growing desire to do justice to the 'plurality' of Irish traditions. The most comprehensive attempt of its kind, the *Anthology* was nevertheless attacked for its paucity of women's writing; uncoincidentally, perhaps, all 22 of its editors were male. Two further volumes in 2002 addressed the imbalance, although by this time Field Day, as a critical project, had closed down, its task of redefining cultural debate largely completed.

Further reading

McCormack (1986). Richards (1988). Richards in Hughes (ed.) (1991). Richtarik (1995). Roche (1994).

film   Film made an early appearance in Ireland, and its importance in representing Ireland to the world beyond, and to itself, increased throughout the twentieth century. However, the making of films in both the Free State and Northern Ireland was difficult, for all but the first two decades of the century. The cost of making film, and the level of expertise required, rose sharply after WWI, as did the stranglehold of film distribution networks. Occasional documentaries apart – these being less capital intensive than features, and sometimes non-profit-making – no Irish-based film industry developed in the decades following Partition. This did not mean that films were not made in Ireland, or about Ireland, or that Irish film actors, directors and technicians did not exist; rather, these were based abroad, or assembled in Ireland for externally financed and directed productions. However, with the 1960s – in line with the MODERNIZATION of other aspects of Irish life – there was a concerted effort by the government in the REPUBLIC to foster a film industry. The decade also saw the start of structural, technical and viewing revolutions in film; these involved new filming practices, equipment miniaturization and digital technology, and the spread of TELEVISION and video. Today, partly as a result, it is possible to speak of an Irish film industry and film culture. At the same time, film-making, which tends by its very nature to be international, continues to raise issues of AUTHENTICITY and to pose problems for attempts to define what 'Irish' film is.

The first filmed images of Ireland were shown in 1897. Louis Le Clerq produced the first Irish documentary in 1904, and the first Irish feature film appeared in 1907. *The Colleen Bawn* (1911), based on BOUCICAULT's play, became the first of many subsequent adaptations of Irish literary works to film. The rise of the popularity of film also paralleled the events leading to the EASTER RISING; as a result, the medium was politicized early on. Thus, protests took place at government films advocating conscription in WWI, for example, and Irish features and documentaries such as *Ireland a Nation* (1914), *Knocknagow* (1918) and *Irish Destiny* (1926), which marked stages in the growth of NATIONALIST political self-realization, were CENSORED by British authorities. A tradition of defining the nation in (usually documentary) film would continue until 1960, its most famous creations being *Man of Aran* (1934) and *Mise Éire/I am Ireland* (1959).

The first of these was made by John Grierson and Robert Flaherty; set on the rugged coast of Aran, it told the story of an archetypal peasant family battling with the elements to wrest a bare livelihood from their surroundings. The film was a success not so much because it was accurate (several crucial details were faked), but more because it chimed with the austere self-reliant ethos of DE VALERA's Ireland of the 1930s. *Mise Éire* was the first of an intended trilogy of films about national emergence; made by George Morrison, it dealt with the period 1893–1919, weaving together archive material and featuring a notable soundtrack by Seán Ó RIADA. Despite its heroic narrative, however, it was at odds with the national redefinition occurring around it. Only one of the two successors, *Saoirse?/Freedom?*, was made, and it did not have the same critical or popular success. From this point on, documentary was turned to critical analysis of the founding ideals of the state, just as, in Northern Ireland, it would become a potent tool for exploring the uncomfortable aspects of the TROUBLES.

In the meantime, popular cinema flourished in Ireland as elsewhere. By 1916 there were 150 cinemas and screening-halls, including 30 each in DUBLIN and BELFAST; by 1923, 1,000 worked in Dublin cinemas alone. In 1934 there were 190 cinemas in the Free State alone; by the peak of film's popularity, in 1954, annual admissions were 54 million. However, this was in the face of opposition by the conservative establishments of both the post-Partition states. Not only were films deemed to be *risqué* or violent attacked, but film *per se* was the target of clerical authorities in the South who maintained that 'we cannot be sons of the Gael and citizens of Hollywood at the same time'. Like jazz and other new cultural forms, film was seen as inherently degrading and menacing of indigenous culture, and was accordingly heavily censored. In Northern Ireland a similar authoritarian trepidation was displayed towards film as popular cultural form.

Nevertheless, popular British film of the 1930s and 1940s often made use of Ireland and Irish materials. Thrillers and features of the same period include *Captain* BOYCOTT (1947) and *Odd Man Out* (1947). The last two were made immediately after WWII when J. Arthur Rank was trying to challenge the market domination of Hollywood, and were aimed at capturing an Irish audience. The second, directed by Carol Reed, is a stylish and atmospheric gangster movie owing something to the film *noir* and Italian neo-realism of the time. Unlike most films set in Ireland, a grittily industrial and blitzed Belfast is the backdrop for an IRA man (James Mason) carrying out one last operation, hunted by the police, and dying in the arms of his girlfriend Kathleen (Kathleen Ryan). As in the earlier American Oscar-winning *The Informer* (1935), by John Ford (based on Liam O'FLAHERTY's novel), when not seen sentimentally or comically Ireland tends to be perceived in terms of its recent violence. In this sense *The Informer* complements Ford's later romantic comedy, *The Quiet Man* (1952), in which John Wayne plays an Irish-American returning to his ancestral home and claiming the hand of a local beauty played by Maureen O'Hara. In this case the film's action turns on the main character's ignorance of local customs, with the presumed Irish penchant for violence taking the form of a fist-fight for dowry money. However, the lush, impossibly vivid and idealized countryside, not to mention the name of the ancestral home – 'Inisfree' – show the film to be commenting on, as well as complicit in, Hollywood stereotypes of Ireland.

The LEMASS government established a national film studio at Ardmore in 1958. The aim was to attract external money and expertise for films, in an era when the major companies had moved to a package system of film-making, hiring facilities rather than maintaining their own. However, few of the spin-off benefits which were hoped for ever materialized. Irish technicians did not gain expertise when outside companies used Ardmore, because their own technicians enforced a monopoly. Ardmore could only stay afloat by making TV series and adverts. Two of the better big-budget films of this period made in Ireland reflect the continuing ambivalence of Irish representations in Anglo-American film. *Ryan's Daughter* (1970), by David Lean offered a

Madame Bovary-type tale of love and adultery set in 1916 Ireland. Lean's voyeuristic attraction to and fear of the dramatic Kerry setting meant he fostered a mood of 'wild romance' which dwarfed the characters, and stressed the archaic 'backwardness' of their society. Perhaps predictably, it was attacked in Ireland and England respectively for its 'immorality' and lack of coherence. However, it was popular, in Ireland as elsewhere, and won several Oscars; it also provided a significant boost to the local economy. By contrast, *Barry Lyndon* (1975) by Stanley Kubrick, an adaptation of a Thackeray novel set in the eighteenth century, and was a relative commercial failure. It follows the fortunes of an Irish adventurer (played by Ryan O'Neal) who achieves social success only to tragically lose his precious only son. With little dialogue, and slow-moving action, the film tests the viewer, indirectly raising questions concerning identity, integrity, social displacement and aesthetic value.

For contemporary Irish film-makers new challenges were being presented by the strains of MODERNIZATION and the Troubles. Documentary became critical in works such as *The Irishmen* (1965) by Philip Donnellan, an investigation of the condition of Irish EMIGRANTS in England, *The Rocky Road to Dublin* (1968) by Peter Lennon (which cast a cold *cinema verité* eye over the Republic's shortcomings), and Richard Mordaunt and the Berwick Street Film Collective's *Ireland: Behind the Wire* (1974), exploring the rise of the CIVIL RIGHTS movement, the British presence, and INTERNMENT in Northern Ireland. A similarly quizzical and critical stance informed the short features of the time, such as Bob Quinn's *Poitín* (1978), Pat Murphy and John Davies's *Maeve* (1981), Joe Comerford's *Traveller* (1982) and Cathal Black's *Pigs* (1984). These films respectively demythologized the West, offered a feminist critique of the sexism of REPUBLICANISM and the British Army (through a character identified with her namesake in the TÁIN), raised the issue of anti-TRAVELLER racism, and traced the victimization of a gay man living in a Dublin squat. The second and third reflect the fact that they were made at the time of the 1980–81 HUNGER STRIKES; all four exposed the flaws in Irish modernization, but also revealed a new sense of momentum among indigenous film-makers and the availability of new sources of finance, particularly from television companies. Thus, Channel 4 helped fund *Eat the Peach* (1986), a more commercial, but quirky and thought-provoking film about a man who builds a wall-of-death; similarly, Granada Film co-sponsored *Joyriders* (1988), while Joe Comerford's *Reefer and the Model* (1988) received funding from the Irish Film Board.

New tax legislation in 1987 in the Republic also encouraged more inward invest-ment in film. Although the FIANNA FÁIL government at this point removed institutional support for smaller and indigenous Irish films, the period was to see the release of unprecedentedly successful externally funded works, including Jim Sheridan's *My Left Foot* (1989) and Neil JORDAN's *The Crying Game* (1992), as well as the powerful smaller-budget films *December Bride* (1990), based on Sam Hanna BELL's novel, *The Field* (1990). Some of these, including *My Left Foot* and *December Bride*, may be regarded as examples of the burgeoning genre of 'Irish heritage' film, one continued in *The War of the Buttons* (1995) by John Roberts, for example, or *Angela's Ashes* (1999), by Alan Parker. Some, though by no means all, of these films had a degree of POSTMODERN self-reflexivity concerning the dangers of nostalgia and the flight from modernity. Others, such as Alan Parker's *The Commitments* (1991), from Roddy DOYLE's novel, or the Mike Newell-directed *Into the West* (1992), specifically located the threat of modernity in Dublin itself. These turned, respectively, to a new ethnic identity (northside Dubliners as 'the blacks of Ireland', in the tale of a soul band's almost-rise to stardom), and to escape from the city in search of a valorized West in which Travellers are seen as the essential Irish.

In the 1990s a number of important institutional advances have been made by Irish film. The ceasefire in Northern Ireland and the 'CELTIC TIGER' prosperity in the Republic boosted confidence, and with the FINE GAEL-LABOUR coalition of 1992 the Galway TD Michael D. Higgins was appointed Arts Minister. Higgins realized the importance of the emergent indigenous film culture, as well as of big budget productions, and furthered the establishment of a National Film Archive and an Irish Film Centre in 1992. In 1993 he opened a new Irish Film Board, and attempted to balance between commercialism and the kind of cultural excellence which would require government and Irish, rather than Anglo-American, funding. As well as smaller films, larger ones continued to be made, notably Neil Jordan's massively successful biopic *Michael COLLINS* (1996); intelligently, Jordan's film appropriated a series of US genres in order to make his own statement of cine-matic independence on the 75th anniversary of the Easter Rising and at a crucial moment in the Northern peace process.

The TROUBLES had often been imaged in film in terms of 'love across the divide' – most notably in *Cal* (1983), directed by Pat O'Connor, in which a lowly young IRA operative is involved in, and destroyed by, his affair with the widow of an RUC man. More complex, less lyrical, explorations of the effects of violence came later, notably in the trilogy of films by Jim Sheridan and Terry George – *In the Name of the Father* (1993), *Some Mother's Son* (1996) and *The Boxer* (1998). The first was based on the harrowing experience of the Guildford Four who, like the Birmingham Six, were wrongly convicted of an IRA bombing in 1974. Like many other recent Irish films, this one focused on the subject of images of fatherhood (in a sense this was the subject of *Michael Collins*), in this case the relationship of Gerry Conlon to his father, Giuseppe, who tragically died before being released from prison. Equally, but differently disturbing, was Thaddeus O'Sullivan's *Resurrection Man* (1998), dealing with the sadistic sectarian mentality of the Shankill Butchers, in a rare excursion into the world of working-class LOYALIST paramilitarism.

Further reading

McLoone and MacMahon (eds) (1984). Pettitt (2000). Rockett, Hill and Gibbons (1988).

Fine Gael   The second major political party in the Republic, after Fianna Fáil, it was formed from a merger between the Blueshirts, Cumann Na nGaelhead and other right-wing parties in 1933 and led until 1944 by William Cosgrave, its co-founder. It has never been able to govern outright, but has always been the dominant power in the coalitions into which it has entered; these are those of 1948–51 and 1954–57 (when its leader was John A. Costello), 1973–77 (when its leader was Liam Cosgrave), 1981–82 and 1982–87 (when its leader was Garret FitzGerald) and 1995–97 (the 'Rainbow' coalition, when its leader was John Bruton).

More right-wing and less populist than Fianna Fáil, Fine Gael began by representing the interests of large farmers, white-collar workers and the professional classes. It attempted to diversify its base, largely unsuccessfully, by an attempted move in a social democratic direction in the 1960s. During the 1980s, the party launched a 'constitutional crusade' in order to endorse a pluralist society (one purpose of this being to allay the fears of Northern Irish Protestants concerning the Republic). The deflationary policies the party was pursuing at the time tended to undermine these attempts.

Finnian, St (*d.c.*549)   One of the most important Irish saints after St Patrick, Finnian's main importance was as a monastic reformer and educator. Finnian was born in Co. Carlow. He was educated in Wales where he became a monk. He returned to Ireland and founded several monasteries, including Clonard, near Kinnegard, Co. Meath, and Aghowle, Co. Wicklow. The establishment of Clonard helped to inspire a series of further monasteries in Ireland. Finnian became renowned for teaching a series of important Irish saints and ecclesiastical figures, including St Columba and St Brendan the Navigator.

FitzGerald, Garret (1926–)   Born in Dublin, educated at UCD, and an Economics lecturer there until 1973, FitzGerald was one of the few politicians with the training to grasp the detail of the complex processes of modernization in the Irish economy from the 1960s onwards. A Fine Gael TD from 1969, he was leader of the party 1977–87. In government he served as Minister for Foreign Affairs 1973–77, and as Taoiseach in 1981–82 and 1982–87. His attempt to launch a liberal 'constitutional crusade' in 1981 to clarify attitudes on national sovereignty and Northern Ireland proved, in his own words, 'stillborn', a victim of 'the sharp swing to the right in religious as well as political affairs that … marked the first half of the 1980s'. As Taoiseach, however, FitzGerald was central to the New Ireland Forum and in forging the 1985 Anglo-Irish Agreement.

Flight of the Earls   On 4 September 1607 the defeated leaders of the Irish forces in the Nine Years War, Hugh O'Neill, Rory O'Donnell, Earl of Tyrconnell, and Cúchonnacht Maguire, Earl of Fermanagh, together with a number of their followers, assembled at Rathmullen, Co. Donegal, and set sail for Spain. The reasons for their unexpected departure remain something of a mystery, but they may have felt that despite the relatively lenient treatment they received in the Treaty of Mellifont which concluded the war their lands were under threat of confiscation. After the flight they were declared traitors and their lands were confiscated, helping to pave the way for the establishment of the Ulster Plantation. The lords never reached Spain but ended up in Rome where they endured a miserable existence funded by the papacy. The flight was subsequently regarded as a national disaster and there were numerous poetic laments for the loss of the native aristocracy. Fear Flatha Ó Gnímh, a poet who flourished in the early seventeenth century, sees the Irish as a lost and leaderless people in his 'After the Flight of the Earls', which begins, 'God rest the soul of Ireland,/island of faltering steps./The soft-voiced people of Brian/are heavy with grief, I think.'

Friel, Brian (1929–)   Dramatist and short story writer. Born in Omagh, in Co. Tyrone, Friel grew up in Derry city. He was educated there at St Columb's College, then at Maynooth and St Joseph's Teacher Training College, Belfast. He became a full-time writer in 1960, and in 1967 moved to Co. Donegal. Friel began as a short story writer, revealing his dual identification with Derry and rural Donegal which marks his play writing. This began with radio features in the late 1950s and led to time spent with the dramaturge Tyrone Guthrie in Minneapolis in 1963. It was the basis for Friel's first international success, *Philadelphia, Here I Come!* (1964), which was followed by *The Loves of Cass McGuire* (1966) and *Lovers* (1967). All three used experimental dramatic techniques.

To the themes of love, illusion, childhood and adaptation to constraint, which informed this work, were added satire in *The Mundy Scheme* (1969) and social critique in *The Gentle Island* (1971), dealing respectively with politics in the Republic and lurking rural violence. These plays show Friel, like his contemporary Thomas Murphy, exploring the strains of modernization, while *The Freedom of the City* (1973) can be seen as his first Troubles play. Like many poets, Friel's treatment of violence has often been oblique, as in *Volunteers* (1975) and the powerful *Faith Healer* (1979), which offers multiple viewpoints of the same events and is set in a Beckett-like limbo. A more explicit interest in the way history is written is evident in *Translations* (1980), the first play staged by his own Field Day Company. It is set at the time of the Ordnance Survey mapping of Ireland in the 1830s, and the introduction of English into the Irish school system, and raises the issues concerning what is lost (or not) in translation, the slippage between history and myth, and mapping and naming as forms of social control. Internationally acclaimed, it provoked a widespread discussion of cultural politics and history, crystallizing a preoccupation with identity aired in such literary journals as *The Crane Bag*, and in the revisionism debate more generally.

In *Making History* (1988), which dramatizes the life of Hugh O'Neill, some of the dangers of a too abstract debating of the nature of history are evident. However, Friel's work showed renewed energy in *Dancing at Lughnasa* (1990), which reworks the autobiographical concerns of his earliest writing and the interest in pre-1917 Russian writers shown in *Three Sisters* (1981) and *A Month in the Country* (1992), based on Chekhov and Turgenev. *Lughnasa* was another major international success, and was later made into a film. Later plays include *Wonderful Tennessee* (1993) and *Molly Sweeney* (1994), both notable for their dramatic invention. With Tom MURPHY, Friel is generally considered the leading Irish dramatist of his generation.

Further reading

Roche (1994).

Froude, J. A. (1818–1894)   Historian, and author of the controversial study *The English in Ireland in the Eighteenth Century* (1872), which criticized Britain for its mismanagement of the country.

G

Gaelic Athletic Association (GAA)   Founded in 1884 by Michael Cusack (1847–1906), a teacher disillusioned by the spread of English games such as rugby and cricket in Ireland. Drawing on FENIAN and IRB support, the GAA was committed to bringing traditional Irish sports, notably hurling and Gaelic football, back to the centre of Irish life. The Association was seen as part of the new nationalist ethos of late nineteenth- and early twentieth-century Ireland (and Cusack himself would be ruthlessly satirized by James JOYCE in the 'Cyclops' episode of *Ulysses*). The continued popularity of the sports it founded testifies to its success and it remains a major sporting administrator in contemporary Ireland. In Northern Ireland, members of the police and armed forces were for many years banned from membership; this has now been revoked.

Gaelic League   The Gaelic League was founded in 1893 by Eoin McNeill, with Douglas HYDE as its first President. Its aim was to promote spoken and written Irish throughout the country, and to resist the ubiquity of English usage. It was highly successful, running a large network of language classes and reading rooms, and sponsoring a regular festival, An tOireachtas. The League quickly gained a foothold among the urban lower-middle classes, and some of its members went on to participate in the 1916 EASTER RISING. Today it remains active under the name of Conradh na Gaeilge.

Gaeltacht   Name given to IRISH LANGUAGE-speaking districts in Ireland; the largest of these are now in coastal areas in Co. Kerry, Connemara (Co. Mayo and Co. Galway) and Co. Donegal. The Free State government established a Commission on the Gaeltacht in 1925; it recommended making competence in Irish compulsory for all senior civil servants dealing with the areas, economic development and better education. These were only sporadically and partially implemented. A new Gaeltacht was 'planted' in Co. Meath in the 1930s and has survived. But, despite this, the creation of agencies such as Údarás na Gaeltachta (a semi-elected development body), and radio (1972) and TELEVISION stations (Telefís na Gaeilge) (1996), the indefinite survival of the Gealtachtaí is today doubtful.

Gate Theatre (1928–)   The Dublin Gate Theatre Company was founded in 1928 by Hilton Edwards and Mícheál Mac Liammóir, and produced two seasons of plays – including, in the first season, Ibsen's *Peer Gynt* and, in the second, Denis Johnston's *The Old Lady Says 'No!'* – at the ABBEY Theatre's experimental Peacock Theatre. In 1930, Edwards and Mac Liammóir moved the company to a newly created theatre in buildings at the Rotunda Hospital. Since then, the Gate has produced both the classics and, in the early years, new Irish plays by Johnston, Lord Longford and Mary Manning. With the demise of Mac Liammóir in 1978 and Edwards in 1982, and that of Lady Longford in 1980, the Gate's already difficult financial situation became acute. But with Michael Colgan's directorship (1983–) the Gate recovered, producing works including Frank McGuinness's translation of *Peer Gynt* in 1988 and Samuel BECKETT's *Waiting for Godot* in 1989, the latter being succeeded by a Beckett Festival in 1991.

Further reading

Luke (1978).

Gerald of Wales (Giraldus Cambrensis, Gerald of Barry) (?1146–?1220) Gerald was an Anglo-Norman churchman who visited Ireland in 1184 as a secretary in Prince John's expedition to consolidate the NORMAN CONQUEST of Ireland. Gerald wrote two enormously influential books describing Ireland and the Irish based on his observations and experiences in Ireland, *Topographia Hibernica* (*The Topography and History of Ireland*) (1188) and *Expugnatio Hibernica* (*The Conquest of Ireland*) (1189). These works provided the basis of most descriptions of Ireland written in English up to the seventeenth century, forcing the Irish historian Geoffrey KEATING to exclaim that everyone copied Gerald. Other historians were roused to similar fury and tried to combat Gerald's potent influence over perceptions of the Irish. *Topographia Hibernica* is a mixture of prejudice, careful observation and scurrilous gossip (Gerald is very keen to believe any story of the Irish having sex with animals). Gerald describes the Irish as a *gens barbara*, a barbaric race who have no culture, orderly religion or proper society. He does, however, praise the religious spirit of the Irish and records a sly response of the Bishop of Cashel. When Gerald argues that the Irish have not had any martyrs worthy of recognition by the church, the bishop agrees but counters with the observation: 'But now a people has come to the kingdom which knows how, and is accustomed, to make martyrs. From now on Ireland will have its martyrs, just as other countries.' Gerald has to admit that this is 'a reply which cleverly got home'.

Expugnatio Hibernica is a more straightforward historical work describing the events which culminated in Henry II's invasion in 1171. It contains the only record of the LAUDABILITER and also makes stern criticisms of the Anglo-Norman invaders for 'degenerating' and becoming Irish, a theme which recurs time and again in later writings on Ireland. Gerald is a lively and entertaining writer with a keen eye for detail and narrative development whose work always reads well even if his prejudices strike the reader as shocking.

Further reading

Bartlett (1982).

gerrymandering   The fixing of electoral areas to maximize sectarian advantage was practised in certain parts of Northern Ireland after the creation of the state. The most blatant example was in the city of DERRY. Here, the Protestant population who made up two fifths of the population always won three fifths of the corporation seats; while the CATHOLIC population, which made up three fifths of the population, never won more than two fifths of the seats. Gerrymandering involved the drawing of electoral ward boundaries such that the vast majority of the Catholic population were included in a single over-large electoral ward, while the Protestants were made a majority in two smaller ones. 87 per cent of the majority Catholic population in the single ward returned eight seats to the council, while the minority Protestant population, controlling two wards of six seats each, were able to return 12 seats. Controlling the corporation in this way, Protestants were able to monopolize corporation housing and job allocations.

Gibbons, Luke (1950–)   Critic and cultural theorist. From early research on Irish FILM and TELEVISION, collected in *Cinema and Ireland*, Gibbons went on to make influential analyses of the nature of MODERNIZATION THEORY and its applicability to Ireland. In particular, he analysed what he dubbed 'mutant' or 'regressive' modernization; that is, modernization which, precisely because of its belatedness and rapidity (since the 1960s), had skipped over the stages of developing an infrastructure of social justice and civic responsibility which occurred during the longer-term growth of capitalism and bourgeois society elsewhere in the world, and which therefore has no commitment to such values. The cultural 'neo-traditionalism' which accompanied such change, simultaneously asserting the myth of romantic Ireland and its status as 'The Most Profitable Industrial Location in the EEC', was thus unencumbered with a vision of social progress. As a result, neo-traditionalists were able to scapegoat 'backward' rural Ireland in order to distract attention from the problems produced by the conservatism and economic liberalism of the 1980s (see 'CELTIC TIGER', MODERNIZATION).

Further reading

Gibbons (1996).

Gladstone, William Ewart (1809–1898) Liberal politician who, as British Prime Minister for four separate sessions between 1868 and 1894, was responsible for facilitating the Disestablishment of the CHURCH OF IRELAND (1869), and for the LAND ACTS of 1870 and 1881. Seen as an increasingly liberal leader, Gladstone became a convert to the cause of Irish HOME RULE, but failed to secure the passage through parliament of the two Home Rule Bills of 1886 and 1893.

Goldsmith, Oliver (1728–1774) Writer. Goldsmith was the son of a Church of Ireland clergyman, who grew up in Longford and Meath before attending TRINITY COLLEGE, DUBLIN, where he was an unhappy student, often in trouble and mocked because of the smallpox scars that disfigured him. He had a series of experiences after he graduated in 1749, planning to study the law in Ireland, then reading medicine in Edinburgh, and embarking on a tour of the Highlands and Europe, funding himself by playing the flute and singing, before arriving penniless in London in 1756. He worked in a school in Peckham and started his career as an author by contributing to the *Monthly Review*. He wrote a treatise on aesthetics, *An Inquiry into the State of Polite Learning* (1759), and contributed to other periodicals, eventually setting up one himself, *The Bee*, in the same year. He was also writing poetry, and sent drafts of *The Deserted Village* (published 1770) to relations in Ireland. This work describes the devastation experienced by a rural community when a village is cleared to improve the landlord's estate. It contains echoes of Goldsmith's early childhood in Ireland.

For the rest of his life Goldsmith published regularly. He produced *The Citizen of the World* in 1762, a series of letters by a fictional Chinese visitor to England; *A History of England* (1764), again in a form of letters, a work which was a considerable success; *The Traveller, or a Prospect of Society* (1764), which analyses the different societies existing in Europe and suggests that there are numerous ways to live a good life; and his most famous work, *The Vicar of Wakefield*, which appeared in 1766. Its gentle humour, irony and kindness made it an international success. Goldsmith was now a well-known figure in London society, associating with Dr Johnson and James Boswell. In the last years of his life he published plays, including *She Stoops to Conquer* (1773); essays of literary criticism in various periodicals; and yet more histories, one of Rome (1769), one of England (1771) and a *History of the Earth and Animated Nature* (1774). Goldsmith's work makes frequent mention of his upbringing in Ireland, either directly or indirectly. He always expressed a sympathy for exploited and oppressed peasants and developed a democratic ideal of the citizen of the world who should be able to enjoy equality. His work never points the finger at those who others felt caused this misery, but laments human suffering in all its forms.

Further reading

Friedman (ed.) (1966). Swarbrick (ed.) (1984).

gombeen man   A rural loan shark, usually a shop owner or publican.

Gonne, Maud (1866–1953)   Familiar to readers of Irish poetry as the inspiration for many of W. B. YEATS's love poems, Gonne was born in Aldershot; she met Yeats, through the offices of the FENIAN John O'LEARY, in London in 1889. Yeats's first marriage proposal to Gonne was made in 1891; in 1892 he wrote his play *The Countess Cathleen* for her. Gonne prompted Yeats to join the IRISH REPUBLICAN BROTHERHOOD, her own love affair with Ireland commencing in 1882, when her father, an officer in the British army, had been posted to DUBLIN. She vigorously protested evictions in Donegal and sought the release of Irish political prisoners. In 1900, Gonne founded Inghinidhe na hÉireann (Daughters of Ireland). Her beauty and stature contributed greatly to the success of her 1902 performance in the title role of Yeats's NATIONALIST play, *Cathleen Ni Houlihan*. Gonne married Major John MacBride in 1903; and, though the marriage would end in DIVORCE, Gonne kept his name after his execution following the EASTER RISING. Gonne was imprisoned in 1923, her REPUBLICAN beliefs leading her to reject the ANGLO-IRISH TREATY, and devoted herself to helping republican prisoners' families. Her autobiography, *A Servant of the Queen*, was published in 1938.

Further reading

Ward (1991).

Good Friday Agreement (1998)   The Downing Street Declaration in 1993 was a constructively ambiguous shelving of difficult long-term issues between Britain and the Republic in order to bring about the IRA ceasefire. It succeeded in this aim, but could not survive without further momentum towards a more permanent settlement. For the IRA, a ceasefire and the democratic mandate of SINN FÉIN were sufficient to begin all-party talks. But, in 1995, the British government made it clear that by 'renunciation of violence' it meant that disarmament had to be accepted as a principle, and stressed the need for a decommissioning gesture as a necessary prelude to all-party talks. This was unacceptable to either set of paramilitaries, and the IRA broke its ceasefire by bombing Canary Wharf in London in February 1996.

Before this, in 1995, the British and Irish governments had published a 'Joint Framework Document', involving the EU, who were to provide a financial support programme for the North. The governments also tried to break the impasse on decommissioning by putting this and the all-party talks on separate or 'twin track' agendas. Elections were called for May 1996 which would elect a forum for all-party negotiations. However, despite winning its highest vote (15.5 per cent), Sinn Féin were denied entry because the IRA had broken their ceasefire. A weak Conservative government, heavily reliant on UNIONIST support in the Commons, was also a factor in the failure of this process. The IRA did not announce the 'complete cessation of military operations' demanded by the British government until July 1997, after the Labour Party under Tony Blair had won the election in May. In September 1997 Sinn Féin were allowed to enter the all-party talks, making them more inclusive. With support from the Clinton administration in the USA, and the international commissioners (George Mitchell, Harri Holkeri and General John de Chastelain) the Blair government then moved towards the 1998 Agreement.

The Agreement established a devolved Northern Irish Assembly, and North-South and British-Irish Councils, covering the totality of relationships in the two islands. But it made clear the right of the people of Northern Ireland to determine their constitutional future, was inclusive of all political opinion, and supportive of human rights. (Thus, the Agreement's definition of identity notes that it is 'the birthright of all the people of Northern Ireland to identify themselves ... as Irish or British *or both*'.) Crucially, it was built on an existing ceasefire and an ongoing peace process which earlier peace initiatives had lacked. With the electorate of the Republic agreeing to drop the claim in items 2 and 3 of their CONSTITUTION to the entire island, the agreement was passed by 71 per cent of voters in Northern Ireland (with only a bare majority of unionists in favour) and 94 per cent in the Republic. The entire process represented a movement towards recognizing multiple identities, and blurring boundaries.

Government of Ireland Act (1920) The descendant of the Third HOME RULE Bill, this was passed at Westminster at the end of 1920. However, it was constructed to solve the 'Irish Problem' as it had been in 1914, not 1920. The British government had offered a nine-county Northern Ireland to UNIONISTS, anticipating that the religious balance in it would favour eventual reunification. But unionists insisted instead on a six-county statelet which they would be able to completely dominate. Under the circumstances, which included escalating attacks on the North by the IRA, they got their way, and accepted secession from the southern state. The Bill provided for two devolved parliaments, one in BELFAST for the six counties of Fermanagh, Antrim, Tyrone, Down, Londonderry and Armagh; one in DUBLIN for the remaining 26 counties.

NATIONALISTS in the south ignored what had happened, and used the subsequent elections to produce another mandate for SINN FÉIN and hence for an independent REPUBLIC. But they underestimated the conviction of unionists, and by the time the ANGLO-IRISH TREATY of 1921 was signed unionists were already entrenched. The May

1921 elections, while giving the Dáil its Sinn Féin 'mandate', had also confirmed the virtual one-party state in the North by yielding a massive UNIONIST majority.

Grattan, Henry (1746–1820)   Politician, best known for giving the name to Grattan's parliament. Grattan trained as a barrister in DUBLIN, qualifying in 1772 and becoming an MP in 1775. He became a leading PATRIOT spokesman, arguing for the need for free trade to enable Ireland to develop as a prosperous nation, and the case was won in 1779, when Ireland was allowed to trade with the British colonies without any prohibition. Grattan was also instrumental in ensuring that the IRISH PARLIAMENT was granted legislative independence in 1782, for which he secured a personal reward of £50,000 from the Irish Commons, enabling him to purchase a landed estate. Irish parliamentary government was now independent of the British Houses of Parliament, which it had not been since the establishment of POYNINGS's LAW; the Irish judiciary was also made independent of its English counterpart with the Irish House of Lords now becoming the final court of appeal. Irish government was still run mainly by English politicians, but many looked back on the period between legislative independence and the ACT OF UNION (1800) as a golden age of Irish self-government which secured considerable national prosperity. The parliament of these years (1782–1800) was later known as Grattan's parliament, even though Grattan played little part in government, remaining on the opposition benches throughout his parliamentary career in Ireland.

Grattan continued to play an important role in the Irish House of Commons. He criticized government reaction to the disturbances in Ireland resulting after the French Revolution, but had little time for the UNITED IRISHMEN. In the 1790s he argued that the PENAL LAWS should be relaxed, and came to believe in the need for CATHOLIC EMANCIPATION. He opposed the Act of Union when it was first proposed in 1799 and then entered parliament in Westminster to campaign for equal rights for Catholics in 1804, although he came to seem a rather dated figure to a new generation of Irish Catholic leaders such as Daniel O'CONNELL. Lionized as a great Irish patriot in the nineteenth century, who brought constitutional government to Ireland, Grattan is now regarded as a flawed figure who was opportunistic, self-regarding and poor at dealing with the proper business of government, as well as being a man of principle.

Further reading

Kelly (1993).

Gregory, Lady (Augusta) (1852–1932)   Playwright, folklorist and poet. Lady Gregory was instrumental to the founding of the Irish Literary Theatre (see ABBEY THEATRE) in 1897 with George MOORE, Edward Martyn and W. B. YEATS. She would write 40 plays for the theatre, most of which are written in 'Kiltartanese', a synthetic Hiberno-English derived from the Galway dialect, to which she had been exposed since a child at her ASCENDANCY household of Roxborough, and in which she continued to be interested after her marriage, in 1880, to Sir William Gregory of the neighbouring demesne at Coole Park. During the 1890s, Lady Gregory gathered folktales, often with Yeats's assistance, in her native Galway, material that would eventually appear in five volumes, from *A Book of Saints and Wonders* (1906) to *Visions and Beliefs in the West of Ireland* (1920). Her preoccupation with the Irish language produced two influential retellings of Irish epic cycles, *Cuchulain of Muirthemne* (1902) and *Gods and Fighting Men* (1904), the former of which was important to J. M. SYNGE's development as a dramatist. Gregory also aided Yeats's dramatic career, as is evident in her history of the Abbey Theatre, *Our Irish Theatre* (1913), helping him with rural speech in *Cathleen Ni Houlihan* and *The Pot of Broth*. Her first-produced play was *Twenty-Five* (1903), a comedy that set the pattern for many of her subsequent dramas in its concision and realism. She also translated Molière into Kiltartanese, as well as IRISH-LANGUAGE plays by Douglas HYDE. Initially a UNIONIST, Lady Gregory's tireless devotion to the LITERARY REVIVAL changed her political convictions, as is witnessed in the NATIONALISM of the play *The Rising of the Moon* (1907), co-authored with Hyde. There is firm continuity between her early support for the Egyptian nationalism of Arabi Bey, on whom she published *Arabi and His Household* in 1882, and the Irish nationalist historiography of the late play, *An Old Woman Remembers*, a monologue performed by Sara Allgood in 1923.

Her son, Robert, was killed in WWI, and is the subject of elegies by Yeats. Her nephew, Hugh Lane, was drowned when the *Lusitania* sank in 1915, and Gregory fruitlessly sought the return of his valuable collection of Impressionist paintings from London, in accord with Lane's wishes in an unwitnessed codicil to his will. A history of her 'BIG HOUSE', in which many of the luminaries of the Literary Revival had found a welcome, was published in *Coole* (1931).

Further reading

Kohfeldt (1985). Saddlemeyer and Smythe (1982).

Griffith, Arthur (1871–1922)   Political leader and propagandist. Born in DUBLIN and educated by the Christian Brothers, Griffith served an apprenticeship as a printer. After the fall of PARNELL he joined the GAELIC LEAGUE and the IRB. He founded and edited the *United Irishman* (1899–1906) and *Sinn Féin* (1906–1914) to argue for a 'dual monarchy' arrangement for Britain and Ireland, on the model of the Austro-Hungarian Empire, an idea developed in *The Resurrection of Hungary: A Parallel for Ireland* (1904). He also founded Cumann na nGaedheal, the organization which became SINN FÉIN in 1907.

Griffith's principles were conservative and monarchist, and stressed the need for Irish economic self-sufficiency. While opposing violence, and committed to constitutional change, his views – often brilliantly expressed – were nevertheless deeply racist.

His intolerance extended to verbal assaults on SYNGE's plays and hostility to the work of W. B. YEATS and the ABBEY THEATRE.

Although he joined the IRISH VOLUNTEERS and was imprisoned for taking part in the Howth gun-running, Griffith was not a party to the EASTER RISING, and for years he and his party were marginal to more militant NATIONALIST currents. This changed after 1916, however, when Sinn Féin became the political wing of armed republicanism under DE VALERA. Elected as an MP in 1918, Griffith was acting President of the DÁIL ÉIREANN in 1919, and led the delegation which negotiated the ANGLO-IRISH TREATY in October–November 1921; he was instrumental in getting Michael COLLINS and other delegates to make concessions to the British.

Further reading

Younger (1981).

Guinness Guinness, on which the worldwide name of Irish brewing largely rests, began being manufactured after Arthur Guinness took over a disused brewery at St James's Gate in DUBLIN in 1759, leasing it for 9,000 years at an annual rent of £45.00. Following a period of brewing ales, a new product made with roast barley, initially called porter and eventually stout, was launched. By 1833 Guinness was the largest brewery in Ireland, and by 1914 the largest in the world. Among other effects of its prominence, the widespread association of the harp with Ireland is attributable to Guinness' decision in 1862 to use it as a trademark. Throughout the twentieth century Guinness remained the leading Irish brand name, maintaining its position by innovative advertizing as much as the innate 'goodness' of its product.

Hamilton, William Rowan (1805–1865) Born in DUBLIN to a Protestant ANGLO-IRISH family, Hamilton was one of the leading mathematicians of the nineteenth century. Something of a child prodigy, he knew several classical and oriental languages at an early age, wrote poetry, and took a keen amateur interest in astronomy. As a student at TRINITY COLLEGE, Dublin, he continued to outstrip his contemporaries in academic achievement, and was appointed Professor of Astronomy in 1827. In 1828 he published the first instalment of what would become his life's major achievement, a revolutionary theoretical analysis of the science of optics, in *A Theory of Systems of Rays*. This was followed by *A General Method in Dynamics* (1834) and by the publication of his *Lectures on Quaternions* (1853). In 1835 he received a knighthood, and two years later became President of the Royal Irish Academy.

   Hamilton reached pre-eminence in the fields of optics and algebra at a time of major advances in the mathematical sciences throughout Europe, and his work was acclaimed across a wide field of interest. He was also a poet, producing numerous rather intro-spective and, in earlier life, love-sick verses in the manner of Wordsworth, who was a close friend. Like Wordsworth, he believed in the close relationship between the poetic and the scientific mind; both, he suggested, were products of the same spirit of enquiry into the 'higher things' of life. He remains a central figure in a strong tradition of nineteenth-century Irish scientific prowess (see also ASTRONOMY, MATHEMATICS).

Further reading

Hankins (1980).

Hartnett, Michael (Mícheál Ó hArtnéide) (1941–1998)   Poet and translator. Born in Croom, Co. Limerick, in what had recently been a GAELTACHT area, Hartnett developed early a delicate but wiry lyric style in English. He moved to DUBLIN in 1963, co-editing *Arena* with James Liddy, and published *Anatomy of a Cliché* (1968) and a version of the *Tao Te Ching* (1971). The former was based on the *dánta grádha* tradition of Irish medieval love-song. A premature *Selected Poems* appeared in 1970, but a translation of Lorca's *Gipsy Ballads* (1973) reflected time spent in Madrid and also a convincing sense of affinity with the Spanish folk tradition. In 1974 Hartnett returned to Co. Limerick, publishing *A Farewell to English* (1975) and announcing that henceforth he would write only in the IRISH LANGUAGE as a gesture of solidarity with it. His Irish collections include *Adharca Broic* (1978) and *Anhia Niocht* (1985), while *Cúlú Ide/The Retreat of Ita Cagney* (1978) is a poem written simultaneously in Irish and English, and described by Hartnett as 'two versions of the one poem: but what the original language is I don't know'. Hartnett's sense of Munster as a lost cultural heartland echoes Daniel CORKERY, but links to the work of the younger *INNTI* writers (see IRISH-LANGUAGE LITERATURE). Though he translated Nuala Ní DHOMHNAILL's poetry, the indifference which greeted his renunciation of English made it likely that Hartnett would eventually return to it. *Inchicore Haiku* (1985) marked this point and was followed by other collections, some – such as *The Killing of Dreams* (1992) – recapturing the lucidity of his best work. He also translated Ó BRUADAIR (1985) and Pádragín Haicéad (1993).

Further reading

Goodby (2000).

Haughey, Charles J. (1925–)   Politician. Born at Castlebar, of a family involved in the ANGLO-IRISH WAR, educated at UCD, Haughey became a FIANNA FÁIL TD in 1957, and Minister of Justice in 1961. He was responsible for the Succession Act, which guaranteed financial entitlement for widows, and introduced military courts shortly before the IRA called off its 1956–62 campaign. He was Minister for AGRICULTURE 1964–66 and for Finance 1966–70; in the latter post he introduced free travel for old-age pensioners and tax concessions to artists and writers. However, his ministerial successes and brash manner upset some party traditionalists and when Seán LEMASS retired in 1966 Haughey withdrew his challenge in favour of Jack Lynch's, despite being a leading contender.

During the flare-up of the TROUBLES in Northern Ireland in 1970, attempts were made by the IRA in the North to import arms. Lynch accused Haughey and Neil Blaney of not fully subscribing to government policy on Northern Ireland and dismissed them. Sensationally, in May 1970 Haughey was arrested and charged with conspiring to import arms illegally. Although a jury finally acquitted him on all counts, the events led to temporary eclipse. He was recalled to the cabinet as Welfare Minister (where he passed the Health and Social Welfare Act, whose proviso for limited CONTRACEPTION he memorably described as 'an Irish solution to an Irish problem'). When Lynch resigned in 1979 Haughey became party leader and Taoiseach. He lost office in 1981, briefly regained it in 1982, and scraped into power in 1987. Progress was made in reducing the national debt, but after calling a snap election in 1989 Haughey could only keep power by becoming the first leader of his party since DE VALERA in 1932 to enter a coalition, with the PROGRESSIVE DEMOCRATS. Early in 1992 his former Justice Minister Sean Doherty said that Haughey had been aware of phone taps on two political writers as Taoiseach in 1982. He denied this but resigned, and was succeeded by Albert Reynolds.

Haughey was a dominant political figure for nearly 20 years and was among the most controversial of all Irish leaders. This controversy pursued him in his retirement, and he was named in the Beef, McCracken and Flood TRIBUNALS, and in the latter two implicated in accepting gifts and bribes on a massive scale. Haughey's former expansiveness and lavish lifestyle is now read as the expression of a brazen culture of corruption which he has come to symbolize.

health, health service see **medicine and health provision**

Heaney, Seamus (1939–) Poet, critic, dramatist. Born Mossbawn, Co. Derry, Heaney was educated at St Columb's College and QUB. He taught at St Joseph's College and as a lecturer in English at QUB, but – under no little personal threat as violence increased – moved to the REPUBLIC in 1972, where he worked as a freelance writer and then at Carysfort College, DUBLIN. Abandoning this in 1980, he has held part-time professorial posts since at Harvard and Oxford universities. A prolific poet and critic, and member of the FIELD DAY collective, Heaney is easily the most celebrated and influential of all living Irish poets, his many awards being crowned by the Nobel Prize for Literature in 1995.

Heaney began his career in the BELFAST GROUP; his first book, *Death of a Naturalist* (1966), published by Faber and Faber, established the local poetry revival (which included Derek MAHON and Michael LONGLEY) as a national and international presence. Its physically immediate style, drawn from Hopkins, Hughes and Keats, rendered rural life in a way which owed much to KAVANAGH and Wordsworth, with Heaney charting vanishing customs – thatching, eel fishing, farming, turf cutting – and his growing up in, and out of, a life of instinct. These were implicitly shadowed, as in its opening poem, 'Digging', by the buried violence and instability of Northern Ireland itself. Heaney's mapping of a post-Movement poetic onto his fraught un-English terrain and CATHOLIC and NATIONALIST sensibility soon made him an exemplary figure, and not only for his community of origin.

These subjects, explored in growing depth in *Door into the Dark* (1969) and *Wintering Out* (1973), came to a head in *North* (1975). As the TROUBLES erupted, 'Digging's metaphoric equation of excavation and memory was extended to the archaeological dig into the vertical matter of Ireland, contrasted with British (and US) horizontal expansion in 'Bogland'. Despite the possibilities of rapprochement between Protestant and Catholic, canvassed in 'place name' poems such as 'Broagh', exhumed Iron Age sacrifices from Danish bogs (the subject of 'Tollund Man') irresistibly led Heaney in *North* to depicting the present-day conflict as a tribal and racial one, in which IRA devotees of an Irish earth mother goddess shed their blood in the struggle against a masculine principle of empire and rationality. But, while poems such as 'Punishment' and 'Bog Queen' assert minority 'rights on/The English lyric', Heaney is arguably more successful in 'Strange Fruit' where he puts his aestheticizing impulse under closer scrutiny. His fatalistic, ritualistic and gendered terms were attacked by several critics; nevertheless, the impact of *North* on Irish poetry and cultural debate (in journals such as *The Crane Bag*) was immense, even if it left Heaney with the problem of dismantling his elaborate myth of northernness.

This he did in *Field Work* (1979) and *Station Island* (1984), mid-career collections which show him in more elegiac and wary mood respectively, with the figures of Dante and Mandelstam in the former, and Sweeney in the latter, viewed as role models for sceptical engagement, proper sympathy and an ideal poetry. Heaney published a translation of the Middle Irish poem *Buile Suibhne*, *Sweeney Astray*, in 1983, followed by *The Haw Lantern* (1987), *Seeing Things* (1991) and *The Spirit Level* (1996), his 'ceasefire collection'. In these books, Heaney can be seen trying to further escape his being 'mired in attachment', orienting himself towards ends while remaining in touch with origins, through an almost neo-Platonic imagery of weightlessness, light and buoyancy. Successful though this can be, the later poetry does not always escape the blandness suggested by some of his more sweeping critical claims ('In that liberated moment when the lyric discovers its buoyant completion … of self-justification and self-obliteration, the poet … is at once intensified in his being and detached from his predicaments'). His latest collection, *Electric Light* (2001), resembles its immediate predecessors, but with a new consciousness of mortality.

Heaney's output also includes the literary criticism of *Preoccupations* (1980), *The Government of the Tongue* (1988) and *The Redress of Poetry* (1995), *The Cure at Troy* (1990) (an adaptation of Sophocles's *Philoctetes* for Field Day), and a translation of *Beowulf* (1999) which became a best-seller.

Further reading

Andrews (ed.) (1998). Corcoran (1986). Curtis (2001). Deane (1985). Lloyd (1993). Longley, E. (1986). O'Donoghue (1994).

hedge school   In late eighteenth- and early nineteenth-century Ireland, the lack of any formalized education for the rural population led to the teaching of children at informal 'schools', often held in the open air. The figure of the 'hedge-school' teacher features in writing by CARLETON (*Traits and Stories of the Irish Peasantry*) and Brian FRIEL (*Translations*), and the great politician and thinker Edmund BURKE began his education at one.

Hewitt, John Harold (1909–1887)   Poet, curator, critic. Born in BELFAST, Hewitt was educated at Methodist College and QUB, starting work at the Belfast Museum and Art Gallery and rising there until denied promotion on sectarian grounds (he was deemed to be too friendly with 'communists', 'Catholics' and 'theatre people'), after which he moved to be director of the Herbert Art Gallery in Coventry 1957. In 1972 he retired to Belfast, effectively beginning a second literary career there. A left-wing political and cultural activist in the 1930s, Hewitt helped form the Ulster Unit of progressive artists with the painters John Luke and Colin Middleton, and in the 1940s, as lecturer, publicist, associate editor of *Lagan* (1945–46) and contributor to THE BELL, was the chief exponent of Ulster regionalism. As regionalism faded, his energies found more historical and personal outlets. Examples of these are his MA dissertation on the plebeian radical 'rhyming weaver' poets of the late eighteenth century, whom he viewed as forebears (published as *Rhyming Weavers* in 1974), and the autobiographical sketch *Planter's Gothic* (1953).

Although he began writing poetry in the 1920s, Hewitt did not publish in book form until *Conacre* (1943) and *No Rebel Word* (1948). Thereafter silence resumed, despite great private productivity and journal publication, until *Tesserae* (1967) and *Collected Poems* (1968). This reflected the difficulty, for Hewitt as for other poets of his generation (such as Austin CLARKE and Robert Greacen), to gain a hearing in the Ireland of the 1940s and 1950s. Certainly, Hewitt regarded his years in Coventry as an exile, and the very titles of some of his later collections – *Out of My Time* (1974), *Time Enough* (1976), not to mention the 1978 documentary film 'I Found Myself Alone' – can be read as alluding to this silencing and belated reappearance. Other late works

109

include the collections *The Rain Dance* (1978) and *Loose Ends* (1983) and monographs on Luke and Middleton. Hewitt's remarkable dramatization of the roots of sectarian violence, the radio play *The Bloody Brae*, was revived in 1986, some 32 years after its first broadcast.

While he was a symbol of endurance to younger generations of Northern Irish poets, Hewitt's poetry is generally too conservative and four-square to have been a direct literary influence. Nevertheless, in his best work, such as 'The Colony' (which draws parallels between a Roman colony and plantation Ireland), or 'The Coasters', which indicts past indifference towards CATHOLICS, he is a subtle and powerful writer uniquely capable of articulating in verse the dilemmas of the liberal Northern Irish Protestant conscience.

Further reading

Brown (1975). Heaney (1980). McDonald (1997). Ormsby (ed.) (1991).

Hierarchy The Conference of Bishops which acts as a national ecclesiastical apparatus for the Irish CATHOLIC CHURCH.

Higgins, Aidan (1927–) Novelist and short story writer. Born Celbridge, educated at Clongowes, he left Ireland without attending university to embark on the travels which inform his work (in South Africa, Germany, London, Andalusia and Denmark). His early work includes the short story collection *Felo de Se* (1960, republished as *Asylum and Other Stories*, 1971) and the travel writing collected in *Images of Africa* (*Diary 1956–60*) (1971) (republished, with later travel writings, in *Ronda Gorge and Other Precipices*). *Langrishe, Go Down* (1966), which won the James Tait Black Memorial Prize, is Higgins's best-known novel. Set in the 1930s, it is in part a 'BIG HOUSE' novel, telling the tale of an affair between the daughter of an impoverished Ascendancy family and a German student, and develops Higgins's characteristic themes of drift, failure and waste. The modernist allegiances evident in these works appear full-blown in his most ambitious work, *The Balcony of Europe* (1972), which was shortlisted for the Booker Prize. It was followed by *Scenes from a Receding Past* (1977), *Bornholm Night-Ferry* (1983) and *Lions of the Grünewald* (1993). His best work is a salutary corrective to the easy stereotypes of some contemporary Irish fiction. A selection of the shorter fiction, *Flotsam and Jetsam*, was published in 1996. A trilogy of memoirs includes *Donkey's Years* (1995), *Dog Days* (1998) and the projected *The Whole Hog*.

Hillsborough Agreement (1985) see Anglo-Irish Agreement (1985)

Home Rule Home Rule was the principal aim of constitutional nationalists from 1870, when Isaac BUTT formed the Home Government Association (later the Home

Rule League), until 1918. Exactly what Home Rule meant was kept deliberately vague in order to maximize support across the range of Irish nationalist sympathies, but Butt's conception was generally agreed upon: Ireland, Scotland and England would have individual parliaments for domestic affairs while also maintaining a common sovereign, executive, and 'national council' at Westminster for all international matters. Butt's successor, Charles Stewart Parnell, was also tactically vague in his use of the term, thereby drawing the support of agrarian radicals as well as the Catholic Church. At this time unionist fear expressed itself in the slogan 'Home Rule is Rome Rule'. Despite Prime Minister Gladstone's backing of the policy, it was defeated as a Bill in the House of Commons in 1886, and again in 1893 when the House of Lords rejected the Second Home Rule Bill. The third Bill was actually enacted in 1914, but without effect, as it was suspended for the duration of WWI; by the end of the war it was irrelevant, overtaken by calls for a republic. Commentators often point out the irony that the only place where Home Rule came into effect, unionist Ulster, was the area most resistant to it.

Hume, John (1937–) Born Derry, educated at St Columb's College and Maynooth, he founded a housing association and a credit union in Derry. In the late 1960s Hume was a member of NICRA and vice-chair of the Derry Citizens Action Committee before being elected MP for Foyle at Stormont in 1969. Hume had called for a new social-democratic party and became a founder member of the Social Democratic and Labour Party in 1970, emerging as its leading figure and chief policy-maker. He was elected to the power-sharing executive of 1974. Hume was notable for his belief, early on in the Troubles, that European and, later, US input was essential for the initiation of any peace process. He has been an MEP and leader of the SDLP since 1979, and was the architect of the New Ireland Forum in 1983. As well as supporting the Anglo-Irish Agreement of that year, he helped engineer the Downing Street Declaration of 1993, which paved the way for the ceasefires of 1994 and the Good Friday Agreement of 1998. In 1998 he also shared the Nobel Peace Prize with David Trimble. Despite attacks on the sectarian ethos of the SDLP, Hume is commonly agreed to be the outstanding constitutional nation-alist politician of his generation in Northern Ireland.

hunger strikes Although 'fasting to distrain' against a debtor or victimizer was a recognized procedure in the Irish Medieval civil code, the *Senchus Mor*, and was used by the suffragettes, the hunger strike as a weapon of protest dates from the imprisonment of republicans in Frongoch camp in North Wales after the Easter Rising. It was then used by Thomas Ashe, who died in 1917 in Mountjoy prison after force-feeding by the British, and Terence MacSwiney, the Lord Mayor of Cork, who died in Brixton prison after a 73-day hunger strike in 1920. MacSwiney's claim that 'it is not those who can inflict the most, but those who can suffer the most who will conquer' goes to the root of the hunger strike as a public spectacle, its mixture of ascetic bravery and masochistic martyrdom. Both deaths boosted the Sinn Féin cause.

Echoes of MacSwiney's words can be detected in the most famous and momentous use of the tactic, by the IRA in the Maze (formerly Long Kesh) Prison, or 'H-Blocks', in 1980–81. This followed the redesignation in 1976 of those serving sentences for terrorism as having ordinary criminal (rather than political) status, and the consequent withdrawal of privileges. It had initially led the so-called 'dirty protest', in which the prisoners' refusal to wear prison uniform escalated to a refusal to wash or dress, and then to smearing their cells with excrement in protest. The failure of this led in turn to Bobby Sands and nine other republicans starving themselves to death to assert their right to be treated as prisoners of war.

Their hunger strike revealed the intransigence of the Thatcher government, and created enormous international opposition to the British government's stance. But, more significantly, it opened up new political possibilities for the IRA leadership under Gerry Adams via electoral politics and Sinn Féin. Following the election of Sands as MP for Fermanagh-South Tyrone on 9 April 1981 with 51 per cent of the vote, and the election of two more strikers in a general election in the Republic in June, enormous latent sympathy was tapped – not so much for IRA violence as for a political alternative for republican sentiment. When Sands died in May, 70–100,000 walked behind his coffin. Up to this point, the IRA's and Sinn Féin's attitude to Westminster and the Dáil had been that they were irrelevant to what was basically a military struggle. After it, most republicans answered in the negative to Danny Morrison's question at the Sinn Féin *ard fheis* (annual conference) of that year: 'will anyone … object if, with a ballot paper in one hand and the Armalite in the other, we take power in Ireland?'

Further reading

Beresford (1987). Clarke (1987). O'Malley (1990).

hybridity   This is the version of COLONIAL and POSTCOLONIAL criticism most influenced by poststructuralist theory. Its main aim is to challenge the viewing of power relations in an either/or framework, making it possible to deconstruct, and so break out of, the Tweedledum-and-Tweedledee binary opposition of colonizer/colonized. The main theorist of hybridity, Homi Bhabha, defines postcolonial writing in terms of its hybrid in-betweenness and unnerving mimicry of the norms of the metropolitan centre. This quality is threatening to imperial centre and indigenous NATIONALIST alike; something of the disquiet felt by the latter is evident in Daniel Corkery's claim that 'Our national consciousness may be described, in a native phrase, as a quaking sod. It gives no footing. It is not English, nor Irish, nor Anglo-Irish …'. Critics of Bhabha, such as

Robert Young, have attacked hybridity as a metaphor, claiming that it has Romantic organicist overtones, and remains bound to imperial concepts of impurity.

Further reading

Bhabha (1994). Lloyd (1993).

Hyde, Douglas (1860–1949)   A leading cultural activist and Gaelic revivalist, Hyde came from a Church of Ireland background and was educated at Trinity College. In 1893, he became first President of the Gaelic League, and from 1938 to 1945 was first President of Ireland. Renowned as a literary historian, his publications included *The Love Songs of Connaught* (1893) and *A Literary History of Ireland* (1899), but he is most frequently remembered for a seminal lecture series, published as *The Necessity for De-Anglicizing the Irish People* (1892), which stressed the need for Ireland to promote its own language and literature, and to resist the ongoing process of English cultural domination.

inquiries and tribunals   As in the revelations concerning abuse by members of the Catholic Church, a culture of concealment in the political sphere began to implode in the Republic during the 1990s. As a foretaste, the Beef Tribunal (1991–94) investigated malpractice in the beef industry. This included massive tax evasion and gifts to politicians; yet, while some minor business fraudsters were found guilty by the courts, the bigger names with whom they had conspired remained unknown, and the political donations were judged 'normal' practice. However, with the fall of Charles Haughey, the long-time leader of Fianna Fáil, the lid began to lift on more widespread and systematic corruption.

In 1997 Haughey himself appeared before the McCracken Tribunal which had been set up in February that year to investigate payments by Ben Dunne, a leading supermarket chain owner, to politicians. It discovered the existence of Cayman Islands tax havens which were part of a massive tax evasion fraud organized by Des Traynor, Haughey's personal financial adviser, on behalf of 120 of the wealthiest people in the country. Haughey's own evidence to the Tribunal was referred to the Director of Public Prosecutions and he was charged with criminal obstruction. Members of other parties, such as the former Fine Gael Minister Michael Lowry, were also shown to be involved in the scheme.

McCracken's investigations were taken up by the Moriarty Tribunal in October 1997. This inquired into details of the payments, discovering that Haughey had received IR£8,500,000 between 1979 and 1996 from businessmen (not to mention the gift of a J. B. YEATS painting from the businessman and tax exile Michael Smurfit), and that he had appropriated Fianna Fáil political funds for his personal use. It also transpired that a Norwegian telecom company had sent a cheque for $50,000 to Fine Gael on behalf of its Irish subsidiary, which had been awarded a mobile phone franchise by the Fine Gael-led government the year before. The party returned the cheque uncashed in 2001, but the suspicion of ever-widening circles of political bribery and corruption grew.

The Flood Tribunal was established in 1998 and continues to explore irregularities in the granting of planning permissions in North DUBLIN. It found that the former city and county assistant manager, George Redmond, had amassed upwards of IR£1,000,000 in illegal payments from developers and landowners, and that a former Fianna Fáil press secretary, Frank Dunlop, had paid IR£180,000 to Dublin county councillors on behalf of developers seeking to have land re-zoned in their favour. The tribunal also found IR£2,600,000 in unexplained deposits to the Fianna Fáil TD Liam Lawler's bank accounts, and a former minister of the environment was summoned to appear on charges related to his receiving money with a view to granting planning permission.

In 1999 the Public Accounts committee of the DÁIL undertook the Deposit Interest Retention Tax (DIRT) Inquiry into bogus non-residential tax accounts, that is, tax breaks awarded to those who claimed not to be living in the country and therefore exempt from DIRT. It found evidence that the number of bogus accounts ran into the tens of thousands, and IR£173,000,000 was recovered. However, in 2000 it was revealed that the committee's vice-chairman had £135,000 in a Cayman Island account, while a year later another member resigned after it was discovered that she had encouraged and advised people on tax evasion as an employee of the National Irish Bank (she was ordered to pay costs of IR£2,000,000).

By 2002 there were over a dozen tribunals and inquiries investigating more and less blatant forms of corruption in the Republic, as well as issues such as abuse by priests and in church-run industrial schools (see SEXUALITY and CATHOLIC CHURCH). These reflected a new openness and frankness in Irish society, but also the malign effects of economic growth, and the public's unprecedented sense of the betrayal of its trust in church and state authorities.

internment The mass rounding up of (usually) REPUBLICAN militants without trial occurred several times in Ireland in the twentieth century. The first internment was of those captured by the British after the EASTER RISING, and held at Frongoch camp in North Wales (see COLLINS). The largest internment was of over 11,000 prisoners by the Free State after the CIVIL WAR. DE VALERA introduced internment again to curb IRA activities during WWII, and again during their border campaign of 1956–62.

The most recent use of internment occurred in Northern Ireland on 9 August 1971 when it was introduced by the Prime Minister, Brian Faulkner (the successor to Chichester-Clark), to counter the Provisional IRA bombing campaign. Two hundred and sixty men, all CATHOLIC, were arrested; but most active IRA members, aware of the raids in advance, had already left their homes. Moreover, the lists of suspects used by the security forces were out of date and in numerous cases simply inaccurate. Over three years about 2,800 people, some LOYALISTS, were interned, for periods ranging from weeks to years. Internment, apart from attracting adverse international public opinion (increased when the European Court of Human Rights found the treatment of some internees brutal and degrading), was counter-productive. Rather than destroying the IRA, the tactic simply acted as a 'recruiting sergeant' for them in working-class Catholic areas and weakened the position of constitutional NATIONALISTS. Violence escalated dramatically, rising from 174 deaths in 1971 to 467 in 1972. Internment was ended in 1985 and, despite periodic calls from loyalist politicians for its reintroduction, has not been used since.

Irish Citizen Army Founded in October 1913 as a force of about 200 to protect workers involved in the Dublin Lockout from physical intimidation by the Dublin Metropolitan Police, James CONNOLLY became its leader after James LARKIN left Ireland for the USA in Autumn 1914. Although he initially saw the ICA as the nucleus of a workers' militia which would eventually overthrow British imperialism and Irish capitalism, Connolly allied the ICA with the NATIONALIST and middle-class forces of the IRB and the IRISH VOLUNTEERS, and thus also with imperial Germany. Its secretary, Sean O'CASEY, resigned in August 1914 in opposition to Constance MARKIEWICZ being a member while simultaneously being a member of the Irish Volunteers. On the day of the EASTER RISING the ICA numbered 220, of which 38 men and one woman, Connolly's secretary Winifred Carney, occupied the insurgent GHQ in the GPO building. Effectively the ICA as an independent entity ceased to exist when Connolly observed that 'From the moment the first shot is fired there will be no longer Volunteers or Citizen Army but only the Army of the Irish Republic'.

Irish-Ireland An ideological position given its most detailed programme in the writings of D. P. Moran (1869–1936), editor and owner of *The Leader* from 1900, and author of *The Philosophy of Irish-Ireland* (1905), a collection of articles first published in the *New Ireland Review*. Irish-Ireland thinking built on Douglas HYDE's belief in the need to 'de-Anglicize' Ireland, which he had presented in a lecture of 1892. Moran and others, including Arthur Clery and Pádraig Ó Duinnín, promulgated the essentialist belief that Irish identity is fundamentally Gaelic and CATHOLIC, and denounced as 'West-Briton' the writings of the (largely Protestant) leaders of the LITERARY REVIVAL. The nationalist historian, and founder of the IRISH VOLUNTEERS, Eoin MacNeill, invoked the rich civilization of the Gaelic past as justification for a modern independent Irish state. In his often fiery contributions to *The Leader*, Daniel Corkery vociferously espoused the Irish-Ireland rhetoric of Moran; his mature thought on the literary revival is to be found in his *Synge and Anglo-Irish Literature* (1931), in which Synge is singled out from the other revivalists as being faithful to Irish identity in his emphasis on religion, nationalism and land.

Further reading

Brown (1985b). McCartney (1967).

Irish language   Irish is a member of the northern, or Goidelic, branch of the Celtic family of languages, and is often referred to as Gaelic. The Celts arrived in Ireland at the beginning of the Iron Age in *c*.500 BC; by the time of the decline of the Roman Empire a thousand years later, they were known as the Scoti and were encroaching on Wales and Scotland (where different Celtic dialects were spoken). Although most of these settlements disappeared, in Scotland, by the eleventh century, the Scoti ruled a largely Irish-speaking kingdom. It is from this that the modern name for Scotland derives. Following the Anglo-Norman expansion of the Middle Ages, Irish was pushed to Galloway and the Highlands and Islands, where it has developed to become Scots Gaelic. In Ireland itself, despite the introduction of Norman French and English-speaking communities, the Irish language remained dominant, and by the fifteenth century had almost entirely reclaimed its range on the island.

However, it came under renewed pressure from the sixteenth century onwards with plantations of New English settlers. The effects of the policies of Cromwell and the Penal Laws were to eliminate the Irish-speaking aristocracy and the learned classes, and to make the English language yet more central to social advancement, and even survival. By the eighteenth century Irish was almost solely the language of the powerless and dispossessed and despite its extensive use in literature, religion and local affairs the tide was running strongly in favour of English. It has been estimated that in 1800 there were some 2,000,000 Irish speakers, 1,500,000 Irish-English bilinguals and 1,500,000 English speakers. But, although the number of Irish-speakers was to increase, the Famine had a devastating effect on a language already disesteemed and declining in importance, since it had a disproportionately devastating effect on the Irish-speaking rural poor. The 1851 census showed that Irish-speakers, including bilinguals, had been reduced to around 1,500,000; and that, of these, only 12.6 per cent of the under-10 age group spoke the language. By 1891 the figure had declined to 3.5 per cent and the language seemed doomed.

At this point, however, the loss of Irish slowed. This was partly because of the sheer isolation and self-sufficiency of the (chiefly coastal) areas, collectively known as the Gaeltacht, to which it was now confined. But it was also because of the movement to restore the language which began under the auspices of the Gaelic League in the late nineteenth century. Through such organizations, the survival of the language was to be tied to the demand for political independence from Britain. The result was that Irish was designated the first official 'national language' of the Free State when it was founded in 1922. Irish was made a compulsory and integral part of the public education system, with competence in it obligatory for many public-service jobs. This official bilingualism has ensured the continuing use of Irish as the minority language, a status recognized today by the EU, and censuses show that 30 per cent of the population claim some fluency in the language.

Nevertheless, despite its protection and survival, Irish is in a far from healthy state. English has made further inroads into the Gaeltacht zones, where it is now estimated that the number of speakers of Irish as a first language is less than 5,000. This is largely attributable to the need to speak English in order to prosper, particularly given mass EMIGRATION. But it also stems from the unimaginative and ultimately counterproductive methods once employed to teach Irish to children from English-speaking back-grounds, and the failure to ensure the language was maintained in use after school. Without gaelicizing the state and the CATHOLIC CHURCH, the major employers in the mid-century REPUBLIC, the language programme was fated to become tokenistic. Indeed, successive governments failed even to finance a sound economic basis for life in the Gaeltacht areas. The 1960s, however, saw the use for the first time of public protests at neglect of the Gaeltacht. HUNGER STRIKES, vigils, demonstrations, albeit small-scale, marked the beginning of a campaign which has succeeded in attracting some resources to these areas, and extracting from government limited Irish-language radio and TELEVISION provision. The difficulties, but also the potential for future growth and development in the language, have been eloquently testified to by the resurgence of IRISH-LANGUAGE LITERATURE in the twentieth century.

Further reading

Crowley (2000).

Irish-language literature (twentieth century)   The older literary tradition in the Irish language, with a few exceptions, died out towards the end of the eighteenth century. In the nineteenth century the effects of Anglicization, and the death-blow the FAMINE dealt the language, ended its use as a literary medium, although a tradition of folk poetry continued and there is some interesting prose in the form of diaries and memoirs. The last significant works before the century or more of near-silence were the lyrics of Eoghan Rua Ó Súilleabhán (1748–84) and Antoine Ó Raifteirí (Raftery) (1784–1835), the mock-heroic bawdy epic *Cúirt an Mheán Oíche/The Midnight Court* by Brian MERRIMAN (1749?–1803) and the great *Caoineadh Airt Uí Laoghaire/Lament for Art Ó Laoghaire* by Eibhlin Dhubh Ní Chonaill (*fl.*1770).

With the GAELIC LEAGUE at the end of the century a desire to make Irish a literary medium again was born. The efforts of Douglas HYDE were central to this; on the one hand he established the existence of a rich Irish literary tradition, while on the other he encouraged original work in Irish, such as his own play *Casadh an tSúgáin* (*The Twisting of the Rope*) (1903). Many Revival writers, such as J. M. SYNGE, learnt Irish and either wrote in it or allowed it to affect their writing in English. The valorization of ruralism and the West of Ireland in the ideology of the Free State (theorized in the writings of Daniel CORKERY) meant that native speakers who began to write about life in the rural GAELTACHT in the 1920s and 1930s were particularly cherished. These included the Blasket Islanders Peig SAYERS (1873–1958), Tomás Ó Criomhthain (1856–1937), author of *An t-Oileánach/The Islandman* (1929), and Muiris Ó Súilleabháin (1904–50), the author of the autobiography *Fiche Bliain ag Fás/Twenty Years A-Growing* (1933). When such material presented a less idealized, earthier view of Irish country life, however, it was dealt with harshly; *The Tailor and Ansty* (1942), the earthy tales of the *seannachie* (oral storyteller) recorded by Tim Buckley and his wife Anastasia, and translated by Eric Cross, was banned after a four-day debate in the DÁIL. In a different mode, such writing was satirized by Flann O'BRIEN in An *Béal Bocht/The Poor Mouth* (1941).

Yet such folklore and autobiography, though raised to the level of art, consciously chronicled a dying, marginal way of life which had little to say to an Ireland which was slowly modernizing. A truly modern literary movement began in 1950 with *Nuabhéarsaíocht*, an anthology of new poetry by Seán Ó RÍORDÁIN (1916–77), Máirtín Ó DIREÁIN (1910–88) and Máire Mhac an tSaoi (1922–) edited by Seán Ó Tuama. It was designed to gain recognition for a new generation of innovative modernist-influenced Irish poets, poets who outgrew the strictures Corkery had set for an AUTHENTIC Irish writing. Mhac an tSaoi, the first important Irish woman poet in either of the island's two literary languages, used traditional forms to write modern love poetry, protesting against women's subordination to conventional roles, and displaying a detailed knowledge of all aspects of Gaelic tradition, including MYTH. The Kerry GAELTACHT area of Dún Chaoin – a 'seantar cnoc is farraige/place of mountains and coasts' – is seen in her poetry as a land of youth and love. Such poetry was matched by the less idealistic prose writing of Máirtín Ó CADHAIN, most notably in his masterpiece, the novel *Cré na Cille* (1948).

The still more modernist work of Eugene WATTERS apart, the next significant 'wave' of Irish-language writing derived from the radicalization of the 1960s. It was centred on UCC, where Seán Ó Ríordáin lectured, and where Irish-language students and writers grouped themselves around the poetry broadsheet INNTI, founded in 1970 by Michael Davitt and Gabriel Rosenstock. INNTI was always as much a crusade as a publication; when the third edition was launched in the Vienna Woods Hotel in Cork in 1973, it is claimed that over 1,000 people attended. Associated with it were many of the leading Irish poets of the last quarter-century; along with Rosenstock and Davitt these included Nuala NÍ DHOMHNAILL and Liam Ó Muirthile. Unlike their modernist predecessors, these writers do not reject the modern city, although they may well be antagonistic to the powers located within it. This stance was shared by Caitlín Maude (1941–82), a gifted actress, *sean-nós* singer and poet, who is remembered for her posthumous *Dánta/Poems* (1985), and who – as a Gaelic Civil Rights activist and supporter of the H-Block HUNGER STRIKERS in 1980–81 – reveals some of the many political possibilities of writing in Irish. Like Maude, Michael HARTNETT/Micheál Ó hAirtnéide belonged to a slightly older generation than the *INNTI* poets; his lack of acceptance in the Irish-language literary community reveals the limitations on its inclusivity at the time. Cathal Ó Searcaigh, the author of collections such as *Súile Shuibhne/The Eyes of Sweeney* (1983), *Suibhne/Sweeney* (1987) and *An Bealach 'na Bhaile/Homecoming* (1993), is innovative in many ways; his work reflects the influence of US Beat writing and Eastern mysticism, and the later poetry is the first in Irish to proclaim and explore an openly gay sexuality.

Contemporary Irish-language writing has broken down many of the barriers which until only recently existed between what were regarded as separate and antagonistic 'Anglo-Irish' (in English) and 'Gaelic' (in Irish) literatures. Through its radical engagement with – for example – sexual, political and folkloric materials, it has made itself relevant to modern Ireland; while, through creative collaborations and imaginative translation projects, it has – albeit at the risk of being submerged in Anglophone culture – managed to suffuse itself through a more inclusive 'Irish' literature.

Further reading

Bolger (ed.) (1986). Kinsella (1995). Ó Tuama (1995). Ó Tuama and Kinsella (eds) (1981). Sewell (2000).

Irish Parliamentary Party An organized Irish NATIONALIST group of MPs at Westminster can be dated from 1870, when Isaac BUTT founded the Home Government Association. It gained strength from the Land War (see LAND LEAGUE) and the election in 1880 of Charles Stewart PARNELL as the secretary of what then became the Home Rule Confederation of Great Britain. Released from prison in 1882, Parnell effectively created a party organization, harnessing the energies of the Land League, the support of the CATHOLIC CHURCH and the backing of GLADSTONE's Liberal Party. But his divorce case in 1890 meant the Liberals' Nonconformist base prevented Gladstone dealing with Parnell, and both the Catholic Church and Gladstone pressured Irish MPs to change leaders. With Tim Healy playing the role of Brutus to Parnell's Caesar, Parnell was deposed, and the anti-Parnellites and Liberals were able to pass the Second HOME RULE BILL in 1893. Nevertheless, it was the leader of the Parnellites in the 1890s, John REDMOND, who managed to reunite the fragments of the Irish group in 1900, as the United Irish League. With the Third Home Rule Bill secured but unimplemented in WWI, the party failed to sense the increasing weakness of their position on Home Rule, constitutionalism and conscription. Unable to respond radically enough to the EASTER RISING, it was crushingly defeated by SINN FÉIN at the 1918 election.

Irish Republican Army (IRA) The Irish Republican Army (in Irish Óglaigh na hÉireann) was the name adopted by the IRISH VOLUNTEERS in 1919 during the

ANGLO-IRISH WAR as the army of the Republic proclaimed by the first, SINN FÉIN DÁIL Éireann of January 1919. It fought an effective guerrilla war, leading to the ANGLO-IRISH TREATY of December 1921, and the formation of the Free State. The Treaty split the IRA; IRA members who followed Michael COLLINS became the National Army of the Free State, while anti-treatyites kept the IRA name and took up arms against the new state in the CIVIL WAR.

The IRA's allegiance was to the pure 'republican' constitutional claim of the first Dáil, and it consistently refused to recognize later ones, abstaining from taking seats in the Dáil or the Westminster parliament. Only a small minority was left after DE VALERA led the majority into constitutional politics in 1927 as FIANNA FÁIL. This group was finally outlawed by De Valera in 1936. During the 1930s, the first of a series of swings towards socialist politics, followed by a swing towards militarism, was enacted. The result in 1939 was an IRA bombing campaign against Britain, and overtures for support from the Nazi regime in Germany during WWII. De Valera viewed these activities as a threat to Éire as well as to Britain, since they might give Britain pretext for invasion. Accordingly, under General Boland, Free State forces practically wiped out the IRA.

In 1956–62 the IRA launched a bombing campaign against police and military bases near the border in Northern Ireland. After the death of two IRA men, it attracted sympathy and some electoral support, but this soon faded, and the return of De Valera in 1957 led to more repression. With nothing achieved, the IRA leadership began to evolve in a Marxist direction during the 1960s.

The outbreak of the TROUBLES in August 1969 spelt the end of this approach. With attacks widespread against undefended CATHOLIC areas, the Dublin-based leadership was unable to provide either arms or a coherent strategy. A group of Northern members reasserted the supremacy of the physical force tradition in January 1970. When the Official IRA leaders called a ceasefire in 1972 the Northern members set up a 'Provisional' wing committed to military action, with Sinn Féin as its political voice, purged of those with Marxist leanings. The Provisional IRA ('Provos'), or PIRA, was born, and it soon acquired money and arms from sympathizers in the REPUBLIC and the USA. The Marxist wing of Sinn Féin changed into the Workers Party and entered constitutional politics in the Republic.

After BLOODY SUNDAY, the Provos were able to claim the role of defenders of Catholics. Among their most notorious acts were the Birmingham pub bombings in 1974, the assassinations of Earl Mountbatten in 1979, and the attempt to blow up Margaret Thatcher and her cabinet at the Conservative Party Conference at Brighton in 1984.

The purely military strategy had stalled by the late 1970s, however. A supplementary political strategy emerged from the HUNGER STRIKES in 1981 to offer a way out of the impasse, shaped by Gerry ADAMS and the new leadership of Sinn Féin. The eventual abandonment of abstentionism was announced by Danny Morrison's call to take power by a dual strategy using the 'armalite and the ballot-box'. Following the DOWNING STREET DECLARATION of December 1993, the IRA declared a ceasefire in 1994. This enabled Sinn Féin to enter talks with the British and Irish governments. This ended in 1996 with the London Docklands bomb. But a new round of talks began in June 1997 and in December Tony Blair, the new Labour Prime Minister, received Adams and others at Downing Street. This seal of approval on IRA co-operation was the prelude to the GOOD FRIDAY AGREEMENT of 1998 and the ceasefire which has held to the present. But, just as the issue of abstentionism split the IRA in the past, so it has now. Thus, the 'Continuity' IRA, like the Provos in the past, disowned the recent political strategy, and were responsible for the Omagh bombing in 1998 which killed 29 people – the worst single incident of the Troubles in Northern Ireland.

Further reading

Bell (1989). Coogan (2000b).

Irish Republican Brotherhood Revolutionary organization which grew out of the FENIAN movement in the early 1850s. Its formal constitution was drawn up in 1873, and it operated as a complex, secret and democratic society under the general aegis of Fenianism. It was responsible for a number of bombing outrages in England during the 1880s. The IRB was dissolved in 1924. See FENIANS.

Irish Volunteers A NATIONALIST, quasi-paramilitary group of some 180,000 formed by Eoin MacNeill (1867–1945) in November 1913 in response to the formation of the ULSTER VOLUNTEERS. The Volunteers were pledged to fight for full HOME RULE, and to oppose the Partition being argued for by CARSON and CRAIG. Initially opposed by the IRISH PARLIAMENTARY PARTY, John REDMOND managed to gain control of its Provisional Council in June 1914. Nevertheless, the Volunteers were subject to SINN FÉIN influence, while the IRISH REPUBLICAN BROTHERHOOD hoped to use it as a front for their more radical aims. Less well organized than their Ulster counterpart, when they engaged, like them, in gun-running – at Howth on 26 July 1914 – they landed only 1,500 obsolete Mausers and 25,000 rounds of ammunition.

The growth of the Irish Volunteers, like that of their Ulster counterparts, has to be seen in the context of the passage of the Third Home Rule Bill, which became law in May 1914, and the effect of the CURRAGH MUTINY of March 1914. After the passage of the Home Rule Bill an exclusion clause for a six-county Ulster was added in July, but left in suspension. Partition had, in principle, been secured – anathema to Irish nationalists – and the position of constitutional nationalism had been weakened by events. In this light the Howth gun-running, organized by Roger CASEMENT and Erskine Childers, can be seen as a calculatedly open and provocative gesture, intended to highlight the government's failure to intervene in the secretive Larne gun-running, since the police and the army immediately intervened and, in the ensuing disturbance, killed three and wounded 38 civilians. The consequences of this series of events were evaded, not resolved, by the outbreak of WWI a few days later.

Home Rule reached the Statute book on 18 September 1914, suspended for 12 months, or until the end of the war, whichever period should prove longer. Redmond now endorsed the war effort on 20 September, calling on the Irish Volunteers to sign up in the British Army and be willing to fight wherever the army chose to send them, thus 'earning' Ireland the right to Home Rule. This led to the split in the Volunteers between those who trusted British intentions (and her willingness to face down future LOYALIST opposition) and those who did not. The first group (of some 170,000) became the National Volunteers, while the latter group (of around 10,000) retained the name Irish Volunteers. From this minority came those who participated in the EASTER RISING. By 1915, a commemoration organized by Patrick PEARSE, at the funeral of the old FENIAN, Jeremiah O'Donovan Rossa, showed that the IRB was now capable of leading the Irish Volunteers in military action.

J

Jacobite   Name given to supporters of the Stuart dynasty after the English constitutional revolution of 1688 when JAMES II was forced to abdicate in favour of WILLIAM III. Many Irish CATHOLICS were fervent Jacobites for much of the eighteenth century and hoped for the return of the old pretender, James III (1688–1766), and later his son, the young pretender, Charles (1720–88), 'Bonnie Prince Charlie', to re-establish the Catholic dynasty. Much poetry in Irish, notably the work of Aodhagán Ó RATHAILLE, longs for the return of the Stuarts who will save Ireland from the English Protestants. A few Protestants supported Jacobite conspiracies, but the movement was overwhelmingly Catholic. After the defeat of the Jacobite rising in 1745, many Catholics decided that armed struggle was unlikely to succeed and agreed to support the Hanoverian dynasty.

James II (1633–1701)   The last Stuart king who precipitated a constitutional crisis when his Catholicism became public (he was converted in 1669). James was replaced by the Protestant WILLIAM III in the Revolution of 1688. In Ireland he had attempted to achieve the difficult task of retaining English loyalty and supporting Irish Catholics. James chose to rule Ireland through the Catholic Lord Deputy, the Earl of Tyrconnell (1630–91), who placed his co-religionists in key positions in the army, judiciary and civil service. James initially fled to France when he was deposed but then went to

Ireland where he had a natural power base. He landed at Kinsale on 12 March 1689, then assumed control of DUBLIN, as the WILLIAMITE WARS began. When he was defeated at the BATTLE OF THE BOYNE (1690) he fled once again, making himself into a ridiculous figure for posterity.

Jellett, Mainie (1897–1944) Painter. Born in Fitzwilliam Square, DUBLIN, by the time of her premature death Jellett was recognized as Ireland's foremost modernist visual artist. She took early lessons in painting from Elizabeth Yeats, in classes her friend Elizabeth BOWEN also attended, before entering the Dublin Metropolitan School of Art. There, she met William Orpen, whose paintings influence some of her early work. From 1917 to 1919, Jellett studied in London under Walter Sickert, the first major influence in her artistic development. In 1920 she won the Taylor Art Scholarship, and in 1921 she attended André Lhote's Academy in Paris. In 1922, Jellett and Evie Hone went to the studio of Albert Gleizes in Puteaux, near Paris. Gleizes revolutionized her work through introducing her to Cubism, and it subsequently reveals the enabling impact of Braque, Gris and Metzinger. A year later, Jellett exhibited two cubist works at the Dublin Painters' Exhibition, and was derided by George RUSSELL ('AE') in *The Irish Homestead*. 1924 saw a joint exhibition in Dublin with Hone, again attracting hostile reviews. A 1925 exhibition, with the London Group in the Royal Watercolour Galleries, attracted a favourable review from the *Sunday Times*. During the mid-1920s, Jellett was also exhibiting with the Societé des Artistes Indépendants in Paris; while, in 1926, her work appeared with the Dublin Radical Club, an event opened by W. B. YEATS. At this date she began lecturing on art and published an article on Cubism. In the 1930s, Jellett provided a number of backdrops for productions at the GATE THEATRE; and, in 1937, she was commissioned by the Irish government to decorate the Irish Pavilion at the 1938 Glasgow Fair. A memorial exhibition opened at the Dublin Painters' gallery in June 1944, while an exhibition of 1992 at the Irish Museum of Modern Art helped put the different phases of her career in perspective.

Further reading

Arnold (1991).

Jordan, Neil (1950–) Writer and film director. Born in Sligo, Jordan began as career as a writer; the short story collection *Nights in Tunisia* (1976) won the *Guardian* Fiction Prize and was followed by three novels, *The Past* (1979), *The Dream of a Beast* (1983) and *Sunrise with Sea Monster* (1994). For the last two decades, however, he has been Ireland's leading FILM director. *Angel* (1982) generated much debate about its non-naturalistic style, while *The Company of Wolves* (1984) adapted Angela Carter to good effect. *Mona Lisa* (1986) is a London gangster narrative-cum-love story featuring Bob Hoskins. Now commanding Hollywood attention, Jordan's *We're No Angels* (1989) featured Robert De Niro and Sean Penn. His biggest success to date has been

The Crying Game (1992), for which he received an Oscar for Best Original Screenplay and numerous other awards. The film explores the relationship between an IRA man, Fergus and his captive, Jody, a black British soldier, who swears to him, in the event of his death, to find Dil, his girlfriend, in London. When Dil reveals herself to be a male transvestite, Fergus recognizes that he is, nevertheless, in love with her; and, in a violent climax, Dil kills Jude, the IRA woman volunteer sent to hunt down Fergus. The gender and racial dimensions make this a complexly unorthodox 'love across the divide' film, and it has generated much critical debate. Other films combine Irish and US appeals and themes, such as *Interview with the Vampire* (1994) and the impressive biopic *Michael Collins* (1996). This raised conservative hackles in the UK, but has good claims to be Jordan's best work to date, given its masterly compression of events, its willingness to take the narrative into the events of the Civil War, and the effective performances of Liam Neeson and Julia Roberts in its lead roles.

Further reading

Pettitt (2000).

Joyce, James (1882–1941)   Novelist and short story writer. Joyce was born in Rathgar, Dublin. His childhood and youth were dominated by his family's slide down the rungs of the social ladder, owing to his father's intemperate habits. Joyce attended Belvedere College, a Jesuit school, and, resisting an invitation to pursue a religious vocation in the Jesuit Order, went to read languages at the Royal University at St Stephen's Green in 1898. While at university, Joyce compiled collections of poetry, of which only a few poems survive, and became an admirer of Ibsen, contributing an essay, 'Ibsen's New Drama', to the *Fortnightly Review* in 1900. His antipathy to the cultural nationalism of the Irish Literary theatre (see Abbey Theatre) produced a pamphlet, 'The Day of the Rabblement'; and his relations with prominent figures in the Literary Revival, including W. B. Yeats and George Russell, remained frosty in the years following his graduation, and are tartly summarized in a satirical poem, *The Holy Office* (1905). After an abortive move to Paris, ostensibly to study medicine, but where he also met J. M. Synge (and disparaged his play, *Riders to the Sea*), Joyce associated with Oliver St John Gogarty. They would briefly and acrimoniously reside at the Martello Tower in Sandycove in 1904, a cohabitation recalled in Stephen Dedalus's relationship with Buck Mulligan in *Ulysses*. In this year, Joyce compiled a further collection of his poetry, *Chamber Music*, which was eventually published in 1907. The collection is influenced by the interest in Elizabethan lyrics shown during the 1890s, and reads as a successful pastiche of *fin de siècle verse* forms and preoccupations. Joyce also met Nora Barnacle in 1904, their first date occurring on 16 June, the day on which the action of *Ulysses* is set. At this time he was also beginning to develop, out of a rejected essay, his fictionalized autobiography, *A Portrait of the Artist as a Young Man*, a *Künstlerroman* eventually published in 1916 with the aid of Ezra Pound. Dispensing with authorial commentary, the book is claustrophobically focalized through Stephen Dedalus, producing a radical ambiguity as to just how ironic its treatment of the titular artist actually is. Also in 1904, he published three stories in Russell's *Irish Homestead* that would find a place in his collection *Dubliners* (1914), and emigrated, with Nora, initially to Paris, thence to Trieste. There Joyce wrote stories for *Dubliners*, though, owing to a publishing debacle centring on fears of the book's obscenity, the collection did not appear until 1914. Joyce's stinging reaction to the prudery of the publisher was another verse satire, 'Gas from a Burner', which also reprises his dismissive attitude towards the Literary Revival. *Dubliners* itself is a series of thematically interconnected stories, the setting of which is *petit bourgeois* Dublin life, in which Joyce's avowed 'style of scrupulous meanness' explores various forms of social, familial and intellectual paralysis. The stories often subvert the sub-genre to which they belong, in a calculated lack of narrative conclusiveness. The idea for a further story for the collection was the germ for *Ulysses*, serialized in the *Little Review*, and published in book form in 1922. *Ulysses* features the *Portrait*'s Stephen, here shown in relation to two further principal characters, Leopold and Molly Bloom, and within the milieu of Edwardian Dublin. Throughout the text, events in the world of 16 June 1904 are counterpointed by episodes from Homer's *Odyssey*, a procedure characterized by T. S. Eliot, in a 1923 review of the novel, as an example of the 'mythic method' with which Joyce has supplanted conventional narrative forms. For other readers, including Pound, the book's psychological verisimilitude, shown in its powerful use of stream-of-consciousness techniques, and compendious realism, are its prime strengths. As it progresses, Joyce's devices become increasingly innovative, the text's endlessly inventive experimentalism effectively changing its reader's conception of the method and purview of the modern novel. In the year of *Ulysses*'s publication, Joyce began a new 'Work in Progress', which appeared in various magazines and as chapbooks over the next 17 years, to be published in its entirety as *Finnegans Wake* in 1939. Formally more radical than its predecessor, the *Wake* is composed in a 'dream language' and, on the most reductive interpretation, concerns events in the life of the publican, Earwicker, and his family. Yet this is the pretext for a hugely ambitious work that comprises a multilingual allegory of humanity, from its fall to its resurrection, the book's closing words being continued in its opening line, thus emphasizing Joyce's theme of endless cyclical renewal.

Further reading

Attridge (1990). Ellmann (1982).

Kane, Robert (1809–1890)   DUBLIN-born scientist who founded the *Dublin Journal of Medical Science* (1832) and produced an extensive report on the *Industrial Resources of Ireland* in 1834. A leading figure in the ROYAL IRISH ACADEMY, he was knighted in 1846.

Kavanagh, Patrick (1904–1967)   Poet, novelist and journalist. Kavanagh was born on a farm in Inniskeen Co. Monaghan, son of a cobbler and small farmer, and left school at 13. His best-known work, *The Great Hunger* (1942), arises from the clash between his intimate knowledge of the very real deprivation and limitations of Irish rural society and the idealized versions of it prevalent in writing of the LITERARY REVIVAL (*Lough Derg* and *Father Mat*, unpublished in his lifetime, are contemporary but incomplete long poems on related themes in a similar critical-realist vein). It traces the gradual squandering of life and potential, and decline into bitter old age, of the bachelor farmer Patrick Maguire, a victim of inhibition and timidity. It does so in a wide range of metrical forms (jazzy repetition, traditional lyric, irregular verse) and lyric modes (meditative, religious, comic, loco-descriptive, narrative), arranged in 14 sections – matching the number of the Stations of the Cross.

For Kavanagh the 'hunger' of his title is a moral and spiritual as well as an economic condition, and is at the heart of a profound national malaise. 'Irishness', as he put it, 'is a form of anti-art'. His reaction against the dominant poetic style was compounded by his reception in DUBLIN literary circles as a 'ploughman poet' and his realization that this was a role he had prepared for himself in *Ploughman and Other Poems* (1936) and the *bildungsroman, A Green Fool* (1938). *The Great Hunger* overturns the early poetry, while *Tarry Flynn* (1948) more mildly rebukes the first novel. Yet Kavanagh found it difficult to progress thereafter; *Soul for Sale* (1947) is an uneven collection which oscillates, as did he himself at this time, between Dublin and Monaghan. Only a string of personal disasters in the early 1950s could bring him to the point where he rejected his previous work as too sociological, rejecting its 'tragedy' in favour of 'comedy', broadly defined. A new humility and transcendent relish of the everyday and quotidian enters the poetry as a consequence; the 'canal bank poems' celebrate new powers of vision and 'not-caring' in baptismal and birth imagery appropriate to his recuperation beside Dublin's Grand Canal. These poems, many of them reflections on the act of writing, were collected in *Come Dance With Kitty Stobling* (1960).

Kavanagh became a revered figure in his last years, a symbol of the suffering and silencing of his generation of writers; his *Collected Poems* appeared in 1964, and a *Complete Prose* in the year of his death. The conversational tone of his work, his distinction between the 'provincial' and the 'parochial', and precariously maintained balance between the banal and the sublime have been hugely influential in modern Irish poetry (see HEANEY, BOLAND, KENNELLY, DURCAN, MULDOON).

Further reading

Brown (1988). Cronin (1976). Foster (1991). Quinn (1991).

Keane, Molly (1904–1996) Novelist and playwright, born into an ANGLO-IRISH family and raised in Co. Wexford. Her career falls into three phases. From 1926 to 1952, Keane published 11 novels under the pseudonym of 'M. J. Farrell'. These novels document the lives led in the Irish 'BIG HOUSE', and examine generational strife, romance and marriage, in the context of country life and its sport, and against the backdrop of an Ireland rapidly rendering this class an anachronism. Of these, *Taking Chances* (1929), *Two Days in Aragon* (1941) – the action of which occurs during the ANGLO-IRISH WAR – and *Devoted Ladies* (1934) illustrate well Keane's witty and, on occasion, macabre imagination. Between 1938 and 1952, Keane wrote three successful plays, drawing-room comedies of which *Spring Meeting* is the most deftly orchestrated. After two decades of silence, Keane returned to novel writing, publishing, under her own name, her finest novel, *Good Behaviour* (1981), a darkly humorous and compelling dissection of the waning of an ASCENDANCY family. The fastidious detail of this novel, its meticulous attention to the fabric and nuances of life, is also found in *Time After Time* (1983) and *Loving and Living* (1988).

Further reading

Adams, A. (1991). Imhof (1992).

Keating, Geoffrey (Seathrún Céitinn) (c.1580–c.1644) Irish historian and poet. Keating was born in Tipperary, where he attended a bardic school which trained him in the arts of poetry, and started preparing for the priesthood. He completed his education in France, studying at Bordeaux and Reims. Keating returned to Ireland in c.1610 and became a priest in Tipperary, where his fiery reputation drew the unwelcome attention of the English authorities. He went into hiding in 1618 or 1619 and started work on *Foras Feasa as Éirinn* (*Groundwork of Knowledge of Ireland*), supposedly writing the first parts of the history while he was in hiding in the Glen of Aherlow in the Galtee Mountains. When the warrant against him was revoked in 1624, Keating started to examine all the records and historical manuscripts he could find in Tipperary, before travelling to Ulster and Connacht, completing his major work in 1624.

Keating is a significant Irish poet, his best known lyrics being a lament for the fate of Ireland and her people, 'At the news from Fál's high plain I cannot sleep', and a scornful poem about women tempting older men, 'O lady full of guile', both skilful examples of types of BARDIC POETRY. He also wrote two theological treatises, *Saltair*

Mhuire, on the rosary, and *Trí Biorghaoithe and Bháis* (*Three Shafts of Death*). Keating's real importance is as a historian, and his work attempts to establish an Irish identity which is both Catholic and Irish-speaking through the examination of the development of Irish culture and society. His aim is to explain the ancient culture of Ireland to a wide audience and so counter the lies of English historians such as Edmund SPENSER and Richard STANIHURST. Keating compares them to dung beetles who can only see filth and are ignorant of the beauty that surrounds them if only they have the wit to look for it. Keating also hoped to unite native Irish and OLD ENGLISH (Keating was descended from an Anglo-Norman family), whom Keating calls the 'Sean-Ghaill' (Old Foreigners), against the NEW ENGLISH invaders ('Nua-Ghaill', 'New Foreigners'), so establishing what was to be the aim of many Irish politicians and propagandists for the next century and beyond. Keating unsurprisingly sided with the Old Irish led by Eoghan Ruadh Ó Néill during the REBELLION of 1641. *Foras Feasa as Éirinn* is a coherently constructed and painstakingly researched work which tells the story of Ireland and the people who inhabited the island until the coming of the NORMANS in the twelfth century.

Further reading

Cunningham (2000). Keating (trans. Comyn and Dinneen) (1902–14).

Kells, Book of   One of the finest Medieval illuminated manuscripts. The manuscript contains a Latin copy of the four Gospels from Jerome's Vulgate translation (*c*.404). The work is large compared to other manuscripts (33 × 24 cm) and incomplete, containing 340 folios out of a probable 370. The text has been copied out carefully by three scribes in majuscule (the style of large script used in British and Irish monasteries).

The manuscript may have been started at the monastery on Iona, but was completed in Kells in 807, probably transferred because of the danger posed by the VIKING raiders. The book was stolen from the church of Cenannas in 1007, as is recorded in the *Annals of Ulster*, but 'was found after twenty nights and two months with its gold stolen from it, buried in the ground'. It was probably kept in Kells until 1192 and was eventually donated to TRINITY COLLEGE DUBLIN in the late seventeenth century, where it is still exhibited, a page turned each day.

The illuminations are generally regarded as the best examples of Celtic draughtsmanship. Especially notable are the designs of the decorated initials and capitals, as well as the pictures of the Virgin and child, the arrest of Jesus, and the portraits of the Evangelists. The illuminations were produced in a scriptorium by a few masters who were able to make use of numerous assistants to ensure a unity of purpose and execution.

Further reading

Sullivan (1986).

Kennelly, Brendan (1936–) Poet and novelist. Born Ballylongford, Co. Kerry, studied at TCD and Leeds University. Professor of English at TCD since 1973, Kennelly is a prolific and well-known poet whose early work – as in his first collection *My Dark Fathers* (1964) – shows him probing a near-masochistic historical sense, particularly of the suppressed horrors of the FAMINE. His most celebrated and controversial work, *Cromwell* (1983), is a book-length poetry sequence which resurrects Cromwell and plays his dour commonsensical brutality off against comic inventions such as Buffún and The Stomach to produce a carnivalesque satire of Irish images of England and vice versa.

Kickham, Charles J. (1828–1882) Writer and FENIAN, who, having been influenced by the writers of the *NATION*, joined the IRISH REPUBLICAN BROTHERHOOD. His novels include *Knocknagow* (1873), which includes evocative scenes of rural Irish life.

Kildare family The Fitzgerald family held this earldom as the most powerful family in Leinster. They were, along with the Butlers, who held the earldom of ORMOND, and the Fitzgeralds of Munster, who held the earldom of Desmond, the most important family of Anglo-Norman descent in Ireland. The Kildares enjoyed unrivalled power in Ireland from the middle of the fifteenth century, the head of the family almost always occupying the position of LORD DEPUTY, until the disastrous Kildare Rebellion (1534–35), a desperate attempt to prevent what the leading members of the family felt was an imminent loss of power. The Kildares enjoyed a further period of prominence in the eighteenth century but the rebellion saw them lose out to the Ormonds and their NEW ENGLISH rivals.

Further reading

McCorristine (1987).

Kilkenny, Statutes of (1366) The most significant piece of legislation passed by the Irish PARLIAMENT in the Middle Ages. The key aspect of the statutes is their attempt to prevent the 'Gaelicization' of the country and preserve the English identity of the colony surrounding DUBLIN. The statutes decreed that the colonists had to speak English, obey English law, wear English dress and conform to English ways in all other social customs. Intermarriage between English and native Irish was prohibited and the native Irish were not permitted to enter English-speaking monasteries or hold English ecclesiastical appointments. Although much of the statutes was aimed to rationalize and make coherent current practice in a society that felt itself under siege and eroded from within, the Statutes of Kilkenny have become notorious, with some justification, as 'apartheid legislation'. Much of what they tried to prevent happened anyway and many of the clauses had to be suspended so that ordinary life could continue in Ireland.

Kinsale, Battle of   24 December 1601. The battle which effectively ended the Nine Years War. The English forces under Lord Mountjoy defeated the Spanish forces under the command of Don Juan del Águila and the Irish forces led by Hugh O'Neill and Red Hugh O'Donnell. The Spanish landed at Kinsale in September and were confronted by Mountjoy who felt that he had to act quickly before the Irish and Spanish had a chance to combine and overwhelm his army. The Irish, realizing the situation, marched south from Ulster but were defeated when attempting a surprise dawn raid, mainly because they were much better at guerrilla warfare than fighting pitched battles. Águila's forces were unable to take part in the battle and they surrendered on 2 January 1602. Had the Irish and Spanish won the battle they might have been able to end English rule in Ireland, but they lost through a mixture of relatively weak support from Spain and foolhardy tactics which were employed through desperation.

Further reading

Silke (1970).

Kinsella, Thomas (1928–)   Poet and translator. Born in Dublin, educated UCD. His first full collection, *Another September* (1958), showed an accomplished and fastidious lyric poet influenced by W. B. Yeats and Auden; *Downstream* (1962) revealed one with greater ambitions, haunted by Ireland's past in the Famine and the Anglo-Irish War, and by the horrors of WWII. The full significance of the poetry's brooding, sardonic, often Gothic-tinged quality, and of Kinsella's concern with the rapacity of Irish economic development, became apparent in the long title poem of *Nightwalker and Other Poems* (1968). This broke with traditional metrics to adopt the 'enabling forms' of modern American poetry and combines satire on the effects of the Economic Programmes and deadening national stereotypes with the nocturnal wanderings of the central figure through Dublin, under a moon – traditional muse of lovers and poets – sullied by the same urge to technological mastery. Kinsella, now teaching in the USA, had also concluded that English-language and Irish-Language literary traditions needed to be conceived as continuous at a deep level; the immediate result was his translation of the Táin (1969); he would publish more translations with Seán Ó Tuama in *An Duanaire 1600–1900* (*Poems of the Dispossessed*) (1981), and criticism in *The Dual Tradition* (1995). A new poetic direction, signalled in the 'Notes from the Land of the Dead' sequence (1973), shows him interrogating notions of identity, order and disorder, drawing on mythic archetypes in a searching exploration of personal, racial and human history. In 1972 Kinsella founded his own Peppercanister Press with which he has published almost all his subsequent poetry, including *Butcher's Dozen* (1972) a denunciation of Bloody Sunday and the Widgery Report; *One and Other Poems* (1974); *A Technical Supplement* (1976); *The Messenger* (1978); *Out of Ireland*

(1987); and *The Pen Shop* (1997). Kinsella edited the *Oxford Book of Irish Verse* (1976) and has edited Austin Clarke (1973). A *Collected Poems* appeared in 2001.

Further reading

John (1996). McCormack (1987). Skelton (1969).

L

Labour Party (Irish)   Founded in 1912 by James Connolly, James Larkin and William O'Brien as the political wing of the Irish Trade Union Congress, Labour is the oldest political party in Ireland. Historically, it has been hampered by the 'fatal ambiguities' of Connolly's subordination of socialist to nationalist imperatives during the Easter Rising. Its abstention from the 1918 election (to prevent a split between its unionist and nationalist supporters) had serious implications, since the national issue was not resolved in 1918. Thus, while it won 22 per cent of the vote in 1922, it was displaced as the main opposition by Fianna Fáil in 1927. The 1960s saw a revival in its fortunes, and it received 17 per cent of the vote in 1969. In coalition with Fine Gael from 1954–57, it was so again in 1973–77, 1981–82 and 1982–87. Less radical than its British counterpart, Labour has also had to compete for the working-class vote with Fianna Fáil; moreover, the belief that modernization would bring a left versus right polarization from which it would benefit has continually proved false. However, Labour's backing of Mary Robinson's candidature for the Presidency in 1990 boosted them, and they polled their highest vote (333,013) and number of TDs (33) in 1992. That year they entered a coalition with Fianna Fáil for the first time, withdrawing in 1994 because of the Smyth Case. They then formed the 'Rainbow Coalition' with Fine Gael and the Democratic Left. But the dalliance with Fianna Fáil was remembered in 1997, when Labour lost half its seats. (See NILP and SDLP.)

laissez-faire   Principle of non-interference in the economic or political concerns of another party; see Famine.

Land Acts   A series of legislative reforms in the 1870s and 1880s, passed in response to growing land agitation and pressure from the Land League. The 1870 Landlord and Tenant (Ireland) Act enforced tenant rights, while the Land Act of 1881 established the so-called three 'F's, fair rent, fixity of tenure and free sale, and also set up the Land Commission, to assist tenants wishing to purchase their own land. In 1885, the

Purchase of Land (Ireland) Act – also known as the Ashbourne Act – increased the loan limit available to such tenants to 100 per cent of the land value, and in 1891 the Purchase of Land Act (also known as the Balfour Act) created 'land bonds' towards the same end. Finally, the 1903 Irish Land Act (the Wyndham Act) passed a series of measures including, most significantly, a 12 per cent bonus to be paid to landlords on the sale price of their estates.

Land League Founded in 1879 by Michael Davitt, the Land League was the organized campaign against landlordism and the exploitation of Irish tenants. Under the presidency of Charles Stewart Parnell, the League set up a network throughout the country (with the exception of Protestant Ulster), and in 1881 launched a weekly newspaper, *The United Ireland*, as its organ. After the passing of the 1881 Land Act much of the League's activity was declared illegal, and Parnell was imprisoned until 1882. A sister-organization, the Ladies Land League, was also established, with high levels of membership throughout the country. See also Trollope, *The Landleaguers* (1883).

Larkin, James (1876–1947) Labour and trade union organizer. Born in Liverpool and raised in Co. Down, Larkin became an organizer for the National Union of Dock Labourers, leading a strike in Belfast and establishing a Dublin branch of the union in 1907. He founded the Irish Transport and General Workers' Union (ITGWU) in 1908 and was involved in the Irish branch of the Independent Labour Party. Larkin is associated above all with the titanic 1913 Dublin Lockout, when the ITGWU took on the Employers' Federation led by William Martin Murphy, owner of Dublin Tramways and the *Irish Independent* newspaper group. Four hundred and four employers attempted to force some 25,000 workers to renounce the union. Larkin was arrested early in the action, which was thereafter led by James Connolly. The Lockout was controversial; the Catholic Church prevented the children of hungry workers from being looked after by British trade unionist, on the grounds that they would be corrupted by Protestants. George Bernard Shaw, W. B. Yeats, Patrick Pearse and many other leading figures supported the strikers. Stranded in America while fundraising by the outbreak of WWI, Larkin worked as a union organizer there; returning to Dublin in 1924 he was rapturously welcomed, but expelled from the ITGWU by its now anti-socialist leadership. He became an independent Labour TD and was responsible for important pro-labour legislation in the 1920s and 1930s. The ITGWU, the Lockout and Larkin himself are vividly rendered in James Plunkett's best-selling novel *Strumpet City* (1969) and Oisin Kelly's statue of Larkin, in O'Connell Street, is one of the most impressive of modern Dublin statues (see statues (Dublin)).

Laudabiliter The name of the papal bull issued in 1155 by Pope Adrian IV, which gave the English king, Henry II, permission to invade Ireland in order to reform the

Church there. The Irish Church had a reputation for rebelliousness, heresy and being at odds with the rest of Christian Europe in the early Middle Ages, which were the reasons given for the proposed invasion in the Pope's bull. However, Ireland also had a reputation for great learning and the Church had been modernized and reformed considerably a century earlier, making the Pope's actions controversial even at the time. Given that Henry II did not invade Ireland until 1171, it is likely that he made little use of the bull as a means of justifying his actions and only later ages have asserted a strong link between the laudabiliter and the Norman Invasion of Ireland. A complete text of the bull is contained in Gerald of Wales's *Expugnatio Hibernica* (*The Conquest of Ireland*).

Further reading

Richter (1983).

Lavin, Mary (1912–1996) Short story writer and novelist. Lavin was born in Massachusetts and accompanied her mother on her return to Ireland when she was nine. She lived initially in Athenry, her mother's home, and the original for the Castlerampart of many of her stories. Her first collection, *Tales from Bective Bridge* (1943), was succeeded by volumes of short stories, including *The Becker Wives* (1946), *A Single Lady* (1951), *A Likely Story* (1957), *A Memory* (1972) and *A Family Likeness* (1985). Lavin follows Virginia Woolf, on whom she wrote an unfinished dissertation, in concentrating on the momentary visions and fleeting insights of her characters rather than a developed plot. Unlike Woolf, Lavin's style is spare and lean. The conclusions to her stories are often richly ambiguous, as she explores individual morality in the context of an often-uncaring society. Many of her stories concentrate on relationships between women. Lavin was also the author of novels, including *The House at Clew Street* (1945).

Further reading

Bowen (1975). Harmon (ed.) (1979).

Lawless, Emily (1845–1913) Anglo-Irish novelist and poet, the daughter of the third Baron Cloncurry. Her works include 10 novels, including *Hurrish*, 1886, a sympathetic exploration of the position of Irish tenant farmers in the Home Rule era, which was much admired by her friend and correspondent William Gladstone. Other publications included the historical novels *Grania: The Story of an Island* (1892), a tragic love story set in the wild, romantic landscape of the Aran Islands, and *Maelcho*, (1894), a rather sentimental narrative set during the Desmond rebellion. Her historical interests also led to a competent history, *The Story of Ireland* (1884), and to a biography of her much-admired predecessor, Maria Edgeworth. She was a keen naturalist and entomologist, and a poet of some distinction (*With the Wild Geese*

(1902) contains some of her best verse). In later life she became ill and reclusive, and moved to Surrey in England, where she died in 1913.

Lebor Gabála Érenn (Book of Invasions)   One of the key sources of legendary Irish history, the *Lebor Gabála* is a medieval chronicle which traces the history of Ireland from the Creation to the twelfth century. It shows how the ur-Irish originated in Scythia, a large region north of Greece stretching into Asia Minor, which was assumed to be inhabited by fierce barbarian warriors (a tradition which later English chroniclers used in an attempt to show how the Irish had always been barbarians). The ur-Irish then migrated to Babel, Egypt, and finally to Spain before settling in Ireland, which they invaded during the time of Alexander the Great, the first conquest in Ireland's long history of invasions. They acquired the name 'Milesians' meaning sons of Míl Espáine, soldier of Spain. Ireland then suffered a wave of six invasions, the last of whom were the Gaels, providing the island with a mixture of various peoples. These include the Fir Bolg, the Fir Domnann, the Britons and the Picts, as well as such mythological races as the gods of Tuatha Dé Danaan, and their enemies, the Fomoire. The *Lebor Gabála* had a crucial influence on later Irish historians such as Geoffrey KEATING, and may also have been used by English historians in the sixteenth and seventeenth centuries.

Le Brocquy, Louis (1916–)   Painter. Educated at TCD, Le Brocquy is probably Ireland's most internationally respected artist of the last half-century. He became a painter at 22, studying in England and Europe, but was essentially self-taught. He began as an accomplished traditionalist and was elected to the Royal Hibernian Academy in 1949; however, the rejection of his *The Spanish Shawl* for the RHA selection committee in 1942 precipitated his participation in the Irish Exhibition of Living Art, and in the 1940s his subjects were often suggestive of existential isolation (such as TRAVELLERS and prisoners). A new focus on the meaning of the individual human being is dominant after 1956, most famously in the 'White Period' heads, usually of literary figures, such as the *Study for Reconstructed Head of S. B.* (Samuel BECKETT). It is the point at which individuality is still fluid, or disassembled, which interests Le Brocquy; this is evident, for example, in his portrait of a Downs Syndrome child, *Caroline* (1956). Such concerns stem from his belief that it is impossible to ever really know others. As well as a painter and tapestry-maker, Le Brocquy is an outstanding book illustrator, as his pen-and-ink drawings for Thomas KINSELLA's TÁIN (1969) prove. In May 2000, his painting *Travelling Woman with Newspaper* was sold for £1.15 million, a record for a living Irish artist. See ART.

Le Fanu, Joseph Sheridan (1814–1873)   Novelist and short story writer. With Charles Robert MATURIN and Bram STOKER, Sheridan Le Fanu completes the triumvirate of Irish masters of nineteenth-century Gothic fiction. The son of a

CHURCH OF IRELAND clergyman and a relation of Richard Brinsley SHERIDAN on his mother's side, Le Fanu was born in DUBLIN, raised in the Phoenix Park and Co. Limerick, and educated at TCD, where he knew Isaac BUTT. Though called to the bar in 1839 he eschewed law for a life of letters, publishing his first work in Butt's *DUBLIN UNIVERSITY MAGAZINE*; he would later edit the *Magazine* from 1861 to 1869. His first collection, *Ghost Stories and Tales of Mystery* (1851), while suspenseful, displays typically Gothic shortcomings of plot and characterization. The later work *In a Glass Darkly* (1871) represents an advance, swapping the explicitly supernatural for inner, psychological and sexual tensions as the engines of the work. The same is true of Le Fanu's best work, the novel *Uncle Silas* (1864). In recent years critics have identified distinctively Protestant concerns in Gothic and supernatural Irish writing, positing a lineage from Maturin, Le Fanu and Stoker through to W. B. YEATS and Elizabeth BOWEN – with varying degrees of success.

Further reading

McCormack (1991, 1994).

Lecky, W. E. H. (William Edward Hartpole) (1838–1903)   Historian and MP. Born in DUBLIN and educated at Cheltenham and TCD. After travelling in Europe he began teaching in TRINITY, eventually representing the university as a UNIONIST MP at Westminster from 1895 until 1902. In Irish Studies today his *Leaders of Public Opinion in Ireland* (1861) is considered an important diagnosis of the failure of public spirit in the years after the ACT OF UNION. In his era he gained renown first as a historian of European philosophy with the appearance of his *History of the Rise and Influence of Rationalism in Europe* (1865) and the *History of European Morals from Augustus to Charlemagne* (1869); but his major work is the *History of England in the Eighteenth Century* (eight volumes 1878–90). Lecky devoted the last two volumes of this work to Ireland, specifically as a refutation of the anti-Irish polemic of the English historian James Anthony FROUDE. This, and his glorification of GRATTAN's parliament, earned him the admiration of NATIONALISTS, but despite his liberalism he was committed to the Union, particularly in the wake of LAND LEAGUE agitation when he strenuously opposed HOME RULE. He also resigned as a guarantor of W. B. YEATS's Irish Literary Theatre when its politics were revealed. A major library in TCD is named in his honour.

Lemass, Seán (1899–1971)   Born Co. Dublin, Lemass joined the IRISH VOLUNTEERS in 1915 and fought in the GPO during the EASTER RISING. INTERNED in 1920–21, he opposed the ANGLO-IRISH TREATY (1921) and was imprisoned in 1923. As TD for DUBLIN City 1924–69, he helped found and organize FIANNA FÁIL in 1926, and was Minister for Industry and Commerce in every DE VALERA administration from 1932 until 1959. He became Taoiseach in 1959. Lemass's name is inseparable from that of T. K. Whitaker, the Secretary to the Department of Finance, who provided the blueprint for the first

PROGRAMME FOR ECONOMIC RECOVERY (1958–62), and so for later economic programmes. His great achievement was to decouple MODERNIZATION and Anglicization for the first time, redefining the Irish nation in terms of economic viability and breaking with autarky and ideological purism. Lemass re-established free trade with Britain in 1965, became the first leader of the Republic to meet a Northern Irish leader since 1922, and was the driving force behind the committee that tried to revise the wording of the Republic's CONSTITUTIONAL claim to Northern Ireland. He resigned as Taoiseach in 1966.

Further reading

Bew, Gibbon and Patterson (1982).

Lever, Charles James (1806–1872)   Novelist. Born in DUBLIN, the son of an English builder and an Irish mother of CROMWELLIAN descent. Educated at TCD and also travelled extensively on the Continent and to Canada. Returning to Dublin he failed medical exams at the Royal College of Surgeons but passed at TRINITY, and was subsequently appointed to practise in Kilkee, Co. Clare, and Portstewart, Co. Antrim, during a severe cholera epidemic in 1832. Under the guidance of William Hamilton Maxwell, a former soldier in the Napoleonic wars and author of numerous comic novels of military life, Lever began writing *The Confessions of Harry Lorrequer* (1839), first serialized to great acclaim in the *DUBLIN UNIVERSITY MAGAZINE*. This work set the template for many of his subsequent 29 novels: a high-born Irish military hero has a series of largely structureless comic and romantic adventures, often set abroad or in an unspecified past, thereby avoiding difficult aspects of nineteenth-century Irish life. Having shifted his practice to Brussels in 1837 at the invitation of the Secretary to the British Embassy, with the appearance of *Charles O'Malley, The Irish Dragoon* (1841) in the *Dublin University Magazine*, he returned home to edit that publication during its peak in circulation, from 1842 to 1845. Shortly after this he settled in Florence and continued his prolific output, including *The Martins of Cro'Martin* (1856), a darker tale, influenced by William CARLETON, occasionally referred to as Lever's *Bleak House*. His works, running to 36 volumes, long out of print, have been criticized for their 'stage-Irishness' (notably by Charles Gavan DUFFY in the *NATION*), but at his best Lever is a master of character, anecdote and the breakneck narrative.

Further reading

Haddelsy (2000).

Lewis, C. S. (1898–1963)   Scholar and novelist. Born in BELFAST, Lewis is today best known as the author of the Narnia Chronicles for children, which include the classic *The Lion, the Witch, and the Wardrobe* (1950). Lewis's fiction is influenced by the work of another member of the Oxford 'Inkling' group to which he belonged, J. R. R.

Tolkien, in its creation of a consistent imaginative world. Lewis also published acclaimed critical studies, including *Allegory of Love* (1936) and *A Preface to Paradise Lost* (1942). Evident in these is Lewis's religious sense, which he expounded in a number of books, including *The Problem of Pain* (1940), *Mere Christianity* (1952), and the best-selling, and brilliantly devised, *The Screwtape Letters* (1942), written from the perspective of a shrewd devil.

Further reading

Brown (1988).

literacy   The Irish census of 1841 registered that 47 per cent of persons over the age of five were able to read, a number which would increase considerably along with educational expansion in the second half of the nineteenth century.

literary and cultural journals (twentieth century)   Like journals elsewhere, those in Ireland have been marked by disruption, brief lifespans and occasional acrimonious dispute. There has, however, been a thriving if uneven presence of such publications to enliven the cultural scene, with several playing a vital role in transcending the division of Ireland, particularly during the mid-twentieth century, and creating a space for discussion where the public sphere was diminished.

The first journals were by-products of the Literary Revival. *Dana* (1904–05) inaugurated a tradition of nationalist critique of ossified thought and religious orthodoxy, although it is best known now for turning down a draft version of James Joyce's 'A Portrait of the Artist'. Perhaps the most influential journals of the first decades of the century were the *Irish Homestead* (1906–23) and the *Irish Statesman* (1923–30), edited by George Russell ('AE'); Russell not only proselytized for the co-operative movement in their pages, but encouraged and was often the first publisher of almost all young writers of significance, including Patrick Kavanagh. *The Irish Review* (1911–14) also carried literary content and writing on social issues; a number of its contributors were involved in the Easter Rising, reflecting the fusion of literature and politics in these years. *The Dublin Magazine* (1923–25, 1926–58) was one of the longest-running journals of the century. Edited by Seamus O'Sullivan (James Starkey) until its death, it was the main outlet for Padraic Fallon. Despite a reputation for staidness in later years, it was one of the few outlets regularly publishing writing by women. *Ireland Today* (1936–38) was notable for being open to international influences during an isolationist period, publishing early work by Brian Coffey and Denis Devlin, preparing the way for Sean O'Faolain's The Bell (1940–54), the dominant journal of its time.

Both *Irish Writing* (1947–56) and *Poetry Ireland* were published in Cork, and *Lagan*, *Rann* (1948–53) and *Threshold* (1957–61), published in Belfast, were the mouthpieces of Ulster Regionalism; some of the best work of John Hewitt, Roy McFadden and W. R.

RODGERS appeared in their pages. *Envoy* (1949–51), a DUBLIN journal edited by John Ryan, was as exceptional as it was short-lived, including as it did work by Samuel BECKETT, Mary LAVIN and Francis STUART, as well as European postwar writers and philosophers such as Jean-Paul Sartre and Martin Heidegger. *Kavanagh's Weekly* in 1952 was a quixotic attempt to produce a weekly broadsheet and fill the gap left by *Envoy*, written by Patrick Kavanagh and his brother Peter; it foundered after just 12 issues.

It was the 1960s which saw the revival of the literary journal on a significant scale. In that decade *Poetry Ireland* was revived under the editorship of the short story writer and poet John Jordan (it has run to the present day, as *Poetry Ireland Review*, the Republic's chief poetry journal), while Dublin also saw the writer James Liddy's *Arena*, Hayden Murphy's *The Holy Door* and *Poetry Broadsheet* (1967–78) (which published concrete poetry among other innovative writing), and the *Irish University Review*, revitalized after 1966 under the editorship of the TCD scholar Lorna Reynolds. One of the most interesting journals of the time was *The Lace Curtain* (1969–1974, 1978), established by the leading experimental poet Trevor Joyce and the poet and translator Michael Smith. This published an unprecedented range of poetry in translation, as well as championing the cause of experimental poetry and the 1930s modernists; it also set up New Writers' Press and published Michael HARTNETT and Paul DURCAN. *The Lace Curtain* had little time for the more genteel *Dublin Magazine*, the main outlet of the young poets centred on TCD, but this also throve in the intense atmosphere of the time. In Northern Ireland, *The Honest Ulsterman* (1968–), founded by the poet James Simmons, was – and has remained – the main literary outlet for northern writers.

Literary critical journals, in which the balance was weighted in favour of criticism rather than new writing, appeared in the 1970s, marking the increased institutionalization of Irish literary study in the academy. Chief among these titles were *Atlantis* (1970–73) and *The Crane Bag* (1977–85). The latter, edited by Richard Kearney and Mark Patrick Hederman, broached many the debates on modernity, POSTCOLONIALISM and postnationalism which would be developed by the FIELD DAY COMPANY. A less urgent, more academic, but equally significant journal has been the *Irish Review* (1986–), which has been edited from CORK and BELFAST, and is perhaps the most important journal for Irish Studies.

New literary journals have emerged with less frequency since the high point of the 1960s; among the most notable are *Cyphers* (1975–) and *Metre* (1996–). Successors to *The Lace Curtain* in fostering international experimental writing were the *Belle* (1978–80) and *the Beau* (1981–84), edited by the poet Maurice Scully, and *the Journal* (1998–), edited by Billy Mills and Catherine Walsh, both also leading contemporary experimental poets.

Further reading

Joyce in Coughlan and Davis (eds) (1995). McCormack (1985). Ryan (1975).

Literary Revival   Designates a period of enormous cultural productivity in Ireland from the late 1880s to the early 1920s. During these years, many writers self-consciously devoted themselves to the task of defining and constructing a national literature. The revival had its roots in many areas of Irish cultural activity in the nineteenth century: the political ballads of the Young Irelanders; the enthusiasm for the collecting and dissemination of folkloric materials; research into Irish manuscripts by various amateur antiquarians and, latterly, professional academics; a renewed interest in the poetry and fiction of earlier Irish writers, including James Clarence Mangan and William Carleton. In his 1923 Nobel acceptance speech, W. B. Yeats would add a further instigation for the emergence of the Revival: the fall of Charles Stewart Parnell, in 1892, the effect of which, said Yeats, was that Irish nationalism was redirected from specifically political aims, pre-eminently Home Rule, into the cultural sphere. The politicizing of the Irish populace, he argued, through the plays and poetry of the Literary Revival, including his own *Cathleen Ni Houlihan*, was to be instrumental in the gestation of 1916 Easter Rising. Yeats's thesis has not gone unchallenged by Revisionist historians; nevertheless, it usefully emphasizes both the intense cultural nationalism of the Revival and Yeats's centrality to the movement. Indeed, Yeats's preoccupation with Celticism predates the Parnell scandal: it is evident in his collection *Fairy and Folk Tales of the Irish Peasantry* (1888); and Yeats would continue to mine the rich vein of Irish folklore in *The Celtic Twilight* (1893 and 1902), an influential anthology whose title set a mood and gave a name to the late nineteenth-century Revival.

Yeats was also a co-founder, with T. W. Rolleston and Charles Gavan Duffy, of the London-based Irish Literary Society (1892), and founded the National Literary Society, in Dublin (1892), which had Douglas Hyde as President. Hyde had published a collection of Irish folktales, *Beside the Fire*, in 1890; his influential anthology of folksongs, *The Love Songs of Connacht*, appeared in 1893. Of equal importance to his folkloric activities was his inaugural lecture to the National Literary Society, 'The Necessity for De-Anglicizing Ireland', in which he spoke of the need to recover Irish language and culture in order to revivify modern Ireland. A year later, Hyde became the first President of the Gaelic League; its newsletter, *An Claidheamh Soluis* (1903–9), promoted modern Irish-language writing, and was edited by Patrick Pearse. In the 1890s, anthologies of Irish poetry and tales were translated, as in Standish Hayes O'Grady's *Silva Gadelica* (1892) and George Sigerson's *Bards of the Gael and Gall* (1897). Irish legends, as preserved in the cycles of literature, were drawn upon in Standish James O'Grady's *History of Ireland: Cuculain and His Contemporaries* (1880), which greatly influenced Yeats, who would adopt Cú Chulainn as a symbolic figure in several poems and plays. Lady Gregory's *Cuchulain of Muirthemne* (1902), a working of the Táin Bó Cuailnge in the Ulster cycle, appeared in 1902 with a preface by Yeats declaring it to be the 'best book that has come out of Ireland in my time'.

Gregory and others, including Yeats, formed the Irish Literary Theatre in 1897, out of which would come the Abbey Theatre. Gregory wrote many plays for the new theatre, though productions would be attacked from the ultra-nationalist Irish-Ireland movement, most notably Yeats's *The Countess Cathleen* and J. M. Synge's *The Playboy of the Western World*. Synge's refusal to idealize the peasantry he depicts in *Playboy* and elsewhere contrasts sharply with the tendency in the work of many Revivalists towards an idealized Celtic pastoral vision. Thus, in the poetry of George Russell ('AE'), the Celt is related, after the fashion of Matthew Arnold, to the spiritual and the natural. Russell's spiritualism is indicative of the unorthodox religious views held by many Revivalists, including Yeats, which led many to an interest in the occult and theosophy.

The 'Celtic Note' of Russell and others is anatomized and critiqued by Thomas MacDonagh in *Literature in Ireland* (1916). Its contrary, for MacDonagh, is an 'Irish Mode' of writing, in which Hiberno-English poetry faithfully reverberates with the speech and literary patterns of Irish. Such a mode can be heard as early as Russell's own 1904 anthology, *New Songs*, in which the tremulous rhythms beloved of much *fin de siècle* Revivalist lyricism give way to more robust folkloric forms, as in the poetry of Padraic Colum. Colum, alongside Russell and Hyde, is mockingly targeted in James Joyce's *Ulysses* (1922), a work that might be seen as marking the end of the Revival. Joyce's urban preoccupations, his concern with lived experience in a modern city, were alien to the nostalgic ruralism of the Revival. The emergence of the Irish Free State, and the ensuing Civil War, also see the Revival's cultural nationalism harshly compromised by political reality.

Further reading

Fallis (1977). Watson (1994).

Longley (Broderick), Edna (1940–)   Born in Dublin, Longley married the poet Michael Longley in 1962 and undertook doctoral research on Edward Thomas at QUB, where she became a lecturer in 1963. She was the chief critical intelligence, together with Philip Hobsbawm, in the Belfast Group, and an early champion both of the work of neglected poets (Louis MacNeice and John Hewitt) and of newer writers (such as Seamus Heaney, Derek Mahon and Paul Muldoon). Her interest in Thomas is extended by her argument, in *Poetry in the Wars* (1986), for the connections between the central English poetic tradition and Northern Irish poetry via the mediating influence of W. B. Yeats, and in opposition to what she regards as the minor disturbances of modernism. Longley is a sensitive close reader of texts, equally pioneering in her work on poets from the Republic, such as Patrick Kavanagh, John Montague, Richard Murphy, Brendan Kennelly and Paul Durcan (whose *Selected Poems* she edited in 1981). A founder and editor of journals such as *Fortnight* and *Irish Review*, and active in the Cultural Studies Group, she has been one of the most prominent figures in Irish intellectual life, and one of the few stable elements in the Northern Irish cultural scene over 40 years. Her other publications include *The Living Stream* (1994), which intervenes in the Revisionism debate, and *Poetry and Posterity* (2000).

Further reading

Kirkland (1996). Longley, E. (1994). McCarthy (2000).

Longley, Michael (1939–)   Poet. Born in Belfast, educated Belfast Academy and TCD. Married to the critic Edna Longley, he was associated early on with the Belfast Group, though work collected in *No Continuing City* (1969) shows a metrical fastidiousness and smoothness at odds with its generally expressivist preferences. Influenced by the Metaphysicals John Clare, Edward Thomas, Keith Douglas and Louis MacNeice (the last of whom he has edited), Longley shows a concern for the mundane, the chancy, and the mildly grotesque. Certain of these aspects are intensified and darkened in *An Exploded View* (1973), *Man Lying on a Wall* (1976) and *The Echo Gate* (1979). In these books, the Belfast of the Troubles is counterbalanced to some degree by the rural retreat of a cottage in Carrigskeewaun, Co. Mayo, and a fascination with flora and fauna (Longley is a genuinely green poet, and was engaged in the struggle in the 1980s to preserve the wildflower habitat of the Burren in Co. Clare from a crassly conceived visitor centre). The early poetry is collected in *Poems 1963–83* (1985). A poetic silence coincided with the demands of his post as Arts Council Officer in the 1980s; but, resigning from this in 1991, he has returned to a rich vein of writing which has produced *Gorse Fires* (1991), *The Ghost Orchid* (1995) and *The Weather in Japan* (2000). A Fellow of the Royal Society for Literature and Aosdána, Longley has been for many years an important and resilient presence in the cultural life of Northern Ireland. A sense of humour rare in contemporary Irish poetry marks his poems and the short memoir, *Tuppenny Stung* (1994).

Further reading

Corcoran (1999). McDonald (1997).

Lord Deputies (Lord Lieutenants) of Ireland   Title of the chief governor of Ireland. Until the reign of Henry VII, English monarchs had relied on powerful Irish families to rule Ireland, most frequently the Fitzgerald family, Earls of Kildare and Desmond. When Poynings Law made the Irish parliament subordinate to the authority of the English parliament by requiring the Lord Deputy to ask the English king and Privy Council permission to summon it, it became more obvious for the post to be given to an Englishman, and after the Kildare Rebellion of 1534 the post went to powerful English magnates for over a century.

   The Deputyship or Lieutenantship provided the holder with enormous power but could also be a poisoned chalice which destroyed careers or even led to the execution of ambitious politicians such as Lord Leonard Grey (*d*.1541) and Thomas Wentworth,

Earl of Strafford (1593–1641). It could also leave the holder in substantial debt, a common complaint of one of the more successful holders of the office, Sir Henry Sidney (1529–86), who was Lord Deputy three times (1565–67, 1568–71 and 1575–78). Throughout the sixteenth and seventeenth centuries the vice-regent attempted to subdue Ireland and make it loyal to the English Crown. This often led to intense rivalry between governors and a stop-start policy which oscillated between a hard-line approach and a more reconciliatory approach to the native Irish and Old English. The intense rivalry between Sidney and Thomas Radcliffe, Earl of Sussex (chief governor, 1556–64), led to a confusing series of abrupt changes in the middle years of the sixteenth century and, later on, complaints from the Old English led to the recall of the hard-line Arthur Lord Grey de Wilton (chief governor 1580–82), whose rule was extravagantly praised by his New English supporters such as Edmund Spenser. After 1596 the role attracted the title of Lord Lieutenant, a sign of its importance for the English Crown, although the fact that English rule was now unchallenged meant that the office-holder only had to visit Ireland for meetings of parliament. From 1567 the Lord Lieutenant resided in Ireland although the role became virtually irrelevant after the Act of Union and it was finally abolished in 1922.

Further reading

Brady (1994).

Lover, Samuel (1797–1868)   Novelist, dramatist and balladeer, best known for his *Legends and Stories of Ireland* (1831), *Rory O'More* (1837) and *Handy Andy* (1842).

loyalism   Loyalism is the oldest of the Protestant ideologies, with its roots in the sixteenth- and seventeenth-century conflict between planter and native, Protestant and Catholic, loyal and disloyal subject. Strictly speaking, it consists of a belief in the irreconcilability of these two sides, and an intense loyalty to the Crown and its institutions (in that order), conditional on the Crown's defence of the Protestant community and its rights. Thus, the Orange Order is a loyalist institution. Historically, loyalism was strongest in 'border territory' west of the Bann River where displacement, settlement and resistance, as in 1642, had been most intense. However, its strongholds now include working-class Protestant population concentrations in Belfast and other towns in the province.

Loyalism was renewed as a mass movement by the response to the Land League and Home Rule crisis from 1885–86 onwards, and crucially to the Third Home Rule Bill of 1911–14. The Ulster Unionist Council and James Craig created the Ulster Volunteer Force which, with collusion from the authorities, was able to land huge quantities of arms at Larne in April 1914. With Sir Edward Carson providing charismatic leadership for Ulster Protestants, loyalism was able to give unionism military backing for its confrontation with the government over the implementation of the Bill, which was suspended for the duration of the war. The threat of loyalist arms was then crucial to securing favourable terms from the British State for Protestants when Partition occurred in 1920.

Thriving on the mentality of the 'border territory' and at times of threat, real or apparent, loyalism exists in generalized form throughout the Protestant community in Northern Ireland. After a period of quiescence, it was reactivated in its most virulent form by the demands for Catholic equality made by the CIVIL RIGHTS MOVEMENT. New loyalist forces then developed, politically around Ian PAISLEY, and paramilitarily in the ULSTER DEFENCE ASSOCIATION (UDA) and the Ulster Freedom Fighters (UFF), as well as a revived UVF. These were intended to counter the lack of a loyalist armed presence after the disbanding of the B-Specials, and they were responsible for many sectarian murders of Catholics, including the horrific car-bombings in DUBLIN in 1975, as well as killings of nationalists and republicans. Allegations of collusion between the UDR and army forces and loyalist paramilitaries in targeting their victims have frequently been made.

Loyalism's greatest fears, of 'sell-out' by a Westminster government acting against the Crown's best interests and 'LUNDYISM' (i.e. betrayal from within), were both realized, to varying degrees, with the ANGLO-IRISH AGREEMENT of 1985 and the GOOD FRIDAY AGREEMENT in 1998. However, following the IRA ceasefire of 1994, loyalist paramilitary groups followed suit, some gravitating towards politics. Even so, and despite some tempering and tactical adjustment, loyalist political ideology and its perpetually embattled frontier identity remains intact, and is a major factor in determining the freedom for manoeuvre of the mainstream unionist parties.

Further reading

Bardon (1992). Miller (1978).

Lundy, Lieutenant-Colonel Robert *(fl.1698)* Soldier. As military governor of Londonderry during the JACOBITE siege by the army of James II in 1689, Lundy argued the indefensibility of the city and sabotaged its defence. He was widely viewed as a traitor by the sheltering Protestant population. A citizens' revolt overthrew Lundy (whose name has been synonymous with treason within LOYALIST ranks ever since) and the siege was resisted. The annual MARCHES of the Londonderry Apprentice Boys commemorate his downfall.

McCarthy, Thomas (1954–)   Poet. Born in Cappoquin, Co. Waterford, and educated at UCC, McCarthy has worked since for Cork City Library. He is the author of *The First Convention* (1977), *The Sorrow Garden* (1981), *The Non-Aligned Storyteller* (1984), *Seven Winters in Paris* (1989) and *The Lost Province* (1998). In his work sentiment is given bite by the use of politics as a way of mapping emotional states and family complexities (he was a youthful activist for Fianna Fáil). The poetry also, unusually, sheds light on the 1940s and 1950s, unromantic decades of emigration and stagnation; the same period is explored in McCarthy's Glenville trilogy of novels, published in the 1990s. *The Non-Aligned Storyteller* is one of the few collections by a poet of his genera-tion from the Republic to stand comparison with those of his Northern Irish contem-poraries. A collection of memoir and criticism, *Gardens of Remembrance* (1998), offers insights into the 1970s and the tangled roots of his work.

Further Reading

Goodby (2000). Kerrigan (1998).

MacDonagh, Thomas (1878–1916)   Poet and literary critic, executed for his role in the Easter Rising of 1916. He had joined the Irish Volunteers in 1913, and, during the Rising, was in command of the Volunteers at Jacob's Factory. Much of his drama, and some of his poetry, reflects his revolutionary beliefs: the play *When the Dawn is Come* (1908) imagines a victoriously nationalist future, while the fervour of the hero of *Pagans* (1915) is matched by the nationalist zeal of a number of poems and ballads. MacDonagh also wrote a satirical play about the craze for theosophy, *Metempsychosis* (1912), lampooning W. B. Yeats's spiritualism in the beliefs of Lord Winton-Winton de Winton. Of his poetry, *Songs of Myself* shows the influence of Walt Whitman, and *Lyrical Pieces* (1913) includes MacDonagh's famous version of Cathal Mac Giolla Ghunna's 'An Bonnán Buí', 'The Yellow Bittern'. In 1911, MacDonagh took up a lectureship at UCD, and founded the *Irish Review* with Padraic Colum, James Stephens and Mary Maguire. His academic work consists of two works of literary criticism: *Thomas Campion and the Art of English Poetry* (1913), originally his MA thesis, and *Literature in Ireland*, published posthumously in 1916. The study of Campion is as much a treatise on prosody as a reading of the English poet. *Literature in Ireland* also investigates rhythm, identifying a quintessential 'Irish Mode', in which Irish poetry in English is inflected by Gaelic literary and Irish speech patterns.

Further reading

Norstedt (1980).

McGahern, John (1934–)   Novelist and short story writer. Born in Dublin but raised in Co. Cavan, McGahern went to UCD and taught in Clontarf. His first literary success came with the novel *The Barracks* (1963); like Brian Moore's first novel, this avoids the *bildungsroman* structure of James Joyce's *Portrait of the Artist* by its sympathetic adoption of the viewpoint of a victimized female narrator. His second novel, *The Dark* (1966), experiments with a protagonist who is variously 'I', 'he' and 'you', proceeding via a series of interwoven stories. Another displaced *bildungsroman*, its more graphic dwelling on sex led to it being banned by the CENSORSHIP Board. McGahern was dismissed from his teaching post, and he left Ireland for London, Spain and the USA. *The Leavetaking* (1974) draws on these experiences; so, too, in a different way, does his fourth novel, *The Pornographer* (1979), a salacious and often comic account of a Dublin writer of pornography who is shown surviving the death of a much-loved aunt and a broken relationship before he moves back home to the countryside. In one sense it is an attempt to show Irish censors what real pornography looks like. McGahern's masterpiece is *Amongst Women* (1990), a scrupulously compassionate examination of the familial power relations surrounding an ageing farmer-patriarch and IRA veteran, Moran, and his daughters. The decrepit house in which they live is allegorical of the Free State, in a variation on the 'Big House' novel. It won numerous prizes and has been filmed; it also survived the outcry over McGahern's first play at the Abbey, *The Power of Darkness* (1991), a disturbingly bleak vision of Irish life without the indirection of his prose work. Three accomplished collections of short stories – *Nightlines* (1970, *Getting Through* (1978) and *High Ground* (1985) – show him to be a master of the form.

Further reading

Cahalan (1988). Sampson (1993).

McGee, Thomas Darcy (1825–1868)   Poet and journalist who returned to his native Ireland from America, where he had been editor of the *Boston Pilot*, and affiliated himself to the NATION. After his involvement in the 1848 Rising, he escaped to America and later moved to Canada, where he continued his involvement in political life. He was assassinated in 1868, probably by one of the young Fenian brotherhood, of whom he had become openly critical. His poems are generally sentimental patriotic setpieces, and he also wrote several volumes of Irish history, including *A Popular History of Ireland* (1862).

Further reading

Vance (1990).

MacGreevy, Thomas (1893–1967)   Poet and critic. A close friend of Samuel Beckett, whom he met in Paris in the late 1920s and introduced to James Joyce, MacGreevy was, with the slightly younger Denis Devlin and Brian Coffey, one of the 1930s group of Irish poetic modernists. Like Beckett's, MacGreevy's work is highly experimental. His single collection, *Poems* (1934), shows the influence of, among others, T. S. Eliot, on whom he wrote the first published critical monograph, *Thomas Stearns Eliot* (1931). MacGreevy's most ambitious poem, 'Crón Tráth na nDéithe' (1929), is, in part, a reworking of Eliot's *The Waste Land* in a Dublin scarred by the Civil War, though the poem also shows the influence of Joyce's *Ulysses*. He also wrote a study of Richard Aldington. This reveals the impact on his theories of avant-garde poetry of serving in the British Army during WWI (during which he was wounded). MacGreevy was a prolific art critic, publishing works on Poussin and J. B. Yeats. He was appointed Director at the National Gallery in 1950, a position he held until his retirement in 1963.

Further reading

Jenkins (1994). Mays (1995).

McGuckian, Medbh (1950–) Poet. Born in Belfast and educated at QUB, where she was taught by Seamus Heaney, she became a teacher before publishing the pamphlets *Single Ladies* and *Visions of Johanna* (both 1980), collected in her first collection, *The Flower Master* (1982). McGuckian's work represents a wholly new direction in Irish poetry, breaking with the mimetic style and recovery of lost histories which characterize the verse of Eavan Boland in a poetry of subjective innerness and imagistic and syntactic density. This recalls, in its difficulties and rewards, the work of European modernists such as Rilke and Mandelstam, of Hart Crane, and French feminist theorists of *écriture féminine*. The 'flower-master' of the first book's title is, at one level, the Baudelaire of *Les fleurs du mal*, but McGuckian makes strange inherited symbolist tropes of exoticism and gender by setting them in domestic interiors, and focusing on female rites of passage, boundary states, and openings such as doors and windows. The tenor is more sorrowful in her second collection, *Venus and Mars* (1984), behind which lies the experience of marital breakdown. Subsequent collections include *On Ballycastle Beach* (1988), *Marconi's Cottage* (1991), *Captain Lavender* (1994) and *The Shelmailier* (1998). The first three collections were reissued, substantially revised, in 1993, 1994 and 1995.

Further reading

Murphy (1998). Wills (1993).

MacNeice, Louis (1907–1963) Poet, radio playwright and critic. Born in Belfast, MacNeice was the son of the local Church of Ireland rector. He was educated in England and at Oxford, where he read Classics. *Blind Fireworks* (1929) toys with modernist and Romantic models, while the political concerns of the decade are evident in

Poems (1935). Often associated with Auden, with whom he collaborated in *Letters from Iceland* (1937), MacNeice was in truth an original poet of flux and surfaces (captured in 'Snow's 'The drunkenness of things being various'), who eschewed party-line poetry in favour of a more sceptical socialistic humanism. He caught and scrutinized the end-of-decade, pre-war mood more sharply than any of his contemporaries in *The Earth Compels* (1938) and *Autumn Journal* (1939), a long verse diary-cum-meditation occasioned by the Munich Crisis, which reflects with typical melancholy flair on Spain, Ireland, work, London, marriage, and his own amusedly ironic, but angst-ridden and unstable self.

In 1936, MacNeice had written a well-received version of Aeschylus' *Agamemnon*; joining the BBC in 1941 he found a new outlet for his dramatic talents in its Features Department, and his best-known work in this medium was *The Dark Tower* (1946). The power of his poetry, however, waned, as witnessed by *Plant and Phantom* (1941), *Springboard* (1944) and *Holes in the Sky* (1948), even as it attempted to engage with the responsibilities posed by WWII. *Autumn Sequel* (1953) shows the difficulty of adjusting to the changed postwar climate, despite a memorable tribute to Dylan Thomas. In his last decade, however, MacNeice attuned himself to the dark currents of the Cold War and middle age by drawing on parable, riddle, nursery rhyme, and authors as unlike each other as Samuel BECKETT, John Bunyan and Edmund SPENSER. These affinities – which he discusses in the 1963 Clark Lectures at Cambridge (published as *Varieties of Parable* (1965) – resulted in the poems collected in *Visitations* (1957), *Solstices* (1961) and *The Burning Perch* (1963). These reflect his growing interest in questions of belief and his Ulster Protestant background, although they offer no consolation in the normal sense of the word.

MacNeice's interest in relativity, flux and mixture of surface, his rejection of binaries and concern with (self-)betrayal make him typically Irish in the tradition which is concerned with the inadequacies of tradition – one which places him in the company of other Protestant-background writers, such as Francis STUART and Elizabeth BOWEN.

Further reading

Longley, E. (1988). McDonald (1997). Stallworthy (1995).

Mahon, Derek (1941–) Poet, translator, scriptwriter and journalist. Born in Glengormley, a suburb of BELFAST, Mahon was educated at the Royal Belfast Academical Institution and TCD, where he studied modern languages. He has worked as a teacher in Ireland, the USA and Canada, in London as a journalist and adaptor of fiction (often Irish) for TV, and has been writer in residence at the New University of Ulster and TCD. He now lives in New York and DUBLIN.

Reflecting his lack of identification with his Protestant middle-class background, Mahon's early poetry, collected in *Night Crossing* (1968), makes a virtue of deracination and travel, dwelling on social and aesthetic margins, in a verse of great formal poise whose greatest debt is to Louis MacNeice. While his pantheon of 'alternative' icons ranges from Malcolm Lowry to Marilyn Monroe, Mahon displays a particular affinity for French culture, as shown in his accomplished translations of de Nerval, Jaccottet and Molière, underlining the metaphysical temper of his work and its existential concerns. *Lives* (1972), revealed him coming under pressure to justify his wryly detached persona as the conflict in Northern Ireland entered a bloodier phase; the opening piece, a poem of self-reproachful, brief return to Belfast, rhymes 'bomb' with 'home'.

The distance from violence is harder to preserve in *The Snow Party* (1975), where an elegiac mood informs an awareness of the inextricability of culture and barbarism, particularly in 'A Disused Shed in Co. Wexford', one of the most discussed and celebrated of all Troubles poems. From its characteristically obscure subject matter – abandoned mushrooms – the poem sweeps out to include all the forgotten of history in a vision of catastrophe which links to Mahon's millenarian and apocalyptic concerns. *Poems 1962–1978* was followed by *The Hunt by Night* (1982), incorporating the pamphlet *Courtyards in Delft* (1981), which showed some disturbance of the delicate equipoise of the earlier poetry; the title poem of the pamphlet, which links Ulster, the Netherlands and apartheid South Africa, has been seen as reductive. Nevertheless *Antarctica* (1985) saw Mahon push to the logical terminus of his journey into desolate and extreme symbolic landscapes.

After a long silence, during which he edited the *Penguin Book of Contemporary Irish Poetry* (1990) with Peter Fallon, Mahon returned to poetry with *The Hudson Letter* (1995) and *The Yellow Book* (1997), in which for the first time (and with mixed success) he attempted longer, discursive poems.

Further reading

Deane (1985). Kennedy-Andrews (ed.) (2002). Longley, E. (1986).

Manchester Martyrs In September 1867 a police van containing two Fenian prisoners was travelling from Manchester courthouse to the county jail when it was ambushed, allowing the prisoners to escape. An unarmed policeman was accidentally shot dead in the raid. Of the 29 men subsequently arrested, five were convicted of murder. One of these was later pardoned, another had his sentence commuted, but the remaining three – William O'Meara Allen, Michael Larkin, and William O'Brien – were hanged. As the trial itself was poorly conducted and the incriminating evidence highly questionable, there was uproar in Ireland. The three men quickly became the 'Manchester Martyrs', at once symbols of resurgent Irish nationalism and English injustice. Popular support for Fenianism rose – even the Catholic Church sided with those they had formerly opposed. Predictably, the incident deepened anti-Irish feeling among many in England.

Mangan, James Clarence (1803–1849)   Poet. Perhaps the most enduringly attractive and enigmatic Irish poet of his century, Mangan was born into poverty in DUBLIN in 1803 and remained there throughout his life. A dark melancholia pervades most of his characteristic work, whether in the form of Irish ballads or his 'translations' (often Mangan originals presented as such) from Irish, German, Spanish, or Arabic. These 'translations' highlight Mangan's use of anonymity and pseudonymity both as literary techniques and as indices of an unstable sense of self. His protean ability is also demonstrated by the fact that he contributed to both the *Nation* and the *Dublin University Magazine*, despite their antithetical politics.

For a time Mangan was employed by the ORDNANCE SURVEY, fostering an interest in Irish folklore and antiquities and inspiring important works such as 'Dark Rosaleen' and 'Lament Over the Ruins of Teach Molaga'. He also displayed an acute sense of psychological suffering and inner torment, no doubt fuelled by his addiction to alcohol and opium, as demonstrated in the poem 'The Nameless One'. This quality, which earns favourable comparisons with Poe, endeared him to modernists such as the young James JOYCE and W. B. YEATS (see 'To Ireland in the Coming Times'), and, more recently, with songwriter Shane McGowan. Mangan died of cholera in 1849.

Further reading

Shannon-Mangan (1996).

marches and parades   Parades are central to religious, political and cultural identity in Northern Ireland and are held during a summer-long 'marching season'. The most important for Protestants are those on 12 July, the anniversary of the BATTLE OF THE BOYNE in 1690, and on the 12 and 18 August (commemorating the start of and relief of the siege of DERRY). There are also numerous other feeder parades, 'little Twelfths', church parades, social, arch, banner, hall, occasional and competitive parades. Although there are marches by CATHOLIC and NATIONALIST groups (such as the Ancient Order of Hibernian), marching is overwhelmingly an expression of Protestant LOYALIST identity (of 3,314 in 1997, 2,582 were classified as 'loyalist' and 230 as 'republican' by the RUC). Most parades are organized by the ORANGE ORDER, the Apprentice Boys of Derry, and smaller organizations such as the Black Institution.

Marches are essentially about staking out territory and symbolically demarcating it. In one sense they are triumphalist assertions of superiority; this is one reason why the CIVIL RIGHTS tactic of marching had such an impact (and why the Apprentice Boys' parade in Derry on 12 August 1969 triggered the events leading to the arrival of British troops). They make clear on an annual basis where members of the majority and minority, in any given district, can and cannot 'walk'. But they also celebrate belonging (as a novel like Glenn PATTERSON's *Burning Your Own* shows). The potency of loyalism, as observers have argued, lies in a set of cultural practices concerned with the public display of symbols of Protestant identity. Along with other forms of street culture – union flags, painted kerbstones, wall murals – marches have become increasingly elaborate and central to working-class loyalists in proportion to how they feel their standing has been weakened since the 1960s. Many marches have become more aggressive, with a marked growth, for example, in the number of the rowdier 'Blood and Thunder' or 'Kick the Pope' bands. Insecurity results from economic decline on (largely male) occupational identity; the dispersal of inner-city Protestant communities in BELFAST; and the results of the TROUBLES, particularly following DIRECT RULE. Parades and marches are potentially more charged and aggressive than hitherto, as symbolized by events in recent years at DRUMCREE. Effectively, marches have shifted from being celebrations of unionist class cohesion and state hegemony to being occasions of loyalist working-class self-assertion and dissent at the current form of the state.

In 1998 the Public Processions Act (Northern Ireland) established a Parades Commission and required 28 days' notice of parades to be given to the police. In the same year, state forces prevented the Drumcree march. Although marches retain their central symbolic importance, these developments mean that they can no longer be regarded as a right.

Further reading

Bell (1985, 1990). Bryan (2000).

Markiewicz, Countess Constance (née Gore-Booth) (1868–1927) Revolutionary and feminist, she was born into the ANGLO-IRISH ASCENDANCY; her family's 'BIG HOUSE' is Lissadell, Co. Sligo. She studied at the Slade in London, where she met and later married the Polish Count Casimir Markiewicz. In 1909, she founded Fianna Éireann, a republican youth organization, and, like her sister Eva Gore-Booth, was a feminist activist and advocate of labour reform. Markiewicz was sentenced to death for her part in the EASTER RISING, a sentence later commuted to imprisonment owing to her gender. She sided with SINN FÉIN when the ANGLO-IRISH TREATY caused a split in the republican movement, and did not enter the DÁIL until 1926, as a member of Éamon DE VALERA's FIANNA FÁIL. Markiewicz is the subject of W. B. YEATS's 'On a Political Prisoner' and both she and her sister are elegized in his 'In Memory of Eva Gore-Booth and Countess Markiewicz'.

Further reading

Coxhead (1979).

mathematics Irish mathematics has its origins in seventeenth-century cartography and surveying, but it was after the foundation of the ROYAL IRISH ACADEMY in 1785, and subsequently the updating of the TRINITY COLLEGE syllabus in mathematics by Bartholomew Lloyd in the 1820s, that several world-class mathematicians emerged in

Ireland. These included the geometrist James MacCullagh, his student George Salmon, renowned algebraist and, from 1888, provost of Trinity College, and the astronomer and physicist William Rowan HAMILTON. In 1849 George Boole (1815–64) was appointed to the Chair of Mathematics at UCC, where he wrote, in 1845, *The Laws of Thought*, and, in 1847, *The Mathematical Analysis of Logic*. He lent his name to 'Boolean' algebra, the basis of logic in modern computing. Later outstanding Irish mathematicians included George Gabriel Stokes (1819–1903), a leading mathematical physicist who became Lucasian Professor of Mathematics at Cambridge University. The most prominent Irish mathematician of the twentieth century was J. L. Synge who made important contributions to relativity theory.

Mathew, Father (1790–1856)   Tipperary-born Catholic priest who worked for relief of the Irish poor, particularly during the Famine. Best remembered for establishing and leading the national temperance movement, which grew to significant proportions in nineteenth-century Ireland. See ALCOHOL.

Further reading

Kerrigan (1982). Townend (2002).

Maturin, Charles Robert (1782–1824)   Novelist. Born in DUBLIN, attended TRINITY COLLEGE, Dublin, and was ordained as a CHURCH OF IRELAND minister before turning to literature. *The Wild Irish Boy* (1808), his second novel, designed to profit from the success of LADY MORGAN's *Wild Irish Girl* (1806), and *The Milesian Chief* (1812) can both be read as attempts to explain Ireland to an English readership. After initial success as a playwright with *Bertram* (1816) a series of flops sent him back to the novel, and he published *Melmoth the Wanderer* in 1820. This lengthy work is an acknowledged masterpiece of Gothic literature, whether this is in spite of, or thanks to, its many digressions, confused and confusing multiple plots and exotic locations. In the preface Maturin admits that a book revelling in perversity, cruelty, and extremes of psychological abnormality is perhaps odd for a clergyman, but he claims that his inadequate salary justified it. He died in poverty in Dublin in 1824, having for many years been a solitary, haunted figure. The anti-Catholicism of his work notwithstanding, Maturin was especially popular on the Continent for many years: Balzac wrote a sequel to *Melmoth*; Baudelaire proposed translating it; the *fin-de-siècle* decadents championed its extravagances; and, when he came to Paris to die, Oscar WILDE paid tribute by signing himself 'Sebastian Melmoth'. Also, in Nabokov's *Lolita* (1955) the car in which Humbert and his prey wander about America is, fittingly, a 'Melmoth'.

Maynooth   St Patrick's College at Maynooth is the main seminary for the training of Catholic priests in Ireland. Created by an Act of Parliament in 1795, it was supported

151

by a government grant, controversially increased by Sir Robert PEEL in 1845. Throughout much of the nineteenth century the seminary was seen to favour French styles of religious training, and its independence was often resented by Irish clerics – notably Paul Cullen, Archbishop of Armagh and later DUBLIN – who saw its continentalism as a rebuff to domestic Catholicism. Maynooth was declared a university in 1896 and since 1910 has been affiliated to the National University of Ireland. (See William CARLETON's tale 'Going to Maynooth'.)

medicine and health provision   Before the seventeenth century medical treatment in Ireland was limited for the most part to traditional or folk remedies supplied by local apothecaries and herbalists. The profession advanced significantly, however, under the auspices of Thomas Molyneux (1661–1733), a natural historian and Professor of Medicine at TCD, who became the State Physician in 1702. Medicine was one of the few professions which remained open to Catholics under the PENAL LAWS, a factor which increased the numbers entering the field. By the nineteenth century a strong school of medicine had emerged in DUBLIN, with the establishment of the Rotunda – the oldest midwifery and maternity hospital in Europe – and the College of Surgeons, which trained apprentice medics in anatomy. Skilled Irish doctors now began to travel abroad to practise, with many serving in the Napoleonic Wars. Notable medics of the period include James Macartney (1770–1843), a leading pathologist, William Wallace (1791–1837), who made a significant breakthrough in the understanding of secondary syphilis, and Francis Rynd (1801–61), a specialist in cardiac disorder. William WILDE, father of Oscar, was a renowned aural and ocular surgeon, and his fellow antiquarian Whitley Stokes wrote landmark studies on the stethoscope and various respiratory disorders.

Despite the many successes of individual medical practitioners, public health in Ireland remained desperately poor, with the major diseases of typhus, cholera and smallpox afflicting the population. During the nineteenth century the government passed a series of Fever Acts, in an attempt to control the spread of disease, and in 1847 the Central Board of Health was established in the wake of the FAMINE, which had revealed on a dramatic scale the inadequacy of Irish health care. Towards the end of the century there were various improvements in medical education, including the admission of women to study at the College of Surgeons in 1885, but health problems persisted, with tuberculosis remaining a widespread killer.

Irish contributions to medical knowledge in the twentieth century range from minor advances, such as Adrian Stokes' provision of the British Army's first mobile laboratory in WWI, to Vincent Barry's pioneering chemotherapy of tuberculosis and leprosy. But the most important advances have arguably been in the field of disease eradication and the provision of mass public health care systems. Into this category falls the successful campaign to eradicate tuberculosis, achieved by the late 1940s, an achievement linked with the name of Dr Noel Browne, the Minister for Health in John

A. Costello's coalition government of 1948–1951. Browne's name is also synonymous with the Mother and Child Bill furore of 1951. Under the proposals of this Bill, which enacted proposals made by the previous Fianna Fáil government, aid was to be given to nursing mothers and children under the age of 16. This was opposed by both the Catholic Church and doctors as a violation of Catholic social doctrine and 'socialized medicine' respectively, although the threat to the monopoly on social provision and to medical fees probably played a greater role in their protests. Under pressure, Browne was abandoned by his Cabinet colleagues and resigned from the government. Northern Ireland, was covered by the generous provisions of the British National Health Service after 1948. Hospitals in the Republic were funded from the Hospital Sweep Stakes lotteries, and a Health Act of 1953 improved services, raising the proportion of patients entitled to either free or reduced hospital treatment from 30 per cent to 85 per cent of the population. In the 1960s the Catholic Church moderated its bitter opposition to the welfare state, although attempts to extend the health service during the 1973–77 government were dropped after opposition from the medical profession. Nevertheless, the pressure of what has been called the 'demonstration effect' – whereby Irish people demand social provision on a par with that elsewhere – forced a substantial increase in state expenditure on social welfare from the mid-1960s. By 1980 the share of national output devoted to it was close to the European norm despite the fact that GDP per capita was still well below EEC levels. Even so, the general rundown of the public health sector has led to an increasingly privatized tier of medicine, with private health insurance covering over 40 per cent of the population, while Northern Ireland's health service suffers from the problems of underfunding and overcentralization endemic to the British system.

Further reading

Barrington (2000).

Meehan, Paula (1955–) Poet. Born in Finglas, Dublin, Meehan was educated there, at TCD, and Eastern Washington University. Her poetry frequently deals with love and relationships (particularly those between mother and daughter), cities, and childhood, her own and those of others. The difficulty of establishing a space for women's voices is not as apparent in Meehan's work as in that of the pioneer generation of modern women poets, but their libertarian strain is developed, and there is an awareness of working-class origins: 'I wanted to find you Connolly's Starry Plough,/The flag I have lived under since birth or since/I first scanned nightskies and learned the nature of work.' Her collections include *Reading the Sky* (1986), *The Man Who Was Marked by Winter* (1991) and *Pillow Talk* (1994).

Merriman, Brian (c. 1749–1805) Poet. Reputedly of illegitimate birth, Merriman was born in Ennistymon, Co. Clare, and later moved with his mother and stepfather to near Lough Graney in Feakle where he taught in a HEDGE SCHOOL and farmed before moving to Limerick in 1802. His celebrated poem *Cúirt an Mheán-Oíche/The Midnight Court* was written about 1780. It is a 1,000-line poem of great energy and comic eloquence, which draws on the rich tradition of burlesque medieval love-songs and ideas associated with European Courts of Love literature. In the poem the speaker is arraigned by an AISLING figure and haled before the all-female court of Queen Aoibheal at Craig Liath. Here he is charged, together with Irish manhood in general, with a lack of sexual prowess and amorousness at a time women are pining for lack of love. His accusers reject the economic arguments for celibacy, restraint or arranged marriage in favour of sexual fulfilment and fertility; the debate reflects growing sexual restraint and tensions in contemporary Irish society, anticipating the demonizing of sexuality by the CATHOLIC CHURCH and FAMILISM. Just as the speaker is about to be punished, by being 'flayed' and flogged', he awakes, and the dream-vision fades. An earthy but sophisticated celebration of sexual and erotic energy, the poem remained popular among Irish speakers despite official disapproval. The best-known translation is that by Frank O'CONNOR, and Merriman is now the subject of an annual summer school.

Further reading

Ó Tuama (1981).

Meyer, Kuno (1858–1919)   Translator and editor. Meyer was born in Hamburg, and studied CELTIC culture in Leipzig. He founded the important *Zeitschrift für Celtische* in 1896. In 1903 he established in DUBLIN the School of Irish Learning with the aim of introducing a rigorous philological programme in the IRISH LANGUAGE. From the school emerged the first wave of Irish teachers for the National University of Ireland, while its journal, *Érui*, founded in 1904, promoted and disseminated advances in the study of Irish. Professor of Celtic at Berlin from 1911, his numerous publications include the influential *Selections from Ancient Irish Poetry* (1911).

Further reading

Ó Lúing (1992).

Mitchel, John (1815–1875)   Journalist, activist and historian. Born in Co. Londonderry, the son of a Presbyterian minister, educated at TCD and worked as a bank clerk in DERRY and a solicitor in Banbridge, Co. Down. After their second elopement he married Jane Verner in 1837. Inspired by Thomas DAVIS and the YOUNG IRELAND movement, he joined the REPEAL Association in 1843, and began writing for the NATION in 1845, eventually becoming one of the two or three most influential journalists of his century. Finding the NATION insufficiently radical, he founded *The United Irishman* in 1848, and urged armed insurrection against the Crown; he was promptly arrested, convicted of treason by a packed jury, and sentenced to 14 years' transportation. Sent to Van Diemen's Land (Tasmania) via Bermuda, he escaped to the USA in 1853 where he became an ardent supporter of slavery and the Confederacy during the American Civil War. His interest in Irish affairs also continued, being involved with the FENIAN movement until he quarrelled with its leaders. Days before his death in 1875 he was elected, disqualified as a felon, and re-elected as MP for Tipperary. Mitchel's most famous work is his *Jail Journal* (1854), in which he accuses the British government of using the FAMINE as a deliberate instrument of genocide. This work had great influence, particularly among the diaspora; later, Patrick PEARSE would call it 'one of the holy books of Ireland: the last gospel of the New Testament of Irish nationalism, as Wolfe TONE's *Autobiography* is the first'.

modernization and modernization theory Although frequently viewed as 'backward', Ireland has frequently been a testing ground for various forms of advanced social policy, by the British state, and in its own right (since Independence) in the South. Thus, railways were introduced early in Ireland; but they served an economy based on the extraction of surplus wealth and population, rather than the more even economic development of the island. Political modernization, in the form of the UNION of 1800, meant a reduction of autonomy, and economic modernity, in the form of a drastic adjustment of population to the market, took the form of the FAMINE. While for UNIONISTS in the North the fruits of technology concentrated in nineteenth- and early twentieth-century BELFAST (but absent from DUBLIN) were self-evidently the reward of a more 'rational' faith and modern work ethic, this was hardly the case for the CATHOLIC minority there.

After partition, Northern Ireland experienced modernization as part of the UK, particularly after 1945, with the introduction of the welfare state and, later, regional aid. The shortfall in tax revenues was made up by the British exchequer, thus concealing Northern Ireland's incapacity for self-development. Moreover, modernization carried a heavy price for STORMONT insofar as the Education Act (1947) introduced by Westminster produced an articulate and confident Catholic intelligentsia during the 1960s; while the inability of unionists to accept the structural flexibility necessary to economic development (i.e. to end sectarian discriminatory practices) was a major cause of the TROUBLES.

In the Republic, postwar modernization was delayed until 1959, when the first programme for ECONOMIC DEVELOPMENT was put into action. However despite the current 'CELTIC TIGER' expansion, the uneven results of the modernization project (which foundered badly in the 1970s and 1980s) have produced scepticism towards the idea of permanent economic growth. This in turn, can be linked to an older sense that – given the traumatic past consequences of modernization – progress and betterment were by no means to be seen as the inevitable outcomes of advanced technology, or industrialization.

The model of modernization which has been most commonly used to describe

Ireland since the 1950s, however, has been a form of 'modernization theory' influential in the academic humanities. It derives from US social sciences post-1945 as promoted by Clarke Kerr, and suggests that the main forces for change and development in any given society are technology, entrepreneurialism and capital investment. Under these influences, it is claimed, societies change in structure and in division of labour. They 'converge', moving away from being 'traditional' (that is, based on personal social relationships, extended family networks, identities defined in local terms, clientelist politics) to being 'modern' (meritocratic, based on the nuclear family, with diffuse relationships, and a bureaucratic relationship with authority). Ideological struggle is replaced by bureaucratic bargaining; and such changes generally take place smoothly. (An oppositional variant on this model adopted by some socialists saw industrialization as beneficial, not because it fulfilled capitalist promises, but because it would inevitably develop the working class and so bring European-style left-right politics to Ireland, replacing NATIONALIST and sectarian politics. Unfortunately, this produced a complacent belief in its inevitability, and a fatally passive attitude to events.)

That certain aspects of both of these forms of 'modernization theory' have been proved correct is undeniable. Thus, the nuclear family is on the wane in Ireland, and the corruption of clientelist politics is being exposed as never before; likewise, the election of Mary ROBINSON, the IRISH LABOUR PARTY candidate for the 1990 Presidential election, was a major mould-breaking event, and the Labour party captured a record number of Dáil seats in the 1992 election. Nevertheless, there is no sign that the 'traditional' is being abandoned in Ireland, and in some ways it is increasingly being prized as a marketable commodity. This may be related to the more general issue of the ways in which the Irish experience can be seen to question the universal validity of Western post-Enlightenment narratives of progress, and the extent to which it represents a highly uneven example of development. This is the model assumed in the 'metropolitan colonial' reading of Irish experience, and (rather differently) in Luke GIBBONS's notion of 'regressive modernization'. Both variants, in turn, can be seen as bearing on the recent debates over so-called REVISIONIST Irish history, and on the extent to which nationalism and modernization may be related, rather than mutually exclusive, forces.

Further reading

Cairns and Richards (1988). Cleary (2000). Gibbons (1996). McCarthy (2000). O'Toole (1988). Thornley (1964b).

Montague, John (1929–) Poet, short story writer, critic. Born in Brooklyn, Montague was sent at the age of four to be brought up by relations in Fintona, Co. Tyrone. He was educated at UCD and a series of American universities. As a contributor to THE BELL's 'Young Writers Symposium' in 1951, Montague had already defined the challenge of postwar Irish writing to be that of reflecting the country's transition between a dying rural way of life and a yet-to-emerge urban one. His own work is marked by a similar in-betweenness, emerging as it does between the 1930s modernists and the Heaney generation, Northern Ireland and the Republic, Ireland and America, and Anglophone and Francophone cultures. The potential fruitfulness of this condition is evident in his first four poetry collections – *Forms of Exile* (1958), *Poisoned Lands* (1961), *A Chosen Light* (1967) and *Tides* (1970) – which draw on his rural background and use erotic candour to critique puritan Ireland in a verse which mixes traditional metrics with those of poets Montague encountered in the USA, such as Robert Creeley and Gary Snyder. Yet, as violence flared in the North, Montague's secular and cosmopolitan vision folded back on its sources in the long, composite epic of Irish modernity, *The Rough Field* (1961–72). His major achievement, this consists of 10 linked sequences, each collaged with woodcuts and extracts from tracts and documents, and weaves Irish history from the sixteenth century onwards together with that of the Montague family and the poet himself; maternal abandonment is mapped across the dispossession and decay of the ancient Gaelic world. Although Garvaghey is seen as being at one with the political flashpoints of DERRY, BELFAST, Berlin, Paris and New York, the poem ends with a mythicizing elegy for its vanishing rural world, using the NATIONALIST figure of a *cailleach*, or crone. Later works, such as *A Slow Dance* (1975) and *The Great Cloak* (1978), push the use of myth and feminine archetypes (as well as Montague's assumption of bardic status) yet further. He turned to a plainer treatment of his past in *The Dead Kingdom* (1984), which is a more subtle and cohesive, if ultimately less striking work than *The Rough Field*.

Further reading

Coughlin in Hughes (ed.) (1991). Johnston (1997). Quinn (ed.) (1989).

Moore, Brian (1921–1999) Novelist. Born in BELFAST, Moore rejected a medical career and the constraints of his native city and CATHOLIC upbringing, EMIGRATING to Montreal in 1948. Early experiences there as a proof-reader gave him the material for his comic novel *The Luck of Ginger Coffey* (1960). Earlier, *The Lonely Passion of Judith Hearne* (1955) and *The Feast of Lupercal* (1957) had dealt with the struggle to find personal autonomy in puritanical and repressive Belfast society, a struggle repeated in *The Emperor of Ice-Cream* (1965), set in the city during WWII. Like other post-JOYCEAN male Irish novelists, Moore escapes the pull exerted by *A Portrait of the Artist* by presenting his narrative from a female viewpoint in *Judith Hearne*, and his ability to empathize with his female characters is also marked in another two of his most impressive works, *The Temptation of Eileen Hughes* (1981) and *Cold Heaven* (1983).

Moore moved to the USA in 1959, and *An Answer from Limbo* (1962), *I Am Mary Dunne* (1968) and *Fergus* (1970) have American settings which contrast with the deterministic world of the Belfast fiction. Responsibility for one's actions is now shifted to oneself. *Fergus*, an experimental novel, was followed by another, *The Great*

Victorian Collection (1975), but a more realistic style is in evidence in other 1970s novels, which include *Catholics* (1972), dealing with MODERNIZATION and the CATHOLIC CHURCH, and *The Mangan Inheritance* (1979). *Black Robe* (1985), a tale of Jesuit missions in seventeenth-century Canada, and *The Colour of Blood* (1987), which has an Eastern Bloc setting, explore the nature of belief. Moore's TROUBLES thriller, *Lies of Silence* (1990), suffers from being rather predictable, but his final works, *No Other Life* (1993) and *The Statement* (1995), show him continuing the main trends of his career, in work which moves beyond Catholicism towards ethical indeterminacy.

One of the few post-WWII Irish novelists with a genuinely international reputation, Moore is often overlooked because of his DIASPORA status, and mordant critique of religion and of his native city.

Further reading

O'Donoghue (1990).

Moore, George (1852–1933)   Novelist, born at Moore Hall, Co. Mayo. On the death of his father in 1873, Moore went to Paris with the intention of becoming a painter; his memories of this period and milieu are treated in his aestheticist autobiography, *Confessions of a Young Man* (1888). Turning his ambitions from the visual to the verbal arts, Moore began to write poetry; then, taking Zola as a model, Moore wrote two naturalist novels: *A Modern Lover* (1883), which was banned by Mudie's lending library, and *A Mummer's Wife* (1885), both unflinching in their exposure of the patriarchal abuse of WOMEN. In the same year as the latter novel appeared, Moore responded to the banning of his first by Mudie's in his pamphlet *Literature at Nurse*, a coruscating attack on the CENSORSHIP imposed by the lending libraries. *A Drama in Muslin* (1886) continues Moore's interest in representing women's lives, and also engages with social iniquities in contemporary Ireland. *Parnell and His Island* (1887) is a swingeing collection of essays on Irish topics.

Esther Waters (1894) provoked heated debate due to its frank depiction of such fictionally controversial issues as childbirth. Though still indebted to Zola, the novel is nevertheless one of the best realist fictions in English of its time. Moore's *Celibates* (1895) is a collection of thematically interrelated short stories. After this point, Moore's career became intertwined with the LITERARY REVIVAL: a meeting with W. B. YEATS in 1897 culminated in a collaborative play, *Diarmuid and Grania* (1901). Moore's principal contribution to the Revival was a collection of short stories, *The Untilled Field* (1903), which he wrote with the intention that they be translated into the IRISH LANGUAGE as an aid to the GAELIC LEAGUE. Experimenting with narrative form, Moore went on to write a novella, *The Lake*, in which he deployed a 'melodic line' in an attempt to register the movement of his major character's consciousness. Moore's involvement in the Revival is a major subject of his autobiographical masterpiece, the three-volume *Hail and Farewell* (1911, 1912,

1914), a book that angered many fellow Revivalists for its biting account of their eccentricities and, on occasion, absurdities.

Moore left Ireland for London in 1911. His later novels include the historical romances, *The Book Kerith* (1916), *Héloïse and Abelard* (1921) and *Aphrodite in Aulis* (1930).

Further reading

Cave (1978). Dunleavy (ed.) (1983). Frazier (2000). Hone (1936).

Moore, Thomas (1779–1852) Poet. Born in DUBLIN, the son of a CATHOLIC grocer, Moore was educated at TCD (among the first Catholics to attend) where he was a friend of Robert EMMET. Despite being interrogated about the matter by college authorities, Moore was not involved in the 1798 rebellion; throughout life his NATION-ALISM was more constitutional than revolutionary. Moving to London, Moore quickly established himself in the literary scene, first with the *Odes of Anacreon* (1800), then with best-selling collections of vaguely licentious verses and political satires, invariably advocating CATHOLIC EMANCIPATION. His reputation rests largely on the *Irish Melodies* (10 numbers, 1808–34), the lyrics he set to music adapted from traditional airs (see MUSIC). A natural performer, the combination of his expressive delivery and diminutive stature made his renditions irresistible to Regency society. Often drawing on events in Irish history and legend, the *Melodies* crystallized an iconography for generations, conferring tragic dignity and respectability on Irish culture for audiences throughout Europe. With the success of the Oriental verse romance *Lalla Rookh* (1817), Moore's fame was rivalled only by Sir Walter Scott and his close friend Lord Byron. In 1818 he went into continental exile until 1822, after which he turned increasingly to prose. His biography of Byron (1830), whose memoirs he had been complicit in destroying in 1824, remained the standard work until well into the twentieth century. Despite his happy marriage and the phenomenal popularity of his writings, Moore's life was often difficult: he was rarely financially secure and his five children all died young, factors hastening senility in 1849 and death in 1852. Before W. B. YEATS self-consciously displaced him, Moore was unquestionably Ireland's national poet.

Further reading

De Vere White (1977).

Morgan (Lady) (1776?–1856) Novelist. If Lady Morgan's date of birth is difficult to ascertain, her place of birth is no more certain: family legend has it that she was born at sea between Ireland and England. This is fitting, as in her life and writings she often laid bare many of the tensions in ANGLO-IRISH relations of the time. Her father, Robert Owenson (originally MacOwen), a Protestant of Catholic ancestry, was an actor, and much of her childhood was spent backstage in Dublin theatres or on tour; her mother was an English Methodist. With her third book, *The Wild Irish Girl: A National Tale* (1806), came literary celebrity. In the guise of a love story between the eponymous Glorvina and the English Horatio, Morgan employs sublime scenery, learned antiquarian footnotes, and pro-Irish propaganda to dramatize and explain Ireland to an English audience. Later works, such as *O'Donnell* (1814), *Florence Macarthy* (1818), and *The O'Briens and the O'Flahertys* (1827), expand upon Irish themes, but have much in common with her works set in India and Greece, as questions of women and colonialism are revisited. In 1812 she married Sir Charles Morgan, a physician. She was an outspoken advocate of Catholic Emancipation. Besides novels, she also published biography, travel literature, and a study of women throughout history. She died in London in 1856. Long overshadowed by Maria Edgeworth, Morgan's work is increasingly valued by literary historians.

Muldoon, Paul (1951–) Poet. Born in 1951, in Collegelands, Co. Armagh. Muldoon's career began with *New Weather* (1973), accepted by Faber when he was still an English student at QUB. Indebted to Seamus Heaney, the poetry is more playful and oblique than his early mentor's, indebted to Frost and MacNeice and often deconstructing Heaney's rural pieties. *Mules* (1977) and *Why Brownlee Left* (1980) develop a range of Muldoon themes – a semi-rural childhood, his father, drugs, hybridity, Native Americans, sex (for pleasure as opposed to procreation), violence, alternative existences – and narrative strategies, such as allegory. A growing architectonic skill, at the level of book and poem, is also evident, as is a sophisticated intertextuality. The first major fruit of this is *Quoof* (1983), whose virtuosic 'The More a Man Has, the More a Man Wants' – a sequence of 49 'crumbled sonnets' – draws on the Winnebago Indian trickster cycle, IRA gun-running and the hunger strikes, and remains one of his outstanding achievements. *Meeting the British* (1987) and *Madoc – A Mystery* (1990) follow and reflect on his 1986 move to the USA, when Muldoon left his job with the BBC for a post at Princeton University. *Madoc* is a mock epic whodunnit 'faction', which imagines Coleridge and Southey founding a pantisocratic community in the USA in the 1790s. This 'what if' tale is framed by a short futuristic narrative, and each of the 233 sections has the bracketed name of a philosopher for a title. *Madoc* marks the limit of a tendency for each long poem to increasingly dominate the lyrics it accompanied, and offers a critique of the violence inherent in Western thought, presenting genocide and atrocity in the deadpan tone of a postmodern epic. In the last decade, two libretti, *Shining Brow* (1992) and *Bandana* (1999), have appeared; the first introduces Muldoon's use of repetition, the possibilities of which are more fully explored in *The Annals of Chile* (1994) and *Hay* (1999). The long poem 'Yarrow' which concludes *Annals* is Muldoon's answer to the demand made in the verse journal *Prince of the Quotidian* (1992) that he do justice to his fraught relationship with his dead mother. Its phenomenally complex rhyme scheme does not detract from the poignancy of this work, although the more plainly grief-stricken 'Incantata', an elegy for a former lover, attracted more critical acclaim. By contrast, *Hay* quirkily charts the pleasures and perils of middle-age sprawl in America, haunted by memories of violence in Northern Ireland. *To Ireland, I* (2000), his only critical work, collects four Oxford lectures in the form of an alphabetical trawl of Irish authors. Muldoon's ninth collection, *Moy Sand and Gravel*, appeared in 2002. In his ludic and fiction-making powers, Muldoon's work recalls his modernist predecessors, as it does postmodernists such as Borges, Nabokov and Kundera. Often seen as the leading Irish poet of his generation, he has been enormously influential, and his work displays a mastery of form from the shortest lyric to the longest and most complex narrative.

Further reading

Wills (1998).

Munster Plantation   This was first established in the early 1580s after the final defeat of the Desmonds (the Fitzgeralds) who had rebelled against Tudor attempts to control and organize the Irish aristocracy from DUBLIN. The lands of the Fitzgerald earldom were confiscated and sold off to English settlers in what was the first large-scale effort to establish an English colony in Ireland (there had been a number of previous, largely unsuccessful attempts in Ulster, Leix and Offaly and CORK before the 1580s). The first plans granted 12,000 acres of land to undertakers who agreed to remove the native Irish and repopulate the area with English settlers. However, the inaccurate nature of the survey and the fact that the English administrative centres in Dublin were committed to the rule of law meant that many land disputes occurred, many being judged in favour of the native Irish. When the NINE YEARS WAR broke out, the dispersed nature of the colony made it an easy target for the Irish forces of Hugh O'NEILL and the English fled to the towns and to England, one of these being Edmund SPENSER, who was made sheriff of Cork. When O'Neill was eventually defeated the colony was re-established with some success. Richard Boyle, first Earl of Cork (1566–1643), made a fortune out of his land dealings on the plantation, helping him to become the richest man in the British Isles, and others made lesser fortunes. A number of prosperous towns were established including Youghal and Kinsale, and the population grew to some 14,000 in 1612 and 22,000 in 1641, helping to establish a wealthy Protestant class in the region.

Further reading

McCarthy-Morrogh (1986).

Murphy, Richard (1927–)   Poet. Born in Galway, Murphy spent part of his childhood in Ceylon (now Sri Lanka) where his father worked in the Colonial Service. He was educated in England and lived briefly in Crete before settling on Inishbofin Island.

Archaeology of Love (1955) reflects these wanderings. Murphy bought and restored a sailing boat, writing about it in 'The Last Galway Hooker', a poem collected in *Sailing to an Island* (1963). Typically, the poet is shown being tested against the elements, whether in sailing and building, or in teaching local TRAVELLER children to read, an outsider who only half-belongs, but who is fascinated by the craft and spontaneity of the life around him. Murphy's most comprehensive achievement, *The Battle of Aughrim* (1968), weaves a crucial episode in the WILLIAMITE WARS with more recent episodes in Irish and imperial history, while exploring the Protestant-Catholic split in his own family. Even nearer the dilemmas of POSTCOLONIALISM is its companion piece, 'The God Who Eats Corn', set in Rhodesia at the time of Independence and white takeover. Murphy's later collections include *High Island* (1974) and *The Price of Stone* (1985), while *The Mirror Wall* (1989) returns to Sri Lanka. An autobiography, *The Kick* (2002), gives a fascinating account of his life and times.

Further reading

Foster, J. W. (1991). Goodby (2000).

Murphy, Tom (1935–) Playwright. Born in Tuam, Co. Galway, Murphy left school aged 15 and became a metalwork teacher at Mountbellew. He wrote a one-act play, *On the Outside* (1959), before *A Whistle in the Dark* (1960) was rejected by the ABBEY THEATRE, whose manager refused to believe that its violence could be a true reflection of Irish life. Set in Coventry, it depicts the violent clannishnes of an Irish FAMILY, split by EMIGRATION. After its successful performance in London, and the Abbey's rejection of a second play, *The Fooleen* (1961; later *A Crucial Week in the Life of a Grocer's Assistant*, 1969), Murphy emigrated to England where he became a full-time writer, chiefly for TELEVISION, returning to Ireland in 1970. Experimental theatre techniques are deployed in *The Morning After Optimism* (1971), a fairy-tale-like play in which James and Rosie, a pimp and his whore, encounter their better selves in a dream-forest. *The Sanctuary Lamp* (1975) is an expressionistic drama which caused controversy for its supposed anti-clericalism. Like this play, Murphy's next, *The Blue Macushla* (1980), dealt with another false sanctuary – in this case the night club of the title. Murphy enjoyed some notable triumphs in the 1980s. *The Gigli Concert* (1983) was a hugely successful work based on Goethe's *Faust*; *Conversations on a Homecoming* (1985) presented the disillusionment of the 1970s after the hope of the previous decade; and, in what is perhaps his finest play, *Bailegangaire* (1985), the toothless, senile Mommo (a kind of latterday Cathleen Ni Houlihan), attempts to tell the tale of how a small town acquired its name of 'the town without laughter' (i.e. 'Baile gan gaire'). The second and third of these plays were the result of a fruitful period in collaboration with Galway's Druid Theatre (1983–85). Murphy's plays explore, in language of great power and generally in contemporary settings, the strains of MODERNIZATION in Irish society and the Irish family, articulating the violence which can arise when ideals and rule systems fail to change with circumstances. As a result of his restless energy and versatility, Murphy is generally regarded, with Brian FRIEL, as one of Ireland's two leading living playwrights.

Further reading

O'Toole (1987). Roche (1994).

music   The Irish were noted for outstanding musical ability as early as the twelfth century, GERALD OF WALES finding 'commendable diligence' in the Irish 'only in the case of musical instruments'. Music at this early period was written for noble families, or for monastic and church use, or belonged to an unrecorded folk tradition. The earliest extant music written down in Ireland are twelfth-century plainsong fragments, and a gradual from the same period is associated with a monastery at Downpatrick, Co. Down. Better-known is the three-part colophon *Cormacus scripsit hoc psalterium*, from the early thirteenth century, the *Dublin Troper* (*c.*1360), and pieces for DUBLIN churches also dating from the fourteenth century. Instrumental music sources date from the sixteenth century, and include the *Dublin Virginal Manuscript* (*c.*1570), Ireland's oldest keyboard anthology, and volumes of lute music transcribed from English, French and Dutch originals. The Irish harp had reached a peak of development in the sixteenth and seventeenth centuries, as the Dalway harp of 1621 shows; however, from the seventeenth century there was a decline in native Irish music and standards of instrument making which can be traced to the decline of the native nobility under the impact of PLANTATION, dispossession and war.

For the PENAL LAW era the record of Irish music is that of an imitation of the music scene in London, as the patronage of native Irish music by Gaelic families died out and it became an adjunct of fashionable Anglophone society in Dublin. A lively musical scene saw the spread of societies and concerts, although ASCENDANCY musical life had little time for the cultivation of serious European musical forms, such as opera. One exception was oratorio, and Handel's *Messiah* was famously given its first performance in Dublin in 1742. Turlough Carolan (1670–1738) was the most important Irish composer of the time, and is significant in that his work accommodates the European tradition (especially of Italian composers such as Geminiani), and the native Irish tradition from which he originated. An Irish harper-composer, Carolan was the last major figure in an ancient line and the only one of whom much is known. Charles Burney's description of the Irish bard/harpist as 'little better than that of piper to the *White Boys* and other savage and lawless ruffians' reveals how this native tradition was viewed by the leading English musical historian of the time. Nevertheless, Carolan's achievement was understood by Irish commentators, chief among them Joseph Walker in his *Historical Memoirs of the Irish Bards* (1786).

A Celticist counter-current, prefiguring Romanticism, showed itself at this time; proper scholarly scrutiny came with the first Irish music festival of modern times, the Belfast Harp Festival of 1792. This gathered together all the nation's remaining harpists in an attempt to preserve disappearing airs, and it also witnessed the emergence of Edward Bunting. Bunting's *Ancient Music of Ireland* in three volumes (1796, 1809, 1840) and *General Collection of the Ancient Irish Music* (1797) were landmarks in the Anglophone recognition of the native repertory. As this suggests, music in Ireland in the nineteenth century became a politicized expression of identity. Antiquarian activity led to debates about AUTHENTICITY and adaptation, and although the airs Bunting reproduced were 'adapted for the pianoforte' when Thomas MOORE used them in his *Irish Melodies* (1808–34) disagreement began in earnest. Bunting claimed that Moore had misrepresented the airs he adapted by making them excessively melancholy; in the words of one critic, he 'converts the wild harp of Erin into a musical snuff-box'. The issue in question – whether or not an expression of Irish essence, musical or literary, could survive the translation into a new medium – is typical of Irish culture in the nineteenth century.

Building on Moore's success, melodic songs and folk ballads came to be seen as the true musical expression of Irishness. This can be seen in the use of ballads in the propaganda of YOUNG IRELAND, as well as by the young W. B. YEATS and others. At the same time, music halls and, in particular, opera performances were also extremely popular in the nineteenth century; their glory-days are recalled in James JOYCE's story 'The Dead' (*Dubliners*). Even so, native and Anglophone-European traditions of music continued to develop in separate courses. Collectors of native music (including Forde, Pigot, Goodman and George PETRIE, author of *The Ancient Music of Ireland* (1855)) worked at a time when linguistic, social and cultural differences between Protestant and Catholic, town and country, Ascendancy and peasant, were hardening. Simultaneously, Irish composers strove to work either wholly in the European musical tradition or in adapting it to national material. John Field (1782–1837), who lived in England and Russia, was the most innovative within the European tradition. An internationally renowned pianist, he developed an intimate style of playing most evident in his nocturnes, a form which he invented and which had a huge influence on Chopin.

Later in the century, Michael William Balfe (1808–70) was a highly successful baritone singer throughout Europe and composed phenomenally popular operas such as *The Bohemian Girl* (1843). But for later Romantic composers NATIONALISM, and its effect on the arts, could not be ignored. Sir Charles Villiers Stanford (1852–1924) and Sir Herbert Hamilton Harty (1879–1941) were the outstanding names associated with this development. Harty, composer and conductor of national prominence in Britain, wrote an *Irish Symphony* (1904) and tone poems such as *With the Wild Geese* (1910) which assimilate Irish subject matter within European musical structures. Several English composers were strongly drawn to Ireland and Irish subject matter; thus, Arnold Bax (1883–1953) was attracted to W. B. YEATS's poetry, writing pieces such as *Into the Twilight* (1908) and *The Garden of Fand* (1913), and playing a role in Irish musical life. This tradition was continued by Constant Lambert, and the half-Irish Kerry-based Ernest John Moeran (1894–1950) who composed original songs (such as *Seven Poems of James* Joyce (1929)) and other works. Such Romantic symphonic music was matched by a movement in the Catholic Church to spread the liturgical use of the music of the Counter Reformation, driven by the Maynooth-based German priest-musician Heinrich Bewerunge.

The growth of musical nationalism resulted in the foundation of the Dublin Feis Ceoil (Festival of Music) 1897; this created a format of classes and competitions which was eventually copied throughout the country. Nevertheless, the politics of the times polarized debates over the relative merits of traditional and European-derived 'art' music. They were further complicated by the upheavals following the Easter Rising and the arrival of musical modernism. Composers often found it easier to sidestep issues of identity; nor did such uncertainty prevent individual performers, such as the singer John McCormack (1884–1945), from enjoying international success, like Balfe before them.

Since WWII, musical resources in Ireland have expanded markedly. There are opera festivals and seasons at Belfast, Dublin, Wexford and Waterford, international competitions, and a flourishing National Symphony Orchestra. This has been reflected in the development of musical education and musicology; Ireland's greatest contribution to the latter being that of Francis (Frank) Harrison (1905–87), editor of *The Eton Choirbook* (1956–61), while Aloys Fleischmann's *Music in Ireland* (1952) was also a landmark. Frederick May (1911–85), a pupil of Vaughan Williams, is often seen as being the most original composer of his generation, his *String Quartet in C minor* being one of the first significant modernist works by an Irish composer. Brian Boydell (1917–2000) was a more prolific composer whose works, such as *Megalithic Ritual Dances* (1956), are in a tonal, but Hindemith-inflected, style. Raymond Warren (1927–99), Seán Ó Riada (1930–71) and John Kinsella (1932–) represent a generation which came of age in the era of modernization, the mainstream resurgence of traditional music and the development of more eclectic, postmodernist musical languages. Their success has been built on by younger composers, from Northern Ireland and the Republic, such as Raymond Deane, Piers Hellawell, Kevin O'Connell, Jane O'Leary and Kevin Volans, while an Association of Irish Composers and a Contemporary Music Centre reflect the rate at which Irish music has developed in the last 20 years. Whatever the status of European-derived contemporary 'classical', its current health and energy, with or without those indigenous energies, cannot be denied. (See TRADITIONAL MUSIC, ROCK AND POP MUSIC.)

Further reading

Boydell (ed.) (1979). Gillen and White (eds), 5 vols (1990–). Hogan (1966). White (1998).

mythology Irish pagan mythology survives in the writings of Christian monks, who have generally cast the material at their disposal in terms of Christian belief. The surviving material is not always coherent and the beliefs of pre-Christian Ireland have had to be reconstructed from other sources: Classical, Welsh and British. The key figures who appear in the mythological Irish cycles are as follows:

Brigit (Brighid): Goddess of poetry and learning (Caesar compares her to the Roman goddess Minerva). She was also associated with prophecy and divination.

Cormac mac Airt: King of ancient Ireland who inaugurated a golden age owing to his leadership abilities and skills as a lawmaker.

Deirdre: Her tragic story is told in *Longes mac nUislenn* (*Exile of the Sons of Uisliu*). Deirdre was the daughter of Fedlimid, who gave a great feast at which she was born, only for a Druid to predict that she would cause great sorrow. Although the guests wanted her killed, King Conchobor had her brought up in secret, planning to marry her. Deirdre decides that she will marry Noisi, who is understandably reluctant to form a union with her as he knows of the prophecy, but she forces him, using her magic powers. Conchobor chases them out of Ireland but they return, mistakenly believing that they have the promise of safekeeping. Conchobor kills Noisi and Deirdre has to endure marriage to Conchobor until she manages to kill herself a year later.

Donn: God of the dead. He inhabited Tech Dunn, a tiny barren island off the south-west coast of Ireland, where the Irish have to go when they die.

Édaín: The most beautiful maiden in Ireland. She married Midhir, whose bitter first wife, Fuamhnach, took a terrible revenge on her, turning her into a pool of water and then a giant fly of great beauty. She was able to comfort her husband with her humming until Fuamhnach had her blown out to sea where she was blown by the wind and buffeted by the waves for seven years until she ended up in the golden goblet of the wife of the king of Ulster. Having been swallowed, she was then reborn as Édain, over a thousand years after her initial birth.

Ériu: Goddess who represents the ancient land of Ireland. In some works she is seen to be welcoming hostile invaders, a foolish decision that costs her people dear.

Fionn mac Cumhaill: Hero of the Fionn cycle, one of the most popular cycles of Irish tales. Fionn was the leader of a band of warriors (Fianna) who existed as outlaws. Fionn was immensely brave and resourceful and had the gift of insight. He completed a series of heroic deeds, including saving Ireland from invasion.

Goibhniu: The pre-eminent smith in Irish mythology, also credited with healing powers.

Lug (Lugh): The most honoured of all the Celtic gods. Julius Caesar compared him to the Roman God, Mercury, 'the inventor of all the arts', although the Celtic figure occupied a more important position in their mythology. He had a widespread cult in Ireland and many saints were honoured for destroying shrines and temples dedicated to him. He was also honoured as the god of war, and his skills included metalwork, poetry, history, sorcery and harping. He was permitted to enter TARA, the seat of the Irish high kings where the gods assembled, when he would list the great range of his skills.

Macha: A goddess of war, often forming a triad with Medb and Morríghan.

Medb (Mebh): Queen of the men of Connacht who invaded Ulster to fight the Uliad in the TÁIN BÓ CUAILNGE. Her name means the intoxicating or intoxicated one. She occupies the role of the powerful *femme fatale* of Irish mythology, sleeping with numerous kings and so compromising, weakening or leading them to their doom. She is also represented as a powerful and bitter harpy who will stop at nothing to get her way.

Morríghan: The form of Medb as fearsome battle-goddess.

Oghma: A heroic strongman who was also the inventor of letters.

Further reading

Mac Cana (1983).

Nation   Nationalist newspaper founded by leading members of the YOUNG IRELAND in 1842, notably Charles Gavan DUFFY, Thomas DAVIS, and John Blake DILLON. An instant success, the paper gained a readership of approximately 250,000 within a year, publishing ballads, poetry, political comment and news of progress in the REPEAL movement. Its contributors included several major political and literary figures of the day, including John MITCHEL and Speranza (Lady WILDE). The *Nation* was part of a vibrant publishing enterprise led by Duffy, who also edited a book of popular nationalist poems and ballads from the newspaper, entitled *The Spirit of the Nation*. (See also NEWSPAPERS.)

National Gallery of Ireland and Municipal Gallery of Dublin   The National Gallery is situated in Merrion Square, DUBLIN, and was founded in 1854. The Gallery's first director was the portrait painter George Mulvaney, who gathered an important collection of Spanish, Dutch and French paintings. Alongside the national collection of European Old Masters, including works by Caravaggio and Rubens, the gallery also holds the Yeats Collection, featuring numerous works by J. B. YEATS. Its benefactors include Nathaniel Hall, who bequeathed 500 oils and watercolours, and George Bernard SHAW. The art dealer Hugh Lane, nephew of Lady GREGORY, gave 21 pictures during his period as curator and, in his will, left his house and property, apart from 39 continental pictures, to the gallery. Hugh Lane's contribution to the visual arts in Dublin centres primarily, however, on his establishment of the Municipal Gallery of Modern Art in 1908. Through his aunt, Lane was in contact with many of the architects of the LITERARY REVIVAL. Subsequent to a visit to Dublin in 1901, in which Lane viewed an exhibition of paintings by Nathaniel Hone and John Butler Yeats, he began to campaign for a gallery of modern art in Dublin. In 1904, Lane mounted the first ever exhibition of contemporary Irish art abroad, at the Guildhall in London. In Dublin, he gathered together a major collection of modern art, including 39 Impressionist artworks from his own collection. The Municipal Gallery of Modern Art opened in January 1908 in temporary premises in Harcourt Street, Dublin. Controversy ensued, when in 1913 Dublin City Council rejected Sir Edward Lutyens' design for a permanent home, a 'Bridge of Sighs' across the Liffey, the council's decision clearly coloured by their disapproval of the Impressionist paintings. Lane promptly moved his pictures to the National Gallery in London. W. B. YEATS expressed the outrage felt by many over the council's behaviour in a poem collected in his *Responsibilities* (1914). Lane drowned in the sinking of the *Lusitania*, off the coast of Co. Cork, in 1915. Shortly before his death, Lane added an unwitnessed codicil to his original will stating that, if a suitable venue was provided, he wished to bequeath the paintings to the Dublin gallery. As the codicil had problematic legal status, the National Gallery in London did not return the paintings. A permanent site for the Municipal Gallery was found in 1929, in the former residence of the Earl of Charlemont. Eventually, in 1959, agreement was reached between the Dublin and London galleries to share the paintings.

nationalism   Expressions of Irish nationalism have a long history dating from the time of the REFORMATION, but its emergence as a sustained political ideology can be pin-pointed to the 1790s, when the fears of Irish patriot politicians at the threatened loss of the independent IRISH PARLIAMENT created by GRATTAN combined with revolutionary impulses imported from France and America by the UNITED IRISHMEN. The call for an independent Ireland subsequently became a regular fixture of Irish political life. In the nineteenth century, a nationalist agenda formed the basis for the REPEAL movement under Daniel O'CONNELL, and inspired the political and cultural policies of the YOUNG IRELANDERS and the *Nation* activists. Though briefly dormant after the failure of the 1848 Young Ireland rebellion, nationalism re-emerged in a more violent form with the FENIANS during the 1860s, drawing support from an Irish diaspora in the USA. As the political field in the latter decades of the Victorian era became increasingly polarized, Irish nationalism – fuelled by the agitation of the Land War (see LAND LEAGUE) and the promise of HOME RULE – moved on to the parliamentary stage under the inspired leadership of PARNELL, whose IRISH PARLIAMENTARY PARTY represented a significant voice in the public and political arena.

From its beginnings as a means of reclaiming political autonomy and religious equality, Irish nationalism developed during the nineteenth century into a considerable cultural force. Under the auspices of Thomas DAVIS and the *Nation* group, it found popular forms of expression in literature and music (see CULTURAL NATIONALISM), and in the 1880s and 1890s developed a powerful cultural wing through the activities and networks of organizations such as the GAELIC LEAGUE, dedicated to the preservation of the Irish language, and the GAELIC ATHLETIC ASSOCIATION, which sought to promote the playing of Irish games over their English counterparts. Most importantly, however, in terms of its future direction, and despite the input of significant numbers of Protestant activists during the nineteenth century, nationalism in Ireland developed close links with the hierarchy of the Catholic Church, and gradually came to be identified as a predominantly Catholic political ideology.

The defeat of PARNELL also advanced this change in nationalism in the early twentieth century, since the failure of the Irish Party for a generation led to the emergence of more militant and exclusivist strains of nationalism and REPUBLICANISM. In some ways this was reflected in cultural developments in the LITERARY REVIVAL, as the cosmopolitan and aristocratic values of writers such as W. B. YEATS and J. M. SYNGE were displaced by those of the Catholic nationalist middle classes, who were becoming dominant in politics. The issue of independence was now increasingly polarized along Catholic–Protestant, North–South lines. Lack of understanding by nationalists of the strength of feeling for the Union by Northern Protestants, and Protestant feelings of superiority to Catholics, led to the crises of the years after 1911. The nationalist victory of the Third HOME RULE Bill was delayed by WWI and potential LOYALIST resistance leading to the EASTER RISING, the ANGLO-IRISH WAR and Partition. As a result, the Free State was to be dominated by two nationalist parties, FINE GAEL and FIANNA FÁIL, while unionist rule of Northern Ireland from STORMONT was perhaps even more monolithic. At this point, the dialogue between nationalists and unionists in Ireland halted for almost half a century. Nationalism turned inwards and became territorial; a desire for self-sufficiency dictated the economic protectionism of DE VALERA from the

1930s and his irredentist 1937 CONSTITUTION, while an idealized vision of the nation, based on Revival images of the peasantry of the West, fed cultural stagnation, CENSORSHIP, and an IRISH-LANGUAGE policy which failed to halt its decline.

In the 1960s MODERNIZATION briefly challenged the arrested development of nationalism. LEMASS's pragmatism led to discussions with O'NEILL, and the unlinking of economic progress from Britishness. The TROUBLES in Northern Ireland, however, reactivated many of the old polarities, by subjecting them again to the pressure of militant republicanism and LOYALISM. After 1969, nationalist thinking could only evolve slowly and painfully. As during the LITERARY REVIVAL period, many of these initially took a cultural form, such as the poetry of Seamus HEANEY, and the drama and criticism of the FIELD DAY COMPANY. The involvement of both FINE GAEL and FIANNA FÁIL in the ANGLO-IRISH AGREEMENT, and the role of the SDLP in brokering the move by SINN FÉIN into democratic politics, began a sea-change in nationalist attitudes, in Northern Ireland and the Republic, symbolized in the 1998 referendum which deleted Articles 2 and 3 of the CONSTITUTION. Secularization and political scandal mean that these developments have been accompanied by a reduction of the links between nationalism and Catholicism. Similarly, the dominance of the two main parties in the Republic has been weakened during the 1990s. Nor should Mary ROBINSON's redefinition of Irishness in 1991 in terms of the DIASPORA be underestimated. Finally, not least of the factors in the modernization of nationalism has been the Republic's orientation of itself towards the EU. This has led some commentators, such as the philosopher Richard Kearney, to argue the case for postnationalism. In the short term, then, it seems possible that nationalism is again acquiring a contemporary, more pluralist identity.

Further reading

Boyce (1995). Kearney (1997). Kee (2000).

neutrality　This has been seen as a defining policy of the identity of the Republic since 1939, and it refused to join NATO in 1949. Although LEMASS said the nation accepted it would have to lose neutral status in order to qualify for EEC membership, this was not demanded of it in 1973 when it joined. It is the only non-NATO member of the 12 states, and the only non-member of the allied Western European Union, a fact which has made Irish troops very successful as UN peacekeepers. However, a referendum on 27 May 1987 over the Single European Act endorsed, among other things, a European defence community, and the Republic is now part of the European Rapid Reaction Force and the Partnership for Peace (1999). Neutrality has not yet ended, but may do soon.

New English　Name given to the English settlers in Ireland who came over in the sixteenth century. They were distinguished from the OLD ENGLISH, who arrived in the wake of the NORMAN INVASION, and the two groups were bitter rivals and fought for control over colonial Ireland. The New English were virtually all Protestant in religion and outlook and were keen to portray their rivals as degenerate Catholics who were worse than the poor native Irish because they should know better than to oppose the policies of the Crown. The New English believed that they should replace the Old English in positions of power, administration and government and in their published writings, as well as their unpublished correspondence, argued that Ireland was so unruly that it needed to be completely reconquered. One of the most vociferous spokesmen of the New English was EDMUND SPENSER, who argued that the Irish were descended from the savage Scythians whose degenerate habits had infected Irish society. Other prominent authors include Fynes Moryson (1566–1630), who acted as Lord Mountjoy's secretary during the NINE YEARS WAR, and whose account of his travels throughout Europe, *An Itinerary* (1617), attacks the Irish as lazy, violent, ignorant and dirty; Barnaby Rich (1540?–1617), a prolific pamphleteer and author of romances, who makes a similar case, arguing that Irish savagery was 'bred in the bone'; and John Derricke (*fl.*1581), whose *Image of Irelande* (1581) contains a series of high-quality woodcuts which show Henry Sidney conquering the wild natives.

Further reading

Foster, R. F. (1988). Moody, Martin and Byrne (eds) (1976).

New Ireland Forum   A group consisting of constitutional (i.e. non-paramilitary supporting) NATIONALIST Irish political parties, which met in DUBLIN in 1983 (IRISH LABOUR PARTY, FIANNA FÁIL, FINE GAEL and the SDLP). Its aim was to establish jointly agreed policy on the future of Ireland, and to allay Protestant fears as to what this might be. Although at one stage there was to be a submission to it by the UDA, it ended up being a solely Irish nationalist exercise. It was also overshadowed by the constitutional amendment on ABORTION in the REPUBLIC, which showed an illiberalism there at odds with what the Forum was attempting to demonstrate. Its report, published in 1984, outlined three possible solutions for a future Northern Ireland: joint sovereignty; a federal Ireland; and a united Ireland. Margaret THATCHER, the British Prime Minister, famously rejected all three with the words 'Out, out, out!' However, the Forum gave the SDLP a role at a time when it had a very small one; it demonstrated that the political parties in the Republic, however partially, were prepared to come to grips with the difficulty and complexity of the crisis in Northern Ireland; and it helped maintain the impetus of the Anglo-Irish intergovernmental process which had begun in 1980, as the signing of the 1985 ANGLO-IRISH AGREEMENT would demonstrate.

Newman, John Henry (1801–1890)   Oxford divine who converted to CATHOLICISM, appointed as first Rector of the new Catholic University in DUBLIN (see QUEEN'S

Colleges) in 1854. He resigned four years later, partly as a response to the clash of approach between English and Irish Catholicism. Author of *The Idea of a University, Defined and Illustrated* (1852).

newspapers   Ireland has an illustrious history of newspaper production, dating from the printing of a regular news-sheet, *An Account of the Chief Occurrences in Ireland together with some Particulars from England*, in 1659. Since the late seventeenth century thousands of publications have appeared, some lasting only a few weeks or months, though the *Belfast News-Letter*, founded in 1737, is still in print today and is the oldest daily newspaper in the British Isles.

Ireland's first regular newspaper, founded in 1703, was *Pue's Impartial Occurrences*, which was affiliated to a coffee house of the same name and appeared three times a week. 1706 saw the emergence of the *Dublin Gazette*, and in 1725 the *Dublin Journal* appeared. The *Freeman's Journal*, founded in 1763, however, was one of the first Irish papers to focus primarily on Irish – rather than English – events, and it was to become the main reading matter for the educated classes in the following century. The *Northern Star*, the radical organ of the United Irishmen, founded by Samuel Neilson in 1792, remains one of the earliest and most important campaigning newspapers to have appeared in Ireland, and was the subject of a play by Northern Irish playwright Stewart Parker in 1984.

Eighteenth-century newspapers were limited largely to a Protestant readership and field of interest, but social and political changes in the nineteenth century saw the emergence of a Catholic readership and press. Inevitably, papers were allied to factional interest: the *Nation*, founded in 1842, was one of the most successful political newspapers of the nineteenth century, but many others such as John Mitchel's *United Irishman*, which was dedicated to sweeping English influence out of Ireland, or the Fenian paper *The Celt*, also marked out clear political territory while contributing to the evolution of a strong Irish print culture. Indeed, the steady increase in newspaper circulation from the mid-century onwards was closely linked to political movements, with the Repeal and later the Land League reading rooms helping to create a regular and eager readership throughout the country. Large-scale emigration also established a significant readership of Irish newspapers abroad, particularly in the USA.

Politics aside, however, staple Irish newspapers of the nineteenth century, such as the *Dublin Evening Post*, or the *Packet*, were geared to the world of advertizing, in response to the rise of a middle-class readership in the capital. *The Irish Times*, which began publication in 1859 as the first penny daily newspaper, catered largely for middle-class Protestant interest, with the *Irish Independent* providing a Catholic counterpart from 1891, and eventually incorporating the *Freeman's Journal*. The regions had their own provincial publications, such as the *Cork Examiner*, or Belfast's liberal paper the *Northern Whig*, both printed daily from 1868. For the more leisured classes, there were numerous periodicals and journals such as the Dublin University

MAGAZINE or the *Dublin Penny Journal*, which produced a steady diet of fiction, political comment, literary criticism and sketches.

The Irish press in the late nineteenth and early twentieth centuries was clearly a partisan one. *The Irish Times*, today the best-known broadsheet, and the *Irish Independent* reflected the aspirations of the Protestant and Catholic middle classes respectively; both were subject to the attentions of the contending sides during the CIVIL WAR. *The Irish Worker* was a powerful organizing force among the Dublin working classes before and after the heroic Dublin Lockout. REPUBLICANS defeated in the war lacked a voice until 1931 when the *Irish Press* was founded. During the 1930s and 1940s the DE VALERA government brought severe and successful actions to stifle the socialist and communist press, a suppression which became more general during World War II, particularly of publications which complained that De Valera had betrayed the founding principles of the state. The most gifted newspaperman of the mid-century was R. M. Smylie, the editor of the *Irish Times* (and employer of Flann O'BRIEN, among others). From the 1960s, younger and more irreverent reporters, including John Healy (*Irish Times*), Tim Pat Coogan (*Irish Press*) and Louis MacRedmond (*Irish Independent*), revitalized Irish journalism. The period also saw the emergence of exceptional women journalists, such as Mary Kenny (*Irish Press*), Maeve Binchy and Mary Maher (*Irish Times*) who changed the nature and tone of journalism. The same problems faced elsewhere have affected Irish journalism, including the development of new specialisms and niche interests, reflecting a more complex and fragmented public sphere and marketplace. This has had mixed results. Irish-language newspapers gradually declined, but the satirical journal *Phoenix*, similar to the British *Private Eye*, held its own, and Irish newspapers abroad have flourished; while in Tony O'Reilly, owner of the Independent Group, Ireland has one newspaper magnate of international stature.

Further reading

Brown, S. (1971).

Ní Chuilleanáin, Eiléan (1942–)   Poet and academic. Born in CORK to a well-known REPUBLICAN family, Ní Chuilleanáin studied at UCC and Oxford before becoming a lecturer at TCD. Her work, like that of Michael HARTNETT, is informed by a deep sense of Munster as a repository of the past; 'Site of Ambush', the title poem of her second collection (1975), alludes to IRA ambushes of the Black and Tans (see ANGLO-IRISH WAR) while the 'Cork' sequence from *The Rose-Geranium* (1981) deals with her native city. Yet the poetry is the opposite of political in any obvious sense; the latter work evokes the damp atmospheres and textures of the city, giving a vague sense of enclosure, rather than specific locales or individuals. It is, moreover, verbally dense and textured, a poetry of the processes of perception rather than of realistic or mimetic representation. Nevertheless, there are poems, such as 'Wash' from *Acts and Monuments* (1972), her first volume, which show a woman poet using and challenging masculine dominance within the Irish lyric tradition, and others, such as 'The Second Voyage', which rewrite myth (in this case that of Odysseus) from female perspectives. Later collections show a new concern with foreign landscapes and translation, as a concept rather than as a practice; these include *The Magdalen Sermon* (1989) and *The Brazen Serpent* (1994). A selected collection of poems, *The Second Voyage*, appeared in 1977. Less of a figurehead than her contemporary Eavan BOLAND, Ní Chuilleanáin is nevertheless a central member of the generation of women who established themselves as a major presence in Irish writing from the 1960s.

Further reading

Kerrigan (1998).

Ní Dhomhnaill, Nuala (1952–)   Poet. Born in Lancashire to Irish parents, Ní Dhomhnaill was brought up in the Dingle GAELTACHT, and studied English and Irish at CORK where she was a member of the group of Irish poets associated with the journal *INNTI* founded by Michael Davitt (see IRISH-LANGUAGE LITERATURE). She lived for several years in the Netherlands and Turkey before returning to the Kerry Gaeltacht in 1980. Abroad, Ní Dhomhnaill came to realize 'the vitality of belief enshrined in [Irish] folklore', and her first collection, *An Dealg Droighin/The Thorn of the Blackthorn* (1981) made available new resources and a reinterpretation of tradition to Irish poetry, particularly in a series of poems about Mór, the Munster fertility goddess, and CÚ CHULAINN. *Féar Suaithinseach/Famine Grass* (1984), her second collection, takes this a stage further, reshaping Irish MYTH as well as using folkloric material, and incorporating totally contemporary settings and notions. Her 'alliance of feminism and folklore' handles such subjects as anorexia ('Fianaise an chailín I ngreim "Anorexia"/Evidence of the girl anorexic') and female sexual desire ('Oiléan/Island'), mingling freely Black & Decker drills and fairy trees; moreover, Ní Dhomhnaill is equally inventive in her disruption of traditionalist metrics. In her third collection *Féis/Festival* (1993), the themes of the earlier work are brought into line with experience in middle-class DUBLIN.

Ní Dhomhnaill's use of folklore and myth is distinguished by its contemporary concerns, which draw it away from archaeology and elegy, and by its feminist charge. Both can be seen working together in some of her most disturbing poems. 'An Bhatrail/The Battering', for example, alludes to the Kerry Babies Case of 1984, in which a young woman was bullied by officials into a confession of infanticide (and another died a lonely death in childbirth), bringing it into shocking juxtaposition with the folk belief in kidnapped babies and changelings. Ní Dhomhnaill is also innovative in her attitude to the English language and translation, which she has actively courted and manipulated. *The Astrakhan Cloak* (1992) is a poetry collection but also a collaboration with Paul MULDOON, some of whose tropes (such as Hy Breasil and the *immram*) she uses in it. No single poet has been more responsible for the growth of Irish-language poetry than Ní Dhomhnaill, and she remains its outstanding contemporary figure.

Further reading

Haberstroh (1996).

Nine Years War (1593–1603)   Name for the war fought between the Irish and the English in Ireland which proved to be the most serious threat to English control of Ireland in the sixteenth and seventeenth centuries. There were numerous rebellions against English rule in the sixteenth century, the most important of which were the Kildare Rebellion (1534–35) and the second Desmond Rebellion (1579–83). However, these had been predominantly local affairs which never really took on a national character (although the Desmond Rebellion did have considerable papal and Spanish support which meant that it was brutally crushed by the English authorities, most notably in the infamous massacre at Smerwick (1581)). The Nine Years War was an altogether more serious affair and it is generally accepted by historians that had the Spanish sent more aid to the Irish then the English forces might well have been defeated.

The Nine Years War began over a series of disputes over land titles which made the lords in Ulster fear that the Crown was planning to break up their estates. A rebellion broke out which involved the allegiance of men whose families were usually bitter rivals, Red Hugh O'Donnell, whose lands were mainly in Donegal, and Hugh O'NEILL, Earl of Tyrone. O'Neill initially pretended to be acting as an officer of the Crown while encouraging his relatives to rebel, as he already had hopes of aid from Spain. He was finally declared a traitor in June 1595.

The conflict developed as a guerrilla war with the Irish regularly ambushing their more heavily armed but often tactically naïve opponents. Famous victories were achieved at Battle of the Ford of the Biscuits (7 August 1594), when soldiers heading for the besieged castle at Enniskillen lost their supplies trying to cross the River Arney; Clontibret (27 May 1595), when Hugh O'Neill secured his first victory over the forces led by Henry Bagenal, the leader of the English troops in Ulster; and, most famously, the Battle of the Yellow Ford (14 August 1598), which was the worst defeat on Irish soil suffered by English forces in the sixteenth century; 800 English troops were killed, including Bagenal, and the forts at Blackwater and Armagh had to be abandoned. That October, the MUNSTER PLANTATION was largely destroyed and the English forced to flee their lands.

The Irish forces controlled most of Ireland outside the towns by the end of the sixteenth century. The appointment of Robert Devereux, second Earl of Essex, with an army of 16,000, the largest army recruited by the English Crown in the sixteenth century, raised English hopes of a swift end to the war. However, Essex's disastrous expedition concluded with him signing an ignominious truce with O'Neill when they met alone in September 1600. O'Neill attempted to play the Catholic card and tried to unite both OLD ENGLISH and native Irish against the English. The English were, quite rightly, afraid that they might lose control of Ireland. They were saved because Spanish aid was disappointing both in terms of its size and the speed with which it was dispatched to Ireland, and because an astute military tactician was appointed to oversee the final stages of the war, Charles Blount, Lord Mountjoy (1563–1606).

Mountjoy was highly successful in establishing a series of small garrisons throughout Ireland which enabled English forces to respond quickly to Irish raids and so minimize their effectiveness.

The war effectively ended in 1601, when the English defeated the combined Irish and Spanish forces in the only pitched battle of the campaign at KINSALE. O'Neill's forces were rounded up or surrendered and he went into hiding, finally submitting in March 1603 when the Treaty of Mellifont was signed. Although he was pardoned and allowed to keep his lands, O'Neill fled Ireland with Hugh O'Donnell in 1607, an event later known as the FLIGHT OF THE EARLS. Despite the huge cost of the war, England had regained control over Ireland and the way was paved for new initiatives such as the Londonderry Plantation.

Further reading

Ellis, S. (1985). Morgan (1993).

Norman Invasion   After invading England in 1066 under William the Conqueror, the Normans established themselves as the ruling dynasty there, spreading through-out much of England and into Wales. In the following century, during the reign of Henry II (1154–89), the Normans turned their attention to Ireland. Henry was keen on the possibility of establishing his rule over Ireland from early on in his reign, but the first invading forces were led by Richard fitz Gilbert, better known as Strongbow, who formed an alliance with Diarmait Mac Murchada, King of Leinster, who was prepared to use any means to win his lands back. Having married Mac Murchada's daughter, Strongbow succeeded him as King of Leinster when Mac Murchada died in 1171. In order to curb Strongbow's excessive power Henry first of all threatened to confiscate his land, before deciding to invade Ireland himself to establish his rights as king which he did in 1171, agreeing to recognize Strongbow as lord of Leinster. Although he had to leave Ireland to quell the revolt of his son, Henry had obtained control over most of Ireland and he was recognized as the overlord of much of Ireland in 1175 with the signing of the Treaty of Windsor. Henry left the running of his Irish dominions to Hugh De Lacy, a Norman colonist, and subsequently made his son, John, lord of Ireland with the plan to make him its king. John led an expedition to Ireland in 1185, principally to bring Hugh de Lacy to heel. Vivid descriptions of this expedition, the progress of the Norman Conquest and Norman perceptions of the Irish are provided in the writings of GERALD OF WALES, who travelled to Ireland as part of John's entourage. The conquest was justified by the LAUDABILITER.

Further reading

Cosgrove (ed.) (1987).

Northern Ireland Labour Party (NILP)   The NILP, based on the powerful BELFAST labour movement and industrial working class, was, for many years, the main challenge to the Ulster UNIONIST Party, and capable at times of unrest of exposing the subordination of working-class interests within the Protestant bloc. By the same token, however, its appeal for Protestant workers was underwritten by an endorsement of the union with Britain, which was associated with progress and hence with socialist reform. This contrasted with the revolutionary republican socialist tradition of CONNOLLY, limiting its appeal to Catholics, and the constitutional issue weakened attempts to forge Catholic-Protestant class unity. Nevertheless, the NILP was seen as a major threat by the Unionist Party, which changed the electoral system for STORMONT elections in 1929 from PR-STV (Proportional Representation-Single Transferable Vote) to a plurality system in order to strengthen its control. Elections thereafter became more or less a sectarian head count, and the potential for the NILP's development was halted. Even so, it challenged unionism in WWII and in the late 1950s, as unemployment rose in traditional industries. Unionists were forced to embrace MODERNIZATION and replace BROOKE with O'NEILL. NILP policy in the 1960s anticipated that of the CIVIL RIGHTS movement, calling as it did for the application of British standards in local government, housing allocations and an end to sectarian discrimination. It was unable to win a Westminster seat, however, despite attracting cross-community support in Belfast, and the sectarian polarization of the early 1970s spelt its demise.

Further reading

Walker (1985).

O'Brien, Edna (1930–)   Novelist and short story writer. Born in Co. Clare, O'Brien achieved a sensational best-selling success with her first three novels; *The Country Girls* (1960), *The Lonely Girl* (1962, later reprinted as *The Girl with Green Eyes*) and *Girls in Their Married Bliss* (1963). All three are coming-of-age novels set in a repressive and puritanical Ireland, and deal frankly with female desire; all three were banned. O'Brien's later works include *Casualties* (1966), *A Pagan Place* (1971), *The High Road* (1988) and *Wild December* (1999). She has also published short story collections, among them *The Love Object* (1968) and *Lantern Slides* (1990).

A prolific, fluent and stylish writer, O'Brien's writing is marked by a liberatory urge, although (as the title like *The Love Object* suggests) this can be ambiguous; her characters both rebel to find and are victims of their belief in romantic love. Escape is frequently symbolized in the form of a man, who then abuses their trust. O'Brien avoids mother-daughter relationships in her work, unlike many other women writers;

in her memoir *Mother Ireland* (1976) they are significant by their absence, a rejection of a nation-as-mother which has a critical bearing on the nationalist gendering of Ireland, while her analyses of masochism resemble those of Jean Rhys and other more obviously proto-feminist writers. A genuine innovator, at her best O'Brien is a daring writer who subtly weaves female assertiveness and stereotypes of vulnerability to explore darker themes of compulsion, violence and reparation.

O'Brien, Flann (Brian O'Nolan) (1911–1966)   Novelist and columnist. O'Nolan was born in Strabane, Co. Tyrone; his family moved to DUBLIN in 1923. His comic ability was first realized in the UCD student magazine, *Comthrom Féinne*, in which the first of his multiple personae, Brother Barnabas, appeared. A short-lived co-venture with his brother, the magazine *Blather*, produced another mask for O'Brien's wordplay: Count O'Blather. O'Brien became a civil servant in 1935, continuing work on his novel, *At Swim-Two-Birds*, which was published in 1939. A modernist comic masterpiece, drawing upon sources as diverse as American cowboy fiction and Old and Middle Irish narratives, the novel owes much to James JOYCE's *Ulysses* in its complex self-reflexivity. Joyce admired the book, but it was not a commercial success, and O'Brien failed in his attempt to secure a publisher for his second novel, *The Third Policeman*, completed in 1940 and published posthumously in 1967. A darker work than its predecessor, the plot of *The Third Policeman* turns on an eternal recurrence of crime and punishment. An innovative novel, it includes lengthy speculations on the dangers of molecular transference risked by cyclists and their machines, and a bogus critical apparatus concerning the theories of the scientist de Selby. In 1940, O'Brien was invited by the editor of *The Irish Times*, R. M. Smyllie, to write a column. 'Cruiskeen Lawn', under another of O'Brien pen-names, Myles na gCopaleen, ran from 1940 until his death. The column became a national institution, entertaining its readers with the wordplay of O'Brien's literary duo, Chapman and Keats, characters such as The Brother, and satirical jibes at the establishment. O'Brien parodied the conventions of works of IRISH-LANGUAGE LITERATURE, such as Tomás Ó Criomhthain's *An tOileánach* (*The Islandman*), in *An Béal Bocht* (1941)/*The Poor Mouth* (1964). With the reissue of *At Swim-Two-Birds*, O'Brien's achievement was belatedly recognized. *A Hard Life* (1961), though a far less adventurous novel, was a commercial success. His final completed novel, *The Dalkey Archive* (1964), is, to some degree, a rewriting in a slightly more conventional format of *The Third Policeman*.

Further reading

Cronin (1989). Hopper (1995).

O'Brien, William Smith (1803–1864)   Nationalist politician. O'Brien's involvement with YOUNG IRELAND and his leadership of the 1848 rising elevated him into the pantheon of Irish nationalism, but it also eclipsed his earlier achievements. Born into a landowning Protestant family, but also acutely conscious of ancestral connections to the ancient Irish family of O'Brien of Thomond, he was educated at Harrow and Cambridge before becoming MP for Ennis in 1828. Though a Tory, he supported CATHOLIC EMANCIPATION. Over time he became convinced of the injustice of the ACT OF UNION and joined the REPEAL movement in 1843, deputizing as leader for the jailed Daniel O'CONNELL the following year. Within Young Ireland O'Brien was a moderate like Thomas DAVIS before him, and, though a revolutionist in theory, in practice he aimed to win support from the landowning classes, reluctantly advocating violence only as a last resort. Spurred by the FAMINE and a series of revolutions across Europe, this last resort was reached in 1848, resulting in an abortive rising to which the vast majority of the hungry populace remained indifferent. After a week, O'Brien surrendered at Ballingarry, Co. Tipperary. He was convicted of treason and transported to Tasmania. Pardoned in 1854, he returned to Ireland two years later, a spent force whose last political activism was to denounce FENIANISM. A STATUE of him was erected in DUBLIN in 1870, making him the first rebel to be so honoured.

Ó Bruadair, Dáibhí (c.1625–1698)   Poet. Ó Bruadair was born in Barrymore, Co. Cork, where he was trained in a bardic school (although he probably did not come from a bardic family). He lived for most of his life in Limerick, where he was supported by a number of patrons, including the Bourkes and the Fitzgeralds. A long poem, 'Woe to that man who leaves on his vagaries', if it can be read as an autobiographical piece, indicates that he spent his last years in poverty, working as an agricultural labourer. Ó Bruadair laments that ploughing is 'a thirsty task … with a weapon I never employed when I was rich' and looks back nostalgically to the time when his 'speech was fluent Latin and cunning English!/I could describe a flourish to dazzle the scribes!' (his use of English and Latin showing how BARDIC POETS worked for various masters in Ireland in the seventeenth century).

Ó Bruadair's work is noted for its skill, eloquence and range. His poems also chronicle the fate of the traditional forms of Irish life in the seventeenth century, the decline of the Gaelic aristocracy and the persecution of the Catholic Church. Many of his poems pour scorn on the vulgar English settlers and the self-interested Irish who profit from them. 'Mairg nach fuil 'na dhubhthuata/(O It's best be a total boor') proclaims that only the ill-educated and the stupid can prosper in the new Ireland after the Cromwellian land settlement: 'O it's best be a total boor/(though it's bad be a boor at all)/if I'm to go out and about/among these stupid people'. In other poems Ó Bruadair blames the Irish themselves for their lack of faith and argues that they have brought their own fate upon themselves.

Ó Cadhain, Máirtín (1906–1970)   Novelist, short story writer, academic. Born in Cois Fharraige in the Connemara GAELTACHT of Co. Galway, Ó Cadhain is by common agreement the greatest prose writer in the IRISH LANGUAGE since the seventeenth century. He trained as a school teacher but was dismissed from his post in 1936 for IRA activities and INTERNED 1940–44. He worked as a translator in the DÁIL after 1947 and became a lecturer in the Department of Irish at TCD in 1956.

Ó Cadhain's early stories, collected in *Idir Shúgradh agus Dáiríre* (1939) are in line with the dominant LITERARY REVIVAL ethos, but his work developed far greater depth and complexity during the 1940s. His masterpiece is his only published novel, *Cré na Cille/Churchyard Earth* (1948). Dismissed by early critics as an insult to the people of the GAELTACHT, it is now regarded as the major prose work in modern Irish. The 'characters' of the novel are bodies lying in a churchyard who, having brought all of the gossipy spite of their lifetimes with them, spend their time in ceaseless talk (their predicament can be related to Ó Cadhain's internment). One dead woman's monologue, for example, centres on the complaint that her living relations have had her buried in a 15-shilling grave, rather than a guinea plot. Irish is used with a modernist relish for exploiting its full lexical and syntactic possibilities, blending dialect and literary models, and testing the limits of language itself (JOYCE is an acknowledged model). With KAVANAGH's *The Great Hunger* and Flann O'BRIEN's *An Béal Bocht*, *Cré na Cille* is one of the great 1940s anti-pastoral deconstructions of urban idealizations of rural life. For all this, the English translation of the novel remains unpublished.

In his later short stories, Ó Cadhain concentrated on presenting life in what he saw as the dehumanizing wasteland of the modern city; a selection of translations, edited by Eugene WATTERS, was published as *The Road to Brightcity* (1981).

Further reading

Kiberd (1993). Ó Tuairisc *et al.* (1981). Welch (1993).

O'Casey, Sean (1880–1964) Playwright. O'Casey was born into a working-class Protestant family in DUBLIN. He joined the IRB, the GAELIC LEAGUE and the Irish Transport and General Worker's Union, was secretary of the IRISH CITIZEN ARMY, and was involved in the Lockout in 1913. In 1914 he distanced himself from the growing nationalism and militancy of the ICA, although he wrote *The Story of the Irish Citizen Army* (1919). The first of his acclaimed Dublin trilogy of plays, *The Shadow of a Gunman*, was produced at the ABBEY THEATRE in 1923, followed by *Juno and the Paycock* (1924) and *The Plough and the Stars* (1926). They deal with Irish political events, and their impact on working-class people, in the period from the EASTER RISING of 1916 to the Irish CIVIL WAR. With their slum settings, vividly rendered speech, and remarkable modulations of dramatic pace and register, these plays were as bold as anything produced at the Abbey since J. M. SYNGE. Like Synge's *The Playboy of the Western World*, the plays probed the touchy issue of national self-representation; in particular, the *Plough* shocked its audience by driving a wedge between the rhetoric of

Republicanism and the brutality that can derive from it. As with Synge's play, O'Casey's caused a riot and thus provoked W. B. YEATS into an eloquent defence of the dramatist he saw as the natural successor to the author of the *Playboy*. O'Casey largely spent the remainder of his life in England. Plays written in England include *The Silver Tassie* (1928), which powerfully exploits expressionist techniques in its rendering of the anguish caused by WWI, and *The Star Turns Red* (1940), which treats the confrontation between socialism and fascism, a subject further explored in *Red Roses for Me* (1942). O'Casey's later plays, *Cock-a-Doodle Dandy* (1949), *The Bishop's Bonfire* (1955), *The Drums of Father Ned* (1959) and *Behind the Green Curtain* (1962), are highly innovative in form, and expound either dystopian or utopian prospects for humanity. Alongside his full-length plays, O'Casey wrote a number of one-act dramas, and, from 1939 to 1954, six volumes of partly factual, partly fantastic, *Autobiographies*.

Further reading

Hunt (1980). Kosok (1985).

O'Connell, Daniel (1775–1847)   Politician. Born in Co. Kerry, educated locally and in Northern France on the eve of the Revolution (where he acquired a life-long antipathy to violence), O'Connell then read law in London and was called to the Irish bar in 1798. His rise to prominence in Catholic politics began in 1800 with a speech against the ACT OF UNION, and progressed steadily while he developed his oratorical skills as 'the Counsellor'. His political priority in these years was the granting of CATHOLIC EMANCIPATION, and to this end he formed in 1823 the Catholic Association, funded by vast numbers of small subscriptions, known as 'the Catholic Rent'. The massive popular support for the Association, bolstered by mass-meetings and a militant rhetoric demanding rights, not concessions, established O'Connell as a folk-hero in Ireland and, following his election as MP for Clare in 1828, a powerful figure in Westminster. After the granting of Emancipation in 1829, O'Connell earned the soubriquet 'the Liberator' and set about campaigning for the REPEAL of the Act of Union. This was a highly sensitive subject that never won support of either liberal Protestants at home or sympathetic MPs at Westminster; moreover, as the YOUNG IRELAND movement adopted Repeal as a core tenet of their policies, it looked increasingly likely that violence might ensue. Accordingly, under the threat of military intervention, O'Connell cancelled his last 'monster meeting' at Clontarf (symbolic site of BRIAN BORU's clash with marauding foreigners) in 1843. Shortly after this, O'Connell was convicted of conspiracy and imprisoned for several months before a successful appeal. Upon his release his health deteriorated, as did relations with the Young Ireland movement. He died at Genoa in 1847, while on pilgrimage to Rome. His body was returned to DUBLIN but his heart was interred in Rome. His popularity was demonstrated by the half-million or so who turned out in Dublin for the laying of the foundation stone of his memorial statue (see STATUES). Since then, O'Connell's reputation has not fared particularly well: his constitutionalism and later conservatism has excluded him from the apostolic succession of republican heroes in extreme nationalist historiography; on the other hand, his demagoguery and sectarian appeal makes him a poor model for more liberal sensibilities. W.B. YEATS would disparage him as 'the Great Comedian', in the poem 'Parnell's Funeral'.

Further reading

McDonagh (1991).

O'Connor, Frank (Michael O'Donovan) (1903–1966)   Novelist, short story writer, dramatist, critic and translator. Born in CORK, O'Connor left school at 12 but continued to read, encouraged by Daniel CORKERY. Supporting the anti-treatyites during the CIVIL WAR, he was INTERNED in 1923, after which he established himself in DUBLIN literary circles. Together with W. B. YEATS he founded the Irish Academy of Letters to oppose CENSORSHIP. He served as a director of the ABBEY THEATRE 1935–39, publishing his best novel, *Dutch Interior*, in 1940 (it was banned).

O'Connor was a master of many genres whose reputation is mainly based on extensive translations of Irish poetry, collected in *Kings, Lords and Commons* (1959), and on his short stories, selected in *My Oedipus Complex and Other Stories* (1963). The stories are studies of mood, atmosphere and small but significant detail and incident. In such work the models are invariably Russian and French, particularly Chekhov and Maupassant.

In 1951, isolated in Ireland, O'Connor moved to the USA where he was lionized as a lecturer, and produced insightful critical works; these included *The Lonely Voice* (1963) and *The Backward Look* (1967). Welcomed back to Ireland in the 1960s, he published two volumes of autobiography, *An Only Child* (1961) and *My Father's Son* (1968). Although his deprecation of James JOYCE, and the element of predictability in some of his work have led to neglect of O'Connor since his death, a revival of his fortunes is now overdue.

Further reading

McKeon (1998). Sheehy (1969). Wohlgelernter (1977).

Ó Direáin, Máirtín (1910–1988)   Poet. Born on Inishmore, one of the Aran Islands. A civil servant in DUBLIN from 1938, he started to write and publish poems. *Rogha Dánta/Collected Poems* (1949) is considered by many to be one of the most significant collections of poetry in modern Irish; one of its chief concerns is the anomie of urban existence, with the city's inhabitants severed from a fructifying relationship with locality. Similar themes are developed in *Ar Ré Dhearóil* (1963) in a tersely compelling poetic diction.

Further reading

Sewell (2000).

O'Donovan, John (1809–1861)   Historian and Gaelic antiquarian scholar, who was appointed to head the Topographical section of the Ordnance Survey memoir, where he influenced the young Samuel Ferguson. He later became Professor of Celtic Studies at Queen's University in Belfast, and published his annotated edition of *The Annals of the Four Masters* between 1848 and 1851.

O'Faolain, Sean (1900–1991)   Short story writer, novelist, editor. Born John Whelan in Cork city, and influenced as a young man by Daniel Corkery and the ideas of Irish Ireland, he joined the Irish Volunteers in 1918, and was a director of propaganda for the IRA during the Irish Civil War. O'Faolain's republican zeal and its subsequent waning are the subject-matter of many of his early short stories, collected in *Midsummer Night Madness* (1932), a volume censored for its alleged obscenity. His historical novel, *A Nest of Simple Folk* (1934), takes an elderly man's extremist politics, which lead to his death, as an instance of the necessary dangers of life-affirming rebelliousness. *Bird Alone* (1936), a novel, also centres on the self-empowerment derived from nonconformity; and the critique of idealized conceptions of Irish identity and nationhood is explored in *Come Back to Erin* (1940), in which cold water is dashed over an Irish American's expectations of the old country. This concentration on the social and cultural reality of Ireland, often obfuscated by much of the political rhetoric of the mid-century, continues in his later collections of stories, which include *The Heat of the Sun* (1966). The ethical dimension to the fictional form in which he excelled relates to O'Faolain's work as a cultural critic, since the demystifying impulse of many of the stories is of a piece with his role as founding editor of The Bell from 1940 to 1946.

O'Faolain was also the author of biographies of Éamon De Valera (1933), Daniel O'Connell (*The King of the Beggars*, 1938) and Hugh O'Neill (1942); a critical book, *The Vanishing Hero* (1956), which addresses the relative absence of heroism in modern fiction owing to its paucity of feeling; a study of nationality, *The Irish* (1948); two travel books; and an autobiography, *Vive Moi* (1964), which, in part, constitutes a record of his youthful politics.

Further reading

Harmon (1966, 1994).

O'Flaherty, Liam (1896–1984)   Novelist. Born on Inishmore in the Aran Islands, O'Flaherty served in the Irish Guards during WWI, saw fighting at the Somme, and was discharged in 1917 suffering from shell shock having been wounded in a bombardment at Langemarck. A period of aimless drifting and odd jobbing followed, recalled in his first volume of autobiography, *Two Years* (1930). He became a communist thereafter and briefly occupied the Rotunda under the self-styled title of Chairman of the Council of the Unemployed. His radical politics led him to visit

Russia; his subsequent disillusionment with communism is the subject of *I Went to Russia* (1931). His caustic observations on the Irish Free State comprise the satirical *A Tourist's Guide to Ireland* (1929). O'Flaherty's first two novels, *Thy Neighbour's Wife* (1923) and *The Black Soul* (1924), are informed by life on the Aran Islands, and, in the second work, by Flaherty's wartime experiences. He achieved considerable success with his novel *The Informer* (1925), filmed by John Ford, in which the Irish CIVIL WAR forms the background to a study of persecution and betrayal. O'Flaherty's hard-edged realism caused his fiction to be linked to the plays of Sean O'CASEY, but his early novels are almost myopically focused through their central protagonists. With *The House of Gold* (1929) and *Skerret* (1932), he showed himself capable of observing an Irish social milieu in a more dispassionate, albeit highly critical, fashion. A wide historical purview is provided in O'Flaherty's trilogy of novels, *Famine* (1937), *Land* (1946) and *Insurrection* (1950), which documents the development of Irish NATIONALISM from the perspective of closely bound groups of characters. O'Flaherty was a prolific short story writer, in English and Irish, the latter collected in *Duil* (1953). Latterly, he shunned the media, ending his life a virtual recluse.

Further reading

Sheeran (1976).

O'Grady, Standish James (1846–1928)   Journalist and historian. Born in 1846 in Co. Cork and educated at TCD, O'Grady practised law in DUBLIN before discovering, at 24, *An Introduction to the Study of the History and Antiquities of Ireland* (1772) by Sylvester O'Halloran (1728–1807). This prompted him to devote his life to Irish history and MYTHOLOGY. His first major work was his two-volume *History of Ireland* (1878–80), a retelling of ancient Irish myths including the heroic cycle centring on Cú CHULAINN. This had a profound effect on writers of the LITERARY REVIVAL period, especially George RUSSELL ('AE'), Lady GREGORY and W. B. YEATS, who called O'Grady 'the father of the Irish Revival'. In politics O'Grady was a UNIONIST, expounding his views in *Toryism and the Tory Democracy* (1886) and his journal, the *All-Ireland Review* (1900–06). When this journal ceased he effectively withdrew from public life, moving to England in 1918 and dying on the Isle of Wight a decade later – by which time the mythic personae he had resuscitated to embolden the ANGLO-IRISH aristocracy seemed to have taken on an agency of their own among middle-class NATIONALISTS. O'Grady is often confused with his near-namesake Standish Hayes O'Grady (1832–1915), also a scholar and antiquary.

O'Leary, John (1830–1907)   Politician and writer. O'Leary was a FENIAN who was initially linked to the YOUNG IRELAND movement. Briefly imprisoned after the 1848 rising, he travelled to America on behalf of the Fenians, and also worked as joint editor of their journal, the *Irish People*. He settled in Paris before returning to Ireland in 1885, publishing his *Recollections of Fenians and Fenianism* in 1896. He was to influence the young W. B. YEATS, and features in the refrain of the poem 'September 1913': 'Romantic Ireland's dead and gone/It's with O'Leary in the grave.'

O'Neill family   The dominant family in Ulster for most of Irish history. Although eclipsed for much of the eleventh and twelfth centuries by the Mac Loughlins, the O'Neills usually held power over their neighbours. The O'Neills often assumed the high kingship of Ireland throughout the Middle Ages, showing that they were also one of the most powerful dynastic families in Ireland.

Further reading

Mathews (1907).

O'Neill, Hugh (?1550–1616)   Second Earl of Tyrone and third Baron of Dungannon, leader of the Irish army in the NINE YEARS WAR. Hugh O'Neill is one of the key figures in Irish history in the sixteenth and seventeenth centuries and his life has been the subject of subsequent literary and popular historical works such as Sean O'FAOLAIN's *The Great O'Neill* (1942) and Brian FRIEL's *Making History* (1989), which see O'Neill as a figure caught between English and Irish culture.

O'Neill was brought up by Sir Henry Sidney in the 1550s, probably in various houses in Ireland, and was employed by the Crown to fight his kinsmen in the 1570s, building up a series of allegiances which made him a powerful player in the faction-ridden world of Ulster politics. He became Earl of Tyrone in 1585 and caused a scandal when he eloped with Mabel Bagenal, the daughter of Sir Henry Bagenal, Marshal of the Queen's Army. In 1594 he was inaugurated to the O'Neillship with the consent of the English government but by 1595 it was clear that he was plotting against Crown forces and negotiating with Spain as the NINE YEARS WAR broke out. Hugh scored a series of remarkable victories against the English and by the end of the century he controlled most of Ireland outside the towns. He was defeated by Lord Mountjoy at the battle of Kinsale and fled into exile in 1607, an event known as the FLIGHT OF THE EARLS. He lived in Rome until his death under the protection of Pope Paul V. His request to return to Ulster was refused by the English authorities.

Hugh O'Neill inspired Irish writers and activists, especially after his death, and troubled and enraged the English. Because he had been educated by a prominent English aristocrat and was notably affable and cultured he was seen as an especially dangerous traitor who could never be trusted. A series of pamphlets and poems were published describing his threat to English civilized values, and his rebellion was associated with the rise of the antichrist because of his links with Catholic Spain. In reality O'Neill was probably a skilful politician and military leader who was superior to many of his English counterparts who inhabited the same world in which he lived.

Further reading

Hadfield and McVeagh (eds) (1994). Walsh (1996).

O'Neill, Shane (*c.*1530–1567)   Ulster chieftain. O'Neill was elected to the O'Neillship in 1559 and became the most powerful leader of the O'NEILLS in the 1550s and early 1560s. He was recognized as a serious opponent of the crown and the LORD DEPUTY, Thomas Radcliffe, Earl of Sussex (1523–83), mounted three very expensive attempts to defeat Shane's forces in Ulster (1560, 1561, and 1563). Despite these attacks Shane was able to consolidate his power in Ulster. In 1562 he submitted to Elizabeth in London in a ceremony that exposed the huge gulf between English and Irish societies. Shane and his entourage arrived in traditional Irish costume, scented with human urine, and proceeded to howl and wail as a means of expressing their subjection to the queen to the horror and amusement of the English court (although Shane was clearly stalling for time by appearing as a naïve savage to disguise his real ambitions). Shane was accepted as the holder of the O'Neillship, but the arrival of Sir Henry Sidney as Lord Deputy in 1563 saw the resumption of hostilities. Shane looked to Scotland for help and was assassinated by the MacDonnells, the Scottish rivals to the O'Neills in Ulster, who probably killed Shane after striking a deal with Sidney.

Further reading

Brady (1999).

O'Neill, Terence (1914–)   Born in London, educated at Eton, Captain in the Irish Guards 1939–45, O'Neill was a STORMONT MP for Bannside 1946–70. He took over from Basil BROOKE as leader of the Unionist Party and Prime Minister of Northern Ireland in 1963. O'Neill was a modernizer who shared aims with his counterpart in the REPUBLIC, Seán LEMASS. Realizing change had to occur if UNIONISM itself was to survive, O'Neill met Lemass, in an historic meeting, visited a Catholic school, and adopted policies for attracting companies, such as Goodyear, from the USA, in order to offset the unemployment created by the decline of traditional industries. Reform, however, required a more skilled and flexible workforce and meritocratic structures in order to succeed; and these an ossified sectarianism proved incapable of granting. It has been argued that O'Neill's embrace of change was aimed more at marginalizing the NORTHERN IRISH LABOUR PARTY than to deal with CATHOLIC grievances, and he eventually angered both NATIONALISTS and LOYALISTS. By May 1969, when he resigned in favour of James Chichester-Clark, the Unionist monolith was already weakened and the state destabilized.

Further reading

Bew, Gibbon and Patterson (1996). Cairns and Richards (1988). O'Neill (1972).

Ó Rathaille, Aodhagán (?1670–1729)   Poet. Ó Rathaille was born in Scrahanaveel, Co. Kerry, where he was well educated, enabling him to speak Latin and English. His family, who appear to have been reasonably well off, were sub-tenants of the MacCarthys, tenants of Sir Nicholas Browne, the descendant of Elizabethan settlers who was favourable to the native Irish, having become a Catholic and a JACOBITE. Browne's estates were confiscated after the BATTLE OF THE BOYNE and his tenants had to leave. Ó Rathaille's family moved to Corcaguiney, Co. Kerry and lived in reduced circumstances. In *c.*1708 he composed 'Is fada liom oíche/The drenching night drags on', a lament for the fall of the Irish aristocracy, specifically the MacCarthys, as well as his own misfortunes. In it, Ó Rathaille complains that he has to eat dogfish and winkles, poor food that he would not have touched in his youth. The storm that engulfs him in the night serves as a symbol of Ireland's chaos. In 'Do shiúlaigh mise an mhumhain mhín/I walked all over Munster mild', Ó Rathaille revisits Togher Castle (Co. Cork), a former MacCarthy stronghold, and finds it occupied by English settlers.

Ó Rathaille led an itinerant and impoverished life until his death. He wrote a number of 'aisling' poems (allegorical dream visions describing the unfortunate fate of the Irish). In 'Gile na gile/Brightness most bright' he narrates his encounter with a beautiful maiden who represents Ireland. She is betrothed to the Stuart pretender, but cannot marry him because she is imprisoned by a troop of goblins who force her to marry 'a lumbering brute'. Ó Rathaille reflects that there can be no solution until 'our lions come over the sea'. In 'An Aisling/The Vision', the poet sees 'a pleasant flock of joyous girls' on top of a hill who light three candles hoping to lead the Jacobite forces back to Ireland. The poet feels inspired until he wakes up 'nerve-shaken, downcast and morose' when he realizes what the real situation is. Humorous verse, such as 'Ar choileach a goideadh ó shagart maith/A good priest's stolen cock', shows the range of his work.

He also wrote poems for the Brownes lamenting their poverty and their inability to help him recover his previous status. 'Cabhair ní ghairfead', probably written during his final illness, links his own suffering to that of the occupied Irish people, whose 'proud royal line is wrecked'. Ó Rathaille died in 1725 and was buried with the MacCarthys in Muckross Abbey, Killarney.

Ó Riada, Seán (1931–1971)   Composer. Born John Reidy in CORK, Seán Ó Riada took a B.Mus. from UCC, and became assistant musical director at Radio Éireann in DUBLIN in 1956, musical director at the ABBEY THEATRE in 1956, and lecturer at UCC in 1962. Ó Riada was the most influential composer of his generation, starting his career as a composer in the European classical art MUSIC tradition, equally able to compose in modal, chromatic and serial styles. Ó Riada also set Kinsella's translation of the TÁIN for a 1970 RTÉ production, and following his death was commemorated in Kinsella's *A Vertical Man* (1973). Some of his best-known scores were film music, most memorably for *Mise Eire* (1959) (see FILM), in which he employed lavish Mahlerian orchestration to impressive effect.

Ó Riada's most lasting significance, however, probably lies in his bringing together of classical music and Irish TRADITIONAL MUSIC in the 1960s. This arose out of an interest in Irish song initially centred on Turlough Carolan (1670–1738), an Irish composer who used native melody under the influence of Italian composers like Corelli. Ó Riada recorded Carolan's music, using a harpsichord instead of a harp, and also collected the traditional music issued in the three-disc set *Our Musical Heritage*. He founded the group Ceoltóirí Chualann (later The Chieftains) to play his arrangements of such music, their style based on his concept of group playing which emphasized 'the essentially solo effect' of the music. The group was organized with the discipline of a classical music ensemble and changed the way traditional music was perceived and performed. In Ciaran CARSON's words,

> the tune, in Ó Riada's hands, could now be dissected into various motifs; harmony was allowable. While most traditional musicians viewed these developments with some suspicion, they were acclaimed by a wider audience, and a music until now confined to parish halls … suddenly became respectable; adulatory notices appeared in the *Irish Times*.

Further reading

Freyer and Harris (1981).

Ó Ríordáin, Seán (1916–1977) Poet. Born in Ballyvourney, Co. Cork, into an Irish-speaking community, in 1938 he was diagnosed as suffering from tuberculosis. Despite the drastic effects of the disease, Ó Ríordáin believed there was a link between his ill health and his writing: he wrote his first published poem while convalescing in a sanatorium in North Cork. A first collection, *Eireaball Spideoige* (1952), marks the first major encounter between literary modernism and IRISH-LANGUAGE poetry, as well as displaying a thorough knowledge of traditional IRISH-LANGUAGE LITERATURE. Ó Ríordáin's later collections are *Brosna* (1964), *Línte* (1971) and the posthumously published *Tar Éis mo Bháis* (1979). Like Brian COFFEY's, his work is informed by a neo-Thomist philosophy, which, in his case, led to a belief that poetic utterance is a form of prayer. An existential preoccupation with identity colours Ó Ríordáin's work, along with an overriding need to isolate the essential being of individual subjectivity and the national spirit; for Ó Ríordáin, this can only occur through the medium of the Irish language. In Cork, Ó Ríordáin was friends with the literary critic and short story writer Daniel CORKERY and the Irish scholar Seán Ó Tuama. In 1969 he took up a lectureship in the Irish Department at UCC, in which role he influenced younger Irish-language poets including Nuala NÍ DHOMHNAILL and Michael Davitt.

Further reading

Sewell (2000). Welch (1993).

Old English (Sean Ghaill) Description used for the descendants of the Anglo-Norman settlers from the twelfth century onwards. It was used in the second half of the sixteenth century to distinguish the early English colonists from the NEW ENGLISH arrivals as the Tudors sought to bring Ireland more fully under English control. The Old English, many of whom lived in DUBLIN, resented the assumption of control by the second wave of English colonists and often tried to communicate directly with the monarch or Privy Council to press their own case, an important intermediary being Thomas Butler, tenth Earl of ORMOND, Elizabeth I's cousin, who was much resented by the New English. Generally, the Old English argued the case that they could govern and control the native (or 'wild') Irish using existing institutions and legal frameworks, while the New English favoured military solutions, which they would oversee. Richard STANIHURST, a member of a prominent Old English family, championed the Old English in his 'Description of Ireland' published in the influential Holinshed's *Chronicles* (1577, 1587). He memorably claimed that the Old English spoke a pure Chaucerian English, so preserving true Englishness in Ireland. The Old English were predominantly Catholic, so started to side more and more with their fellow Irishmen and women in the seventeenth century as Protestant English control was more forcefully asserted, dividing Ireland into the Protestant ascendancy and Catholic majority after the 1641 REBELLION and WILLIAMITE WARS.

Further reading

Canny (1987). Lennon (1978). Moody, Martin and Byrne (eds) (1976).

Ordnance Survey Between 1824 and 1836, the British government undertook to produce a six-inch-scale survey map of Ireland. This map would be crucial to various statistical, taxation and engineering ventures, and represented the continuing expansion of state administration and intervention in Ireland after the ACT OF UNION. In the early 1830s, however, under the dynamic leadership of Captain Thomas Larcom, the Ordnance Survey took on an additional emphasis on human enquiry, as the project began to document the environment and social conditions of each region. In 1832 Larcom drew up a detailed checklist for his officers, which included questions on the habits and traditions of the people concerned, their living conditions, feast-days, holidays, religious practices and recreation.

The resultant expansion in workload led to the establishment of the Topographical Department of the Survey, which coordinated the skills of various notable individuals including the artist George PETRIE, the Gaelic scholars John O'DONOVAN and Eugene O'Curry, and the poets Samuel FERGUSON and James Clarence MANGAN. This group was united in its concern for a Gaelic ARCHAEOLOGICAL, topographical and ANTIQUARIAN heritage, and its reports were aimed at producing, ultimately, a comprehensive 'Memoir' of information relating to each county covered by the survey. Despite what many at the time saw as the immense value of this work, the government suspended funding for the Memoir research in 1842. The existing material remains an important resource for economists, cultural historians and anthropologists of nineteenth-century Ireland.

In his 1981 play *Translations*, the playwright Brian FRIEL drew on the history of the Ordnance Survey Commission in the north-west of Ireland, highlighting the various political and cultural confusions which arose from the translation of Irish place names into English.

Orangeism, Orange Order   The Orange Order is an organization dedicated to the protection of Protestant LOYALIST interests in Ireland. It was founded in 1795, taking its inspiration from the memory of WILLIAM III, Prince of Orange, and his victory over Catholic JACOBITE forces of JAMES II at the BATTLE OF THE BOYNE in 1690. After its formation and the establishment of the Grand Lodge in Dublin in 1798, the Order spread quickly throughout Ireland, with particularly strong support in Protestant Ulster. Though it initially opposed the ACT OF UNION, fearing that it would pave the way for Catholic Emancipation, Orangeism gradually came to be identified with Union as the defensive bulwark of Irish Protestant loyalism.

In 1825, the Orange Order was temporarily outlawed under the Unlawful Societies Act, leading to the dissolution of the Grand Lodge and the formation of a substitute network, the BRUNSWICK CLUBS. It re-emerged, however, in the mid-1840s, re-establishing the Grand Lodge in 1847, expanding its profile and gaining crucial support from the middle classes and many members of the Irish gentry. While the activities of the Order were largely community-based, charitable and evangelical, it retained a strict anti-papist policy, and in the latter decades of the Victorian era became closely allied to the forces of Ulster UNIONISM. By the end of the century, largely as a result of EMIGRATION, Orangeism had spread beyond Ireland to Britain, the USA and Canada, where several major Orange Lodges still exist.

For much of the twentieth century, the role of the Orange Order remained central to organizing and articulating loyalist identity. After Partition, however, this was almost wholly confined to Northern Ireland, where it has served, as previously, to unify the different strata of Protestant society. The defining period was the HOME RULE crisis of 1911–14, when the Ulster Unionist Council, led by James CRAIG, organized the ULSTER VOLUNTEER FORCE through the local Orange Lodges (which supplied it with many of its recruits), and the signing of the Solemn League and Covenant in 1912. In this way, as before, the Order signalled its various overt and covert links with the political and physical force wings of loyalist unionism.

Occasional cracks have appeared in the monolith of Protestant solidarity, most often when working-class rank-and-file and middle-class leadership interests conflicted. This might take the form of reasserting Orangeism's supposedly radical roots (as with the Independent Orange Order, founded in 1903), or through temporary defection from sectarian to class politics in the shape of the NORTHERN IRELAND LABOUR PARTY (as in the 1930s and 1950s). Such splits were eventually defused by appeals for unity and accusations (usually exaggerated) of the threat to the Union. Just as the Orange Order helped contain dissident energies, so it also supported and shaped the policy of the unionist political parties. Informally, its political influence is pervasive; formally, the Order nominates 25 per cent of the delegates to the Ulster Unionist Council, the coordinating body of the local unionist party organizations, which in turn have authority over party policy.

After loyalism was sealed with blood in World War I and following the ANGLO-IRISH WAR, Orangeism increasingly viewed itself in a wider British and imperial, as opposed to an Irish, context. Partition reinforced further its purely Ulster identity. While Orange Lodges dwindled in the Free State with the general Protestant decline there, in Northern Ireland the Order acquired greater influence than ever. Indeed, it was almost (if never totally) synonymous with power in the state, and its celebrations and MARCHES enjoyed public status. Thus, Craig could claim in 1934 that he coveted the office of Grand Master of the Orange Institution of Co. Down 'far more than I do being Prime Minister', adding 'I am an Orangeman first and a member of this parliament afterwards'.

As the main cohesive force in Northern Irish Protestant society, Orangeism succeeded in containing its tensions for almost 50 years. But its ideology and monopolistic position rendered it incapable of dealing with modernizing forces and nationalist claims for equality from the 1960s onwards. Nor was it capable of incorporating and articulating the hardline LOYALIST response, this being best achieved by the maverick Ian PAISLEY, or the working-class unionism embodied in the Progressive Unionist Party. Thus, while the Order is still a potent force, as the annual protests at DRUMCREE and its influence in the Unionist Party testify, Protestant unity has slowly but irrevocably fragmented.

Further reading

Bryan (2000). Edwards (1999). Haddick-Flynn (1999).

Ormond family Earldom of the Butler family of Munster, along with the KILDARES and the Desmonds, one of the three most powerful Anglo-Norman families in Ireland. The title was granted to the Butlers in the mid-fourteenth century and they wielded significant power in south-west Ireland, having been granted the palatinate of Tipperary, enabling them to administer the law without outside interference. This privilege was later resented by the NEW ENGLISH in the area, who felt that the earls of Ormond enjoyed greater royal prestige than their most exalted ranks.

Owenson, Sydney see **Morgan (Lady)**

P

Paisley, Ian Kyle (1926–)   Born Co. Armagh, ordained Evangelical minister 1946, co-founder of Free Presbyterian Church of Ulster 1951, Ian Paisley has been the best-known voice of intransigent religious LOYALISM in Northern Ireland of the last 40 years. He came to prominence agitating against the demands of the CIVIL RIGHTS Campaign, and was elected to STORMONT and Westminster parliaments in 1970. Paisley's own Democratic Unionist Party, drawing on working-class loyalist disaffection with upper- and middle-class unionism, was founded in 1971. He supported the ULSTER WORKERS' COUNCIL STRIKE in 1974, and the DUP became the second-largest UNIONIST party. Paisley has been an MEP since 1979, and launched a 'Carson trail' in 1980 to protest against what he called the Thatcher-Haughey 'conspiracy'. Opposing POWER SHARING in any form, Paisley tried to block implementation of the ANGLO-IRISH AGREEMENT after 1985, and SINN FÉIN participation in the Northern Ireland Assembly before the GOOD FRIDAY AGREEMENT in 1998. Though still a substantial political force, he is not today as influential as he once was.

Further reading

Bruce (1986).

Pale, The   The name given to the English-speaking area in Ireland in the Middle Ages. The Pale was traditionally the area around DUBLIN which was under the suzerainty of the English Crown. It was also defined by its occupants as the 'land of peace' as opposed to the 'land of war' outside, where the Gaelic Irish dominated. It tended to expand and contract according to the state of the conflict and tension between the two sides, but later came to consist of the counties of Dublin, Meath, Louth and Kildare, which were the counties that most resembled English society. The Pale effectively disappeared after the NINE YEARS WAR when the Tudors were able to secure control over the whole of Ireland.

Parker, Stewart (1941–1988)   Poet, playwright and journalist. Born in East Belfast, and educated at QUB, Parker began writing as a poet in the BELFAST GROUP, publishing two poetry collections before turning to drama. His plays show a love of theatricality, a taste for the surreal and an infectious zest for life, and he wrote prolifically for radio and TELEVISION as well as the stage. This work includes *The Kamikaze Ground Staff Reunion Dinner* (1980) (for radio), and *I'm a Dreamer, Montreal* (1979), *Iris in the Traffic* and *Ruby in the Rain* (both 1981) and a six-part TELEVISION play on versions of the Deirdre MYTH, *Lost Belongings* (1987), which attacks the punitive aspects of Northern Irish society. Parker's ability to cross between different cultural levels and forge HYBRIDS is reflected in his 1970s ROCK AND POP MUSIC column for the *Irish Times* called 'High Pop', an ability which informs stage plays such as *Spokesong* (1974) and *Catchpenny Twist* (1977). 'Three Plays for Northern Ireland' – *Northern Star* (1984), *Heavenly Bodies* (1986) and *Pentecost* (1987) – deal with the UNITED IRISHMEN, the career of BOUCICAULT and the ULSTER WORKERS' STRIKE of 1974, offering an overview of the forces of both breakdown and redemption through charity and compassion.

Further reading

Richards (1988).

Parliament   Parliaments originated from the need for kings to discuss matters of state with their more important subjects (hence the name derived from 'parley', meaning 'discussion'), often as a means of extracting revenue from them in return for some political concessions. The earliest recorded parliaments in Ireland date from the thirteenth century and in 1297 the knights and lords from Ireland were summoned to DUBLIN to attend a parliament and the same group was ordered back in 1300 to subsidize the king's military budget. As the English king came to require more serious funding to finance his wars with France, parliaments were summoned with more regularity in London and Dublin. In Ireland the same process occurred as funds were sought to fight the Gaelic threat to the English colony.

The Irish parliament developed in the fifteenth century as an instrument of government where legislation relating to Ireland could be discussed and established by the MPs who came from Anglicized Irish backgrounds or were part of the colonial elite itself. When the Irish parliament supported the claims of Perkin Warbeck to be the legitimate heir to the English Crown, Henry VII supported the imposition of POYNINGS'S LAW, which decreed that the Irish parliament must defer to the English parliament. As the sixteenth century continued the Irish House of Commons began to contain more English settlers who now dominated its proceedings as spokesmen of the NEW ENGLISH. The OLD ENGLISH, who had initially co-operated with the wishes of the Crown, now resisted this new domination of what had been their political arena, causing considerable disruption of government plans in the first half of the seventeenth century. In the longer term they were less successful. By the Restoration, after the devastating effect of the Oliver CROMWELL's Land Acts, only one Catholic was returned to the Restoration parliament of 1661–66. In the eighteenth century the Irish parliament represented the interests of the Protestant ANGLO-IRISH, until challenges to this dominance came from inside and outside the house. PATRIOTS such as Henry GRATTAN started to criticize the unrepresentative nature of the Irish House of Commons inaugurating a period of political debate and conflict after legislative independence was achieved in 1782. The ACT OF UNION (1800) then dissolved the Irish parliament until it was reformed as the DÁIL ÉIREANN in 1919.

Parnell, Charles Stewart (1846–1891)   Politician. Born Avondale, Co. Wicklow, in 1846, the son of a Protestant landlord, and educated at Cambridge. He was HOME RULE MP for Meath (1875–80) and CORK city (1880–91), fast winning the soubriquet 'the uncrowned king of Ireland', as president of the LAND LEAGUE (1879), chairman of the IRISH PARLIAMENTARY PARTY (1880), and a key player in the 'New Departure', a policy which effectively united constitutionalists with more radical elements. Vitally, Parnell's wide appeal also drew the CATHOLIC CHURCH into actively supporting Home Rule. In 1880 Parnell began an affair with Katherine ('Kitty') O'Shea, a development tolerated by her husband, a fellow Home Rule party member, as long as it promised political and financial rewards; when these dissipated in 1889 he filed for DIVORCE, precipitating Parnell's downfall. The couple married in June 1891, provoking denunciation from the Catholic Church. Parnell died several months later, in England, his party bitterly divided, his reputation in tatters. Despite having little interest in literature himself, his dramatic rise and fall had a great influence on many writers of the LITERARY REVIVAL period, particularly W. B. YEATS (see the poem 'Parnell's Funeral'), and James JOYCE, who draws on Parnell's legacy in *A Portrait of the Artist* and his short story 'Ivy Day in the Committee Room'. Both writers traced many of the ills of their society to the downfall of 'the Chief'.

Patrick, St (*fl.*fifth century)   Patron saint of Ireland. Patrick's birthplace is unknown and he could have been born in Wales, Scotland or France. He was the son of Calpurnius, a British deacon and a minor official in the Roman Empire, and the grandson of a priest. He was captured by Irish pirates when he was 15 and forced to herd pigs in Antrim for six years for a chief named Milchu. He escaped back to Britain after a series of adventures on the continent and began to study for the priesthood in France. He led a mission to Ireland and started to destroy the Druidic religion which flourished there and establish Christianity as the official religion, baptizing thousands as he traversed the country. According to legend he established Armagh as the official centre for Christianity in Ireland. Other legends have Patrick expelling all the snakes from Ireland, and using the shamrock to explain the Trinity to his flock. Patrick's extant writings comprise his *Confessions*, an autobiographical account of his mission to Ireland, and a *Letter to Coroticus*, a British chief who enslaved and killed some of Patrick's converts. The cult of Patrick developed in the Middle Ages and the shrine, St Patrick's Purgatory, Lough Derg, Donegal, became an important site of pilgrimage in the twelfth century. Patrick's feast day is 17 March.

Patrick's Day Broadcast (1943)   This particular address to the nation by Éamon DE VALERA has been seen as a point of divergence between rural reality and the IRISH-IRELAND ideal of national self-sufficiency. In it he claimed that 'the Ireland we have dreamed of would be the home of a people who valued material wealth only as a basis of a right living, of a people who were satisfied with frugal comfort and devoted their leisure to things of the spirit; a land whose countryside would be bright with cosy homesteads, whose fields and villages would be joyous with sounds of industry, with the romping of sturdy children, the contents of athletic youths, the laughter of comely maidens; whose firesides would be forums for the wisdom of old age.' At the time, however, thousands were already streaming from the land to work in Britain, and EMIGRATION would accelerate in peacetime. The broadcast is contemporary with Patrick KAVANAGH's poem *The Great Hunger* (1942), which criticizes the peasant ideal.

Patriot   Name given to Protestants in the late eighteenth century who committed themselves to defending Irish interests and so tried to build bridges with Catholics. In general they opposed restrictions imposed on Ireland's freedom by English dominance and English laws, making them in favour of free trade and opposed to POYNINGS'S LAW, as well as the PENAL LAWS against the Catholics. Some patriots were angry that the ANGLO-IRISH had fewer rights than their English counterparts; others were more concerned to reform political and social life in Ireland and place adherents of each religion on an equal footing. Patriotism declined in the early nineteenth century after the defeat of the uprising of 1798 led to a more cautious and reactionary political climate. Notable patriots include SWIFT and Grattan.

Patterson, Glenn (1961–)   Novelist. A leading younger Northern Irish novelist, linked in the late 1980s with fellow BELFAST writer Robert Macliam WILSON by a media eager for new TROUBLES fiction, Glenn Patterson is the author of four novels: *Burning Your Own* (1988), *Fat Lad* (1992), *Black Night at Big Thunder Mountain* (1995) and *The International* (1999). Patterson's originality lies in the way his deceptively quiet and realistic style is played off against elements of fantasy, games-playing and autho-rial manipulation. Although Belfast and the Troubles figure in his work they are never merely a backdrop, but rather provide a climate of uncertainty within which tradi-tional narrative and character are established only to be unravelled by the forces of memory and a POSTMODERN present.

Further reading

Goodby (1999). Patten (1995).

Paulin, Thomas Neilson (1949–)   Poet and critic. Paulin grew up in BELFAST and was educated at Hull and Oxford universities. His first collections, *A State of Justice* (1977) and *The Strange Museum* (1980), owe much to a disenchanted Hardyesque English tradition. However, a fascination with the state and notions of civility and disorder reveal his Northern Irish background and the influence of the TROUBLES, and *Strange Museum* takes the Russian poet Osip Mandelstam as a figure for the pure artist resisting near-intolerable duress – an implicit comparison between Stalinist Eastern

Europe and Northern Ireland which other Irish poets would use. *Liberty Tree* (1983), written in the shadow cast by the Falklands War and the HUNGER STRIKES, plays an earlier earnestness off against a new playfulness and use of vernacular. The subject is, more clearly than before, the decline of Ulster PRESBYTERIANISM from its radical past in the UNITED IRISHMEN to a 'servile defiance that whines and shrieks/For the bondage of the letter', and 'The Book of Juniper', which uses 'liberty trees' planted in the eighteenth century to symbolize an 'equable republic', remains one of Paulin's most impressive achievements. Its historical vision and lyric condensation recur in the 'The Caravans on Lüneburg Heath', from *Fivemiletown* (1987), and *The Invasion Handbook* (2002), which treat WWII and the descent into it. A *Selected Poems* appeared in 1993.

Paulin's critical reputation was established in the early 1980s with his denunciation of critical theory in a celebrated exchange in the *Times Literary Supplement*. This provides the context for his first essay collection, *Ireland and the English Crisis* (1984). As a director of FIELD DAY, he advocated the use of Hiberno-English as a literary medium in *A New Look at the Language Question* (1983), and wrote several plays. Other critical works include *Minotaur: Poetry and the Nation State* (1992) and *The Day-Star of Liberty: William Hazlitt's Radical Style* (1999).

Further reading

Hughes, in Graham and Kirkland (eds) (1999). Wills (1993).

Pearse, Patrick (1879–1916)   Revolutionary and writer. Pearse was executed for his part in the EASTER RISING of 1916, during which he was commandant-general of the REPUBLICAN forces. He was a founder member of the IRISH VOLUNTEERS in 1913 and a member of the IRB. He had been active in the GAELIC LEAGUE since 1896, and had founded a school, Sgoil Enda, in 1907 to advance Irish education. His candid views on education were published as *The Murder Machine* (1916). His political writings include a collection of essays, *From a Hermitage* (1915), and several works of Irish political NATIONALISM, including *The Spiritual Nation* (1916) and *The Sovereign People* (1916). Pearse wrote several plays, the best known of which, *The Singer* (1915), advocates the ideal of self-sacrifice in the service of the nation. In Irish, he wrote two collections of short stories, *Iosagan* (1907) and *An Mháthair/The Mother* (1916), the prose style of which reflects living speech patterns rather than literary convention. Pearse wrote poems in both English and Irish, the latter experimenting with Gaelic prosody and poetic forms.

Further reading

Edwards (1993).

Peel, Sir Robert (1788–1850)   British politician. Probably best remembered in British history as the bridge between eighteenth- and nineteenth-century Toryism and the modern Conservative Party, Peel's parliamentary career was indelibly marked by Irish affairs – and vice versa. His first seat was as MP for Cashel (1809); as chief secretary for Ireland (1812–18) he established the Peace Preservation Force (1814) to counter rural agitation. Dubbed 'peelers', and unpopular with both peasants and landlords (who were obliged to pay for the service whether it was called for or not), the Force was replaced in 1822 by a permanent, national constabulary. An extremely able and tactical politician, Peel had long been a strenuous opponent of CATHOLIC EMANCIPATION and, in more personal terms, of Daniel O'CONNELL (the pair very nearly duelled in 1815), yet when the measure appeared inevitable he was instrumental in securing the assent of George IV to its enactment. As Prime Minister (1841–46), he resisted calls for REPEAL; instead, he won over moderate Catholics from the Repeal movement with several propitiatory measures. These included tripling a state grant to MAYNOOTH seminary, creating the QUEEN'S COLLEGES, and reforming control over Catholic charities – all of which contributed significantly to the modernization of the CATHOLIC CHURCH in Ireland and facilitated the consolidation of its social control. Many of these and other reforms were unpopular with the British establishment and Peel's government was defeated in 1846; yet his (admittedly brief) handling of the FAMINE is often favourably compared to that of his successors.

Penal Laws   Refers to a series of acts passed in the 1690s designed to prevent the Catholic clergy and laity from having any influence on Irish life and society. While Catholics had been discriminated against in the seventeenth century after the final completion of the Tudor conquest, they still exercised some power in Irish society. After the WILLIAMITE WARS Protestants became more determined to prevent Irish Catholics from participating in Irish public life.

The first penal laws were passed in 1695, preventing Catholics from possessing weapons and forbidding them from either going abroad to secure an education or teaching in and running schools within Ireland. The Bishops' Banishment Act (1697) expelled most senior Catholic clergy from Ireland by 1 May 1698. An Act of 1704 decreed that the few who were permitted to stay had to register with the relevant authorities. The Act to Prevent the Further Growth of Popery (1704), the most draconian and important of the penal laws, prevented Catholics from inheriting land or from buying land from Protestants. It also forbade Catholics from taking out leases longer than 31 years and decreed that Catholic estates had to be divided equally between male heirs on the death of the head of the family as a means of breaking up Catholic land owning. Catholics were not allowed to: serve as Members of Parliament (an Act of 1728 forced them to forfeit the right to vote); practise law; serve on juries; serve in local government; or join the army or navy. Agitation against the Acts began on a large and carefully organized scale in the second half of the eighteenth century, starting with the CATHOLIC COMMITTEE, which was supported by a number of liberal Protestants. The UNITED IRISHMEN also took up their cause, although the defeat of their revolutionary aims may have helped to set the cause back some years. The Catholic Relief Acts (1774–93) started to dismantle the extent of the penal laws. Impetus was provided by the French Revolution and the fear of rebellion spreading to Ireland if reform was not implemented, as much as a benevolent desire to right a series of wrongs. Catholics were permitted to: lease land under more favourable conditions, and eventually buy land once again; hold some government offices; teach in schools; practise the law; vote; and serve in the army and navy once again. It was only with the act establishing Catholic Emancipation in 1829 that equality before the law was achieved.

The penal laws clearly had a major effect on Irish religion and society, but their most pernicious influence was on Catholic landed society rather than all groups of Catholics in Ireland (Catholic traders and businessmen were relatively unaffected by the laws). The very harshness of the laws meant that they were not always rigorously enforced and the Catholic Church was not suppressed as the devisers of the penal laws had intended.

Further reading

Bartlett (1992).

Petrie, George (1789–1866) Antiquary and painter, one of the Ordnance Survey Memoir group and a member of the Royal Irish Academy, best known for his antiquarian studies (*The Ecclesiastical Architecture of Ireland* 1845), and for his highly popular picturesque landscapes of rural and peasant Ireland. (See also music.)

Phoenix Park murders On 6 May 1882, the newly appointed Irish Chief Secretary Lord Frederick Cavendish and the Under Secretary T. H. Burke were assassinated with knives in Phoenix Park on the outskirts of Dublin. A group known as the Invincibles were held to be responsible, and the murder encouraged Prime Minister Gladstone to keep in place his tough coercion policies. Samuel Ferguson wrote two dramatic monologues, 'At the Polo Ground' and 'In Carey's Footsteps', in response to the event. (See also Trollope.)

Plunkett, Sir Horace Curzon (1854–1932) Visionary economic activist and politician. The son of Lord Dunsany, Plunkett launched a co-operative campaign aimed at putting Irish rural workers and farmers in charge of their own economic destinies in 1889. He started a shop on his estate in Dunsany in 1895, Co. Meath, followed by another in Doneraile, Co. Cork, where a co-operative bank was also established. Plunkett's aim was to overcome the existing haphazard processing and marketing of produce and to shift power away from middlemen and dealers.

In 1894 when Plunkett founded the Irish Agricultural Organization Society (IAOS) there were 33 co-operative creameries and 13 co-operative agricultural societies; by

1915, these figures were, respectively, 344 and 219. Although UNIONIST MP for South Dublin, by 1911 he supported HOME RULE, and after Independence he was made a member of the Senate. However, he left Ireland in 1923 after the burning down of his home. His writings include *Ireland in the New Century* (1904) and *Noblesse Oblige* (1908).

The co-operative movement, in which Plunkett was the leading spirit, played a major role in improving standards in the diary industry and helping small farmers become self-sufficient. It was always hampered by insufficient capitalization; nevertheless, the movement was a remarkable success – some creamery co-operatives went on to rank among the largest firms in Ireland. The ethos and principle of co-operation, while not as effective in other areas (e.g. the meat sector), and on the retreat in today's market environment, has had a major beneficial effect on Irish rural life. See AGRICULTURE.

Further reading

Smith (1961).

Plunkett, St Oliver (1629–1681)   Catholic archbishop and martyr. Born in Co. Meath and ordained in Rome, Plunkett went to Ireland as archbishop of Armagh in 1670, with the daunting task of rebuilding the church after its reverses of the previous years during the Confederate War. He was arrested in 1679 and executed in London during the panic after the allegations of a Catholic plot to assassinate the king and overthrow the government organized by the perjurer, Titus Oates (1649–1705). Few believe that Plunkett was guilty of the charge of treason brought against him that he planned to organize a French invasion of Ireland. However, his attempts to reform the Irish Church and improve its discipline had made him many powerful enemies and a number of Franciscans testified against him. He became a symbol of the oppressed Irish Catholic Church and was beatified in 1920 and canonized in 1975.

Poor Law   Introduced to Ireland in 1838, based on the English model of 1834. The Poor Law Amendment Act introduced a national system of poor relief, financed largely by rates imposed on landowners. Workhouses for the sick, elderly and destitute were established in each district under the control of a local Board of Guardians. For most, the workhouses were a desperate last resort, and were completely overburdened during the FAMINE years of the mid-nineteenth century.

pop music see **rock and pop music**

population   There are no accurate figures for the population of Ireland before the nineteenth century. Sir William Petty made a probably over-generous estimate of 1,100,000 in 1672; this, however, is not likely to have been much above the eighth-century level, an indication that near-continuous wars, famines and plagues in the interim had kept the population static. Yet by the end of the seventeenth century it had probably reached 2,000,000. Evidence suggests that in the early eighteenth century the population continued a slow growth, reaching 3,000,000 by the 1770s. From this point on, there was a population explosion with a gap in famines and a high birth rate. On the eve of the Famine, in 1841, the Irish population was 8,175,124 and, at 254 people per square mile, it was one of the most densely populated countries in Europe.

The Famine precipitated a dizzying drop in population. By 1851, it had fallen to 6,552,386, a drop of nearly 20 per cent; in 1881 it was 5,174,836; in 1901 4,458,775. At this point, the depopulation of what would soon become Northern Ireland began to bottom out; in 1946, it had risen from its low point of 1,236,952 in 1901 to 1,334,168. The population of the Republic continued to drop after Independence, down to a low point of 2,818,341 in the census of 1961. Since then the population of Northern Ireland has grown a little to reach about 1,600,000, while that of the Republic has increased by about 50 per cent, thanks to economic expansion, reaching 3,840,000 in 2001, its highest level for the 26-county area since 1881. It is important to note that depopulation was not evenly spread. The effects of the Famine, and emigration since, disproportionately affected the poorest classes of the rural West of Ireland. Thus, while by 1979 the population of the eastern province of Leinster (which contains Dublin) had risen to 88 per cent of its 1841 figure, that of the western province of Connacht was only 29 per cent.

Factors which may maintain the increase include the peace process in Northern Ireland, which may slow emigration, and the fact that the Republic has one of the youngest populations in Europe, 38 per cent of which is under the age of 25, together with a booming economy. However, pre-Famine population levels have not yet been restored, and Ireland remains the only country which has fewer inhabitants today than it had 150 years ago. Effectively, the 'missing' population has been displaced (and multiplied) in the Irish diaspora, which has been estimated at 40–70,000,000.

Further reading

Brody (1973).

postcolonialism and colonialism Debates over the colonial status of Ireland have recently acquired increased importance to readings of Irish culture, if not so much of politics, history and economics. This development follows the expansion of colonial and postcolonial literary studies as an academic subject from the 1960s, which gave rise to work by literary theorists such as Gayatri Chakravorty Spivak, Ashis Nandy and Homi Bhabha. They, in turn, drew on earlier political theorists of colonialism, such as Franz Fanon. The conditions under which the 'postcolonial' emerged as a discipline were also deeply influenced by the more general political, critical and theoretical climate of the time, one conditioned by varieties of structuralism and poststructuralism (especially that of Jacques Derrida). Most Irish critics, in the 1960s and 1970s, were uninterested in these radical new developments; thus, while some (such as D. E. S. Maxwell) made contributions to the early development of postcolonialism in Irish literary studies, it was not until after Edward Said's *Orientalism* (1979) and the FIELD DAY COMPANY's intervention into cultural debate in the early 1980s that it acquired a full-blown postcolonial trend. In brief, the notion of the 'postcolonial' was intended to oppose the compartmentalization of history into 'before', 'during' and 'after' phases' for the colonial experience, and to see it rather as an open-ended, continuing one. The applicability of this to Ireland, where many kinds of colonization occurred over a long period of time, and where the island remains divided despite British withdrawal from part of it, is easy to grasp.

Nevertheless, the text which popularized the term 'postcolonial' (*The Empire Writes Back*) makes a point of excluding Irish literature on the grounds of Irish complicity in British imperialism, and this as late as 1989. It was also against the current of Irish historiography, which was, and is, in a largely REVISIONIST, anti-nationalist (and thus anti-colonial-interpretation) mode. Even so, the case that Ireland's history is a colonial one is irrefutable. The attempt to subjugate the island and its population by the British state was a more or less continuous feature of Irish history from the NORMAN Invasion onwards. What is more debatable is the nature of the colonial experience which ensued, its legacy, and its modern relevance. Thus, historians have focused on the degree of usurpation of native Irish land, the legal status of CATHOLICS under the PENAL LAWS, and the extent of English attempts to stifle Irish trade and manufacturing industry. One crucial issue has been the degree of British complicity in the astonishingly high death and depopulation caused by the FAMINE, and the inconceivability of its occurring elsewhere in the UK; conversely, others have pointed to the dismantling of ASCENDANCY landlordism in the LAND ACTS.

The idea that the REPUBLIC acquired nominal independence in 1921 but, hampered by Partition, remained a neo-colonial dependency, has often been made by NATIONALISTS, REPUBLICANS and Marxists. Up to a point this, too, is accurate; the Free State kept many of the structures it inherited, such as its civil service and legal institutions, even though it attempted to eradicate other aspects of British influence. For its first half century the southern state remained dependent on Britain as its main trading partner and recipient of emigrants. By the same criteria, Northern Ireland was an even more unviable entity, wholly dependent on direct British subsidy and state power. More profoundly, its sectarian divisions are a legacy of COLONIZATION and PLANTATION. Yet Northern Ireland's strategic importance, sometimes used to advance the colonial case, has long gone in an era of nuclear missiles. The presence of the British state there is better explained by its entrapment by the boundaries it allowed UNIONISTS to fix in 1925, the desire to minimize the (already considerable) political embarrassment it causes, and the wish of a well-armed majority of the population to remain British citizens.

Arguably, the Republic at least no longer has a neo- or postcolonial relationship with Britain. While Britain is still its single largest trading partner, the USA almost matches it, while the EUROPEAN UNION outstrips either. Moreover, by far the greatest amount of inward investment now comes from the USA. Similarly, the very manner in which the Troubles have been ended reveals British post-imperial weakness in Ireland, in the sense that it finally had to concede negotiating roles to the Republic, the USA and the EU, and a quasi-administrative role to the Republic. While British power is still substantial, recent Irish experience might be equally explained by the context of larger globalizing forces to which the former imperial power is now also subject. Many of the arguments which see dependency as the source of Irish ills, like those of neo-colonialism, tend to shift the focus away from divisions within Irish society, implicitly endorsing a nationalist belief that 'full' independence is the absolute prerequisite for solving all problems. Yet, despite the fact that this has not occurred, the 'CELTIC TIGER' economy has made the Republic one of the top 25 richest countries in the world. If the colonial legacy still festers, such remarkable growth surely proves that there is no ideal 'nation state' developmental model.

A variant on this position is that of the philosopher Richard Kearney, who has proposed 'postnationalism' as a means of understanding the Irish present, arguing that the emancipatory aspects of nationalism can be separated from the regressive ones by critiquing the extent to which past Irish nationalism has mirrored, in the very process of refuting, the categories of British nationalism. Postnationalism challenges Irishness based on a singular, island-bound identity, and disperses it among the multiple identities available in a Europe of the regions, of awareness of the DIASPORA, and of a globalized economic system.

Nevertheless, cultural perceptions never tamely follow facts. Liam Kennedy has claimed, on the basis of the latter, that any Irish claim to 'third world' status is wholly untenable. Comparisons with (for example) Algeria, Namibia and Egypt are, as he convincingly demonstrates, economically fallacious. But, though his arguments are empirically irrefutable, it has been claimed that Kennedy does not account for the extent to which apparently purely subjective discourses, such as that of long historical suffering, may have acquire material agency. In the words of Luke GIBBONS, 'Ireland is a first world country with a third world memory', and that memory can been seen to have had a very palpable influence upon events. It is precisely this aspect of Irish reality which many cultural commentators and critics would say constitutes a 'post-colonial' culture. The difficulty then becomes one of negotiating a postcolonial reading which does not fall into the trap of becoming merely a rehashing of older nationalist approaches. The most thoroughgoing attempt to apply a postcolonial approach to Irish writing to date, Declan Kiberd's *Inventing Ireland* (1995), has been seen by some critics as failing to achieve this aim.

What is certain is that Irish colonialism, postcolonialism or decolonization is a complex and in some ways contradictory phenomenon. One way of grasping its dialectical and ambivalent nature is to view Ireland as having been a 'metropolitan colony', which enjoyed some (limited) rights of the imperial centre, while suffering grievously in an inferior, subject position to it. Even so, Ireland's size, NEUTRAL status, record of participation in the United Nations, and unparalleled history of resistance to (as well as implication with) British power, continues to lend it an anti-imperial authority unique among European nations.

Further reading

Ashcroft, Griffiths and Tiffin (1989). Bhabha (1994). Cairns and Richards (1988). Eagleton (1995). Graham and Hooper (eds) (2002). Kearney (1997). Kiberd (1995). Lloyd, D. (1993). McCormack (1994). Said (1978). Smyth (1998).

postmodernism Ireland's relative industrial underdevelopment, until very recently, makes it an unlikely candidate for a site of postmodernism as defined by theorists of the phenomenon such as Jean-François Lyotard, Frederic Jameson and Michel Foucault. However, it has been argued by Fintan O'Toole and Luke GIBBONS, among others, that experience of the fragmentation caused by COLONIALISM, mass EMIGRATION and dislocation, and current globalization represents a form of paradoxical post-modernism, i.e. one attained before the achievement of modernity, as usually under-stood. That the 1980s and 'CELTIC TIGER' industrialization has occurred in such post-Fordist industrial sectors as pharmaceuticals and computers is taken to strengthen this argument. This postmodernism is a POSTCOLONIAL variety, a product of Irish membership of the EU zone, low corporation taxes, and a cheap yet skilled labour force. Its anomalousness is the reason why it has not been recognized hitherto by European or Anglo-American models of development.

Postmodern culture, understood as one in which depth is rejected for surface, past and future for the immediate present, the 'real' for simulacra, and in which eclectic mixings of 'high' and 'low' occur is, again, apparently at odds with the 'back-ward look' and quest for AUTHENTICITY and rootedness which characterizes much Irish culture. Moreover, the formal experimentalism of much postmodern art seems alien to an Irish preference, since the 1920s at least, for realist description and inward-looking lyric modes. However, while modernism was certainly marginalized in Ireland, the progression from modernism to postmodernism is not seen as a necessarily chronological one by theorists of the postmodern. Thus, the eighteenth-century novel *Tristram Shandy*, by STERNE, is often regarded as an exemplary postmodern text. This hints at the way the DIASPORIC dimension of Irish writing, in particular, enforces different (if overlapping) experiences of time and space, and may result in displaced, innovative artistic practices. Moreover, several Irish modernists – the James JOYCE of *Finnegans Wake*, the Flann O'BRIEN of *At Swim-Two-Birds*, and the Samuel BECKETT of *Godot* – are frequently treated as proto-postmodernists. Seen in this light, Ireland looks more central to debates about postmodernism than might at first appear. Among current Irish writers, Paul

MULDOON and John BANVILLE might also be regarded as showing distinct post-modernist inclinations.

Further reading

Gibbons (1996). Jameson (1991). O'Toole (1997).

power sharing After proroguing STORMONT in March 1972, the problem for the British government was to find a form of democratic system for Northern Ireland which did not involve the complete majoritarian dominance of Stormont. As a result, in 1973, William Whitelaw proposed a devolved assembly with executive power sharing (i.e. between political representatives of the nationalist and unionist communities) and a Council of Ireland. The ALLIANCE Party and the SDLP accepted this, while a moderate majority of the UNIONIST Party (calling themselves the 'Official Unionists' and led by Brian Faulkner, Chichester-Clarke's successor) did so, if guardedly. There were elections for the Assembly in June 1973, which gave 26 per cent of the vote to the Official Unionists, 22 per cent to the SDLP, and 9 per cent to the Alliance Party. However, unionist parties opposed to the proposals polled 35 per cent of the vote, a majority of Protestants.

A power-sharing executive was agreed in 22 November 1973, giving due representation to all parties represented in the Assembly. On 9 December, under the Sunningdale Agreement, British and Irish Prime Ministers, along with executive representatives, agreed to the establishment of a Council of Ireland. The principle established was that a solution to the TROUBLES required tackling the three-way relationship between London, BELFAST and DUBLIN. For Faulkner, this was a purely nominal concession, since the Irish government had 'fully accepted' that there could be no change in the status of Northern Ireland until a majority of the population agreed it. Nevertheless, he was immediately repudiated by the Ulster Unionist Council and was forced to resign as party leader. He was succeeded by Harry West. Although he continued to be supported by most Official Unionist MPs, and remained chief of the Assembly executive, his position was weakened. At the same time, however, the executive assumed office, effectively ending direct rule, at the beginning of January 1974.

In the general election in February 1974, Faulkner and his supporters were routed by the United Ulster Unionist Council (UUUC) formed to bring together all the shades of unionist opinion against him. Both the IRA and the UUUC now attempted to destroy the authority of the executive and the Sunningdale Agreement. Faulkner and the Assembly limped on until May 1974 until its bluff was called when the Ulster Workers Council mounted a general strike (the ULSTER WORKERS' COUNCIL STRIKE) with the UUUC and brought it down, ending power sharing for 25 years.

Poynings's Law An act passed in the Irish PARLIAMENT in 1494 having been introduced by the LORD DEPUTY, Edward Poynings, which decreed that the Lord Deputy and his council in Ireland had to ask the English monarch's permission to hold a parliament in Ireland and to obtain his or her approval for any bills that were to be introduced. The aim was to restrict the power and freedom of manoeuvre of the Lord Deputy, specifically the KILDARE family who had often occupied the post, rather than bind the Irish parliament as a subordinate institution to its English counterpart. This, however, was the way the law was subsequently perceived and how it often worked until it effectively ceased to function when legislative independence was achieved in 1782. It could also function as a means of preventing the will of the Lord Deputy from becoming law automatically and allowing opposition MPs to refer proposed legislation back to England for approval or modification.

Presbyterianism   In Ireland Presbyterianism is largely restricted to the north-east and was imported in the early seventeenth century with the establishment of the ULSTER PLANTATION which was populated by a large number of low-church Scottish Protestants. While some remained inside the CHURCH OF IRELAND in the early years of the seventeenth century, most were purged by Thomas WENTWORTH, the Lord Deputy, when he tried to unite the official church under the doctrine of Arminianism.

Presbyterians believe that the church should be governed by its elders and so tend to regard the Church of Ireland's episcopalian structure (government by bishops who are appointed, not elected) as far too close to CATHOLICISM to constitute a reformed church. They also tend to be committed to the doctrine of predestination and believe that mankind is too wicked to save itself by its own efforts and needs to be saved by the intervention of God. Irish Presbyterianism has often been characterized as a faith which has two distinct and not always congruent sides. There is a fierce sense of independence and self-righteous belief that refuses to compromise with other churches because Presbyterians believe that they alone hold the true doctrine of Christianity and see all opposition as a sign of their opponents' worldly weakness. There is also a more ecumenical side to Presbyterianism which derives from the democratic form of church government adopted and stresses the equality of all men and women in the eyes of God, and has often played a significant part in political reform in Ireland, notably the UNITED IRISHMEN.

Presbyterianism was granted official sanction in the Toleration Act of 1719, which allowed Presbyterians the same rights of worship as their Church of Ireland counterparts. However, they were still forced to pay tithes (church taxes) to the official church which, given the fact that most were lowly tenant farmers, ensured that many emigrants to America in the eighteenth century were Presbyterians.

In the early nineteenth century Presbyterianism continued to be a major influence on the culture and identity of Ulster. Its links to the political radicalism of 1798 were seriously undermined, however, by a series of public debates in the late 1820s between the fundamentalist and unionist Henry Cooke, and the advocate of 'New Light' liberalism Henry Montgomery. The resultant schism of 1829 weakened the profile of

Presbyterianism in Ireland, though the presence of the Dissenters would remain a major consideration in the campaign for the Disestablishment of the Church of Ireland later in the century. The liberal Remonstrant Synod, followers of Montgomery, remained in a minority; joining with the Presbytery of Antrim and the Synod of Munster, they formed the Non-Subscribing Presbyterian Church in Ireland and, in the early 1990s, had some 4,500 members. Followers of Cooke, in the Synod of Ulster, formed the Presbyterian Church in Ireland in 1840, and remain today by far the largest Presbyterian church, with around 400,000 members.

Perhaps the most remarkable modern Irish literary expression of Presbyterianism is that of the poet W. R. Rodgers, who was himself a Presbyterian minister from 1935 to 1946, and in whose work Christian doctrine is often retold in vivid, even sensual, terms. Another literary work which helps complicate a too-rigid understanding of Presbyterianism is Sam Hanna Bell's novel *December Bride* (1951). The twentieth century saw the emergence of one new Presbyterian Church in Northern Ireland, the Ian Paisley-led Free Presbyterian Church, which was founded in 1951. This church accused the main Presbyterian body of 'modernism', and was vehement in its opposition to ecumenicism, secularism and the Roman Catholic Church. Paisley, originally from a Baptist background, became its first and (to date) only moderator. By 1990 there were 11,500 members in over 50 congregations, one of which was in the Republic.

Further reading

Brooke (1987). Bruce (1986). Stewart (1989).

Progressive Democrats   Political party founded in 1985 as a split from Fianna Fáil and Fine Gael, they were a product of the ideological climate generated in the Western world by 1980s economic neo-liberalism. Their aim was to hold the balance of power between the larger parties and use this in order to insist on neo-liberal legislation of the kind pursued by those leaders (privatization, cutting of public expenditure, etc.). They have formed coalition governments with Fianna Fáil in 1989–92, and since 1997.

Protestantism see **Ascendancy, Anglo-Irish, Catholicism, Church of Ireland, Patriot, Presbyterianism, Reformation, Stormont, loyalism**

Queen's Colleges   Created by the P<small>EEL</small> government of 1845 as one of a series of measures aimed at mitigating demands for R<small>EPEAL</small>, the colleges (at B<small>ELFAST</small>, C<small>ORK</small>, Galway and later D<small>UBLIN</small>) were intended to provide non-denominational third-level education in Ireland. Highly controversial, they were resisted by many members of the Irish Catholic clergy, and denounced by O'C<small>ONNELL</small> as the 'godless colleges'.

radio see **television and radio**

Rebellion of 1641   A key event not just in Ireland itself but also in the developing conflict between the British Crown and the parliamentary forces, often now called the War of the Three Kingdoms rather than the English Civil War. The rebellion broke out in Ulster on 22 October under the loose command of Sir Phelim O'N<small>EILL</small> and Rory O'More, each of whom headed a different faction of rebels. The rebellion was principally motivated by a fear that the property rights of native aristocrats would be attacked by the parliamentary forces loyal to the puritan administration that now ran Ireland after the execution of Thomas W<small>ENTWORTH</small>, although there was also some opposition to the U<small>LSTER</small> P<small>LANTATION</small>. The rebellion developed into an unstable and confusing conflict between a combination of O<small>LD</small> E<small>NGLISH</small> and native Irish forces (known as the Catholic Confederates, after the signing of the Confederation of Kilkenny, 7 June 1642) against Irish Royalists and supporters of the developing parliamentary faction in Ireland. Although the rebellion may have been intended as more of a show of force than an attempt to expel the English from Ireland, it quickly developed into a religious struggle with the leaders of the rebellion split between royalists and Catholics keen to establish an independent Ireland.

The rebellion developed into the Confederate War in the following decade. Eóghan Ruadh Ó Neill returned from service abroad to lead the Confederate army in 1642, allied with the dogmatic and uncompromising papal nuncio, Cardinal Rinuccini, who arrived in Ireland in 1645. James Butler, first Duke of O<small>RMOND</small>, led the opposing crown forces, becoming L<small>ORD</small> L<small>IEUTENANT</small> in 1644. After a truce the crown forces were defeated at the Battle of Benburb (1646) and Ormond offered the Confederates exemption from the Oath of Supremacy if they ended the conflict. Rinuccini countered by threatening excommunication for those who accepted these terms and the war continued. The war was effectively ended by CROMWELL's campaign in 1649, and the confiscation of Catholic land legitimized in subsequent Act of Settlement (1652) and Act of Satisfaction (1653).

The conflict soon became notorious for the extensive massacres of Protestants that took place. However, these were undoubtedly exaggerated in such propagandist works as Sir John Temple's *Irish Rebellion* (1646), a widely read work, which claimed that 300,000 Protestants had been murdered in a premeditated uprising plotted by the Irish and the Spanish who used the excuse of loyalty to Charles I for their own evil ends. Temple's work contains a number of graphic woodcuts depicting unspeakable acts of violence, and the work mainly contains a list of atrocities described at great length (children boiled alive, unborn infants ripped from their mothers' wombs, adults drowned in rivers, and so on). When Oliver Cromwell massacred the inhabitants of Drogheda and Wexford he claimed that he was only behaving as the Irish Catholics had done, indicating the hold that works such as Temple's had on the English Protestant imagination, and they were reprinted regularly well into the nineteenth century.

Modern estimates suggest that some 4,000 Protestants were killed in the uprising, and perhaps an equal number of Catholics in reprisals. The evidence is largely contained in the sworn depositions of Protestants collected in TCD library, statements which demand careful and sceptical analysis.

Further reading

Canny (2001). Mac Cuarta (ed.) (1993).

Redmond, John (1856–1918)   Politician. Redmond was leader of the Parnellite minority of the IRISH PARLIAMENTARY PARTY (IPP) from 1891 to 1900, when he reunited the party. He gained Liberal Party support for the Third HOME RULE Bill in 1912. Redmond believed that by supporting the war effort in WWI Ireland would earn the right to Home Rule, although this had been suspended in 1914 after being passed in the Commons, largely due to the opposition of Ulster UNIONISTS. His appeal to NATIONALISTS to enlist in the British Army at a speech at Woodenbridge on 20 September swayed most IRISH VOLUNTEERS, but left a rump of 10,000 unconvinced. These became the reservoir for the EASTER RISING. Although he opposed the executions of PEARSE, CONNOLLY and the others, Redmond and the IPP were soon swept away by events; he died not long before his party were crushed by SINN FÉIN at the election of 1918.

Further reading

Mansergh (1960).

Reformation and Counter-Reformation The inspiration for the Reformation began when Martin Luther challenged the right of the church to interpret the scriptures. Its spread throughout Europe was complicated and uneven, but before the seventeenth century the continent was split into two hostile camps of Protestants keen to reform the church and Catholics loyal to the papacy. This split was confirmed by the Council of Trent (1545–63) when the papacy assembled its church leaders to plan a concerted opposition to the advance of Protestantism by establishing a better-educated and more militant clergy.

The Reformation and Counter-Reformation in Ireland cannot be separated from the history of religion in England. The Reformation was inaugurated in England when Henry VIII, who had been a loyal servant of the church, sued for an annulment of his marriage to Catherine of Aragon because she had previously been married to his elder brother, Arthur (which Henry felt explained why he and Catherine had failed to produce a male heir). With Henry making himself the head of the church in England he also had to make himself the head of the church in Ireland. This was duly performed in the Reformation parliament in Ireland (1536). There was, of course, significant opposition to the new changes in church government and doctrine in England but the problem was far more serious in Ireland. The vast majority of the population adhered to the Catholic Church and opposed the Protestant state. Catholicism became a central constituent of an Irish identity defined against a Protestant Englishness, a division accepted by both sides. John Bale (1495–1563), who was bishop of Ossory for a brief period in 1552, prefaced his account of his experiences in Ireland, *The Vocacyon* (1553), with a woodcut depicting the English Christian and the Irish papist, showing that religious identities had become elided with national ones. Later in the century Hugh O'Neill was able to launch a serious challenge to English rule by uniting the various factions in Ireland under the banner of Catholicism. While there were attempts to convert Ireland to a more radical Protestantism during the reign of Edward VI (1547–53), Elizabeth (1558–1603) and James (1603–25) accepted that compromises had to be made. The Bible was translated into Irish (1558), a labour which helped to preserve Irish as a language rather than ease its replacement by English by making the Irish loyal Protestant servants of the crown as some of the sponsors of the work hoped. Trinity College was established (1592) to rival the Catholic seminaries and train Protestant ministers. The Reformation made no more real progress under James, although he established Ulster as a Protestant province through the establishment of the Ulster Plantation.

Historians are divided about the lack of progress of the Reformation in Ireland. Was it always doomed to failure? Or could Protestantism have taken root in Ireland if it had not been so clearly united to English coercion? It is clear that Catholicism also flourished because of a systematic campaign of conversion after the first Jesuit mission arrived in 1542. In 1570 Pope Pius V declared that Elizabeth was a heretic and should be deposed by loyal Catholics, an act that had disastrous consequences for

English Catholics but helped to fuel resistance in Ireland. The papal envoy, James Fitzmaurice, sent over to help the Irish during the Desmond Rebellion, declared Irish military efforts to be a holy war. There was concerted resistance to English rule after the Spanish Armada (1588). There was also a concerted attempt to reform the Irish Catholic Church in the 1590s when the Irish seminary was established at Salamanca in 1592. Although the exact level of success of the Catholic Church in controlling religious life in Ireland cannot be measured, it had enough support in the 1640s to establish the Confederate alliance and oppose the Protestant forces led by Oliver CROMWELL.

Further reading

Corish (ed.) (1985). Ford (1997).

Repeal and the Repeal Movement Repeal of the ACT OF UNION and the restoration of the Irish Parliament in DUBLIN was the focus of much nationalist activity once CATHOLIC EMANCIPATION had been granted in 1829. The calls for Repeal were led by Daniel O'CONNELL, who hoped to secure the measure from the progressive British government that was instigating wide reforms at home; in this he was disappointed, a vote in parliament on the motion in 1834 being defeated by 523 votes to 38. Repeal was then effectively sidelined until the advent of the YOUNG IRELAND movement and their newspaper the *NATION* at the start of the 1840s. O'Connell soon returned to the issue, employing the politics of mass agitation that had served so effectively in the campaign for Emancipation. 1843 was, he declared, the Repeal Year, resulting in a series of 'monster meetings', the greatest of which was due to take place in Clontarf, only to be banned by Prime Minister PEEL. The Young Irelanders and O'Connell soon came to disagree about the direction the Repeal movement should take, the former advocating decisive violent action, the latter arguing for more constitutional methods. After O'Connell's death in 1847 and the failed rising of 1848 the demands of the Repeal movement abated for a time before finding new expression as FENIANISM and, in time, re-emerging as calls for HOME RULE.

Republic of Ireland (1949) In the CONSTITUTION of 1937, the Free State was referred to as Éire (Ireland). In 1948, a clearer redefinition occurred when a coalition government under John A. COSTELLO of FINE GAEL deprived FIANNA FÁIL of power for the first time since 1932. At this point the External Relations Act still allowed the British monarch to appoint and receive envoys and ratify treaties on behalf of the Free State. To end this, Costello's government enacted a Republic of Ireland Act in 1948 and symbolically declared a Republic on Easter Monday 1949. This broke the final links with the Commonwealth.

However, the Republic continued to enjoy economic, social and trading relationships not normally granted to foreign states (the right of its citizens to vote in British elections, and to travel there without a passport or visa, for example). For reasons of expediency, the British state treated the Republic as if it were still a Commonwealth member.

Westminster responded to the declaration of a Republic by passing the Ireland 1949 Act. This allowed Irish citizens to benefit from exemptions contained in the British Nationality Act. On the negative side (for those desiring reunification), in response to UNIONISTS' demands for confirmation of their British status, it also declared that no part of Northern Ireland would cease to be a part of the UK without the consent of STORMONT.

The declaration of the Republic, an attempt to steal some of Fianna Fáil's anti-colonial clothing, was therefore a paradoxical act. For some REPUBLICANS, the Republic already existed (even if it was not yet fulfilled territorially). To them, legislative ratification of a Republic was therefore both an impertinence and a reminder of territorial incompletion. On the other hand, the declaration was an assertion of moderate republican intent which ended a humiliating constitutional relationship with Britain. Nevertheless, it could also be read as an acceptance of the circumscribed territory of the partitioned state.

Further reading

Ryan (ed.) (2000).

republicanism   In its purest form republicanism is an eighteenth-century European political philosophy for organizing society without a monarchy and hereditary aristocracy. It received its greatest endorsements and practical tests in the American and French Revolutions at the end of the eighteenth century, and it was these which informed Irish republicanism. But, although republicanism as an expression of Irish nationalist separatist aspirations can be traced to the UNITED IRISHMEN's revolt in 1798, republicanism was slow to spread in nineteenth-century Ireland. The YOUNG IRELAND movement of the 1840s attempted to 'Gaelicize' republicanism, but in cultural terms this failed to occur before the rise of the LITERARY REVIVAL in the 1890s; in the meantime, republicanism had fused with a rural tradition of clandestine armed resistance to landlordism represented by groups such as the DEFENDERS. In the post-FAMINE period, this can be seen in the rise of the FENIANS in the 1850s and the IRISH REPUBLICAN BROTHERHOOD.

Republicanism held minority appeal as long as constitutional nationalism made advances, as it did with the IRISH PARLIAMENTARY PARTY and the campaign for HOME RULE in the late nineteenth century. Thus, SINN FÉIN separatism, under Arthur GRIFFITH before World War I, envisaged not an Irish Republic but a Dual Monarchy, along the lines of Austria-Hungary, reflecting Irish society's deep conservatism; nor did republicanism, as elsewhere, acquire an anti-clerical agenda. In 1916, the EASTER RISING, a republican and socialist revolt under PEARSE and CONNOLLY, had little popular support; it was the peculiar circumstances of WWI and British brutality which generated majority support for independence. Even so, a majority of the population supported the compromise of the Anglo-Irish Treaty in 1921. Still, the new state was informed with a republican ethos, and this intensified after Fianna Fáil came to power in 1932. The 'Gaelicization' of republicanism was marked during the mid-century, even though it conflicted with the realities of poor economic performance and mass emigration. In the 1960s, however, Fianna Fáil, as the mainstream republican party, was able to redefine its republicanism in terms of managerialism and economic openness, rather than of autarky and isolation. This ideological modernization coincided with a related, but opposed Marxist, anti-imperialist critique of the state emerging among the leadership of the IRA. Yet, with the breakaway of the Provisional IRA, a tradition of reading Irish history as undiluted victimhood and resistance resurrected 'physical force' republicanism in Northern Ireland. Moreover, in the Arms Trial (1970), Fianna Fáil itself revealed that it had yet to break free of the thought-patterns of the militant republicanism from which it had emerged.

Loyalism's focus on the Crown (as opposed to the democratic structures of the British state) reveals the extent to which it is militant republicanism's mirror image. It was in an attempt to deconstruct this violent circularity that attempts were made, in the late 1970s, to elaborate a more utopian, idealist and non-violent form of republicanism. This can be seen in the notion of the 'Fifth Province' which was first floated by Mark Patrick Hederman and Richard Kearney in *The Crane Bag* (see literary journals). This idea took its cue from the fact that there was, in medieval Ireland, a central, fifth province, called Midhe (Middle); this, for Hederman and Kearney, and later for members of the Field Day collective, came to symbolize a Platonic republican ideal of a future united Ireland beyond contemporary polarization and violence. Although mocked at the time, it can be argued that the notion has been partly echoed in the shift away from violence to a peace process by the IRA and Sinn Féin, with their ceasefire and acceptance that a more inclusive republic, or elements of one, are best achieved through democratic engagement.

Revisionism A term applied to purportedly value-free history, often used pejoratively. Broadly speaking, it applies to a research-based, empirically detailed historical study which, since the late 1950s, has supplanted nationalist- and unionist-biased Irish history. The second of these, often termed 'Whig' history, can be traced back to J. A. Froude in the nineteenth century, whose account of Irish history justified the progressive mission of British rule, adducing the more economically advanced Belfast area as proof of his argument. Froude was opposed in his time by W. E. H. Lecky, the founder of a modern nationalist historical tradition (although Lecky himself was in favour of the Union and opposed Home Rule). After Independence, a version of nationalist history which saw the previous 800 years as totally dominated by the struggle against Britain was dominant in the Free State. It was against this 'mythic' and simplified Irish history that the historians described as Revisionist have opposed themselves, pointing to what they see as the disjointed, sporadic and sometimes positive aspects of British activities in Ireland.

The Revisionist historiographical achievement is complicated by the claim sometimes made by its practitioners that it is accurate because it is 'value-free'. Critics of this claim point out that, philosophically speaking, it is impossible to be totally objective. Moreover, they note that many Revisionist historians reject the possibility of the existence of larger historical patterns and rhythms in advance because their focus is, almost by definition, reliant on a detailed and therefore often limited focus on an isolated period or phenomenon. This means that within the very methodology of these historians certain 'values' are implicit. Crucially, some argue, the apparently objective stance is effectively an endorsement of the status quo – frequently seen by anti-Revisionists as that of the European-inclined ruling- and middle-classes embarrassed by, and seeking to disown, uncomfortable aspects of the nation's past. Moreover, by too great a reliance on material facts, their opponents suggest that Revisionists have evaded the importance of less quantifiable discourses of national destiny or self-image as factors motivating action. Against this, Revisionist historians have countered by arguing that much of what passes as discourse theory or post-colonial interpretations of Irish history is actually old nationalist history in disguise. Anti-Revisionists are seen as symptomatic of a national difficulty in coming to terms with MODERNIZATION and as clinging on to comforting illusions concerning Irish exceptionalism and self-privileging victimhood.

It can be argued that both sets of historians, anti- and pro-Revisionist, have tended to regard certain areas of the historical record – such as women's and working-class history (see FIELD DAY) – as peripheral. This is just one example which suggests that the debate will continue, and that there is no simple or single answer to these several conflicting interpretations of Irish history. What is certain, however, is that, just as the most important recent achievements in Irish cultural studies have relied on new theoretical approaches, so the major advances in Irish historiography have been sustained by a 'Revisionist' insistent focus on empirical detail, and this in turn points to the inadequacy of the term itself.

Further reading

Boyce and O'Day (eds) (1996).

Revival see **Literary Revival**

Robinson, Mary (1944–) Born in Co. Mayo and educated at TCD and Harvard University, Robinson became at 25 TCD's youngest professor of law and subsequently a barrister and senator. She achieved prominence through her support for reform, championing human, civil and, in particular, women's rights in areas such as DIVORCE and CONTRACEPTION. In 1990 she stood as an independent candidate for President with the support of LABOUR and other smaller parties; and, aided by the FIANNA FÁIL candidate's implication with Charles HAUGHEY in a cover-up, she scored a triumph against all the odds. Robinson soon became the most popular ever holder of the office, breaking with its moribund traditions in a series of symbolic yet powerful gestures which included the reading of poetry by Paul DURCAN and Eavan BOLAND at her inauguration, overtures towards Northern Protestants, and the placing of a candle in the window of the presidential residence, Áras an Uachtarán, to symbolize a welcome to the global 'family' of the Irish DIASPORA. Robinson represented, and advanced, the ideals of those hoping for a more tolerant, pluralist Irish society. In 1997, she stepped down to become the United Nations High Commissioner for Human Rights. She resigned from it in 2002, citing interference from the newly elected Bush administration in the USA as the cause.

rock and pop music   For various reasons (cultural, logistical and technical) Ireland was slow to develop a pop and rock music industry in the 1950s and 1960s, although a distinctive musical youth culture quickly emerged. Individual artists, such as Gary Moore, Rory Gallagher and VAN MORRISON achieved international fame in this period, but usually by relocating to England or the USA. The first Irish rock band of international note were Thin Lizzie, founded in the late 1960s. They were fronted by Phil Lynott, perhaps the first person of colour to achieve public prominence in Ireland; their repertoire included a rock version of the traditional Irish ballad 'Whiskey in the Jar'. A more extensive exploitation of the rock crossover with TRADITIONAL MUSIC was practised by Horslips, inventors and purveyors of 'Celtic rock' in the early 1970s.

At this stage the Irish influence on the course of popular music was felt mainly through Irish-descent musicians in Britain, following the examples of John Lennon and Paul McCartney (both of whom later wrote songs expressing Irish NATIONALIST sympathies). This fruitful tradition encompasses such innovative groups as Dexy's Midnight Runners, headed by Kevin Rowland, whose album *Searching for the Young Soul Rebels* (1980) infused Stax soul with a specifically West Midland Irish sense of alienation (in a Birmingham remembering the 1974 pub bombings) while successor works *Too-Rye-Ay* (1982) and *Don't Stand Me Down* (1983) charted a course through use of Irish folk trappings to rejection of racist stereotyping. Other bands showing a distinctive Irish-informed sense of dislocation within British society included the Sex Pistols, whose lead singer Johnny Rotten (John Lydon) was, like Rowland, of Irish parentage. The Pistols' most notorious single, 'God Save the Queen' (1977), was a withering attack on the monarchy in the year of the Silver Jubilee, and only kept from the number 1 spot by the rigging of sales figures, while the title of Lydon's autobiography – *Rotten: No Irish, No Blacks, No Dogs* (1991) – speaks for itself.

Other examples of this phenomenon include the Smiths, fronted by Morrissey, who were massively influential pioneers of Mancunian lyric angst, and Oasis, arguably the biggest British band of the 1990s, based around the brothers Liam and Noel Gallagher. Elvis Costello, né Declan McManus, was the most impressive songwriter of the post-punk New Wave, creating a string of classic albums which included *My Aim Is True* (1977), *This Year's Model* (1978) and *Armed Forces* (1980); the later *Spike* (1987) contains overtly Irish instrumentations and ballads. The London-Irish sense of self-assertion found a direct outlet in the much-acclaimed Pogues. Led by their lyrically brilliant, hard-living lead singer Shane McGowan, the Pogues released albums such as *Rum, Sodomy and the Lash* (1985) which spliced traditional music and punk, and ranged from scabrous satire to haunting elegy. Their chief progeny in Ireland were the Saw Doctors from Tuam in Co. Mayo, who flourished in the mid-1990s.

In Ireland itself, the dominant popular musical medium in the 1950s and 1960s was the showbands, large ensemble groups which mixed current pop and rock cover versions in sets which provided opportunities for dancing and mingling with the opposite sex. These declined in the face of competition from the international rock and pop industry. Part of the gap was filled by traditional music, which incorporated elements of rock and reached new creative heights through groups such as the Bothy Band in the early 1970s. This success led to ever more ambitious attempts to mix musical styles, seen at its most successful in Moving Hearts and the career of Paul Brady. A healthy tradition of Irish-based rock bands of originality and merit definitely established itself from the punk period, which produced two outstanding bands – Stiff Little Fingers and the Undertones, in BELFAST and DERRY respectively – and DUBLIN's Boomtown Rats, fronted by Bob Geldof (Geldof would go on to organize the Band Aid fundraiser for aiding Ethiopian FAMINE victims, and the international Live Aid concert in 1986). One response to the take-off which helped maintain it was the introduction by RTÉ of Radio 2, a popular music channel, in 1979. These developments produced a range of innovative bands in the 1980s, such as the Hothouse Flowers, the Fatima Mansions, In Tua Nua and one band with a global reputation, U2. The 1980s also saw the development of a market for Celtic-theme easy listening, one catered to by leading singers such as Mary Black, formerly of De Danaan, and Enya, formerly lead singer of the IRISH LANGUAGE traditional group Clannad.

The granting of tax breaks to resident creative artists by the government in the Republic, which would do so much for the Irish FILM industry, helped make Dublin a centre of the recording industry from the late 1980s; some musicians, such as Elvis Costello, even relocated there. The Irish-black association, drawn on by CIVIL RIGHTS campaigners in Northern Ireland, was now made at a musical level in Ireland, as in the film *The Commitments* (1991), just as it had been by Dexy's a decade before. The traditional edginess of Irish musicians was maintained in the 1990s by perhaps the most provocative of them all, the singer Sinead O'Connor. O'Connor's career began through the good offices of In Tua Nua and U2 and trailed a quantity of controversy which was never quite matched by her musical output; her second album *I Do Not Want What I Have Not Got* (1990) is her best, while the success of her cover of Prince's

'Nothing Compares 2U' single of the same year was massive, but unrepeatable. However, O'Connor's gestures – publicly ripping up a photo of the Pope, boycotting a concert when 'The Star-Spangled Banner' was played and withdrawing from the Grammy Award ceremony – raised important political issues, even if they could also be confused and contradictory.

The best-known Irish acts since the mid-1990s have been noted more for conformity than rebellion; this may be linked to the 'CELTIC TIGER' prosperity of the Republic and of the peace process in Northern Ireland. They include The Corrs and Boyzone, one of a rash of 'boy bands' of the period.

Further reading

Campbell (1998). Clayton-Lea and Taylor (1992). O'Connor (2001). Prendergast (1987, 1992).

Royal Irish Academy   The Royal Irish Academy was founded in 1785 to promote the study of science, polite literature, and ANTIQUARIANISM. Its membership from the outset comprised academics, clergymen, lawyers, members of parliament, and assorted nobility. By the mid-nineteenth century, when figures such as George PETRIE, Samuel FERGUSON and William WILDE were members, the Academy had become the most important and prestigious learned society in the country. The findings of the Academy were published in *Transactions* (1787–1907) and *Proceedings* (1836 to the present), both exemplary journals. The Academy's work in cataloguing and translating ancient Irish texts did much to transform thinking about the Irish past, while the rigorous scholarship it fostered in this field did much to debunk the speculation of more amateurish antiquarians. The library of the Academy holds Ireland's largest collection of ancient manuscripts as well as many other valuable documents and artefacts relevant to the study of Irish culture.

Russell, George see **'AE'**

S

Sayers, Peig (1973–1958)   Storyteller. Sayers was born in Dunquin, Co. Kerry, and, through marriage, went to live on the Great Blasket Island. Her fame as a storyteller led, through the offices of Máire Ní Chinnéide, to the dictation of her classic autobiography, *Peig* (1936), to her son, Micheál Ó Gaoithín. For generations of schoolchildren, *Peig* was a not-always-welcome rite of passage in the IRISH LANGUAGE. But the book is necessary reminder of the hardships and rewards of island life in her lifetime, and reveals great narrative skill in its construction and phrasing. A collection of some 360 of her stories, recorded by Seosamh Ó Dálaigh, is held by the Irish Folklore Commission.

Further reading

Coughlan (2003).

sex and sexuality While Irish CATHOLIC attitudes to the place of sexual activity before the FAMINE seem to have been consistent with those of similar societies of the time in Europe, the values of the last century and a half have been shaped by the response to it, known as FAMILISM, which controlled population growth on the land through deferred marriage and widespread celibacy. This produced a low marriage rate, high celibacy rate and large FAMILY size; couples married late, but had large families. While Irish Protestants tended to follow British and general Western trends to smaller family sizes, and more liberal attitudes to sex, these did not apply to Irish Catholics.

The Catholic Church played a crucial part in these processes. Given its central role to the stabilization of post-Famine Ireland, it was able to exercise a good deal of influence on the ethos of the Free State, giving it a theocratic cast which was confirmed in the 1937 CONSTITUTION. The Church's attitude to relations between the sexes was patriarchal, based on the belief that responsibility for Original Sin lay with women, and that this placed the onus on them to prevent sexual sin. Sexual passion was controlled through the inculcation of guilt concerning sexual matters, and through an extensive clerical monitoring of the penitent's sexual being through confession. In this climate, sex and sin became almost synonymous. Women, from this point of view, were regarded as complementing men, but subordinate to them. They were effectively defined by their childbearing biological function as 'naturally' destined for home-making and family-rearing, and work after marriage was either prevented or frowned upon. Within this moral economy, however, women's presumed greater ability to control sexual passions was seen as revealing their potentially distinctive, refined nature. This potential was focused on the figure of the Virgin Mary, who combined the otherwise exclusive roles of virgin and mother. A role model for women to aspire to, Mary was nevertheless, in her flawless perfection, an unattainable ideal, and thus one which ultimately confirmed female weakness.

The church's binding of sex to reproduction has powerfully shaped the role of sex in Catholic Irish society, because it defined it rigidly in terms of the family unit, with the family unit in turn seen as the cornerstone and paradigm for society as a whole. This made it difficult to envisage sexuality in non-heterosexual terms, as a personal right, or as an experience to be enjoyed for its own sake; or to recognize the validity of less orthodox family arrangements (this is one reason why the disconnection of sexuality from reproduction has been such a central preoccupation for so many Irish writers). Because there is so much at stake, issues which from a secular or liberal viewpoint appear as private matters of conscience and lifestyle – such as CONTRACEPTION,

DIVORCE and ABORTION – acquired a public and bitterly contentious character. Nevertheless, in liberal compliance with a ruling from the European Court of Human Rights in Strasbourg, in June 1993 the Justice Minster Maire Geoghegan Quinn set the homosexual age of consent at 17 – the same as for heterosexuals, and lower than in the UK, where it remains 18.

The hypocrisy, concealment and abuse of power which results from long suppression of sexual matters was revealed in the 1990s in a series of devastating scandals and exposures. These began with the SMYTH CASE, and that of Éamon Casey, the Bishop of Galway, who was revealed to be the father of a teenage son. They have continued ever since, with 48 priests and religious brothers now convicted of child abuse, over a score of further cases awaiting trial, and more than 400 legal actions resulting from alleged abuse in industrial schools run by the church awaiting settlement. In one recent case, a priest who was the subject of complaints of the sexual abuse of children was transferred by Cardinal Desmond Connell, the Bishop of Dublin and leader of the church, to a hospital that treated children; the hospital was not informed of the complaints.

Further reading

Foucault (1990).

Shaw, George Bernard (1856–1950)   Playwright and socialist activist. Shaw was born in DUBLIN but spent most of his life in London, where he began his literary career as a novelist and reviewer. There he became involved in politics, and in 1884 joined a newly formed socialist party, the Fabians, marking the beginning of a life-long commitment to humanitarianism and non-revolutionary socialism. Shaw continued to support himself with journalism and review work, but soon his keen interest in music led him towards the stage. In 1885, he was asked to collaborate on a play, which was eventually entitled *Widowers' Houses* and performed at London's Royalty Theatre in 1892. Heavily influenced by Henrik Ibsen, the work dealt with the social ills of unscrupulous landlords and their treatment of overcrowded, exploited tenants. This was followed by *Mrs Warren's Profession*, which, controversially, dramatized the subject of prostitution, and was refused a licence by the Lord Chamberlain. Along with a third play, *The Philanderer*, these pieces were grouped together under the title of *Plays Unpleasant*, and were followed in 1898 by a series of *Plays Pleasant*: *Arms and the Man*, set in the Bulgarian/Serbian war, *Candida*, *The Man of Destiny*, and *You Never Can Tell*. In these works, Shaw displayed his skill for social and romantic comedy without abandoning his tendency towards political or philosophical comment.

Shaw married an Irish heiress, Charlotte Payne Townsend, in 1898, by which time he had adopted a highly disciplined lifestyle as a strict, non-smoking, teetotal vegetarian. Idealism – and its attendant problems – were appropriately the subject of his *Plays for Puritans*, written in this period. He also remained deeply interested in Ireland and Irish affairs, and in 1904 produced one of his best-known works, written specifically for the Irish stage, *John Bull's Other Island*. The satirical edge of this comedy lies partly in its reversal of national stereotypes: its protagonists are Irishman Larry Doyle, an arch-realist, and sentimental English dreamer Tom Broadbent. This was followed a year later by a somewhat darker play, *Man and Superman*, which dealt with questions of power and evolution, and in 1913 by one of Shaw's most popular works, *Pygmalion*, in which the engaging character of Liza Doolittle is taken from the streets to be educated and re-created by the ambitious phoneticist Henry Higgins.

The outbreak of WWI deeply depressed Shaw, destroying much of his earlier optimism. His response, in 1920, was *Heartbreak House*, a Chekhovian study of defeated hopes. In 1923 he wrote what many consider his masterpiece, *St Joan*, a play based on the life of Joan of Arc, who had been canonized in 1920. The play explores how the individual spirit responds to and resists the forces of conformity and orthodoxy. Meanwhile Shaw continued his political work, travelling, writing pamphlets and lecturing across the world, despite his declining health, and in 1926 was awarded the Nobel Prize for Literature. His also continued to write plays, and had produced over 50 by the time of his death. In addition, he penned commentaries on subjects which included Ireland, the war, socialism and the contemporary stage, published his correspondence and much of his early journalism, wrote several more novels and added extensive and involved explanatory prefaces to some of his plays. His reputation as the foremost modern Irish-born dramatist and man-of-letters remains intact, and he is recognized as a major influence on contemporary Irish theatre.

Further reading

Bentley (1947). Gordon (1990). Grene (1984). Holroyd (1988–91).

Sheridan, Richard Brinsley (1751–1816) Dramatist and politician. Sheridan came from an established ANGLO-IRISH literary family and was educated in DUBLIN and in England. After a relatively dissolute youth Sheridan began writing for the stage after eloping with his wife in order to make money. His first play, *The Rivals* (1773), was a great success and was quickly followed by a series of farces and comic operas. He became manager of the Drury Lane Theatre in London in 1776 and wrote his major works, *The School for Scandal* (1777) and *The Critic* (1779), for performance there. Sheridan later played an important role in English politics, supporting Edmund BURKE when he impeached Warren Hastings. Sheridan lost all his money when the theatre burnt down in 1809 and lost his seat in parliament in 1812. His last years were blighted by illness and debt, but his brio and panache meant that he retained many admirers.

Sinn Féin 'Sinn féin' translates variously as 'ourselves', 'we ourselves' and 'ourselves alone'; the term was chosen by the GAELIC LEAGUE as its motto of national self-sufficiency, and it became synonymous not only with Irish political independence around the turn of the nineteenth century, but with what Arthur GRIFFITH, its founder, referred to as 'the de-Anglicization of Ireland'. At this stage the party's programme was for an independent Ireland under the British monarch – more radical than the HOME RULE programme, but short of full REPUBLICAN independence. Despite its prominence as a political ginger group, this first Sinn Féin party, formed in 1907, was a relative failure; it lost the one by-election it contested and faded. After 1913 the IRISH VOLUNTEERS took over the role of radical NATIONALIST challenger to John REDMOND's IRISH PARLIAMENTARY PARTY (IPP); unlike Sinn Féin, they were neither passive nor pacifist in their outlook.

However the usefulness of the slogan meant that Sinn Féin soon became a target for the Volunteers after the EASTER RISING. They entered it and took it over as a political vehicle for attaining separatist ends and the party thus played a far more prominent role in events than could have been expected. This second, revived but altered Sinn Féin had over 1,200 branches by 1918, and in the general election of December beat the IPP, winning 73 of the 105 Irish seats at Westminster. Just before this, Griffith had been ousted as president of his party by DE VALERA, the senior survivor of 1916. In January 1919, the Sinn Féin MPs set up their own Irish parliament, the DÁIL.

After the ANGLO-IRISH WAR, Sinn Féin was as divided over the ANGLO-IRISH TREATY, as were the IRA and the Dáil, and after the May 1922 elections, as CIVIL WAR loomed, it disintegrated again, torn between the factions. Voters had endorsed the pro-treatyites by 92 to 36 seats in May, and these decided to leave Sinn Féin to form a new party, CUMANN NA NGAEDHEAL. De Valera made what was now a third Sinn Féin the political wing of republicanism after 1923, but its inflexible abstentionism led him and his supporters to break with it to form FIANNA FÁIL in 1926. However, as De Valera's policies of national isolation and protectionism show, he tried to put certain 'sinn féin' principles into effect during his years in power.

Since the 1920s the purist republicanism of Sinn Féin has meant that it has effectively been an auxiliary political force to successive forms of the IRA. It has oscillated throughout its existence between simply existing as an adjunct to 'physical force' republicanism and subordinating this wing to the political struggle. It has also wavered between social radicalism (following the Official IRA in the 1960s, for example) and conservatism (usually more associated with the 'physical force' element). The latest phase of Sinn Féin political revival – effectively its fourth incarnation as a mass party – flows from the Provisional IRA strategy of the 'armalite and the ballot box' which originated in the HUNGER STRIKES of 1980–81. Its success has allowed Gerry ADAMS and the Provisional IRA's former leaders to gradually damp down the military wing of republicanism, and to win a substantial share in the government of Northern Ireland. Sinn Féin is also trying to make headway in the REPUBLIC. Having shown their willingness to take part in the democratic political process, it is likely that they will also make gains there.

Further reading

Feeney (2002).

Smyth Case   The case of the paedophile priest Brendan Smyth illustrated the growth of awareness of the sexual abuse, particularly of children, by representatives of the Catholic Church, and, simultaneously, the limits of power of state institutions. In 1994, the Fianna Fáil Taoiseach Albert Reynolds insisted on appointing Harry Whelehan, then Attorney General, President of the High Court. Because Whelehan had previously prevaricated in the extradition of Smyth to Belfast to stand trial for child sex abuse committed in Northern Ireland, Fianna Fáil's coalition partners, the Irish Labour Party, resigned from the government. Reynolds resigned and was replaced by Bertie Aherne. It was then revealed that Fianna Fáil ministers had known of a precedent for swifter extradition in an earlier and similar case and had effectively been covering this up. Labour then turned to Fine Gael and the Democratic Left to form a 'rainbow coalition'. The case proved that public morality could not be flouted for party gain with impunity, since Whelehan was a political appointment. As a result, the method of making judicial appointments was altered to limit the influence of party bias. But it also revealed the effect of showing live the proceedings of the Dáil on television; the electorate was able to judge the behaviour of its representatives at first hand and act accordingly.

Social Democratic and Labour Party (SDLP)   Formed in August 1970 out of the unified political activity of the Catholic population of Northern Ireland of the 1968–1969 period, and funded by political parties in the Republic, the SDLP filled something of the gap left by the shattering of the Northern Ireland Labour Party and the marginalized Nationalist Party. It was broad front of moderate nationalists, overwhelmingly Catholic, and prepared, tentatively, to co-operate with the Stormont regime. Initially, its leading figure was the established socialist politician Gerry Fitt (who resigned from the party as a protest against its increasingly confessional coloration in 1979, and became Lord Fitt in 1983). However, as a vehicle for the Civil Rights generation, it rapidly brought Fitt's successor John Hume into prominence. The SDLP, if limited in the socialist aspect of its appeal, still commands the majority of the votes of the Catholic population of Northern Ireland, although at times it has been displaced by Sinn Féin. It has been central to the expression of moderate nationalist opinion, and was instrumental in brokering with both unionists, Sinn Féin and the IRA in order to end the Troubles.

'Somerville and Ross' (Somerville, Edith (1858–1949) **and Martin, Violet** (1862–1915))   Collaborating novelists and short story writers. Cousins, Somerville and Ross began their literary collaborations soon after meeting in 1886. Their best work draws directly on the foxhunting, horse-riding lifestyles of the minor gentry milieu they both grew up in. Their popular reputation rests on the comic short stories in *Some Experiences of an Irish R.M.* (1899) and two subsequent collections, but it is the earlier novel *The Real Charlotte* (1894) that is regarded as their masterpiece.

Brilliantly combining superficial sheen with dark irony, this tale of a 'Big House' in decline has earned favourable comparison with Turgenev. Their work has been accused of perpetuating stage-Irish stereotypes, but this is to miss the many subtleties of their achievement. Though the authors maintained a distance from the literary society of their day, their correspondence provides remarkable insights into their numerous intellectual concerns. Both were spiritualists as well as suffragists, and Martin's death in 1915 did not stop the collaborations – at least according to her cousin. Both names appeared on further publications such as *The Big House at Inver* (1925), though the later work suffers a falling-off in style. Somerville died at Drishane in 1949.

souperism   Refers to the practice of proselytizing at the same time as offering food (often in the form of soup) to the poor, reportedly a popular tactic of Protestant evangelicals during the Famine.

Spenser, Edmund (1552?–1599)   Poet, civil servant and colonial administrator. Spenser is arguably the most important English non-dramatic Renaissance poet. Having published an influential work, *The Shepheardes Calender* (1579), he emigrated to Ireland as secretary to the new Lord Deputy, Lord Grey de Wilton, in 1580. Spenser spent most of the rest of his life in Ireland and came to regard himself as Anglo-Irish rather than English in identity (the preface to his poem, *Colin Clouts Come Home Againe* (1595) refers to his Irish house as his home, and favourably contrasts the society of fictional shepherds in Ireland to the jealous backbiting at the English court). He held a variety of civil service posts in and around Dublin, before moving to the newly established Munster Plantation in the late 1580s where he occupied a large estate at Kilcolman, Co. Cork. Spenser appears to have been active in local politics, but now enjoyed the status of a gentleman landowner, although he fought a bitter and protracted legal suit with Lord Roche over the rights to his estate. Spenser's house was destroyed in 1598 as the Nine Years War reached a climax. His family fled to Cork where Spenser was made sheriff. Spenser died in early 1599 in Westminster, having crossed the Irish Sea to bring letters from the desperate colonists to the Privy Council requesting urgent military aid.

Ireland plays a key role in much of Spenser's poetry, most notably in his *magnum opus*, *The Faerie Queene* (1590, 1596). The poem describes a series of allegorical quests by knights in an imaginary fairyland which is often a version of the contemporary British Isles. Key events take place in Ireland, especially in the later stages of the poem when the failure to subdue hostile rebellion in Book 5, the Book of Justice, leads to the chaos and violence present throughout the pastoral Book 6, the Book of Courtesy. A fragment of Book 7, discovered later and published in 1609, contains a mythical story in which Diana abandons Ireland, then the fairest island in the world, to chaos, when she is seen naked by Faunus. The implication is that Ireland's fall from grace will trigger disaster for the world. Spenser also wrote *A View of the Present State of Ireland* (*c.*1596), a prose dialogue which recommends a violent solution to Ireland's ills, claiming that peace and prosperity will not happen until England has reconquered the island. This was not published until 1633, but circulated widely in manuscript.

Further reading

Coughlan and Davis (eds) (1989). Hadfield (1997). Maley (1997).

Stanihurst, Richard (1547–1618)   Historian, poet and classical scholar. Stanihurst was educated in Kilkenny and at University College, Oxford, where he was taught by the Jesuit martyr, Edmund Campion (*d.*1581). Campion wrote a sympathetic *History of Ireland* in Stanihurst's house when he went into exile in 1569 which argued that the native Irish were ignorant but not inherently wicked as many NEW ENGLISH authors argued and that Ireland needed a better education system rather than a full-scale invasion to make it a civil and obedient country. Stanihurst made extensive use of Campion's *History* when he wrote his own 'History of Ireland' for Raphael Holinshed's *Chronicles of England, Scotland and Ireland* (1577), giving prominence to a relatively benign interpretation of the situation in Ireland for an English audience. Stanihurst argued that the OLD ENGLISH were the best governors of Ireland and should be allowed to reform the country as they saw fit.

Stanihurst publicly declared his allegiance to CATHOLICISM soon afterwards and emigrated to the Netherlands where he wrote a second history of Ireland in Latin, *De Rebus in Hibernia Gestis* (Antwerp, 1584). This work argues the Irish must unite under the banner of Catholicism and oppose the English Protestants, a key theme in the work of many Irish writers and historians of the seventeenth century such as Geoffrey KEATING and Philip O'Sullivan Beare (1590?–1634?), author of *Zoilomastix* (c.1626) (although O'Sullivan Beare objected to Stanihurst's Old English viewpoint and was instrumental in having the work banned by the inquisition in Portugal). Stanihurst now praises the religious devotion of the native Irish and no longer regards them as savages who need to be educated. Stanihurst also completed an important translation of the first four books of Virgil's *Aeneid* into quantitative verse, which some have suggested owes a debt to BARDIC POETRY. Stanihurst spent his last years in exile in Spain trying to help engineer a Spanish succession to the English throne.

Further reading

Lennon (1981).

statues (Dublin)   As symbols of particular ideologies, statues in DUBLIN have played an important role in the assertion political sympathies, both in their erection and in their destruction. Until the mid-nineteenth century the statuary of the second city of the British Empire was almost exclusively of an imperial cast (more neutral are the late eighteenth-century allegorical figures that adorn the Custom House, Dublin Castle, and the General Post Office (GPO). Following the classical Roman tradition, equestrian statues of WILLIAM III (which features in James JOYCE's 'The Dead'), George I and George II embodied the values of the ANGLO-IRISH establishment. Unsurprisingly, they were also the sites of protest throughout the nineteenth and twentieth centuries, to the extent that today none survives. Similarly, Nelson's Pillar, erected in 1809 (the 'onehanded adulterer' of *Ulysses*), was symbolically dynamited by the IRA in 1966.

In the years after Daniel O'CONNELL's death (1847) NATIONALIST sentiment first asserted itself with commemorative statues of cultural icons with wide appeal – Thomas MOORE (1857), and the masterpieces by John Henry Foley (1818–74) of Oliver GOLDSMITH (1864) and Edmund BURKE (1868) – before moving on to more overtly political subjects (see ART). The most important of these was the O'Connell monument, also by Foley, first proposed in 1862, its foundation stone laid in 1864, and finally unveiled in 1882. Fewer statues were erected in the following two decades – the years of the Land War (see LAND LEAGUE) – until Irish nationalists responded to Victoria's 1897 jubilee with commemorations of the 1798 Rebellion, including the laying of a foundation stone of a never-erected statue of Wolfe TONE. The statue of Charles Stewart PARNELL by Augustus St Gaudens (1848–1907), unveiled in 1911, would provide a late end to nineteenth-century statuary in Dublin were it not for the symbolic history of the Victoria monument by John Hughes (1865–1941) erected in 1908 outside Leinster House, ceremonially removed in 1948, and given as a gift to the Australian people by Charles HAUGHEY in 1987.

The twentieth century saw some notable additions to Dublin's statuary, although there has been a shortage of money, and then of will, since Independence, to commit money to public sculpture. The most famous is possibly the figure of CÚ CHULAINN (1911) by Oliver Sheppard (1864–1941) in the GPO which, although designed before the event, became a memorial to the EASTER RISING. Equally impressive are Oisin Kelly's statues of James LARKIN in O'Connell Street and *The Children of Lir* (1971) in the Garden of Remembrance, Parnell Square. Other sculptors contributing to the cityscape include Hilary Heron with her witty *Crazy Jane* (c. 1960) in Jury's Hotel and the (in)famous *Anna Livia Plurabelle* fountain-statue, erected by the Smurfitt Corporation in O'Connell Street in 1987. Known locally as 'The Floozie in the Jacuzzi', this was the subject of a bravura verbal attack by the critic Ailbhe Smyth, proving that Dublin's sculptures continue to challenge, annoy and amuse its inhabitants as much as they have in the past.

Finally, the Spire, already nicknamed by Dubliners as 'the stiletto in the ghetto', was commissioned in 1998 by Dublin City Council to celebrate the millennium. Designed by London-based architect Ian Ritchie, it was completed 2 years late in January 2003, at a cost of 4.5 million euros. Officially known as the Spire of Dublin, this giant stainless-steel needle-like structure stands in the middle of Dublin's historic O'Connell Street, on the former site of the statue of Nelson, blown up by the IRA in 1966. The structure stands 120 metres high, is 3 metres in diameter at its base and just 15 centimetres at its tip. A powerful light illuminates the top 12 metres, which taper off to a tip of optical glass.

Steele, Sir Richard (1672–1729)   Essay writer and playwright. Steele was born in DUBLIN and went to Oxford University before joining the Life Guards in 1694. Steele took part in a couple of duels and seriously wounded an opponent in 1700. He produced a number of plays soon afterwards, including *The Christian Hero* (1701), *The Funeral* (1701), *The Lying Lover* (1703) and *The Tender Husband* (1705). Steele turned to journalism in subsequent years, forming an important partnership with Joseph Addison (1672–1719) in 1709. They contributed essays to a variety of journals that they established, including *The Tatler* (1709–11), *The Spectator* (1711–12), *The Guardian* (1713) and *The Englishman* (1713–4). Steele's essays are his main contribution to literary history. They are noted for their high moral sentiment and idealism. He continued to play an important role in English intellectual and cultural life until his retirement to Wales in 1724. Steele earned the enmity of Jonathan SWIFT for his support for the Hanoverian dynasty in 1714.

Sterne, Laurence (1713–1768)   Novelist and clergyman. Sterne was born in Clonmel, Co. Tipperary; the English branch of his family were from Yorkshire, while an Irish branch had been settled in the country since the seventeenth century and his childhood was spent largely with relatives of his Irish mother until he was sent to school in Halifax in 1723, and then to Cambridge. He became vicar at Sutton-on-the-Forest in Yorkshire in 1738. Sterne was enthralled by Locke's philosophy at university and other formative influences on his prose included Cervantes, Sir Thomas Browne, Robert Burton and Rabelais. His earliest work was *A Political Romance* (1759), a satire on ecclesiastical lawyers.

The first two volumes of his greatest work, *The Life and Opinions of Tristram Shandy*, were published in 1759, and a further seven appeared before his death nine years later. *Tristram Shandy* was popular enough to be pirated, and, although dismissed by Dr Johnson as too 'odd' to last, it proved to be both phenomenally popular and a milestone in the development of the novel. Sterne was lionized and cashed in on his international reputation with *The Sermons of Yorick* (1760–69) and *A Sentimental Journey* (1768), based on travels in France and Italy in 1762–64. The *Journal to Eliza*, written for Elizabeth Draper, with whom he fell in love in 1764, appeared in 1904.

Tristram Shandy is one of the most radical and innovative works in the history of fiction and has been claimed as a forerunner of both modernist and POSTMODERNIST practice. An artful offhandedness, apparent indifference to rules and a disdain for chronological narrative and sequence mark its style. The digressions from the ostensible narrative of the novel, that of the evolution of Tristram's 'life and opinions', hardly ever tell stories in any traditional sense. Arguably, any plot they offer, as in the Slawkenbergius episode, is subordinate to, and validated by, the impulse to verbal performance. Sterne claims the authority of Locke for the thread of arbitrary association which links ideas, to comic effect, as in the opening account of his narrator's begetting (where his parents' monthly acts of intercourse and clock-winding meet in absurd cross-purposes to disperse the 'homunculus' Tristram's vital animal spirits). Yet, as this suggests, just as important is the juxtaposition of seriousness and trivia which Locke's model of perception permits, and Sterne's relation of it to the eighteenth-century cult of sensibility. The latter was a subject which he returned to ironize in *A Sentimental Journey*, this time in the character of the figure who links both books, the clergyman Yorick – Hamlet's emblem of humour and mortality, and one with which Sterne himself came to increasingly identify. Yet, true to the tradition of learned wit, *Tristram Shandy*'s characters are scarcely 'rounded' in any psychologically coherent sense, memorable though Walter Shandy, Widow Wadman, Uncle Toby and the others are. Similarly, *Tristram Shandy* also queries the transparency and communicative function of language with its non-typographical squiggles, marbled and blackened pages, and insistence on the materiality of the book: '… we have got thro' these five volumes (do, Sir, sit down upon a set – they are better than nothing) …'

Though the 'Irishness' of Sterne, in any narrow sense, is disputable, his subversive irreverence, buttonholing but knowing tone (anticipating 'stream-of-consciousness' styles), and general attitude to the act of writing have proved particularly influential to later Irish authors, among them James JOYCE, Samuel BECKETT, Flann O'BRIEN, Paul MULDOON and Ciaran CARSON.

Further reading

Ross (2001).

Stoker, Bram (Abraham) (1847–1912)   Theatre manager and novelist. Born in DUBLIN, the son of a civil servant, whom he followed into that profession as a young man, Stoker also took after his father in his love of the theatre and he began contributing unpaid reviews to *The Evening Mail* while in the civil service. He developed a friendship with the great Victorian actor Henry Irving after orchestrating his highly successful visit to Dublin in 1876, and he followed him to London in 1878 as secretary and business manager of the Lyceum Theatre. That same year he married Florence Balcombe, previously the object of Oscar WILDE's affections. The marriage foundered after the birth of their only child, and Stoker began a career of serial womanizing, eventually contracting the syphilis that would kill him in 1912. Critics of Irish literature have looked for merit in *The Snake's Pass* (1891), his second novel, but only because it is set in Ireland; his sole work of enduring merit is the Gothic masterpiece, *Dracula* (1897). The themes, images and preoccupations of this epistolary tale of an aristocratic vampire, his hunters and victims – sex, technology, modernity, blood, invasion and the occult – readily lend themselves to re-workings in other genres and media, making the undead count always our contemporary.

Stormont The Northern Irish parliament was opened by George V in 1921; Stormont, its permanent home on the outskirts of Belfast, was opened by the Prince of Wales in 1932. It is a huge neo-classical edifice with lavish interiors, situated on a hill, approached by a long wide avenue and fronted by a statue of Sir Edward CARSON in a defiant stance.

The institutions of the Northern Ireland government run by the Stormont parliament were liberal democratic in form, with a free press and elections. However, 'manipulations and modifications' of the system increased already preponderant UNIONIST power. A PR voting system and new constituency boundaries introduced by Westminster in 1919 had increased non-unionist representation by allowing nationalists to win control of certain local authorities. When some of these refused to recognize the new Northern Irish parliament in 1921, it dissolved 21 of them, handing over their functions to government commissioners. These abolished the PR and boundary changes, returning the councils to unionist control (thereafter maintained, in some cases, by GERRYMANDERING). In 1929 the voting system for Stormont itself was also changed to guard against the threat to unionism posed by the NORTHERN IRELAND LABOUR PARTY.

The refusal by MPs of the main opposition Nationalist Party to take their seats at Stormont until 1925, their occasional boycotts of it, and their constant identification with the Free State, undoubtedly gave unionists more of a free hand than they would have otherwise had in establishing total dominance. Nevertheless, at a ratio of 4 MPs to 1 in favour of unionists (despite a population differential of only 2:1) there was a distinct limit to what representatives of the CATHOLIC community could accomplish.

An unambiguous and unashamedly sectarian ethos permeated parliament, government and state as a result. In legal and security terms, this was based on the Civil Authorities (Special Powers) Act of 1922, passed at the height of the IRA campaign to destabilize Northern Ireland. Despite the threat's temporary nature, the Act was made permanent in 1933. Two armed police forces existed; the Special Constabulary (which included the B-Specials), made up largely from former ULSTER VOLUNTEER FORCE (UVF) members, who became notorious among Catholics for sectarian abuses; less sectarian was the Royal Ulster Constabulary (RUC), formed in 1922. Both were overwhelmingly Protestant in composition. Sectarian discrimination was also institutionalized in the civil service, public employment, and in public housing allocation. Close ties existed between unionist politicians and LOYALIST organizations such as the ORANGE ORDER and Ulster Unionist Council. The parliament's and the state's innately sectarian biases were well expressed by Craig himself in 1934, with the words 'all I boast is that we are a Protestant Parliament and a Protestant state'.

Successive Westminster governments of different political hues gave unionists a free hand in running Northern Ireland for 50 years. So great was unionist domination that the only Bill sponsored by a non-unionist member of Stormont ever passed there was the Wild Birds Act (1931). Paternalistic and complacent, it presided not merely over discrimination, but also a poor public health, housing and social welfare record. Its air-raid defence planning for the population of BELFAST in WWII was also woefully inadequate. Though Stormont accepted welfare state subventions after 1948, the real machinery of government in Northern Ireland had always functioned at local authority level, and it was there that the grievances which led to its downfall continued to fester before finding expression in the CIVIL RIGHTS movement. The government's capacity to keep order broke down in August 1969 when the penultimate Northern Ireland Prime Minister, James Chichester-Clarke, had to call in the army, and in 1972 the Northern Irish parliament was suspended in favour of DIRECT RULE by Westminster.

Further reading

Bew, Gibbon and Paterson (1996). Buckland (1979).

Stuart, Henry Francis Montgomery (1902–2000)   Novelist. Born in Australia, brought up in Co. Antrim, Stuart attended Rugby, and married Iseult Gonne, daughter of Maud GONNE, at the age of 18. He soon moved from the Protestantism of his background to embrace CATHOLICISM and militant REPUBLICANISM, supporting opponents of the treaty in the CIVIL WAR. Following a false start in poetry, Stuart turned to fiction with *Women and God* (1931), *Pigeon Irish* (1932) and *Try the Sky* (1933). His taste for the scapegoat role, indulged in his republicanism and relations with W.B. YEATS's ménage, was made shockingly real, however, when he travelled to lecture in Nazi Germany a month after the invasion of Czechoslovakia and stayed for the duration of the war, broadcasting over German radio in praise of Irish neutrality, IRA attacks in England, and, on one occasion, Adolf Hitler.

Twice briefly arrested after WWII by the French, Stuart moved to Paris where he published the trilogy of novels which make up his greatest achievement, *The Pillar of Cloud* (1948), *Redemption* (1949) and *The Flowering Cross* (1950). In these the moral and social chaos of war and its aftermath are explored through female characters who have suffered torture and sexual violence but, in a Christian anarchist manner which recalls Dostoyevsky, retain the ability to forgive and forge new relationships. Like BECKETT's great trilogy of the same period, it was virtually ignored until Stuart gained later fame. In the meantime he moved to London with his companion Gertrud Meissner, where he published a further five novels in the 1950s, before moving to Ireland to work on a 'memoir in fictional form'. The resultant work, *Black List, Section H* (1970), is on the same level of achievement as the trilogy. It gained Stuart an audience and made it clear that he was a major, if, for many, unpalatable presence in Irish letters.

His later work, in which his republicanism was inflected by the Northern Irish TROUBLES, continued in the experimental vein of *Black List, Section H,* and included *Memorial* (1973), *A Hole in the Head* (1977), *The High Consistory* (1981) and *Faillandia* (1985). These novels, which often fuse sexual and religious experience, consolidated his critical reputation and maintained his scapegoat appeal among younger writers, such as Paul DURCAN. Despite such recognition, his writing raises and confronts (as well as avoiding) some of the most intractable and painful moral issues of the twentieth century and represents one of the extreme achievements of Irish literature.

Further reading

McCartney (2000). Welch (1993).

Swift, Jonathan (1667–1745)   Author, politician and clergyman. Swift, whose father was English, was born in DUBLIN, and educated at TRINITY COLLEGE Dublin. After some time working in England he returned to Dublin in 1694 where he was ordained as an Anglican priest. He oversaw a parish in Co. Antrim, then spent time in London and Dublin occupying a variety of posts. Swift became well connected in London, working for the Tory party and socializing with some of the major English poets and authors of the day, Richard Steele, Joseph Addison, and Alexander Pope. All this time he was writing and publishing poetry and a variety of pamphlets.

Swift returned to Dublin in August 1714 to become Dean of St Patrick's, disappointed that he had failed to secure a similar position in England. He started to write pamphlets dealing with Irish issues and also began *Gulliver's Travels*, which was published in 1726. He also wrote a number of pamphlets attacking Protestant sects and defending the Church of Ireland, and helped to start a newspaper, *The Intelligencier*, which commented on literature and social issues in Dublin. A collected volume of his works was published in 1735, including the poetry he had been writing all his adult life. The last years of Swift's life were blighted by the death of many of his closest friends. In 1742 he was certified insane and was looked after by friends for the last three years of his life. In his will he left a considerable sum for the establishment of St Patrick's Hospital for the mentally ill.

Swift's work constitutes one of the major achievements of literature in English. Much of his work deals with Ireland and Irish problems which concerned him for most of his adult life. These include *The Drapier's Letters* (1724–25), in which Swift, in the guise of a Dublin shopkeeper, launches a series of attacks on England's subjugation of Ireland. Even more well-known and polemical is *A Modest Proposal* (1729), a shocking satire in which the apparently serious author suggests that Irish babies ought to be eaten as a means of preventing ruinous Irish population growth and providing nutrition for those left alive on the island. The pamphlet even provides a series of cooking suggestions. Swift's anger is aimed at philanthropic schemes designed to alleviate Irish poverty, which are, in effect, no less cruel than the proposed cannibalism.

The third book of *Gulliver's Travels*, the voyage to the flying island of Laputa, contains an obvious satire of the relationship between England and Ireland which was initially censored. Laputa flies above the city of Lindalino to shut out its light and so starve the inhabitants into submission but in doing so nearly comes to grief. Swift is clearly suggesting that the same might happen if England tries to oppress the Irish too savagely. It is possible to argue that all four of Gulliver's voyages relate the history of England and Ireland. The first shows the Lilliputians subjecting their neighbours on the island of Blefuscu; the second shows the giants of Brobdingnag living a self-sufficient existence; the third, the Laputians viciously subjecting their neighbours; and the fourth the rational horses, the Houyhnms, advocating the genocide of their bestial neighbours, the Yahoos. If books one, three and four show the frightening progress of England's oppression of Ireland, then book two reveals an alternative story in which the Irish were allowed to develop without the interference of England.

Further reading

Ehenpreis (1962–83). Hammond (1988).

Synge, John Millington (1871–1909) Playwright. Born in Rathfarnham, Co. Dublin, into an ANGLO-IRISH family, Synge spent his childhood at Crosthwaite Park, Kingstown. An early enthusiasm for naturalism led him to evolution and disbelief in the religion of his clerical family. Synge's interest in the IRISH LANGUAGE was fostered during his time at TCD. He travelled in Europe, and in 1896 met W. B. YEATS and Maud GONNE in Paris, briefly becoming a member of Gonne's militant Parisian Irish League. Partly under Yeats's urging, Synge travelled to the Aran Islands, off the west coast of Ireland, in 1898; he would return to the islands in the summers of 1899, 1900, 1901, and 1902, gathering material for a prose work, *The Aran Islands* (1907). Immersing himself in the IRISH LANGUAGE, he engaged in the translating of Gaelic texts, developing the synthetic Hiberno-English – an English based on the speech rhythms of Irish – later deployed to powerful effect in his plays. Synge's earliest compositions, however, are influenced principally by the aestheticism and decadence of the *fin de siècle*. His first play, *When the Moon has Set* (1901), is equally indebted to others, in this case largely Ibsen, with an admixture of Yeats.

In the following year he wrote his first compelling composition, *In the Shadow of the Glen* (first performed in 1903), a one-act play, which draws upon Synge's understanding of the rural inhabitants of Wicklow. This knowledge is also keenly demonstrated in his 1905 articles on the Congested Districts of Wicklow and Kerry for the *Manchester Guardian*, a collaboration with J. B. YEATS. In 1903 he composed *Riders to the Sea* (produced in 1904), a play set on Aran in which the precariousness and dignity of human existence is juxtaposed with a casually indifferent universe. Both plays became part of the ABBEY THEATRE's repertoire and Synge was made a Director of the theatre in 1905. In the same year, the Abbey produced *The Well of the Saints*, in which a blind couple in Wicklow find their conviction in their own handsomeness dashed by a miracle cure; at the play's conclusion, they choose to embrace their delusion rather than confront reality.

In 1907, Synge's greatest play, *The Playboy of the Western World*, was performed at the Abbey. Prefiguring the audience's reaction to Sean O'Casey's *The Plough and the Stars*, Synge's play prompted a riot at the theatre, apparently at the heroine's use of the word 'shift' (as undergarment). As with O'Casey's, the play, through the Janus-faced figure of Christy Mahon, forced its audience to contend with the pleasing rhetorical mask brutality can wear, the baseness that can lie beneath heroicism. The *Playboy* was an outrage to the shallow pieties of many nationalists who felt it constituted an insult to the rural populace of the western seaboard, an image, for many, of the quintessence of Irishness. Though it derives much of its eroticism from *The Love Songs of Connaght*, a collection compiled and translated by the Gaelic League's President, Douglas Hyde, members of the Gaelic League were offended by its supposed vulgarity.

In the year of the *Playboy*'s controversial staging, Synge was re-afflicted with Hodgkin's disease, which he had first experienced in 1897. During his final illness, he drafted *Deirdre of the Sorrows*, based on a tale from the Ulster Cycle, *Longes mac nUislenn/Exile of the Sons of Uisliu*, which was first performed, in its unfinished form, in 1910. Synge's unjustly neglected mature poetry was published in *Poems and Translations* (1911).

Further reading

Greene and Stephens (1989). Grene (1975). McCormack (2000).

T

Táin Bó Cuailnge (The Cattle Raid of Cooley) The central heroic tale in the Ulster Cycle, a series of mythological works which recount the conflict between the Uliad, the ancient people from whom the name Ulster derives, and the Connachta, who supposedly had a similar relationship to Connacht. The *Táin* survives in three manuscripts, including the Book of Leinster, suggesting that it was a widely read and influential work in early Medieval Ireland. The original version probably dates from the seventh century, but it is likely that it was embellished and adapted in subsequent years. As with many early works of literature it is hard to decide whether the *Táin* was an oral work which was later written down and altered or whether it was composed in written form as an Irish epic or an allegorical commentary on dynastic disputes in Ireland.

The story told is fairly simple. Medb, Queen of Connacht, launches a cattle raid against the Uliad, planning to carry off the Donn (Brown) Cuailnge, their prize bull from Cooley. Her army is opposed by the Ulster hero, CÚ CHULAINN, who blocks their path with a series of *geis* (a taboo which prevents an action being taken, such devices being common in early Irish literature). Fergus, a prominent Connacht warrior who was banished by Cú Chulainn, explains to his fellow soldiers whom they are fighting by narrating the deeds of Cú Chulainn, who is now 17. These include defeating most of a boy-troop of some 150 boys armed only with a toy shield made of sticks and a toy javelin, driving his fist through the skull of a man whom wakes him up, and single-handedly defeating a group of marauders who attack the Ulster boys. Cú Chulainn has to save Ulster alone because the Ulstermen are cursed with weakness after they forced the goddess Macha to enter a race when she was pregnant.

Cú Chulainn defeats the Connacht army when he attacks them at night, wreaking havoc as he did earlier. He then faces a series of opponents, after an agreement is reached with Fergus. After killing the warrior, Etarcomal, who makes the mistake of boasting that he can defeat the Ulster champion, Cú Chulainn defeats all who dare to face him, before he has to fight the wily enchantress, Morrígan. Cú Chulainn defeats her with rather more difficulty, after she appears in a variety of forms: a cow, an eel and a wolf. Cú Chulainn wounds Morrígan and a truce is agreed because he is now exhausted. While he sleeps a troop of Ulster boys fight the Connacht warriors and are all killed. When Cú Chulainn awakes he revenges the deaths of his kinsmen and inflicts terrible slaughter on their enemies. He then kills his foster-brother, Ferdia, in a terrible manner, suffering painful wounds himself. Cú Chulainn at last manages to rouse the Ulstermen from the torpor that Macha has inflicted on them and they defeat the Connacht forces, which retreat. Cú Chulainn agrees to let their champion bull, Finnbennach, fight the Donn, and their encounter concludes the *Táin*. The Donn triumphs and scatters Finnbennach's carcass across Ulster before dying.

The *Táin* is a complex and sophisticated work. The significance of the cattle raid, a subject of other Irish heroic tales, reflects the importance of the possession of herds of cattle in Irish life and the prevalence of cattle raiding as a means of one group asserting power over another. As in most societies in the early heroic age, life in Ireland was dominated by conflict and violence. The tale also deals with political issues of government and kingship, the importance of fate and the relationship between earthly life and supernatural powers.

Further reading

Kinsella (1970).

Talbot, Matt (1856–1925)   Reformed alcoholic who became an inspirational penitent; beatified in 1976.

Tara   The seat of the ancient high kings of Ireland, southeast of Navan, Co. Meath. A series of ARCHAEOLOGICAL remains still exist showing how extensive the original earthworks and fortifications must have been. These date from *c.*2000 BC. Tara also occupies an important place in Irish MYTHOLOGY. It symbolized the unity of Ireland, manifested in the crowning of the high king. He had to mate symbolically with the goddess of Ireland to confirm his right to rule over the Irish. Possession of the site was vitally important during the dynastic wars which took place in Ireland in the fifth and sixth centuries. Tara is frequently referred to in subsequent Irish literature.

television and radio   Public radio broadcasting in Ireland began with the BBC in 1922. Almost from its inception, it was seen as conducive to the creation of a sense of national identity, and from 1927 (when the BBC received its public service mandate), the corporation covered events such as the Grand National and Trooping the Colour. Local unionists exercised considerable control over what was transmitted by BBC Northern Ireland (BBC NI); nevertheless, the relationship between them and Broadcasting House could be strained when Catholic or nationalist-interest material was sent by London, and from 1937 BBC NI was allowed a veto. The frequent broadcasts of popular music, frowned upon by PRESBYTERIANS, also revealed the anomalousness of the Northern Irish state within the UK.

2RN (Radio Éireann after 1937), the broadcasting service of the Free State, began transmitting in 1926. It took the BBC's public-service, non-commercial approach as its model. As in Northern Ireland, broadcasting was rather more closely identified with the state than in Britain (exemplified through DE VALERA's ST PATRICK's DAY BROADCASTS), and RÉ was run as a branch of the civil service until 1953. If, for the BBC, the public-service ethic empowered it to engage in new kinds of cultural activity as well as to integrate the nation (and empire), in the south broadcasting was regarded more as the revival of an already existing nation, whose essence was established. Broadcasting was seen as the relaying of what existed, rather than an agent in its own right capable of creating new cultural forms. This made for increasingly moribund programming, and this (like RÉ's ban on most popular music) meant that southern listeners often tuned in to the BBC.

BBC television broadcasts began in 1947, extending to Northern Ireland in 1953, and it was partly anxiety about transmission 'invasion' from BBC and ITV 'overspill', as well as the general impetus of MODERNIZATION, which led RÉ to set up its own television service under an Act of 1960. Renamed Radio Telefís Éireann (RTÉ), it was funded by advertizing as well as licence revenue. By 1966, it had made possible national participation in such momentous events as the Second Vatican Council, the visit of President Kennedy in 1963, and the 50th anniversary of the EASTER RISING. But RTÉ was soon faced with the question of its integrity as a small, autonomous national service, given soaring production costs; by 1980, 70 per cent of all of its programmes were produced outside Ireland, a proportion not changed by the introduction of a second channel in 1978. This proportion has continued to rise in recent years.

RTÉ's own programme-making has included the Dublin-based soaps *Tolka Row* (1964–68), *Fair City* (1989–) and the 'agri-soaps' *The Riordans* (1965–79) and *Glenroe* (1983–2000), studio-based single plays in the 1960s, and dramatic series in the 1970s and 1980s. Two of the best series of the last decade have been Roddy Doyle's *Family* (1994) and the adaptation of John McGahern's *Amongst Women* (1998). There has also been satire, as in the sketch-based *Hall's Pictorial Weekly* (1971–80), and homegrown sitcoms. News and current affairs such as *Prime Time* have also been crucial in probing scandals, such as the Smyth Case, while coverage of the Gulf War in 1991 was less supine than that on British and US television. Recent documentary series include the high-quality *Irish Empire* (1999) and *Seven Ages* (2000). However, RTÉ's best-known and most durable programme is *The Late Late Show* (1962–), fronted by Gay Byrne, a mixture of informal talk and entertainment based on US chat shows. It has been closely entwined with national life for four decades, airing and altering attitudes towards such taboo subjects as contraception, unmarried mothers, Travellers' rights, infanticide, and the Catholic Church. The adaptation of an imported format to Irish needs can also be seen in RTÉ's use of the Eurovision Song Contest, where Irish successes and consequent responsibilities as hosts permitted a series of marketing exercises on a national scale. One spinoff from this was that the 1994 interval act – a spectacular performance by Irish-Americans Michael Flatley, Jean Butler and a chorus of young, energetic dancers, blending Irish set dancing, ballet and modern dance to a score by Bill Whelan – went on to become the internationally successful stage show *Riverdance*. Its use of diaspora talent and hybrid forms revealed the new national confidence of the 1990s. This period also saw the launch of a commercial channel, TV3, and the belated introduction of Irish-language television broadcasting, in 1996, with Telefís na Gaeilge. Up to this point, provision had been pitiful; in 1975–76, for example, the sum total of RTÉ's Irish-language broadcast was three hours of children's television, representing 0.25 per cent of its output.

In Northern Ireland television has been profoundly shaped by the Troubles. Prior to this, the drama of Sam Thompson and John D. Stewart had caused ripples in the 1960s by exposing sectarianism. During the 1970s this tradition was sporadically continued. Other dramas explored the difficulties of British soldiers stationed in Northern Ireland, often critical of their role, as in Howard Brenton's *The Paradise Run* (1976). The main contribution to Troubles drama in the 1980s came from two Northern Irish writers, Graham Reid and Stewart Parker. Reid's three *Billy* plays (1982–84), investigated loyalist identity through family conflicts. Parker's most ambitious television work was the six-part thriller *Lost Belongings* (1987), which shared its love-across-the-divide theme with much other Troubles drama, but was distinguished by its re-viewing of Ulster Protestantism from a complex, historically informed, Christian-humanist viewpoint. A nationalist and feminist perspective was articulated in Anne Devlin's *A Woman Calling* (1984), *The Long March* (1984) and *Naming the Names* (1987), plays which complicate stereotypes, dramatize internal communal differences, and offer a critique of militant REPUBLICANISM.

In the late 1980s and early 1990s, an increase in CENSORSHIP saw the investigation of Northern Irish issues through drama, docudrama and documentary genres; examples include *Rat in the Skull* (1987), *Blind Justice* (1988), *Chinese Whispers* (1989), *Who Bombed Birmingham?* (1990) and *Shoot to Kill* (1990). The last two were documentaries covering, respectively, the growing outcry over the imprisonment of the Birmingham six, and the suspension of John Stalker, a Manchester policeman, during his investigation of the alleged 'shoot to kill' policy of the SAS in Northern Ireland. Since the ceasefire of 1994 television has been coming to terms with the new conditions; examples include Channel 4's 'The Long War' season appraising the Troubles, and BBC NI's *Give My Head Peace* (1998–), a satirical sitcom which mocks the platitudes and pomposities of the peace process. The last of these is perhaps the closest Northern Irish equivalent to *Father Ted* (1995–97), an Irish-written and Irish-acted anarchic sitcom made for Channel 4. *Father Ted* featured three dysfunctional Irish priests and their housekeeper, isolated on Craggy Island, and explored and exploded stereotypes of Irishness, mocking the CATHOLIC CHURCH, and expressing something of the confidence of the Irish in mid-1990s Britain, as well as in the Republic itself.

Despite opposition from conservatives, television has, by its very nature, acted to liberalize Irish life, even as censorship has limited its reach. Thus, the initial willingness of RTÉ, BBC and ITV to report on CIVIL RIGHTS abuses in Northern Ireland, and then to publicize the severity of the STORMONT response to protestors, was crucial in hastening reform there – this being followed by restrictions, with reporting conditions for BBC NI and Ulster Television (UTV) particularly fraught. In the Republic, RTÉ introduced some censorship to insulate the state against the Troubles; in one incident in 1972, the entire RTÉ executive was dismissed. In 1988–94 the British ban on the voices of republicans was both farcical and damaging to claims for freedom of speech.

Pluralism, heralded by the Annan Report in Britain, altered the BBC and IBA (Independent Broadcasting Association) ethos of paternalistic provision from the early 1980s by arguing for minority representation and the enforcing of work from independents. This has since spread to RTÉ. The contemporary scene is one of a plethora of provision via multi-channel satellite and/or cable networks, reflecting the shift caused by technological and political change, and the challenges from commercial broadcasting. This has weakened the public-service basis of BBC NI and RTÉ, and dissolved the sense of national function, but also showed the futility of trying to police the airwaves, as governments did in the past. In the 1990s, Irish DIASPORA audiences have been supplied with cable/satellite provision from Tara TV in England (1995) and Celtic Vision in the USA (1995).

Further reading

Gibbons (1996). McIlroy (1998). McLoone (ed.) (1991, 1996). McLoone and McMahon (eds.) (1984). Pettitt (2000). Pine (2002).

Thackeray, William Makepeace (1811–1863)   English writer and satirist who toured Ireland and produced, in 1842, his *Irish Sketch Book*, a humorous but often insightful account of the country which many Irish readers found offensive.

Thompson, Sam (1916–1965)   Playwright. Born in BELFAST, Thompson was a painter in the Harland and Wolff shipyard, and worked for the Belfast Corporation after WWII. Sacked for trade-union activities, he was encouraged by Sam Hanna BELL to write about his experiences for BBC radio. Thompson's first full-length play, *Over the Bridge*, shows trade-union solidarity at the shipyard broken by sectarianism, as the largely Protestant workforce victimizes a Catholic worker. The directors of the Ulster Group Theatre dropped the play when it was in rehearsal in 1957. Thompson successfully sued for breach of contract, but it was not performed until 1960. The debate reflected the fear of the UNIONIST establishment, and the tentative moves towards liberalization at the time. Thompson's other plays were *The Evangelist* (1961), about religious hypocrisy, and *Cemented with Love* (1965), exploring political corruption.

Titanic   A 66,000-ton White Star liner, RMS *Titanic* was built at the Harland and Wolff shipyard in BELFAST. She sank with the loss of 1,503 lives after striking an iceberg off Newfoundland during her maiden voyage, early in the morning of 15 April 1912. This fate immediately became symbolic, and it has been mythicized as years have passed. In retrospect, the *Titanic* has been taken to embody UNIONISM and empire (given the much-vaunted unsinkability of the ship); class and sectarian division (given that many of those in the cheapest Steerage Class, who were denied access to the liner's limited number of lifeboats, were poor Irish CATHOLIC EMIGRANTS); and technological arrogance. After WWI, the *Titanic* was seen as epitomizing a golden Edwardian era about to sink into carnage. Recent location of the wreck, and the recovery of artefacts from it, have rekindled interest. The *Titanic* has been remarkably productive of artistic responses, including films (*A Night to Remember* and James Cameron's 11 Oscar-winning *Titanic* of 1997), poetry (Thomas Hardy's 'Convergence of the Twain', Louis MacNeice's 'Death of an Old Lady', Anthony Cronin's 'RMS *Titanic*'), drama (Stewart Parker's *The Iceberg* of 1974), fiction (Beryl Bainbridge's *Every Man for Himself* of 1996), and memoir (such as Mary Costello's *Titanic Town* (1993)).

Further reading

Hawthorn (1996).

Tone, Theobald Wolfe (1763–1778)   Revolutionary leader. Tone was born in Dublin, the son of wealthy Protestants, and educated at Trinity College, where he qualified as a barrister. He had a keen interest in political issues from his student days, arguing that Irish Protestants and Catholics had a common interest and that they should combine to create a united Ireland independent from England. His early pamphlet, *An Argument on Behalf of the Catholics of Ireland* (1791), brought him to the attention of the United Irishmen who invited him to join them. He was made secretary to the Catholic Committee (1792), a group which represented the interests of Catholics and was starting to become more militant in its demands for equality. However, in 1795 he was forced into exile in America after the clergyman and journalist William Jackson (1737–95) revealed to a government spy that Tone and other Irish radicals were forging links with French groups in the hope of organizing an invasion to overthrow English rule. Tone moved to France in 1796 and persuaded the revolutionary government to support an invasion of Ireland. In December of that year a large force of 14,450 troops sailed to Bantry Bay under the command of General Hoche but were dispersed by a storm and did not land on the Munster coast. After this failure a second expedition set off in September 1798 with fewer French troops but was intercepted before it reached land. Tone committed suicide when awaiting execution for treason.

Tone occupies a crucial place in Irish history. He is seen as the inspiration behind Sinn Féin and Irish republicanism, who honour his memory by visiting Tone's grave at Bodenstown, Co. Kildare, every year. His journals, published posthumously, helped to cement his reputation, as a tragic martyr and far-sighted thinker who saw the future course of Irish history (although many historians have challenged this conception of the coherence and depth of Tone's thinking).

Further reading

Elliott (1989).

tourism   Ireland, although not an obvious tourist destination, benefited from the interest in things Celtic from the late eighteenth century onwards, and the 'tour of Ireland' book became a minor literary-pictorial genre (see Thackeray). But it was not until the advent of railways and steam ferries between Ireland, Britain and the Continent that travel for pleasure became a large-scale possibility. Air travel after WWII soon made the country far more accessible for tourists, particularly from North America, where there was substantial interest in Ireland through the diaspora (Bord Fáilte, the Republic's Tourist Board, was established in July 1952). Thus, while in 1960 only 25,000 people visited from the Continent, by 1989 this had risen to 744,000. US visitors rose from 69,000 to 443,000 in the same period. Already, by the mid-1960s, tourism was the single largest industry in the Republic. Overall, the number of visitors to Ireland roughly tripled between 1960 and 1990, and by the late 1990s tourism was worth over £1.5 billion per annum.

Ireland offers, above all else, a level of industrialization and urbanization which is uniquely low in Western Europe, and has a tradition for being carefree, hospitable and friendly (hence the Bord Fáilte slogan of 'cead mile fáilte', or 'a hundred thousand welcomes'). The host of conferences, food festivals – as at Kinsale – and literature festivals – for MERRIMAN, SWIFT, KAVANAGH, JOYCE, SYNGE, and others – show that marketing is not simply a matter of the Lakes of Killarney, the Giant's Causeway, golf courses and luxury hotels. Arguably tourism has had a beneficial impact in parts of Ireland; it has fostered community pride, led to the regeneration of small towns and villages, and been used by environmentalists to strengthen their case. Much tourism is connected with genealogy, ARCHAEOLOGY and history, and TRADITIONAL MUSIC, and this contrasts with more recent developments, such as the Temple Bar drinking area in DUBLIN. However, cut-price flights now mean that Ireland is increasingly cheaper to reach, and with the peace process continuing in Northern Ireland the limits of its capacity for tourism are likely to need serious reassessment in the near future.

Further reading

Cronin and O'Connor in Ryan (ed.) (2000).

traditional and folk music   'Traditional music' is Irish folk music, and is defined by having evolved through a process of oral (as opposed to written) transmission. It also overlaps with 'folk' music in its more common sense (that is, as contemporary songs, usually with guitar accompaniment), although traditional music purists insist on distinguishing between the two. Despite the interchangeability of the terms 'folk' and 'traditional', then, the question of the legitimacy of the influence of other musics on this music is a vexed one, reflecting a perennial concern with AUTHENTICITY. This is well-reflected in the debates concerning the centrality of *sean-nós* ('old style') singing to traditional music. Unaccompanied, intensely charged, highly ornamented, and peculiar to GAELTACHT areas, it has been seen by many (such as Séan Ó RIADA) as the source of all genuine traditional music; others, however, have criticized what they regard as the essentialism of this approach. The point remains that traditional music has been adept in the past at absorbing ballroom music and music-hall song, for example, while debate as to where it ends and begins is one of the things which makes it a living form. In truth, even the most 'traditional' traditional music has been shaped by developments over the last century. Significantly, while it is often seen as a marker of Irishness, performance of traditional music crosses sectarian divisions, and it has not been associated with Celtic, nationalist or Catholic identity to the same degree as the Irish language.

Irish traditional music was usually dance music; reels, jigs and hornpipes are common, and are played in groups of two or three at a time called 'sets'. Increasingly, with the availability of recordings, it has become more a music for listening to. It shares a family resemblance with Cape Breton, Scottish and Eastern US folk musics, and there are different musical 'dialects' within it. Its language is that of variation within the strict limits of a 16-bar form. Due to the non-written nature of its transmission, and the mode of its performance (often in an informal or semi-informal setting), individual melodies are rarely repeated exactly, and are highly context-specific – for any given musician, some tunes may only be played in certain places, or at certain times, or with certain people present. Unlike classical music, additional music typically eschews vibrato, dynamic climaxes and diminuendo, and seamlessness of sound.

The first real collection of Irish folk music was the Neales' *A Collection of the Most Celebrated Irish Tunes* (1726), which was used by Turlough Carolan. Other collections preceded the work of Edward Bunting, and the nineteenth-century collectors, whose labours were given an edge by the threat of the FAMINE to folk culture. Their efforts anticipated the more general attempts to revive Irish culture later in the century of organizations such as the GAELIC LEAGUE. Ironically, however, a major boost to Irish music came from the DIASPORA which the Famine had done so much to augment. Francis O'Neill, a Chief of Police in Chicago, assiduously collected tunes from musicians scattered by EMIGRATION, publishing his greatest collection, *The Dance Music of Ireland* (with 1,001 tunes), in 1907. This is still referred to by Irish musicians as 'The Book'; crucially it focused on dance music, rather than the airs and songs which had appealed most to Victorian collectors.

O'Neill's work coincided with the onset of cheap, mass-produced musical instruments and the beginnings of a music recording industry. Like O'Neill himself, the effect on Ireland came via America, with a stream of recordings by fiddlers such as Michael Coleman (1891–1945) and James Morrison (1893–1947) pouring into Ireland from the early 1920s. Coleman's authority, in particular, was such that his style became a 'standard' which had the effect of tending to homogenize the different styles of playing which existed in Ireland. At the same time the puritanism of the new Free State meant that the house dance, at which dance music was usually played, was on the wane, being broken up by priests and forbidden under the Public Dance Halls Act (1935). The mid-twentieth century, in terms of officially sanctioned folk music at least, was the era of the *céilí*, which involved no-contact dancing, relied on accordions (rather then uillean pipes, fiddles and flute) as promoted by Radio Éireann. Céilí bands began to decline in the 1960s with the mainstream rediscovery of traditional music and competition from rock and pop music. In the 1940s, the government – like the BBC in Northern Ireland – sponsored the transcription of tunes and songs in the countryside. In 1951 the Comhaltas Ceoltóiri Éireann (Association of Irish Musicians) mounted the first annual Fleadh Cheoil (Music Festival). Elsewhere, with mass emigration, music-making in British cities began to influence that in Ireland.

It was the 1960s, however, which brought these developing forces to a head. The newly booming economy in the Republic, together with the folk revival in the USA, made folk music relevant to a young generation, and traditional music helped give

Irish youth culture a distinctive cast. Irish folk acts riding this wave included the Clancy Brothers and Tommy Makem, the Dubliners and Sweeney's Men. Often sweater-clad pub-based ballad-singers with little connection with the music as practised by traditional musicians, their efforts nevertheless re-energized the music. Contemporaneously, advances were also being made by the musicologist Breandán Breathnach (1912–85) who found ways of categorizing and understanding the structures of tunes, while Seán Ó Riada's experiments with traditional music led to his forming of Ceoltóiri Chualann, a group of outstanding solo instrumentalists which established the norm of ensemble playing, including instruments as various as flute, pipes, fiddle, harpsichord and bodhrán drum. Some of the members of the group formed themselves in 1963 into the Chieftains, an internationally successful group who were trailblazers for the music from their very first album, *The Chieftains* (1964).

Ensemble playing enabled traditional music to absorb the modern energies of folk and rock music, and the leading groups of the early 1970s, such as Planxty, the Bothy Band and De Danaan, did so with remarkable success. A new generation of soloists also emerged in the wake of such renewed activity and mainstream interest, including the influential fiddle player Tommy Peoples of The Bothy Band. The oral tradition which defines traditional music often flows through families, such as the Na Casaidigh (Cassidys) of Co. Donegal and the Keanes of Co. Galway; Dolores Keane, a member of the latter, is one of traditional music's outstanding singers, and her album *There Was a Maid* (1978), made with Reel Union, remains a landmark recording. Perhaps the single most influential figure of the last three decades is Dónal Lunny, a musician, arranger, producer and director whose career has taken him through all three definitive progressive folk bands – Planxty, the Bothy Band and Moving Hearts – and the musical direction of the BBC/RTÉ series *Bringing It All Back Home* (1992) (which advanced the much-disputed thesis that much subsequent US ROCK AND POP MUSIC derived from Irish music). Moving Hearts brought acoustic and electric instruments together in a trad-folk 'supergroup' which also included the Dublin singer Christy Moore. At the more raucous end of this spectrum were the Pogues, whose mantle has been inherited in the 1990s by bands such as the Saw Doctors from Tuam, Co. Galway. (See ROCK AND POP MUSIC.) By way of contrast, the Donegal band Clannad pioneered ambient 'Celtic' music, and launched the solo career of their lead singer Enya. Other HYBRID forms include orchestral suites (effectively concertos) for traditional music instruments; the best-known of these is Shaun Davey's *The Brendan Voyage* (1980) which featured Liam O'Flynn on uilleann pipes.

Traditional bands have multiplied since the 1970s, as have standards of playing. Many hybrid forms have arisen as the music has dispersed itself in fusions, and with the rise of 'world music' as a lucrative niche market and such spinoffs as the success of *Riverdance*. Probably the outstanding traditional music group of the last two decades has been Altan, whose albums include *Ceol Aduaidh* (1983) and *Island Angel* (1993).

Among the emergent bands extending the music's range and variety are Cran and Danú, while innovative instrumentalists include Máire Ní Chathasaigh, who has recreated the tradition of the harp in traditional music, and Sharon Shannon, who has brought a new verve and popular appeal to the accordion.

Further reading

Carson (1996). O hAllmhurain (1998). O'Connor (1991). Wallis and Wilson (2001). White (1998).

Travellers Irish Travellers are a nomadic ethnic group of Irish origin. Heavily discriminated against in a society which has long defined itself in monocultural terms, Travellers have in recent years asserted their cultural distinctiveness and struggled to achieve recognition and rights within Irish society. In the report of the Task Force for Travelling People (1995), Traveller culture was officially recognized for the first time, and the 1998 Traveller Accommodation Act required local authorities to provide accommodation facilities for Travellers (although this is still widely flouted). In the 1990s, the Traveller population was estimated at 35,000, with 15,000 of these living in Britain. Of the remainder, most live in the counties of Cork, Dublin, Galway and Limerick.

Traditionally, Travellers were nomads who made a livelihood in tinsmithing and horse dealing. Nomadism played an economic role, by enlarging market access; thus, the wealthiest Travellers tended to be the most mobile. It also brought important social and psychological functions, ensuring the orderly functioning of Traveller society. But the use of plastics, economic decline in the countryside, and restrictions on travel have now made their marginal activities less profitable. Many Travellers have moved into towns, engaging in activities such as waste recycling and scrap dealing.

Travellers face serious accommodation problems due to resistance by local authorities to meet obligations and many live in makeshift and roadside dwellings. Nevertheless, there is a new desire by this once-silenced community to improve its conditions, and in particular to ensure adequate education for its children.

Further reading

Joyce and Farmer (1985).

Trinity College, Dublin (TCD) The first Irish university was finally established in 1592 as a Protestant college modelled on Cambridge, being built on the site of a supposed Augustinian monastery after various earlier plans to found a seat of learning had collapsed. The Archbishop of DUBLIN, Adam Loftus (*c*.1533–1606), was closely involved in the plans, the hope being that it would make a significant difference to the religious allegiance of the Irish. In practice, undergraduates at Trinity came largely from the NEW ENGLISH. Trinity acquired an early reputation for teaching a strongly Calvinist theology not readily designed to appeal to CATHOLICS or to build bridges between the faiths.

As the seventeenth century progressed various attempts were made to change the direction of the university and ensure a wider appeal and impact. William Bedell (1571–1642) who was Provost (1627–9) introduced teaching in Irish to the curriculum, but this reform did not survive his tenure. The college was, as might be expected, caught up in subsequent religious and political conflicts. The puritan character of Trinity was challenged in the 1630s during the reign of Charles I (1625–49) when an Arminian doctrine, emphasizing free will and human merit rather than the failure of man to live up to God's standards, became the official belief of the English and Irish Churches. Many students and teachers opposed such changes. During the Interregnum attempts were made to return Trinity to its puritan heritage but its identity as an Anglican college was established after the Restoration and it became the university which educated the Protestant Ascendancy in the eighteenth century.

Numerous famous Irish thinkers, writers and even rebels attended TCD as undergraduates, including Edmund Burke, Thomas Davis, Wolfe Tone and Robert Emmet (who was expelled for his participation in the United Irishmen movement). Though from as early as 1793 Roman Catholics had been permitted to enter and take degrees at Trinity, restrictions on Catholic attendance continued in various forms and by the nineteenth century the College had become firmly established as a bastion of the Protestant Ascendancy. Numerous individual scholars from Trinity made important contributions to the fields of medicine, mathematics and science in this period. In 1904 the College opened its doors to women undergraduates, and continued to expand as Ireland's foremost centre of third-level education. However, much of its establishment, such as the Provost of 1914–19, Sir John Mahaffy, were bitterly and publicly opposed to nationalism. After Independence, its Ascendancy past and ethos meant that the College was neglected by governments in the 1920s and 1930s, while its Protestant base in the Free State also declined, from 8 per cent to 4 per cent of the population between 1920 and 1970. In 1944, the Archbishop of Dublin forbade Catholics to attend TCD on pain of excommunication, a sectarian measure which maintained its isolation; in 1970, however, this ban was rescinded. The College also drastically reduced its intake of overseas (effectively English) students, opening itself to more students from Ireland. In the 1960s, the College was a crucible for social change, and also developed a lively literary circle. See also architecture, Dublin, Dublin University Magazine.

Further reading

McDowell and Webb (1982).

Trimble, David (1944–)   Politician. Leader of the Ulster Unionist Party since 1995 and MP for Upper Bann since 1990. Trimble was a barrister and law lecturer at QUB, associated with the civil disobedience campaign against the Anglo-Irish Agreement before being elected to the UUP executive. He was also prominent in confrontations between Orange Order marches and Catholic residents at Portadown in 1995, and again at Drumcree in 1996. His leadership was strengthened with the UUP's winning of an extra Westminster seat in 1997, and his political skills were in evidence when he led the UUP into talks at Stormont which included Sinn Féin. Despite bitter criticism from Ian Paisley's DUP, Trimble was then able carry the day in the referendum called to establish a new Northern Ireland Assembly in April 1998. Facing down his UUP opponents, Trimble was elected Northern Ireland's First Minister in July 1998; bravely recasting James Craig's claim, he spoke of 'a pluralist parliament for a pluralist people'. Later that year he and John Hume were jointly awarded the Nobel Peace Prize.

Further reading

McDonald (2000).

Trollope, Anthony (1815–1882) English novelist. First sent to Ireland in 1841 as Deputy Postal Surveyor at Banagher, Trollope later worked for the Post Office in Cork and Belfast. He became deeply interested in Irish affairs, and embarked on an Irish novel, eventually published in 1847 as *The Macdermots of Ballcloran*. This romantic saga deals with the fortunes of the beautiful Euphemia Macdermot, pursued by both the scheming agent on her estate and an equally unscrupulous English police captain. In a similar vein, *The Kellys and the O'Kellys* (1848) presented the tempestuous love affairs of aristocratic Irish heiress Fanny Wyndham. Both novels centre on the complications of financial inheritance and romantic pursuits, but also touch on the increasing political tensions surrounding the Irish land question, a subject to which Trollope would return in *The Landleaguers* (posthumously published in 1883), a work inspired by the Phoenix Park Murders of 1882, and promoting the need for liberal compromise in the face of mounting agrarian violence.

Troubles A euphemism for political violence, applied to the periods 1916–23 and 1968–94. The most recent Troubles have been enormously costly in terms of deaths, injuries, compensation payments and material destruction. In Northern Ireland, a total of 3,376 people were killed and 42,000 injured in the 30 years to 1999, about 3 per cent of the population. This means that almost everyone has been affected in some way by the violence. Overwhelmingly, the victims have been the population of Northern Ireland. In addition, the British government has lost international prestige, both as a result of its actions in Northern Ireland and in the miscarriages of justice by its own legal system.

The most notorious cases involved the wrongful conviction in 1974 of the Guildford Four and the Birmingham Six, following IRA pub bombings in England which killed 26 people. They were followed by the jailing of the Maguire Seven in 1976, and the imprisonment of Judith Ward for the M62 bombing. In each case, convictions were made on the basis of faulty evidence of a single forensic scientist and confessions extorted through violence and intimidation. Gerry Conlon, of the Guildford Four, served 14 years, while his father Giuseppe died in prison; the Birmingham Six were not released until 1991, or Ward until 1992. These and other cases caused the British government to be singled out for its poor human rights record by Amnesty International and the European Court of Human Rights. Society in the Republic has also been distorted, albeit less drastically, through the infringement of civil liberties and by the need for large increases in security expenditure. Troubles violence has not been confined to Northern Ireland; the bloodiest single atrocity of the period was the LOYALIST car bombing of Dublin and Monaghan in 1975, and there were also IRA killings of British soldiers and innocent civilians in Europe. All of this took place at a time of moderately good relations between the Irish Republic and Britain.

The Troubles have been one of the decisive influences on Irish culture and society in the last century, creating the two states on the island in their first phase, and shaking both to their foundations in their second. Both periods feature in all cultural forms, including ART, FILM, MUSIC and TELEVISION. In particular, they have had a profound effect on literature and the writing of history, since the REVISIONIST debate has been shaped by, if it does not always centre on, the Troubles. In literature, their effect can be seen in numerous memoirs of participants, such as those by Ernie O'MALLEY and Gerry ADAMS, in many of W. B. YEATS's most important poems, drama by Sean O'CASEY and novels by Jennifer Johnson, Brian MOORE and Benedict Kiely. In recent poetry the Troubles are mediated more obliquely, but their influence is equally deep and disturbing in the work of Michael LONGLEY, Seamus HEANEY, Tom PAULIN, Paul DURCAN, Brendan KENNELLY and Paul MULDOON.

Further reading

Cairns and Richards (1988). Coogan (1996). Harris (1972). McCann (3rd edn 1993). McKay (2000). Mullin (1990). O'Connor (1993). Whyte (1996).

U2 Dublin rock band, and the one true supergroup to emerge from Ireland. They were formed in 1976 by Paul 'Bono' Hewson (1960–), Dave 'The Edge' Evans (1960–), Adam Clayton (1960–) and Larry Mullen (1962–) while they were still at school. Bono's voice and The Edge's guitar style are the trademarks of the band, clear on the critically acclaimed second album *Boy* (1980) and the internationally best-selling third, *War* (1982). Successive albums such as *The Unforgettable Fire* and *The Joshua Tree*, backed with worldwide tours, have proved enormously popular. Anthemic stadium rock and a commitment to various social good causes marked the band in the 1980s, while an ability to change can be seen in the harder-edged *Achtung Baby* (1991). Later albums include *Zooropa* (1993), *Pop* (1997) and *All That You Can't Leave Behind* (2000).

Further reading

Dunphy (1988).

Ulster Defence Association (UDA)   Formed from a variety of groups in the summer of 1971, the UDA claimed 40,000 members and was the main LOYALIST paramilitary organization of the TROUBLES period. It was involved in the large-scale intimidation and murder of CATHOLICS, and particularly in driving out those living in integrated (mixed-religion) areas of BELFAST. Like other such loyalist groups, its preferred tactic was individual assassination, rather than bombing, as often used by the IRA. The apogee of its power and influence was the ULSTER WORKERS' COUNCIL STRIKE of 1974. In spite of its paramilitary activities, the UDA remained a legal organization, unlike the IRA and UVF. It was finally proscribed in 1992.

Further reading

Bruce (1992).

Ulster Defence Regiment (UDR)   Indigenous Northern Irish regiment of the British Army, raised from April 1970 as a replacement for the B Specials, which had been disbanded for their sectarian attitudes and behaviour towards CATHOLICS. Catholics were encouraged to join the UDR, and Catholic membership soon reached 18 per cent. But this fell to 3 per cent as the IRA targeted them, and because of sectarianism within the UDR itself. UDR members were often part-time and vulnerable to attack; 197 were killed by the IRA. Their image also suffered because some members were implicated in the activities of LOYALIST paramilitaries, or of leaking classified information to such groups. In 1992 the UDR was incorporated into the Royal Irish Regiment.

Ulster Plantation   The British colonization of Ulster which was established after the FLIGHT OF THE EARLS enabled the British Crown to seize the lands of the departed magnates in Armagh, Cavan, Donegal, Fermanagh, Londonderry and Tyrone. The plantation was planned in 1609 providing estates of 1,000–2,000 acres for all the English and Scottish settlers who agreed to establish farms in Ulster. Problems were caused from the outset because the claims of the Irish who had helped the Crown forces in the NINE YEARS WAR were often deliberately ignored and natives received only 20 per cent of the land. It soon became apparent that whatever draconian measures were approved by the government could not be applied because the colony simply would not be viable without the help of native labour. The colonists were often threatened by disgruntled and dispossessed native Irish throughout the seventeenth century. Nevertheless settlers were attracted to the plantation and some 6,500 had emigrated to Ulster by 1630. The establishment of the Ulster Plantation is a key event in modern Irish history and has been instrumental in creating the divided character of contemporary Ireland with the Protestant people of the north-east, many of Scots origin, separated from the Catholic majority in the rest of the island.

Further reading

Moody (1939). Robinson (1984).

Ulster Workers' Council strike (1974)   The general strike against the Sunningdale Agreement and the POWER-SHARING executive headed by Brian Faulkner began on 14 May 1974. Protestant workers, particularly in power stations, walked out, gradually bringing Northern Ireland to a standstill. The UWC, which brought together LOYALIST trade unionists and paramilitaries, enforced the strike at first through violence and intimidation, but it was soon supported by almost all UNIONISTS. The effect was to paralyse the executive, which did not control security. The British Army could have intervened, but the new Labour government was unwilling for it to do so, convinced in any case that the executive was doomed. On 28 May the unionist members of the executive resigned and the government prorogued the Assembly and its executive. In October 1974, in a second general election, there was an overwhelming victory for unionists opposed to power sharing.

Following the strike, the British government realized the weakness of liberal unionism in the face of loyalist fears of abandonment, while the Irish government were made aware of the power of loyalists and British unwillingness to face it down. The SDLP saw that while they could topple STORMONT they had no acceptable replacement. But loyalists themselves could not re-impose a new version of Stormont-style domination; a later, so-called 'constitutional stoppage' in 1977 failed because it was not generally supported by unionists and was firmly opposed by the British government.

Ulster Volunteer Force   Founded by the Ulster Unionist Council in January 1913 as the armed body of LOYALISM, charged to resist the incorporation of Ulster into a united Ireland should Westminster press ahead with the Third HOME RULE Bill. In a publicity (and military) coup it acquired 25,000 firearms and 3 million rounds of ammunition in a gun-running operation at Larne in April 1914. The rise of the UVF provoked the formation of the IRISH VOLUNTEERS in Dublin. The organization was revived as a clandestine paramilitary organization during the 1968–94 TROUBLES.

unionism and the Unionist Party   Since the late seventeenth century, the question of Ireland's status and representation under the terms of a union with Britain had been discussed by writers such as Jonathan SWIFT, and in the eighteenth century by Irish patriots concerned about the future of an independent parliament. Unionism as a political ideology, however, emerged in the nineteenth century, in the wake of the passing of the ACT OF UNION in 1801. The Union itself was seen by many as a means of protecting Protestant interests in Ireland, but sceptics included a large section of Ulster's Protestants, who initially saw the Act as a prelude to CATHOLIC EMANCIPATION and a threat to their political autonomy in the country. As the century progressed, the lines of affiliation shifted, and Protestant loyalists who faced growing Catholic self-assertion through Emancipation and the REPEAL movement came to identify their best interests in the continuation of the Union.

The consolidation of Protestant unionism in the nineteenth century was encouraged by the parallel emergence of the ORANGE ORDER, and by the continuing distinction of Ulster, as a comparatively successful economic unit, from the rest of the island. Towards the end of the century, the Disestablishment of the CHURCH OF IRELAND and later the Land War intensified the perceived pressure on a Protestant minority, sustaining a reactionary unionism which drew support mostly from Ulster, but also from certain sectors of the Protestant and landed classes in the South of Ireland. Unionism now became a coherent and recognized political ideology, with the Unionist Party (UP) within parliament successfully opposing the Irish HOME RULE bills of 1886 and 1893.

In its opposition to the Third Home Rule Bill, unionism prepared for armed opposition to Westminster in 1911–14. Through the Ulster Unionist Council, and the Orange Order, resistance was prepared, with Edward CARSON providing political leadership, and extra-parliamentary protest being orchestrated by James CRAIG. The ULSTER VOLUNTEER FORCE armed LOYALISTS, while the signing of the Ulster Covenant (1912) showed unionism's ideological opposition to 'Rome Rule' from DUBLIN.

The right of a six-county section of Ulster to remain separate from a Home Rule Ireland for the first six years of Home Rule had already been conceded in the 1914 Bill. After WWI this was implemented in permanent form by the Government of Ireland Act of 1920, which made provision for two Irish PARLIAMENTS. When it came to drawing the border and constituency boundaries, their own strength, as well as SINN FÉIN abstention from Westminster, meant that unionists got what they wanted constitutionally and territorially in the new state and its parliament, STORMONT. During the following 50 years, there were threats to Unionist Party domination in 1932, when working-class Protestants and Catholics in BELFAST briefly united against cuts in the Outdoor Relief Rate; in 1943, when Craig's successor, John Andrews, was perceived to be incompetent, and resigned in favour of Basil BROOKE; and in 1958 and 1962, when working-class Protestants began to desert the UP for the NORTHERN IRELAND LABOUR PARTY (NILP).

Terence O'NEILL succeeded Brooke in 1963 and was committed to MODERNIZATION. This was long overdue, yet the attempt to implement it led to the breakdown of UP and, ultimately, of unionist domination, as O'Neill and the party were caught between a loyalist backlash and CIVIL RIGHTS movement demands for more radical reform. In swift succession, O'Neill resigned and was succeeded by Chichester-Clarke in 1969, followed by Brian Faulkner in 1971, while Liberal unionists walked out to found the Alliance Party in 1970 and Ian Paisley won O'Neill's Bannside seat and founded the rival Democratic Unionist Party (DUP) in 1971. At this point, just before the introduction of DIRECT RULE in 1972, unionism as a cohesive force can be said to end. Although the UUP remains powerful, it has broken its link with the British Conservative Party (see Anglo-Irish Agreement 1985), shares the Protestant vote with the DUP and smaller parties such as the Progressive Unionist Party (PUP); and, like the Orange Order, to which it was organically wedded, has witnessed a slow decline in its authority over the last 30 years. While a desire for union with Britain predominates among Protestants, and the Unionist Party remains the largest single force in Northern Irish politics (presently led by David Trimble), the cross-interest unionist alliance once organized to promote this no longer exists in a unified form.

Further reading

Bew, Gibbon and Patterson (1996). Brown (1985a). Gibbon (1975). Jackson (1989, 1990).

United Irish League   An organization established by William O'Brien in 1898 to campaign for the buying-out of landlords, in the interests of tenants, by compulsory purchase. By 1900 it had nearly 100,000 members, and made a powerful base on which the Irish Parliamentary Party could reunite.

United Irishmen   A society which campaigned for the end to English rule of Ireland accompanied by substantial parliamentary reform. The United Irishmen were founded in 1791 in Belfast and Dublin and soon established a number of branches throughout Ireland. They attracted both Catholics and Presbyterians inspired by the American and French revolutions and keen to reform what they regarded as the corrupt oligarchy of Anglo-Irish rule in Ireland. In 1794 the society demanded that universal suffrage be adopted for all elections, a message spread through their newspaper, the *Northern Star* (1792–97), which sold as many as 4,000 copies until the militia broke up the United Irishmen's presses. The Dublin branch of the society was suppressed when William Jackson revealed plans of some radicals to plot an invasion from France. Now that legitimate political expression had been denied them, many United Irishmen became involved in the conspiracies led by Wolfe Tone. By 1798, the year of Tone's doomed invasion, the United Irishmen had some 280,000 members. Many of the rank and file were far more militant than their leaders, who merely wanted constitutional reform, and demanded a democratic republic, or revenge on the Protestants. Such members were often closely linked with radical military organizations such as the Volunteers and the Defenders. The United Irishmen suffered considerably as the government sought to root out subversion. A successful campaign under the command of General Lake (1744–1808) saw most of their national and local leaders arrested (1797–98). The movement faded into insignificance after the failure of Robert Emmet's coup (1803).

Van Morrison (1945–)   Born George Ivan Morrison in East Belfast, the young Morrison was exposed to jazz and blues music during his upbringing and became a member of the Monarchs showband before fronting the rock band Them. However, despite hits such as 'Baby Please Don't Go' and 'Here Comes the Night', he became disillusioned with the London music scene, and moved to New York. His *Astral Weeks* (1969) was one of the most innovative pop albums ever cut while *Moondance* (1970) opened up a spiritual vein later pursued in *No Guru, No Method, No Teacher* (1986), *Avalon Sunset* (1989) and *The Healing Gate* (1997). Irish musical elements became more marked with *The Veedon Fleece* (1974), and culminated in *Irish Heartbeat* (1988), made with the Chieftains (see TRADITIONAL MUSIC). Morrison's Irish soul style, and the often biblical imagery of his songs, results from a blend of pop, rock, soul, traditional, and spiritual and gospel musics – the latter attributable to his Protestant background – making his work an exemplary instance of HYBRID and cross-cultural practice.

Vikings   The relationship between the Vikings and Ireland lasted for nearly 400 years after their first raid on the Irish coast in 795 (probably on Rathlin Island). The Vikings are generally remembered, as they are in England and Scotland, as ruthless plunderers and destroyers of civilized settlement. They usually attacked monasteries and raided Ireland regularly in the early ninth century, taking slaves as well as plunder. By the 830s far larger fleets of Viking ships sailed up the main Irish rivers for a series of sustained campaigns in the summers before returning to Scandinavia in the winters. The first permanent Viking settlements were established in DUBLIN and Co. Louth in 841, and were named longphorts. Dublin developed into a slaving centre, the Vikings bringing prisoners from their raids into Scotland and Northumberland to sell on.

Now that the Vikings were settled in Ireland the native kings started to attack them, managing to expel the Vikings from Dublin in 902, when they retreated to the Isle of Man. However, the Vikings returned in force in 914, landing at Waterford and plundering Munster in the following year. In 919 they defeated the Niall Glúdub, king of the Uí Néills, and leader of combined Irish forces from Ulster, Connacht and Meath. They built, as well as destroyed, founding settlements at Wexford (*c*.921) and Limerick (922). For much of the tenth century Viking kings, ruling in Dublin, dominated the east coast of Ireland and were closely linked to Viking settlements in England, centred at York. The Irish started to have more success against the Vikings towards the end of the century, their first major victory coming at the Battle of TARA (980) when Mael Sechlainn II (Malachi) triumphed, allowing him to seize Dublin in

994. After a series of battles the Vikings were finally defeated by BRIAN BORU at Clontarf, bringing their dominance in Ireland to an end.

As elsewhere in Europe the Viking invasion destroyed and disrupted ordinary life in many coastal areas. They destroyed religious settlements and other communities, although they also served to unite previously hostile factions and dynasties. The Vikings founded or developed a number of settlements which became important Irish towns – Dublin, Wexford, Waterford, CORK and Limerick. They generally established bases for their ships, which then grew into urban centres. They helped to establish trade routes between Ireland and the rest of Europe. However, their impact on Irish ART and literature was more limited and mainly confined to ARCHITECTURE, and their legacy has not inspired much subsequent literature (although Seamus HEANEY's *North* (1975) is one exception).

Further reading

Ó Corráin (1972).

Volunteers   A military force who played an important role in helping to radicalize politics in Ireland in the late eighteenth century. The Volunteers were formed in the late 1770s as a means of protecting Ireland from invasion and establishing law and order when the army had been called to fight in the American War of Independence. There were about 60,000 volunteers by 1782. The ideals of the American revolutions helped to inspire the volunteers who became involved in campaigns to allow Ireland to take advantage of free trade and, more significantly, independence for the Irish parliament. Henry Grattan played a prominent role in organizing the focus and actions of the Volunteers. At the National Convention held in DUBLIN in 1783, the Volunteers produced a plan for reform but by now they were opposed by many influential figures wary of their growing influence. Some of their leaders, most notably Napper Tandy (*c.*1737–1803) wanted to establish a broader-based movement and argued that more working-class members would be of benefit, but others such as the Earl of Charlemont (1728–99) felt that, given the opposition to the growing radicalism of the Volunteers, they should be more cautious in their demands. Although the French Revolution gave further impetus to the causes of the Volunteers, the movement withered in the 1790s as the government sought other means of raising a defence force.

War of Independence see **Anglo-Irish War**

Watters, Eugene Rutherford Louis (Eoghan Ó Tuairisc) (1919–1982)   Poet, novelist, dramatist. Born in Co. Galway, Watters was educated at UCD. His writing in Irish includes three novels, eight plays, and two collections of poetry and *Aifreann na Marbh* (1964), a nine-part requiem for the victims of Hiroshima. An Irish-language activist, he joined the HUNGER STRIKE held in 1966 to draw attention to its plight. His masterpiece, in English, is the long poem *The Week-End of Dermot and Grace* (1964), a highly imaginative modernist reworking of the Diarmid and Grainne legend set in 1945. Neglected because of his bilingualism and modernism, Watters is a fascinating writer whose work raises large questions about the nature and ambitions of modern Irish writing.

Further reading

Ellis and Kelly (eds) (1985). Goodby and Scully (eds) (1999).

Wentworth, Thomas, 1st Earl of Strafford (1593–1641)   Appointed Lord Deputy by Charles I in 1632. Wentworth became one of the most unpopular viceroys because of his 'thorough' policy of increasing the power of the king and the Church of Ireland at the expense of both the Old English and New English (deputies usually risked offending one rather than both of these colonial factions). Wentworth also managed to offend sections of the Irish church by insisting that the High Church style of worship promoted by Charles be practised at the expense of Calvinist forms. He worked hard to try to replace Old English landowners with new settlers, with mixed success. When war broke out in 1639 Strafford returned to England where parliament, worried by the extent of his draconian policies in England and Ireland, had him impeached. Charles, recognizing Strafford's unpopularity, was forced to agree to his execution on 12 May 1641.

Further reading

Kearney (1959).

Whiteboys   Secret societies which proliferated in the early nineteenth century against the backdrop of increasing economic pressures after the Act of Union. Composed largely of peasantry, artisans and agrarian labourers, they were frequently violent, particularly in response to what they regarded as unfair demands for the payment of Church of Ireland tithes. Many groups followed precise rituals, such as the wearing of masks or white shirts when on a raid. According to locality, the groups were also variously known as Whitefeet, Rockites, Shanavests or Ribbonmen. They often went under the leadership of a fictional 'captain': in 1824 Thomas MOORE's *Memoirs of Captain Rock* offered a satirical fake biography of the leader of one such society.

Wilde, Jane Francesca ('Speranza') (c.1824–1896)   Poet and mother of Oscar WILDE, born in Wexford. Under her pen-name 'Speranza', she was a regular contributor to the *NATION*, where her poetry tended towards exclamatory patriotic verse, such as 'The Famine Year':

> Oh! We know not what is smiling, and we know not what is dying;
> But we're hungry, very hungry, and we cannot stop our crying ...

In 1851 she married William WILDE, and after his death in 1876 moved to London, where she held literary soirées, often in conjunction with her son. She is remembered as a vivid personality, and as an important folklorist for her collections, *Ancient Legends, Mystic Charms, and Superstitions of Ireland* (1887), and *Ancient Cures, Charms and Usages of Ireland* (1890).

Wilde, Oscar Fingal O'Flahertie Wills (1854–1900)   Playwright and poet, and essayist, famed for his epigrammatic wit and extravagant dress, and notoriously imprisoned for homosexuality. The son of the eminent surgeon WILLIAM WILDE, and the poet Lady (JANE) WILDE ('Speranza'), he was born in DUBLIN and educated at TRINITY COLLEGE, before moving to Magdalen College, Oxford, to take a degree in classics. At Magdalen, he came under the influence of Walter Pater and the so-called Aesthetic Movement, whose motto, 'art for art's sake', was to become close to his heart. Wilde was a brilliant scholar who, after graduation, threw himself headlong into the literary and theatrical society of London. His early dramatic efforts were subsidized by lecturing, magazine editing and writing children's stories (including The *Selfish Giant* and The *Happy Prince*) In 1884 he married Constance Lloyd. The couple had two sons and appeared settled in family life, but in 1891 Wilde met the handsome, dandyish son of the Marquis of Queensbury, Lord Alfred Douglas, with whom he became infatuated. His private life now became the subject of intense speculation, and it was rumoured that he consorted with male prostitutes. When Queensbury openly referred to him as a sodomite, Wilde took proceedings against him for libel, a rather foolhardy move given the existence of his letters to Douglas and other evidence. At the trial, Queensbury was defended by the unionist barrister Edward CARSON, who skilfully led Wilde into a number of damaging admissions on the witness stand. Queensbury was found not guilty, and, in turn, Wilde was prosecuted on charges of homosexual practice. He spent two years in prison, during which time he wrote *De Profundis*, a long and complex meditation on his persecution, addressed to Alfred Douglas. After his release he penned *The Ballad of Reading Gaol* (1898), as a testimony to his experiences of incarceration. It became a classic work of prison literature:

I never saw a man who looked
With such a wistful eye
Under the little tent of blue
Which prisoners call the sky.

Wilde spent his later years in Paris, where he adopted the pseudonym of Sebastian Melmoth, a reference to the martyr-like protagonist of the novel *Melmoth the Wanderer*, written by his great uncle Charles MATURIN. He continued an occasional relationship with Douglas, but lost many of his former friends as a result of the scandal of the trial. He died in the winter of 1900, and is buried in Père Lachaise cemetery.

Wilde's best works remain his novel, *The Picture of Dorian Gray* (1891), and his four most successful plays, *Lady Windermere's Fan* (1892), *A Woman of No Importance* (1893), *An Ideal Husband* (1894), and finally what many regard as his most accomplished comedy, *The Importance of Being Earnest* (1895). His deftly argued essays, including 'The Decay of the Art of Lying' and 'The Soul of Man Under Socialism', similarly display his genius for witticism but suggest, too, a more serious philosophical and critical intelligence. He remains one of the most colourful personalities of the period, and has subsequently been depicted in numerous satires, films and plays, including Terry Eagleton's play *Saint Oscar* (1990).

Further reading

Ellmann (1987).

Wilde, William (1815–1876) Antiquarian, biographer and surgeon; the father of Oscar WILDE. Married Jane Francesca Elgee ('Speranza') in 1851, and they had three children. The family lived in DUBLIN's fashionable Merrion Square, where Sir William conducted his practice and contributed to numerous scholarly journals, producing, most notably, a comprehensive catalogue of the ROYAL IRISH ACADEMY collection of antiquities.

William III, Williamite Wars William III (1650–1702) became king of England, Scotland and Ireland after the deposition of JAMES II in the revolution of 1688. William came to Ireland in 1690 when James returned from exile to try to re-establish his reign through his Catholic support in Ireland. While William was undogmatic and keen to tolerate as many forms of religion as he could, he has become the symbol of Protestant resistance to Catholicism and has been enshrined as the inspiration for the ORANGE ORDER and UNIONISM in general.

The Williamite Wars lasted from 1689 to 1691. Protestant support for the new English monarch was most pronounced in Ulster. After arriving, James's forces launched an assault on the Protestant stronghold of DERRY but were met with the fierce resistance of the Apprentice Boys who closed the gates to prevent the city being overrun. The city was besieged from 18 April until 31 July 1689 as James tried to starve it into submission, but after serious hardship two ships with supplies managed to break through the blockade and relieve the starving inhabitants after 105 days. The siege marked the first time that the Protestant slogan 'No Surrender' was employed and is celebrated by the annual Apprentice Boys' MARCH every 31 July.

Despite this victory the early stages of the war saw the sides equally balanced after a series of JACOBITE victories in Ulster. William's arrival in the following year led to a decisive victory at the BATTLE OF THE BOYNE, leaving the Jacobites controlling Munster and Connacht. It was only after the capture of Athlone and a further victory at Aughrim (12 July 1690), which enabled the Williamite forces to surround the chief Catholic stronghold at Limerick, that the balance of power tilted firmly in favour of a Protestant victory. The Jacobite forces were split over the prospect of surrender, despite the offer of relatively generous terms, but eventually agreed and the wars ended with the signing of the treaty of Limerick (3 October 1690). The Jacobite forces were allowed to leave for France and Protestant ascendancy was affirmed.

Wilson, Robert McLiam (1964–)   Novelist. Born in BELFAST, educated there and at Cambridge University, which he left before graduating, Wilson published *Ripley Bogle* (1989) to enthusiastic reviews. The novel takes the form of an unreliable autobiography by the narrator, who switches between the present as a tramp in London and a past in the Belfast of the TROUBLES. An ABORTION, a friend's betrayal, his exploitation of the modish appeal of his Northern Irishness are gradually divulged, but the main interest of the novel is the brio of Wilson's prose style. *Manfred's Pain* (1992) is a narrative by an old Jewish man who considers the addiction to violence which ruined him, while *The Dispossessed* (1992) is a documentary account of poverty in 1980s Britain, with photographs by Donovan Wylie. *Eureka Street* (1997), set in a Belfast emerging from the Troubles, was successfully adapted for TELEVISION by the BBC.

women, social position of   Women have played a significant role in modern Irish society, beginning with the formation of a women's section of the LAND LEAGUE in 1880, and continuing in the early years of the twentieth century. Lady GREGORY was a central figure of the LITERARY REVIVAL, while distinguished political figures included Maud GONNE, Hanna Sheehy-Skeffington (1877–1946), Helena Molony (1884–1967), Louie Bennett (1870–1956) and Eva Gore-Booth. Her sister, Constance MARKIEWICZ (1868–1927), was the first woman to be elected to a seat in the British House of Commons. Suffragism and feminism operated as a powerful force in the independence struggle through organizations such as Cumann na mBán (The Society of Women), Inghinidhe na hÉireann (Daughters of Ireland) and the Irish Women's Franchise League, often alongside the radical wing of NATIONALISM. Markiewicz became Minister for Labour in the first DÁIL, and the first Free State government introduced votes for all women over 21 in 1923, well ahead of Britain and many other European states.

Thereafter, the conservative forces behind independence reasserted themselves as a radical social agenda was shelved in favour of the politics of nationalism and self-sufficiency. Markiewicz's post was made a non-Cabinet one, while modernity – as it applied to women's dress, dance MUSIC and other cultural forms – was subject to denunciation and CENSORSHIP. The 1920s, a liberal decade in many countries, was an increasingly repressive one in Ireland, north and south, and, given the emphasis on sexual restriction, particularly so for women. Some women's voices persisted through the 1930s and 1940s, despite the reactionary tide against them, though they were generally isolated. Cultural activity, in particular, saw women finding something of the voice denied to them in the political sphere. The main promulgators of artistic modernism in the visual arts were Evie Hone (1894–1955) and Mainie JELLETT (1897–1943), members of a strong tradition of female organizers and practitioners which includes May Guinness (1863–1955), Wilhelmina Geddes (1885–1955) and Eileen Gray (1888–1976). Apart from well-known women novelists of the period, such as Elizabeth BOWEN and Kate O'BRIEN, there were also poets, such as Blanaid Salkeld (1880–1958), whose work still awaits proper acknowledgement.

The Irish CONSTITUTION of 1937 recognized the family, sustained by women, as the basic unit of social organization, a deliberately narrow and prescriptive definition of women's role in the new state. While women were subject to the marriage bar which applied to state posts, or submitted to a domestic role, given low wages and male unemployment (and the low and late marriage rate), many continued to work and/or emigrate. Unlike other European countries of emigration, where the male-to-female ratio was around 2:1, the Irish ratio was 1:1, leading to intermittent moral panics about the 'spiritual dangers' to which women would be exposed. Though warned to be content with their lot and remain in Ireland, the female emigration rate remained high, with many finding employment as nurses or teachers abroad in order to improve their status and financial independence.

The subservient position of women in Ireland was challenged with the 'second wave' of feminism, as the Women's Movement reached Ireland in the late 1960s and early 1970s. Concerns were the same as elsewhere – violence against women, discrimination and unequal pay and opportunities, media representation of women and so on – and pressure led to the Anti-Discrimination (Pay) Act (1974), which established the right to equal pay for work of equal value, and the Employment Equality Act (1977) which prohibited discrimination on the grounds of sex or marital status, overturning the marriage bar. Such legislation was often diluted, delayed and evaded partly as a result of what was, until the early 1990s, a poor employment situation. In addition, women's legal progress was more often the result of Ireland's membership of the EEC than of indigenous women's groups, indicating a lack of proactive activity which was to be exploited by the Right in the 1980s.

Following the upholding of the appeal by Mary McGee in 1973, embodied in a Bill of 1977, effectively allowing access to CONTRACEPTION, organizations such as the Pro-Life

Amendment Campaign led an attempt, through pre-emptive legislation on ABORTION and DIVORCE, to weaken women's reproductive rights and control of their bodies. This took the form of bitter and divisive referenda in 1983 and 1986, the negative outcomes of which were overturned in 1992 and 1995. The resistance to attempts to reassert conservative social values in the 1980s was fostered by a new generation of women in media and in politics. Journalists such as Mary Kenny, Nell McCafferty and Maeve Binchy appeared in papers such as the *Irish Press* and the *Irish Times*, extending the irreverent critique of earlier lone voices such as that of Edna O'BRIEN. Taboo areas of family life were exposed through TELEVISION and radio; this continued into the 1990s with Marion Finacune's *Liveline* radio talk show. At the same time, women politicians, from Bernadette DEVLIN in Northern Ireland to Mary ROBINSON and Mary McAleese (her successor as President) in the Republic, began to emerge more independently to push women's issues, breaking with the tradition that women in politics had to be the widows or daughters of successful male politicians. As a result, the number of women deputies in the DÁIL has increased from six (in 1977) to 22 (in 1996).

Belying their only slowly improving social position, women continue to be leaders in cultural life in all fields; Máire Mhac an tSaoi and Nuala Ní DHOMHNAILL are, arguably, the leaders of their respective revivals of Irish-language poetry (in the 1950s and 1980s), while Eavan BOLAND and Eiléan Ní CHULLEANÁIN are among the leading Irish poets of their generation, and Edna LONGLEY is the leading contemporary Irish poetry critic. Similarly, the outstanding tradition of women in the visual arts and music has continued with Kathy Prendergast, Jane O'Leary, Alice Maher, Eithne Jordan, Cathy Carman, Sharon Shannon, Marie Barrett, Sinéad O'Connor and Mháire Sutherland. (See ART, ROCK AND POP MUSIC, MUSIC and TRADITIONAL MUSIC.)

Further reading

Beale (1986). Bolger (ed.) (1986). Brown (1985b). Coulter (1993). Coxhead (1979). Innes (1993). Luddy and Murphy (1990). Ní Chuilleanáin (ed.) (1985). Owens (1984). Tweedy (1992). Ward (1983).

World War I (WWI)   As Roy Foster has suggested, 'The First World War should be seen as one of the most decisive events in modern Irish history'. Economically it brought a boom economy; politically, it postponed a showdown on the Third HOME RULE Bill. John REDMOND, leader of the IRISH PARLIAMENTARY PARTY (IPP), was eager to make the case for its enactment by showing Irish loyalty. Initially he suggested that Ireland be guarded by the IRISH VOLUNTEERS, north and south, while recruitment proceeded. Soon afterwards, however, he pledged the Volunteers to fight 'wherever the firing line extends'. This split the Redmondites and radical NATIONALIST Volunteers, with 170,000 supporting Redmond and around 10,000 ignoring him. Tens of thousands of ULSTER VOLUNTEER FORCE members joined the new 36th (Ulster) Division; nationalist recruits, however, were dispersed among different regiments, causing some resentment and suspicion.

While Irish soldiers overall suffered as high a casualty rate as other sections of the British Army, the fate of the Ulster Division at the Battle of the Somme was particularly bloody. In the first two days, 5,500 were killed or wounded, and this has been taken since as sealing the Union in blood, in stark contrast to the 'disloyalty' of the nationalist EASTER RISING. The event is powerfully explored in Frank McGuinness's play *Observe the Sons of Ulster Marching Towards the Somme* (1986), which deals with LOYALISM, violence and sexuality. Meanwhile, in Ireland SINN FÉIN ran an increasingly successful anti-recruitment drive. As support leaked away from the IPP with the execution of the Rising's leaders, so the war which had precipitated it was overshadowed.

Viewing it as a British war, the REPUBLIC has eschewed any official Armistice Day commemoration of Irishmen who died in WWI (or WWII) until very recently; for unionists, however, the Somme remains a mythical battle to rank with that of the BOYNE.

Further reading

Fitzpatrick (1985).

World War II (WWII) World War II was known in Ireland as 'the Emergency'. The term, which was DE VALERA's, conferred a constitutional status on the country's NEUTRALITY (necessary, since it was technically still a member of the British Commonwealth). Neutrality was popular because it boosted the sense that the new nation had made an independent choice (in reality, the Irish authorities repatriated British service personnel while they interned their German equivalents). An IRA attempt to secure German backing for an attack on Britain had little support, and was suppressed. During the war, thousands in Ireland EMIGRATED to work in British factories or to join its armed forces. Despite threats, however, De Valera would not allow Irish territory or ports to be used by the Allies. Criticized by Churchill, he defended the Irish stance in a radio broadcast of 1945 (although some have felt that he took even-handedness too far by signing the condolences book in the German Embassy on the death of Hitler). After the war, Ireland was isolated to some degree by the former Allies.

If the southern state proved itself in war, Northern Ireland was arguably saved by it. Until 1941, it was unprepared, especially for air-raids on BELFAST, which had been thought beyond German bombing range. John Andrews, who had replaced CRAIG in 1940, was seen as incompetent and resigned in favour of Basil BROOKE in 1943. But the war boosted flagging industries and generated prosperity. Northern Ireland was crucial to providing air cover for Atlantic convoys and, because of its distance from reconnaissance, a major site for the assembly of D-Day men and material.

Further reading

Bardon (1992). Fisk (1996).

'X' case (1992)   Like the Kerry Babies Case (see Ní Dhomhnaill) of a decade before, this case crystallized concern with, and opposition to, official Catholic teaching on SEXUALITY and ABORTION. It began when an injunction was taken out by the Attorney General Harry Whelehan to prevent a 14-year-old-girl who had been raped from travelling to Britain for an abortion. Whelehan was a FIANNA FÁIL supporter who held strict puritan views, and the High Court judge who made the ruling was a former Attorney General who in 1973 had attempted to prevent the distribution of a Family Planning Association booklet. Intense anger followed the Court's decision to force the girl to endure the pregnancy, leading to vigils, demonstrations, and school children's walkouts. Under pressure the Supreme Court made a bizarre re-interpretation of the Pro-Life clause added to the CONSTITUTION in 1983, claiming that it allowed abortion if there was a danger of the mother committing suicide. The aftermath of the 'X' case can be traced in the reforms which legalized homosexuality and promoted the use of condoms to combat AIDS.

Yeats, Jack Butler (1871–1957)   Painter, dramatist and prose writer. A son of artist John Butler Yeats and younger brother of the poet and dramatist W. B. YEATS, Jack B. Yeats was born in London and spent his childhood largely in Co. Sligo. The light on the Sligo countryside, he afterwards maintained, prompted his decision to become a painter. After attending the Westminster School of Art, he went to Manchester and worked as a black-and-white illustrator. In 1894 he produced the first cartoon strip version of *Sherlock Holmes*, and contributed to several newspapers and journals including *Punch Magazine*. He also edited and illustrated two monthly publications, *Broadsheet* (1902–03) and *Broadside* (1908–15). His friendship with J. M. SYNGE resulted in illustrated articles for the *Manchester Guardian* (1905) on the Congested Districts in Ireland, and he also illustrated George Birmingham's *Irishmen All* (1913). Yeats's early work romantically portrays various aspects of rural Irish life, as evident in the *Guardian* illustrations that were used to accompany Synge's *The Aran Islands* (1907). Yeats devoted the first 12 years of his career to watercolours (which bear some comparison with those of Turner and Cézanne) before turning to oils *c.*1905. These began as conservatively representational, showing the influence of Honoré Daumier. In the mid-1920s, however, his realism gave way to an intensely expressive vision, the romanticism of his early illustrations metamorphosed, through uninhibited brush-strokes and intense colour, into a volatile and highly subjective vision. In later paintings, such as *A Race in Hy-Brazil* (1937) and *Returning from the Bathe, Mid-day* (1948), these techniques produce dazzlingly radiant canvases with enormous depth of colour. Yeats also wrote plays for children and adults: *La La Noo* (1942) and *In Sand* (1949) were staged at the ABBEY THEATRE's experimental Peacock Theatre. These later plays subvert dramatic convention in ways that resemble the plays of Samuel BECKETT, an admirer of Yeats. In the 1930s, Yeats produced a number of fictionalized autobiographies and fantasies, including *Sligo* (1930), *Sailing, Sailing Swiftly* (1933), and *The Amaranthers* (1936). These innovative prose works bear some comparison with the work of Flann O'BRIEN in their rejection of realist narrative form and modernist self-reflexivity, while their deeply subjective, even idiosyncratic, narrative modes clearly relate them to Yeats's great paintings of this period.

Further reading

Pyle (1970). Rosenthal (1993).

Yeats, William Butler (1865–1939)   Poet, playwright, short story writer, folklorist, publicist and cultural activist. Yeats was the foremost contributor to the Irish LITERARY REVIVAL. Born in DUBLIN to the portrait-painter John Butler Yeats and Susan Pollexfen, daughter of a Sligo merchant, Yeats spent his childhood summers with his maternal grandparents in the West of Ireland. The folk tales he heard in Sligo provided the inspiration for a number of early poems and some of the material for two collections of prose, *Fairy and Folk Tales of the Irish Peasantry* (1888) and *The Celtic Twilight* (1893). The title of the latter collection became a label for the wistful poetic reveries that Yeats and others composed in the 1890s, the apotheosis of which is *The Wind Among the Reeds* (1899). Other important early works include *The Wanderings of Oisin* (1889) and *The Countess Kathleen and Various Legends and Lyrics* (1892).

The folkloric and legendary Irish material in this work was linked to occult interests: Yeats joined the Theosophical Society and the Rosicrucian Order of the Golden Dawn in 1890. His preoccupations with spiritualism and magic informed his interest in William Blake, whose poetry Yeats co-edited in 1893, and can be glimpsed in prose of the time, such as 'Rosa Alchemica', from *The Secret Rose* (1897). Yeats championed Irish literature in this period: *Representative Irish Tales* appeared alongside his own stories *John Sherman and Dhoya* in 1891, and he helped found the National Literary Society in 1892, as well as being active in the Irish Literary Society in London. His 1894 meeting with Augusta, Lady GREGORY would culminate in the founding of the ABBEY THEATRE; much of Yeats's energy at the turn of the century and afterwards was directed towards the creation of a national drama. His own NATIONALIST play *Cathleen Ní Houlihan* was first performed in 1902, with Yeats's great love, Maud GONNE, in the title role. His varied dramatic output includes plays in both verse and prose, the most innovative of which are those modelled after the highly stylized Japanese Noh theatre, such as *At the Hawk's Well* (1921), one of several plays based on the CÚ CHULAINN legend.

Yeats's imagination resembles that of a number of modernists, but he belonged to an older generation than theirs, and the influence of the literary movements of the 1890s is crucial to his poetics. In his first collected poems, the 1895 *Poems*, Yeats grouped a selection of early work drawn from two previous collections under the title 'Crossways', his preface arguing that 'in them he tried many pathways'. His early poetic forays led him not only to Celtic materials, but also to Symbolism, as revealed in the occult hermeticism of those poems he chose to include in 'The Rose' subdivision of *Poems*. Yeats was also deeply involved in English Aestheticism, publishing in *The Dome*, *The Savoy* and *The Yellow Book*: the Celticism of his collection of Irish folklore, *The Celtic Twilight* (1893) is intertwined with the Decadent preoccupations and Paterian style of his short stories, *The Secret Rose* (1897), 'The Tables of the Law' and 'The Adoration of the Magi'. Yeats's Aestheticism, like his Celticism, was fuelled by his antipathy towards aspects of late Victorian Britain, its materialism, utilitarianism and imperialism. His poetic of the 1890s is thus transitional to modernism, rather than high modernist in any formal experimental sense.

By 1900 Yeats had learnt from his playwriting, throwing off the introspection, wavering rhythms and ornate diction of his Celtic Twilight verse. A tough declamatory voice begins to be heard in his poetry; and, by the time of *Responsibilities* (1914), *the Wild Swans at Coole* (1919) and *Michael Robartes and the Dancer* (1921), he was increasingly concerned with public controversy and historical events. These volumes include commentary and interventions into contemporary Irish history – 'Easter, 1916', 'On a Political Prisoner' – and expositions of broader historical processes, as in the apocalyptic 'The Second Coming'. The latter poems are based on Yeats's spiritually inspired historiography, outlined in the poem 'The Phases on the Moon', which had its origins in his marriage in 1917 to Georgie Hyde Lees, whose aptitude as a medium was quickly demonstrated. Yeats would formulate his arcane knowledge of historical cycles and human personality imparted to him via his wife in several esoteric prose works: *Per Amica Silentia Lunae* (1917), and *A Vision* (1925); and it became the very marrow of many of the poems collected in *The Tower* (1928) and *The Winding Stair and Other Poems* (1933). In these volumes, and in his last poems and plays, Yeats perceives his true lineage to be that of the ANGLO-IRISH ASCENDANCY, and proceeds to savage the cultural torpor of the Irish Free State. His nightmarish vision of historical process finds its final expression in the play *Purgatory* (1938), while his patrician disparagement of modernity is given its last articulation in the polemics of the posthumously published *On the Boiler* (1939).

Further reading

Brown (1999). Donoghue (1971). Ellmann (1964). Foster, R. F. (1997).

Young Ireland   The 'Young Irelanders' was the name originally given by Daniel O'CONNELL to the group of journalists, lawyers and poets brought together through the founding of the NATION newspaper in 1842. Led by Thomas DAVIS, Charles Gavan DUFFY and John Blake DILLON, Young Ireland quickly developed from being a splinter of the national REPEAL movement and, under the influence of European romantic NATIONALISM, began to formulate a distinct policy for an inclusivist CULTURAL NATIONALISM. The ethos defined by Davis was of 'the spirit of the nation', a racial identity forged through a shared cultural inheritance which would rise above religious and economic divides.

The Young Irelanders, several of whom were highly educated, middle-class Protestants, were astute in recognizing the increasing power of print to communicate with a large audience. In the *Nation*, they strove for a simple and even simplistic rhetoric, including short poems and anthems amidst announcements for Repeal meetings, celebratory political reports, and commercial illustrations. The newspaper was highly successful and by 1843, a year after its launch, was reaching an estimated readership of 250,000. In addition, the Young Irelanders established a publishing venture entitled 'The Library of Ireland' series, through which they issued popular romantic histories of Ireland and a number of literary works. Of most importance was the publication, in 1842, of *The Ballad Poetry of Ireland*. Edited by Charles Gavan Duffy and including works by several leading writers of the day, this landmark anthology was strategically designed to appeal to popular tastes with its emphasis on accessible ballad forms and romantic nationalist sentiments.

From a cultural perspective, the Young Ireland movement was relatively successful in integrating the interests of an urban intellectual elite with those of the nation as a whole. Politically, their position was difficult, however, as they clashed with O'Connell over the issue of non-denominational education and the direction of the Repeal movement in general. Increasingly, too, this predominantly moderate group was obliged to confront the question of whether violence was legitimate as a means of achieving political goals. Tensions were increased by the cataclysmic impact of the FAMINE and the death of Thomas Davis, in 1845. An extremist wing of the Young Ireland movement which regrouped under the revolutionary, John MITCHEL, and his radical newspaper the *United Irishman*, in 1848, began to adopt a less moderate policy of militaristic republicanism. In 1848, Mitchel and William Smith O'BRIEN led a rebellion which, though quickly suppressed by government forces, became legendary within nationalist ideology, particularly after the leaders of the rising were arrested and several deported.

Z

Zoological Gardens Dublin zoo in the grounds of the Phoenix Park, was founded in 1830 by the Zoological Society of Dublin with animals supplied by London Zoo, making it one of the oldest zoos in Europe. It has long been considered a typically Victorian institution, prompting calls for its closure in the 1980s and early 1990s as animals revealed disorders stemmimg from inadequate conditions. Major improvements have since been made. The zoo's lions have been consistent attractions since the first pair was bought in 1855, the most famous being Cairbre, born in the zoo in 1927, later to become the original mascot for MGM films. Belfast (originally Bellevue) Zoo was opened in 1934. Like its Dublin counterpart its fortunes declined in the mid-century, but it was massively redeveloped in the late 1970s; for its promotion of conservation and breeding it is now held up as a model of its kind. Cork's Fota Wildlife Park, opened in 1983, and run by the Zoological Society of Ireland and University College Cork, represents a new approach to the presentation and study of native and non-native wildlife in Ireland.

Bibliography

This bibliography provides full details of works recommended in relevant individual entries, and also includes works that were especially helpful in the preparation of the Glossary.

Adams, Alice (1991) 'Coming apart at the seams: *Good Behaviour* as an anti-comedy of manners', *Journal of Irish Literature* 20: 27–35.

Adams, Gerry (1986) *The Politics of Irish Freedom*, Dingle: Brandon.

Adams, Gerry (1996) *Before the Dawn*, Dingle: Brandon.

Allen, Kieran (2000) *The Celtic Tiger: The Myth of Social Partnership in Ireland*, Manchester: Manchester University Press.

Allen, Nicholas (2003) *George Russell (AE) and the New Ireland*, Dublin: Four Courts Press.

Andrews, Elmer (ed.) (1998) *The Poetry of Seamus Heaney*, London: Icon Books.

Andrews, J. H. (1975) *A Paper Landscape: The Ordnance Survey in Nineteenth-century Ireland*, Oxford: Oxford University Press.

Arnold, Bruce (1969) *A Concise History of Irish Art*, London: Thames and Hudson.

Arnold, Bruce (1991) *Manie Jellett and the Modern Movement in Ireland*, New Haven: Yale University Press.

Arthur, Paul (2000) *Special Relationships: Britain, Ireland and the Northern Ireland Problem*, Belfast: Blackstaff.

Ashcroft, Bill, Griffiths, Gareth and Tiffin, Helen (1989) *The Empire Writes Back: Theory and Practice in Post-Colonial Literatures*, London: Routledge.

Attridge, Derek (1990) *The Cambridge Companion to James Joyce*, Cambridge: Cambridge University Press.

Bardon, Jonathan (1982) *Belfast: An Illustrated History*, Belfast: Blackstaff Press.

Bardon, Jonathan (1992) *A History of Ulster*, Belfast: Blackstaff Press.

Bardon, Jonathan and Burnett, David (1996) *Belfast: A Pocket History*, Belfast: Blackstaff.

Bardon, Jonathan and Coulin, Stephen (1985) *Belfast: 1000 Years*, Belfast: Blackstaff.

Bareham, Tony (ed.) (1991) *Charles Lever: New Evaluations*, Gerrards Cross: Colin Smythe.

Barrington, Ruth (2000) *Health, Medicine and Politics in Ireland 1900–1970*, Dublin: Institute of Public Administration.

Bartlett, Robert (1982) *Gerald of Wales, 1146–1223*, Oxford: Clarendon.

Bartlett, Thomas (1992) *The Fall and Rise of the Irish Nation: The Catholic Question in Ireland 1760–1830*, Dublin: Gill and Macmillan.

Beale, Jenny (1986) *Women in Ireland: Voices of Change*, Dublin: Gill and Macmillan.

Beames, M. (1983) *Peasants and Power: the Whiteboy Movements and their Control in Pre-Famine Ireland*, Brighton: Harvester.

Beckett, J. C. (1976) *The Anglo-Irish Tradition*, London: Faber.

Beckett, J. C. (1983) *Belfast: The Making of the City*, Belfast: Appletree.

Beckett, Samuel (1983) *Disjecta: Miscellaneous Writings and a Dramatic Fragment*, ed. Ruby Cohn, London: John Calder.

Belford, Barbara (1996) *Bram Stoker: A Biography of the Author of Dracula*, London: Wiedenfeld and Nicolson.

Bell, Desmond (1985) Contemporary cultural studies in Ireland and the 'problem' of Protestant ideology', in *The Crane Bag*, 9: 91–95.

Bell, Desmond (1990) *Acts of Union*, London: Macmillan.

Bell, J. Bowyer (1989) *The Secret Army: The IRA 1916–1979*, Dublin: Poolbegs.

Bentley, Eric (1947) *Bernard Shaw: A Reconsideration*, New York: New Directions.

Beresford, David (1987) *Ten Men Dead: The Story of the 1981 Irish Hunger Strike*, New York: Atlantic Monthly.

Bew, Paul, Gibbon, Peter and Patterson, Henry (1982) *Sean Lemass and the Making of Modern Ireland* 1945–66, Dublin: Gill and Macmillan.

Bew, Paul, Gibbon, Peter and Patterson, Henry (1996) *Northern Ireland 1921–1996: Political Forces and Social Classes*, London: Serif.

Bhabha, Homi K. (1994) *The Location of Culture*, London: Routledge.

Bielenberg, Andy (1991) *Cork's Industrial Revolution 1780–1880: Development or Decline?*, Cork: Cork University Press.

Boland, Eavan (1996) *Object Lessons: The Life of the Woman and the Poet in Our Time*, London: Vintage.

Bolger, Dermot (ed.) (1986) *The Bright Wave/An Tonn Gheal: Poetry in Irish Now*, Dublin: Raven Arts.

Bolger, Pat (ed.) (1986) *And See Her Beauty Shining There: The Story of the Irish Countrywoman*, Dublin: Irish Academic Press.

Bowen, D. (1978) *The Protestant Crusade in Ireland 1800–1870*, Dublin: Gill and Macmillan.

Bowen, Zack (1975) *Mary Lavin*, Lewisburg, PA: Bucknell University Press.

Bowman, John (1982) *De Valera and The Ulster Question*, Oxford: Oxford University Press.

Boyce, D. George (1995) *Nationalism in Ireland* (3rd ed), London: Routledge.

Boyce, D. George and O'Day, Alan (eds) (1996) *The Making of Modern Irish History: Revisionism and the Revisionist Controversy*, London: Routledge.

Boydell, Brian (ed.) (1979) *Four Centuries of Music in Ireland*, London: BBC.

Brady, Ciaran (ed.) (1989) *Worsted in the Game: Losers in Irish History*, Dublin: Lilliput.

Brady, Ciaran (1994) *The Chief Governors: The Rise and Fall of Reform Government in Tudor Ireland, 1536–1588*, Cambridge: Cambridge University Press.

Brady, Ciaran (1999) 'Shane O'Neill Departs from the Court of Elizabeth: Irish, English, Scottish Perspectives and the Paralysis of Policy, July 1559 to April 1562', in Connolly, S. J. (ed.) *Kingdoms United? Great Britain and Ireland since 1500*, Dublin: Four Courts, pp. 13–28.

Brody, Hugh (1973) *Inishkillane: Change and Decline in the West of Ireland*, London: Faber.

Brooke, Peter (1987) *Ulster Presbyterianism: The Historical Perspective, 1610–1970*, Dublin: Gill and Macmillan.

Brown, Stephen (1971) *The Press in Ireland*, New York: Lemma.

Brown, Terence (1975) *Northern Voices: Poets from Ulster*, Dublin: Gill and Macmillan.

Brown, Terence (1985a) *The Whole Protestant Community: The Making of a Historical Myth*, Derry: Field Day Company.

Brown, Terence (1985b) *Ireland: A Social and Cultural History 1922–1985*, London: Fontana.

Brown, Terence (1988) *Ireland's Literature: Selected Essays*, Mullingar: Lilliput.

Brown, Terence (1995) 'Ireland, modernism, and the 1930s', in Coughlan, Patricia and Davis, Alex (eds) (1995), pp. 24–42.

Brown, Terence (1999) *W. B. Yeats: A Critical Biography*. Oxford and Dublin: Blackwell and Gill and Macmillan.

Bruce, Steve (1986) *God Save Ulster: The Religion and Politics of Paisleyism*, Oxford: Oxford University Press.

Bruce, Steve (1992) *The Red Hand: Protestant Paramilitaries in Northern Ireland*, Oxford: Oxford University Press.

Bryan, Dominic (2000) *Orange Parades: the Politics of Ritual, Tradition and Control*, London: Pluto.

Buckland, Peter (1979) *The Factory of Grievances: Devolved Government in Northern Ireland 1921–39*, Dublin: Gill and Macmillan.

Butler, Marilyn (1972) *Maria Edgeworth: A Literary Biography*, Oxford: Clarendon.

Cahalan, J. M. (1984) *Great Hatred, Little Room: The Irish Historical Novel*, Dublin: Gill and Macmillan.

Cahalan, J. M. (1988) *The Irish Novel: A Critical History*, Dublin: Gill and Macmillan.

Cairns, David, and Richards, Shaun (1988) *Writing Ireland: Colonialism, Nationalism and Culture*, Manchester: Manchester University Press.

Campbell, Sean (1998) 'Race of angels: the critical reception of second-generation Irish musicians', *Irish Studies Review*, 6 (2): 165–74.

Canny, Nicholas (1987) 'Identity formation in Ireland: the emergence of the Anglo-Irish', in Canny, N. and Pagden, A. (eds) *Colonial Identity in the Atlantic World, 1500–1800*, Princeton: Princeton University Press, pp.159–212.

Canny, Nicholas (2001) *Making Ireland British 1580–1650*, Oxford: Oxford University Press.

Carlson, Julia (1990) *Banned in Ireland: Censorship and the Irish Writer*, London: Routledge.

Carson, Ciaran (1996) *Last Night's Fun: A Book about Irish Traditional Music*, London: Random House.

Cave, Richard (1978) *A Study of the Novels of George Moore*, Gerrards Cross: Colin Smythe.

Chadwick, Nora (1970) *The Celts*, Harmondsworth: Penguin.

Chadwick, Nora (1997) *The Druids*, Cardiff: University of Wales Press.

Christian, Edwin (1988) *Joyce Cary's Creative Imagination*, New York: P. Lang.

Clark, S. and Donnelly J. Jr. (eds) (1983) *Irish Peasants: Violence and Political Unrest 1780–1914*, Manchester: Manchester University Press.

Clarke, Liam (1987) *Broadening the Battlefield: The H-Blocks and the rise of Sinn Féin*, Dublin: Gill and Macmillan.

Clayton-Lea, Tony and Taylor, Ritchie (1992) *Irish Rock: Where It's Come From, Where It's Going, and Where It's At*, Philadelphia: Trans-Atlantic.

Cleary, Joe (2000) 'Modernization and aesthetic ideology in contemporary Irish culture', in Ryan, Ray (ed.), pp. 105–29.

Comerford, R. V. (1985) *The Fenians in Context: Irish Politics and Society 1848–82*, Dublin: Wolfhound.

Connely, Willard (1949) *Young George Farquhar: the Restoration Drama at Twilight*, London: Cassell.

Connolly, S. (1982) *Priests and People in Pre-Famine Ireland 1780–1845*, Dublin: Gill and Macmillan.

Coogan, Tim Pat (1996) *The Troubles*, London: Arrow Books, Random House.

Coogan, Tim Pat (2000a) *Wherever Green is Worn: The Story of the Irish Diaspora*, London: Hutchinson.

Coogan, Tim Pat (2000b) *The IRA*, London: Harper Collins.

Corcoran, Neil (1986) *A Student's Guide to Seamus Heaney*, London: Faber.

Corcoran, Neil (ed.) (1992) *The Chosen Ground: Essays on the Contemporary Poetry of Northern Ireland*, Bridgend: Seren.

Corcoran, Neil (1997) *After Yeats and Joyce: Reading Modern Irish Literature*, Oxford: Oxford University Press.

Corcoran, Neil (1999) *Poets of Modern Ireland: Text, Context, Intertext*, Cardiff: University of Wales Press.

Corish, Patrick J. (ed.) (1985) *The Irish Catholic Experience: A Historical Survey*, Dublin: Gill and Macmillan.

Cosgrove, Art (ed.) (1987) *A New History of Ireland: II, Medieval Ireland, 1169–1534*, Oxford: Clarendon.

Coughlan, Patricia (2003) 'The Peig Sayers Texts: Self, Social History and Narrative Art', in St Peter, Christine, and Boyle Haberstroh, Patricia (eds), *Feminist Approaches to Irish Texts*, Dublin: Maunsel.

Coughlan, Patricia and Davis, Alex (eds) (1989) *Spenser and Ireland: An Interdisciplinary Perspective*, Cork: Cork University Press.

Coughlan, Patricia and Davis, Alex (1991) '"Bog queens": the representation of women in the poetry of John Montague and Seamus Heaney', in O'Brien Johnson, Toni and Cairns, David (eds), pp. 89–111.

Coughlan, Patricia and Davis, Alex (eds) (1995) *Modernism and Ireland: The Poetry of the 1930s*, Cork: Cork University Press.

Coulter, Carol (1993) *The Hidden Tradition: Feminism, Women and Nationalism in Ireland*, Cork: Cork University Press.

Coxhead, Elizabeth (1979) *Daughters of Erin: Five Women of the Irish Renascence*, Gerrards Cross: Colin Smythe.

Craig, Maurice (1982) *The Architecture of Ireland from the Earliest Times to 1880*, London: Batsford.

Craig, Maurice (1992) *Dublin 1660–1860*, London: Penguin.

Cronin, Anthony (1976) *Dead as Doornails: Bohemian Dublin in the Fifties and Sixties*, Oxford: Oxford University Press.

Cronin, Anthony (1989) *No Laughing Matter: The Life and Times of Flann O'Brien*, London: Grafton.

Cronin, Michael, and O Connor, Barbara (2000) 'From gombeen to gubeen: tourism, identity and class in Ireland, 1949–99', in Ryan, Ray (ed.), pp. 165–84.

Crookshank, Ann and the Knight of Glin (1978) *The Painters of Ireland, c.1660–1920*, London: Barrie and Jenkins.

Crotty, Raymond (1966) *Irish Agricultural Production: Its Volume and Structure*, Cork: Cork University Press.

Crowley, Tony (2000) *The Politics of Language in Ireland 1366–1922*, London: Routledge.

Cullen, Louis Michael (1969) 'The hidden Ireland: reassessment of a concept', *Studia Hibernica*, 9: 148–70.

Cunningham, Bernadette (2000) *The World of Geoffrey Keating: History, Myth and Religion in Seventeenth-Century Ireland*, Dublin: Four Courts.

Curtis, L. P. (1968) *Anglo-Saxons and Celts: A Study of Anti-Irish Prejudice in Victorian Britain*, Bridgeport, CT: University of Bridgeport Press.

Curtis, Tony (2001) *The Art of Seamus Heaney*, Bridgend: Seren.

D'Angeli, Daniel and O'Meara, J. J. (trans.) (1994) *The Voyage of Saint Brendan (Navigato Sancti Brendani Abbatis)*, Dublin: Four Courts.

Daly, Mary (1981) *A Social and Economic History of Ireland since 1800*, Dublin: Educational Company.

Daly, Mary (1985) *Dublin: the Deposed Capital: A Social and Economic History 1860–1914*, Cork: Cork University Press.

Daly, Mary (1986) *The Famine in Ireland*, Dundalk: Dundalgan.

Davis, Alex (2000) *A Broken Line: Denis Devlin and Irish Poetic Modernism*, Dublin: University College Dublin Press.

Davis, Richard (1988) *The Young Ireland Movement*, Dublin: Gill and Macmillan.

Deane, Seamus (1983) *Civilians and Barbarians*, Derry: Field Day.

Deane, Seamus (1985) *Celtic Revivals: Essays in Modern Irish Literature 1880–1980*, London: Faber.

De Búrca, Seamus (1993) *Brendan Behan: A Memoir*, Dublin: P. J. Bourke.

De Man, Paul (1984) *The Rhetoric of Romanticism*. New York: Columbia University Press.

De Vere White, Terence (1977) *Tom Moore: The Irish Poet*, London: Hamish Hamilton.

Donoghue, Denis (1971) *Yeats*, London: Fontana.

Drudy, P. J. (ed.) (1982) *Ireland: Land, Politics and People*, Cambridge: Cambridge University Press.

Duffy, Charles Gavan (1890) *Thomas Davis, the Memoirs of an Irish Patriot*.

Duffy, Charles Gavan (1896) *Young Ireland: A Fragment of Irish History, 1840–45*.

Dunleavy, J. E. (ed.) (1983) *George Moore in Perspective*, Gerrards Cross: Colin Smythe.

Dunleavy, J. E. and Douglas, G. W. (1991) *Douglas Hyde: A Maker of Modern Ireland*, Berkeley: University of California Press.

Dunphy, Eamon (1988) *The Unforgettable Fire*, Harmondsworth: Penguin.

Eagleton, Terry (1995) *Heathcliff and the Great Hunger: Studies in Irish Culture*, London: Verso.

Edwards, Ruth Dudley (1993) *Patrick Pearse: The Triumph of Failure*, Swords: Poolbeg.

Edwards, Ruth Dudley (1999) *The Faithful Tribe: An Intimate Portrait of the Loyal Institutions*, London: HarperCollins.

Ehenpreis, Irvin (1962–83) *Swift: The Man, His Works and the Age*, 3 vols, London: Methuen.

Elliott, Marianne (1982) *Partners in Revolution: The United Irishmen and France*, New Haven: Yale University Press.

Elliott, Marianne (1989) *Wolfe Tone: Prophet of Irish Independence*, New Haven: Yale University Press.

Ellis, Conleth and Kelly, Rita E. (eds) (1985) *Poetry Ireland Review: Special Eugene Watters Issue*, no.13.

Ellis, Peter Beresford (1975) *Hell or Connacht! The Cromwellian Colonisation of Ireland 1652–1660*, London: Hamish Hamilton.

Ellis, Stephen G. (1985) *Tudor Ireland: Crown, Community and the Conflict of Cultures, 1470–1603*, Harlow: Longman.

Ellmann, Richard (1964) *The Identity of Yeats*, London: Faber.

Ellmann, Richard (1982) *James Joyce*, New York: Oxford University Press.

Ellmann, Richard (1987) *Oscar Wilde*, London: Hamilton.

Fallis, Richard (1977) *The Irish Renaissance*, Syracuse: Syracuse University Press.

Fallon, Brian (1994) *Irish Art: 1830–1990*, Belfast: Appletree Press.

Fallon, Brian (1998) *An Age of Innocence: Irish Culture 1930–1960*, Dublin: Gill and Macmillan.

Farrell, Brian (1971) *The Founding of Dáil Éireann: Parliament and Nation-Building*, Dublin: Gill and Macmillan.

Feeney, Brian (2002) *Sinn Féin: A Hundred Turbulent Years*, Dublin: The O'Brien Press.

Fermor, Una Ellis (1954) *The Irish Dramatic Movement*, London: Methuen.

Fisk, Robert (1996) *In Time of War: Ireland, Ulster and the Price of Neutrality 1939–45*, Dublin: Gill and Macmillan.

Fitzpatrick, David (1984) *Irish Emigration 1801–1921*: Studies in Irish Economic and Social History no. 1 (Dundalk: Economic and Social History Society of Ireland).

Fitzpatrick, David (1985) *Ireland and the First World War*, Dublin: Trinity History Workshop.

Fletcher, John (1970) *The Novels of Samuel Beckett*, New York: Barnes and Noble.

Ford, Alan (1997) *The Protestant Reformation in Ireland, 1590–1641*, Dublin: Four Courts.

Ford, A., McGuire, J. and Milne, K. (eds) (1995) *As By Law Established: the Church of Ireland since the Reformation*, Dublin: Lilliput.

Forester, Margery (1989) *Michael Collins: The Lost Leader*, Dublin: Irish Books and Media.

Foster, John Wilson (1974) *Forces and Themes in Ulster Fiction*, Dublin: Gill and Macmillan.

Foster, John Wilson (1991) *Colonial Consequences: Essays in Irish Literature and Culture*, Dublin: Lilliput.

Foster, R. F. (1988) *Modern Ireland: 1600–1972*, London: Penguin Books.

Foster, R. F. (1993) *Paddy and Mr Punch: Connections in Irish and English History*. London: Allen Lane.

Foster, R. F. (1997) *W. B. Yeats: A Life*, vol. 1, *The Apprentice Mage*, Oxford: Oxford University Press.

Frazier, Adrian (1990) *Behind the Scenes: Yeats, Horniman, and the Struggle for the Abbey Theatre*, Berkeley: University of California Press.

Frazier, Adrian (2000) *George Moore, 1852–1933*, New Haven, CT: Yale University Press.

Foucault, Michel (1990) *The History of Sexuality*, vol. 1, Harmondsworth: Penguin.

Friedman, Arthur (ed.) (1966) *The Collected Works of Oliver Goldsmith*, 5 vols., Oxford: Oxford University Press.

Freyer and Harris (1981) *The Achievement of Sean O'Riada*, Chester Springs: Dufour Editions.

Furniss, Tom (1993) *Edmund Burke's Aesthetic Ideology: Language, Gender, and Political Economy in Revolution*, Cambridge: Cambridge University Press.

Gailey, Andrew (1987) *Ireland and the Death of Kindness: The Experience of Constructive Unionism 1890–1905*, Cork: Cork University Press.

Garvin, Tom (1988) 'The politics of denial and of cultural defence: the referenda of 1983 and 1986 in context', *Irish Review*, 3: 1–7.

Gibbon, Peter (1975) *The Origins of Ulster Unionism: The Foundations of Popular Protestant Politics and Ideology in Nineteenth-Century Ireland*, Manchester: Manchester University Press.

Gibbons, Luke (1996) *Transformations in Irish Culture*, Cork: Cork University Press and Field Day.

Gibbons, Luke (2003) *Edmund Burke and Ireland: Aesthetics, Politics and the Colonial Sublime*, Cambridge: Cambridge University Press.

Gibbons, Luke, Rockett, Kevin and Hill, John (1988) *Cinema and Ireland*, London: Routledge.

Gillen, Gerald and White, Harry (eds) (1990–) *Irish Musical Studies*, 5 vols., Dublin: Four Courts.

Glendinning, Victoria (1977) *Elizabeth Bowen: Portrait of a Writer*, London: Weidenfeld and Nicolson.

Goodby, John (1999) '"The prouder counsel of her throat": towards a feminist reading of Austin Clarke', *Irish University Review*, 29 (2): 321–40.

Goodby, John (2000) *Irish Poetry Since 1950: From Stillness into History*, Manchester: Manchester University Press.

Goodby, John and Scully, Maurice (eds) (1999) *Colonies of Belief – Ireland's Modernists*, *Angel Exhaust* no. 17.

Gordon, David J. (1990) *Bernard Shaw and the Comic Sublime*, Basingstoke: Macmillan.

Graham, Colin and Hooper, Glenn (eds) (2002) *Irish and Postcolonial Writing: History, Theory and Practice*, Basingstoke: Palgrave Macmillan.

Graham, Colin and Kirkland, Richard (eds) (1999) *Ireland and Cultural Theory: The Mechanics of Authenticity*, Basingstoke: Macmillan.

Greaves, C. Desmond (1961) *The Life and Times of James Connolly*, London: Lawrence and Wishart.

Greene, David H. and Stephens, Edward M. (1989) *J. M. Synge 1871–1909*, New York: New York University Press.

Gregory, Augusta (1913) *Our Irish Theatre*, New York: Putnam's.

Grene, Nicholas (1975) *Synge: A Critical Study of the Plays*, London: Macmillan.

Grene, Nicholas (1984) *Bernard Shaw: A Critical View*, Basingstoke: Macmillan.

Haberstroh, P.B. (1996) *Women Creating Women: Contemporary Irish Poets*, Syracuse: Syracuse University Press.

Haddelsy, Stephen (2000) *Charles Lever: the Lost Victorian*, Gerrards Cross: Colin Smythe.

Haddick-Flynn, Kevin (1999) *Orangeism: the Making of a Tradition*, Dublin: Wolfhound Press.

Hadfield, Andrew (1997) *Spenser's Irish Experience: Wilde Fruit and Salvage Soyl*, Oxford: Oxford University Press.

Hadfield, Andrew and McVeagh, John (eds) (1994) *Strangers to That Land: British Perceptions of Ireland from the Reformation to the Famine*, Gerrards Cross: Colin Smythe.

Hall, Wayne E. (2000) *Dialogues in the Margin: A Study of the Dublin University Magazine*, Gerrards Cross: Colin Smythe.

Hammond, Brean (1988) *Gulliver's Travels*, Buckingham: Open University Press.

Hanafin, Patrick (2000) 'Legal texts as cultural documents: interpreting the Irish constitution', in Ryan, Ray (ed.), pp. 147–64.

Hankins, Thomas L. (1980) *Sir William Rowan Hamilton*, Baltimore: Johns Hopkins University Press.

Harbison, Peter, Potterton, Homan and Sheehy, Jeanne (1976) *The Archaeology of Ireland*, New York: Scribner's.

Harbison, Peter, Potterton, Homan and Sheehy, Jeanne (1978) *Irish Art and Architecture from Prehistory to the Present*, London: Thames and Hudson.

Harmon, Maurice (1966) *Sean O'Faolain: A Critical Introduction*, South Bend, IN: University of Notre Dame Press.

Harmon, Maurice (ed.) (1979) *Irish University Review: Mary Lavin Special Issue*, vol. 9, no. 2.

Harmon, Maurice (ed.) (1981) *Irish University Review: John Banville Special Issue*, vol. 11, no. 1.

Harmon, Maurice (1989) *Austin Clarke 1896–1974: A Critical Introduction*, Dublin: Wolfhound.

Harmon, Maurice (1994) *Sean O'Faolain: A Life*, London: Constable.

Harris, Rosemary (1972) *Prejudice and Tolerance in Northern Ireland: A Study of Neighbours and 'Strangers' in a Border Community*, Manchester: Manchester University Press.

Hartigan, M. (ed.) (1986) *The History of the Irish in Britain: A Bibliography*, London: Irish History in Britain Centre.

Hawthorn, Jeremy (1996) *Cunning Passages*, London: Edward Arnold.

Heaney, Seamus (1980) *Preoccupations: Selected Prose 1968–1978*, London: Faber.

Hickman, Mary (1995) *Religion, Class and Identity: The State, The Catholic Church and the Education of the Irish in Britain*, London: Avebury.

Hill, Judith (1998) *Irish Public Sculpture: A History*, Dublin: Four Courts.

Hogan, Ita (1966) *Anglo-Irish Music, 1780–1830*, Cork: Mercier.

Holmes, R. F. G. (1985) *Our Presbyterian Heritage*, Belfast: Presbyterian Church in Ireland.

Holroyd, Michael (1988–91) *Bernard Shaw* 3 vols., London: Chatto and Windus.

Hone, Joseph (1936) *The Life of George Moore*, New York: Macmillan.

Hopkinson, Michael (1988) *Green Against Green*, London: Macmillan.

Hopkinson, Michael (2002) *The Irish War of Independence*, Belfast: Queens University Press.

Hoppen, K. T. (1984) *Elections, Politics and Society in Ireland, 1832–85*, Oxford: Oxford University Press.

Hopper, Keith (1995) *Flann O'Brien: A Portrait of the Artist as a Young Post-modernist*, Cork: Cork University Press.

Hughes, Eamonn (ed.) (1991) *Culture and Politics in Northern Ireland 1960–1990*, Milton Keynes and Philadelphia: Open University Press.

Hunt, Hugh (1980) *Sean O'Casey*, Dublin: Gill and Macmillan.

Hutchinson, John (1987) *The Dynamics of Cultural Nationalism: the Gaelic Revival and the Creation of the Irish Nation State*, London: Allen and Unwin.

Hyland, Paul and Sammells, Neil (eds) (1991) *Irish Writing: Exile and Subversion*, Basingstoke: Macmillan.

Imhof, Rüdiger (1992) 'Molly Keane, *Good Behaviour*, *Time after Time*, and *Loving and Giving*', in Rauchbauer, Otto (ed.), pp. 195–203.

Inglis, Brian (1973) *Roger Casement*, London: Hodder and Stoughton.

Innes, C. L. (1993) *Women and Nation in Irish Literature and Society, 1880–1935*, Athens GA: University of Georgia Press.

Jackson, Alvin (1989) Unionist History (i), *The Irish Review*, 7: 58–65.

Jackson, Alvin (1990) Unionist history (ii), *The Irish Review*, 8: 62–69.

Jameson, Fredric (1991) *Postmodernism, or, The Cultural Logic of Late Capitalism*, London: Verso.

Jenkins, Lee (1994) 'Thomas MacGreevy and the pressure of reality', *The Wallace Stevens Journal*, 18 (2): 146–56.

John, Brian (1996) *Reading the Ground: The Poetry of Thomas Kinsella*, Washington, DC: Catholic University of America Press.

Johnston, Dillon (1997) *Irish Poetry After Joyce*, Syracuse: Syracuse University Press.

Jones, H. M. (1937) *The Harp That Once – : A Chronicle of the Life of Thomas Moore*, New York: Henry Holt.

Joyce, Nan and Farmer, Anna (1985) *Traveller*, Dublin: Gill and Macmillan.

Kearney, Colbert (1977) *The Writings of Brendan Behan*, Dublin: Gill and Macmillan.

Kearney, Hugh (1959) *Strafford in Ireland, 1633–1641: A Study in Absolutism*, Manchester: Manchester University Press.

Kearney, Richard (1997) *Postnationalist Ireland: Politics, Culture, Philosophy*, London: Routledge.

Keating, Geoffrey (1902–14) *Foras Feasa as Éirinn*, ed. and trans. Comyn, David and Dinneen, P. S. 4 vols, Dublin: Early Irish Text Society.

Kee, Robert (2000) *The Green Flag: A History of Irish Nationalism*, London: Penguin.

Kelly, James (1993) *Henry Grattan*, Dundalk: Dundalgan Press.

Kennedy, Liam (1996) *Colonialism, Religion and Nationalism in Ireland*, Belfast: Irish Studies Institute.

Kennedy, S. B. (1991) *Irish Art and Modernism: 1880–1950*, Belfast: Institute of Irish Studies.

Kennedy-Andrews, Elmer (ed.) (2002) *The Poetry of Derek Mahon*, Gerrards Cross: Colin Smythe.

Kenner, Hugh (1969) *Samuel Beckett: A Critical Study*, Berkeley: University of California Press.

Keogh, G. and Doherty, G. (eds) (1998) *Michael Collins and the Modern Irish State*, Cork and Dublin: Mercier Press.

Kermode, Frank (1957) *Romantic Image*, London: Routledge and Kegan Paul.

Kerr, D. (1982) *Peel, Priests and Politics: Sir Robert Peel's Administration and the Roman Catholic Church in Ireland 1841–6*, Oxford: Clarendon.

Kerrigan, Colm (1982) *Father Mathew and the Temperance Movement 1838–1849*, Cork: Cork University Press.

Kerrigan, John (1998) 'Hidden Ireland: Eiléan Ní Chuilleanáin and Munster poetry', *Critical Quarterly*, 40 (4): 76–100.

Kiberd, Declan (1993) *Synge and the Irish Language*, Dublin: Gill and Macmillan.

Kiberd, Declan (1995) *Inventing Ireland: The Literature of the Modern Nation*, London: Jonathan Cape.

Kiely, Benedict (1972) *Poor Scholar: A Study of the Works and Days of William Carleton*, Dublin: Talbot Press.

Kineally, Christine (1994) *This Great Calamity: The Irish Famine 1845–52*, Dublin: Gill and Macmillan.

Kinsella, Thomas (1970) *The Táin (from the Irish Epic Táin Bó Cuailnge)*, Oxford: Oxford University Press.

Kinsella, Thomas (1995) *The Dual Tradition: An Essay on Poetry and Politics in Ireland*, Manchester: Carcanet.

Kirkland, Richard (1996) *Literature and Culture in Northern Ireland since 1965: Moments of Danger*, London: Longman.

Knott, Eleanor (1960) *Irish Classical Poetry, Commonly called Bardic Poetry*, Dublin: Cultural Relations Committee of Ireland.

Kohfeldt, Mary Lou (1985) *Lady Gregory: The Woman Behind the Irish Renaissance*, London: André Deutsch.

Kosok, Heinz (1985) *O'Casey the Dramatist*, Gerrards Cross: Colin Smythe.

Lee, Hermione (1981) *Elizabeth Bowen: An Estimation*, London: Vision Press.

Lee, J. J. (1973) *The Modernization of Irish Society 1848–1918*, Dublin: Gill and Macmillan.

Lee, J. J. (1993) *Ireland 1912–1985: Politics and Society*, Cambridge: Cambridge University Press.

Leerssen, J. T. (1996) *Remembrance and Imagination: Patterns in the Historical and Literary Representation of Ireland in the Nineteenth Century*, Cork: Cork University Press.

Legg, Marie Louise (1999) *Newspapers and Nationalism: The Irish Provincial Press, 1850–1892*, Dublin: Four Courts.

Lennon, Colm (1978) 'Richard Stanihurst and Old English identity', *Irish Historical Studies*, 82: 121–43.

Lennon, Colm (1981) *Richard Stanihurst, the Dubliner, 1547–1618*, Dublin: Irish Academic Press.

Lessner, Phyllis (1989) *Elizabeth Bowen*, Savage, MD: Barnes and Noble.

Lloyd, Cathie (1995) *The Irish Community on Britain: Discrimination, Disadvantage, and Racism: An Annotated Bibliography*, London: University of North London Press.

Lloyd, David (1987) *Nationalism and Minor Literature: James Clarence Mangan and the Emergence of Irish Cultural Nationalism,* Berkeley: University of California Press.

Lloyd, David (1993) *Anomalous States: Irish Writing and the Post-Colonial Moment,* Dublin: Lilliput.

Longley, Edna (1986) *Poetry in the Wars,* Newcastle-upon-Tyne: Bloodaxe.

Longley, Edna (1988) *Louis MacNeice: A Study,* London: Faber.

Longley, Edna (1994) *The Living Stream,* Newcastle-upon-Tyne: Bloodaxe.

Longley, Michael (1994) *Tuppenny Stung,* Belfast: Lagan.

Loughlin, J. (1986) *Gladstone, Home Rule and the Ulster Question, 1882–1893,* Dublin: Gill and Macmillan.

Lucas, A. T. (1973) *Treasure of Ireland: Irish Pagan and Early Christian Art,* Dublin: Gill and Macmillan.

Luddy, Maria and Murphy, Cliona (1990) *Women Surviving: Studies in Irish Women's History in the Nineteenth and Twentieth Centuries,* Dublin: Poolbeg.

Luke, Peter (ed.) (1978) *Enter Certain Players: Edwards, MacLiammoir and the Gate 1928–1978,* Dublin: Dolmen.

Lyons, F. S. L. (1971) *Ireland since the Famine,* London: Wiedenfeld and Nicolson.

Lyons, F. S. L. (1977) *Charles Stewart Parnell,* London: Collins.

Lyons, F. S. L. and Hawkins, R. A. J. (eds) (1985) *Ireland under the Union: Varieties of Tension,* Oxford: Clarendon.

MacAnna, Ferdia (1991) 'The Dublin renaissance', *The Irish Review,* 10: 14–30.

McAvera, Brian (1989) *Art, Ireland and Politics,* Dublin: Open Air.

McCafferty, Nell (1985) *A Woman to Blame: The Kerry Babies Case,* Dublin: Attic.

Mac Cana, Proinias (1983) *Celtic Mythology,* Feltham: Newnes Books.

McCann, Eamonn (3rd edn 1993) *War in an Irish Town,* London: Pluto.

McCarthy, Conor (2000) *Modernisation: Crisis and Culture in Ireland 1969–1992,* Dublin: Four Courts.

McCarthy-Morrogh, Michael (1986) *The Munster Plantation: English Migration to Southern Ireland 1583–1641,* Oxford: Clarendon.

McCartney, Anne (2000) *Francis Stuart Face to Face: A Critical Study,* Belfast: Institute of Irish Studies.

McCartney, Donal (1967) 'Hyde, D. P. Moran, and Irish Ireland', in F. X. Martin (ed.) *Leaders and Men of the Easter Rising,* London: Methuen.

McCartney, Donal (1994) *W. E. H. Lecky: Historian and Politician, 1838 – 1903,* Dublin: Lilliput.

McCormack, W. J. (1985) *The Battle of the Books,* Malinger: Lilliputian.

McCormack, W. J. (1986) *The Battle of the Books: Two Decades of Irish Cultural Debate,* Malinger: Lilliputian.

McCormack, W. J. (1987) 'Politics or community: crux of Thomas Canella's aesthetic development', *Tracks: Thomas Kinchella Special Issue,* Dublin Devalues.

McCormack, W. J. (1989) 'Isaac Butt and the inner failure of Protestant Home Rule', in Brady, Ciaran (ed.) *Worsted in the Game, Losers in Irish History*, Dublin: Lilliputian.

McCormack, W. J. (1991) *Sheridan Le Fanu and Victorian Ireland*, Dublin: Lilliputian.

McCormack, W. J. (1994) *From Burke to Beckett: Ascendancy, Tradition and Betrayal in Literary History*, Cork: Cork University Press.

McCormack, W. J. (2000) *Fool of the Family: A Life of J. M. Synge*, London: Weidenfeld and Nicolson.

McCorristine, Laurence (1987) *The Revolt of Silken Thomas*, Dublin: Wolfhound.

McCracken, Kathleen (1995) 'Ciaran Carson: unravelling the conditional, mapping the provisional', in Kenneally, Michael (ed.) *Poetry in Contemporary Irish Literature*, Gerrards Cross: Colin Smythe.

Mac Cuarta, Brian (ed.) (1993) *Ulster 1641: Aspects of the Rising*, Belfast; Institute of Irish Studies.

McDonagh, Oliver (1991) *O'Connell: The Life of Daniel O'Connell, 1775–1847*, London: Wiedenfeld and Nicolson.

McDonald, Frank (1985), *The Destruction of Dublin*, Dublin: Gill and Macmillan.

McDonald, Henry (2000) *Trimble*, London: Bloomsbury.

McDonald, Peter (1997) *Mistaken Identities: Poetry and Northern Ireland*, Oxford: Clarendon.

McDowell, R. B. and Webb, D. A. (1982) *Trinity College, Dublin, 1592–1952: An Academic History*, Cambridge: Cambridge University Press.

McIlroy, Brian (1998) *Shooting to Kill: Filmmaking and the 'Troubles' in Northern Ireland*, Trowbridge: Flicks Books.

McKay, Susan (2000) *Northern Protestants: An Unsettled People*, Belfast: Blackstaff.

McKeon, Jim (1998) *Frank O'Connor: A Life*, Edinburgh: Mainstream.

Mac Laughlin, Jim (1994) *Ireland: The Emigrant Nursery and the World Economy*, Cork: Cork University Press.

McLoone, Martin (ed.) (1991) *Culture, Identity, and Broadcasting in Ireland: Local Issues, Global Perspectives*, Belfast: Institute of Irish Studies.

McLoone, Martin (ed.) (1996) *Broadcasting in a Divided Community: Seventy Years of the BBC in Northern Ireland*, Belfast: Institute of Irish Studies.

McLoone, Martin and MacMahon, John (eds) (1984) *Television and Irish Society: 21 Years of Irish Television*, Dublin: RTÉ.

McMinn, Joseph (1991) *John Banville: A Critical Study*, Dublin: Gill and Macmillan.

McMinn, Joseph (1999) *The Supreme Fictions of John Banville*, Manchester: Manchester University Press.

McRedmond, Louis (ed.) (1996) *Modern Irish Lives: Dictionary of 20th-century Biography*, Dublin: Gill and Macmillan.

Malcolm, Elizabeth (1986) *Ireland Sober, Ireland Free: Drink and Temperance in Nineteenth Century Ireland*, Syracuse: Syracuse University Press.

Maley, Willy (1997) *Salvaging Spenser: Colonialism, Culture and Identity*, Basingstoke: Macmillan.

Mandle, W. F. (1987) *The Gaelic Athletic Association and Irish Nationalist Politics, 1884–1924*, London: Christopher Helm.

Mansergh, Nicholas (1960) 'John Redmond' in O'Brien, C. C. (ed.) *The Shaping of Modern Ireland*, London: Routledge, Kegan and Paul.

Mathews, T. (1907) *The O'Neills of Ulster*.

Maume, Patrick (1993) *Life that is Exile: Daniel Corkery and the Search for Irish Ireland*, Belfast: Institute of Irish Studies.

Maye, Brian (1997) *Arthur Griffith*, Dublin: Griffith College Publications.

Mays, J. C. C. (1995) 'How is MacGreevy a modernist?', in Coughlan, Patricia and Davis, Alex (eds) (1995), pp. 103–28.

Miller, David W. (1978) *Queen's Rebels: Ulster Loyalism in Historical Perspective*, Dublin: Gill and Macmillan.

Miller, Kerby A. (1971 repr. 1985) *Emigrants and Exiles*, New York: Oxford University Press.

Mokyr, Joel (1983) *Why Ireland Starved: A Quantitative and Analytical History of the Irish Economy 1800–1850*, London: Allen and Unwin.

Moody, T. W. (1939) *The Londonderry Plantation, 1609–41: the City of London and the Plantation in Ulster*, Belfast: William Mullen.

Moody, T. W., Martin, F. X. and Byrne, F. J. (eds) (1976) *A New History of Ireland: III, Early Modern Ireland, 1534–1691*, Oxford: Oxford University Press.

Morash, Christopher (1996) *Writing the Irish Famine*, Oxford: Clarendon.

Morash, Christopher (2002) *A History of Irish Theatre*, Cambridge: Cambridge University Press.

Morgan, Austen (1988) *James Connolly: A Political Biography*, Manchester: Manchester University Press.

Morgan, Hiram (1993) *Tyrone's Rebellion: The Outbreak of the Nine Years War in Tudor Ireland*, Woodbridge, Suffolk: Royal Historical Society/Boydell Press.

Moriarty, Dónal (2000) *The Art of Brian Coffey*, Dublin: University College Dublin Press.

Moynihan, Maurice (ed.) (1980) *Speeches and Statements by Éamon De Valera, 1917–1973*, Dublin: Gill and Macmillan.

Mullin, Chris (1990) *Error of Judgement: The Truth About the Birmingham Bombings*, Swords: Poolbeg.

Murphy, Brian P. (1991) *Patrick Pearse and the Lost Republican Ideal*, Dublin: James Duffy.

Murphy, Shane (1998) '"You took away my biography": the poetry of Medbh McGuckian', *Irish University Review*, 28 (1): 110–32.

Ní Chuilleanáin, Eiléan (ed.) (1985) *Irish Women: Image and Achievement*, Dublin: Arlen House.

Norstedt, Johann A. (1980) *Thomas MacDonagh: A Critical Biography*, Charlottesville: University of Virginia Press.

Nowlan, K. B. (1965) *The Politics of Repeal: A Study in the Relations between Great Britain and Ireland, 1841–50*, London: Routledge and Kegan Paul.

O'Brien, Conor Cruise (1992) *The Great Melody: A Thematic Biography and Commented Anthology of Edmund Burke*, Chicago: University of Chicago Press.

O'Brien Johnson, Toni and Cairns, David (eds) (1991) *Gender in Irish Writing*, Milton Keynes: Open University Press.

O'Broin, Leon (1967) *Charles Gavan Duffy: Patriot and Statesman*, Dublin: J. Duffy.

O'Connor, Fionnuala (1993) *In Search of a State: Catholics in Northern Ireland*, Belfast: Blackstaff.

O'Connor, Nuala (1991) *Bringing It All Back Home: The Influence of Irish Music at Home and Overseas*, Chelmsford, MA: Merlin.

Ó Corráin, Donnchadh (1972) *Ireland before the Normans*, Dublin: Gill and Macmillan.

O'Donavan, John (ed.) (1848–51) *Annála Ríoghachta Éireann: Annals of the Kingdom of Ireland by the Four Masters*, 6 vols.

O'Donoghue, Bernard (1994) *Seamus Heaney and the Language of Poetry*, Hemel Hempstead: Harvester.

O'Donoghue, Jo (1990) *Brian Moore: A Critical Study*, Dublin: Gill and Macmillan.

O'Ferrall, Fergus (1985) *Catholic Emancipation: Daniel O'Connell and the Birth of Irish Democracy*, Dublin: Gill and Macmillan.

Ó Gráda, Cormac (1994) *Ireland: A New Economic History 1780–1939*, Oxford: Clarendon.

Ó Gráda, Cormac (1999) *Black '47 and Beyond: The Great Irish Famine in History, Economy and Memory*, Princeton: Princeton University Press.

Ó hAllmhurain, Gearoid (1998) *A Pocket History of Irish Traditional Music*, Dublin: O'Brien.

O'Keefe, Finbar (2002) *Goodnight, God Bless and Safe Home: The Golden Showband Era*, Dublin: O'Brien.

Ó Lúing, Séan (1992) *Kuno Meyer 1858–1919*, Dublin: Geography Publications.

O'Malley, Padraig (1990) *Biting at the Grave: The Irish Hunger Strikes and the Politics of Despair*, Belfast: Blackstaff.

O'Neill, Terence (1972) *Autobiography*, London: Hart Davis.

Ó Raifeartaigh, T. (ed.) (1985) *The Royal Irish Academy: A Bicentennial History 1785–1985*, Dublin: Royal Irish Academy.

Ó Seaghdha, Barra, (1990) 'Ulster regionalism: the unpleasant facts', *The Irish Review*, 8: 54–61.

O'Toole, Fintan (1987) *The Politics of Magic: The Work and Times of Tom Murphy*, Dublin: Raven Arts.

O'Toole, Fintan (1988) 'Island of saints and silicon: literature and social change in contemporary Ireland', in Kennedy, Michael (ed.) *Cultural Contexts and Literary Idioms in Contemporary Irish Literature*, Gerrards Cross: Colin Smythe, pp. 11–35.

O'Toole, Fintan (1990) *A Mass for Jesse James*, Dublin: New Island Books.

O'Toole, Fintan (1996) *The Ex-Isle of Erin: Images of a Global Ireland*, Dublin: New Island Books.

O'Toole, Fintan (1997) *The Ex-Isle of Erin: Images of a Global Ireland,* Dublin: New Island.

Ó Tuairisc, Eoghan and others (1981) *The Road to Bright City*, Dublin: Poolbeg.

Ó Tuama, Seán (1981) 'Brian Merriman and his court', *Irish University Review*, 11: 149–64.

Ó Tuama, Seán (1995) *Repossessions: Selected Essays in the Irish Poetic Heritage*, Cork: Cork University Press.

Ó Tuama, Seán and Kinsella, Thomas (eds) (1981) *An Duanaire, 1600–1900: Poems of the Dispossessed*, Portlaoise: Dolmen.

Ó'Tuathaigh, G. (1972) *Ireland before the Famine, 1798–1848*, Dublin: Gill and Macmillan.

Ormsby, Frank (ed.) (1991) *The Collected Poems of John Hewitt*, Belfast: Blackstaff.

Owens, Rosemary Cullen (1984) *Smashing Times: A History of the Irish Women's Suffrage Movement 1889–1922*, Dublin: Attic.

Parker, Michael (1993) *Seamus Heaney: The Making of the Poet*, Basingstoke: Macmillan.

Patten, Eve (1995) 'Fiction in conflict: Northern Ireland's prodigal novelists', in Bell, A. (ed.) *Peripheral Visions: Images of Nationhood in Contemporary British Fiction*, Cardiff: University of Wales Press.

Pettitt, Lance (2000) *Screening Ireland: Film and television representation*, Manchester: Manchester University Press.

Phelan, J. (1951) *The Ardent Exile: The Life and Times of Thomas D'Arcy McGee*, Toronto: Macmillan.

Pilling, John (ed.) (1993) *The Cambridge Companion to Beckett*, Cambridge: Cambridge University Press.

Pine, Richard (2002) *2RN and the Origins of Irish Radio*, Dublin: Four Courts.

Pitcher, George (1977) *George Berkeley*, Oxford: Oxford University Press.

Prendergast, Mark J. (1987) *The Isle of Noises*, New York: St Martin's.

Prendergast, Mark J. (1992) *Irish Rock: Roots, Personalities, Directions*, Dublin: O'Brien.

Purdie, Bob (1990) *Politics in the Streets: The Origin of the Civil Rights Movement in Northern Ireland*, Belfast: Blackstaff.

Pyle, Hilary (1970) *Jack B. Yeats: A Biography,* London: Routledge and Kegan Paul.

Quinn, Antoinette (ed.) (1989) *Irish University Review: John Montague Special Issue*, 19: 1.

Quinn, Antoinette (1991) *Patrick Kavanagh: Born-Again Romantic*, Dublin: Gill and Macmillan.

Rauchbauer, Otto (ed.) (1992) *Ancestral Voices: The Big House in Anglo-Irish Literature*, Hildesheim: Georg Olms.

Reilly, Tom (1999) *Cromwell, An Honourable Enemy*, Dingle: Brandon.

Richards, Shaun (1988) 'To bind the northern to the southern stars: field day in Derry and Dublin', *Irish Review*, 4: 52–58.

Richards, Shaun (1991) 'Field Day's fifth province: avenue or impasse?', in Hughes, Eamon (ed.), pp. 139–50.

Richtarik, Marilyn (1995) *Acting Between the Lines: The Field Day Theatre Company and Irish Cultural Politics, 1980–84*, Oxford: Oxford University Press.

Richtarik, Marilyn (2000) '"Ireland, the continuous past": Stewart Parker's Belfast history plays', in Mustafa, Shakira, Watt, Stephen and Morgan, Eileen (eds) *A Century of Irish Drama: Widening the Stage*, Bloomington: Indiana University Press, pp. 256–74.

Richter, Michael (1983) *Medieval Ireland: The Enduring Tradition*, Basingstoke: Macmillan.

Ricks, Christopher (1993) *Beckett's Dying Words*, Oxford: Oxford University Press.

Robinson, Philip (1984) *The Plantation of Ulster: British Settlement in an Irish Landscape 1600–1670*, Dublin: Gill and Macmillan.

Roche, Anthony (1994) *Contemporary Irish Drama: from Beckett to McGuinness*, Dublin: Gill and Macmillan.

Rockett, K., Hill, J. and Gibbons, L. (1988) *Cinema and Ireland*, London: Routledge.

Rosenthal, T. J. (1993) *The Art of Jack B. Yeats*, London: André Deutsch.

Ross, Ian Campbell (2001) *Laurence Sterne: A Life*, Oxford: Oxford University Press.

Ruane, Joseph and Todd, Jennifer (1996) *The Dynamics of Conflict in Northern Ireland: Power, Conflict and Emancipation*, Cambridge: Cambridge University Press.

Ryan, John (1975) *Remembering How We Stood: Bohemian Dublin at the Mid-Century*, Dublin: Gill and Macmillan.

Ryan, Ray (ed.) (2000) *Writing in the Irish Republic: Literature, Culture, Politics 1949–1999*, Basingstoke: Macmillan.

Saddlemeyer, Ann and Smythe, Colin (eds) (1982) *Lady Gregory: Fifty Years After*, Gerrards Cross: Colin Smythe.

Said, Edward (1978) *Orientalism*, London: Routledge.

Sampson, Denis (1993) *Outstaring Nature's Eye: The Fiction of John McGahern*, Dublin: Lilliput.

Sewell, Frank (2000) *Modern Irish Poetry: A New Alhambra*, Oxford: Oxford University Press.

Shannon-Mangan, Ellen (1996) *James Clarence Mangan: A Biography*, Dublin: Irish Academic Press.

Sheehy, Maurice (1969) *Michael/Frank: Studies on Frank O'Connor*, Dublin: Gill and Macmillan.

Sheeran, Patrick (1976) *The Novels of Liam O'Flaherty*, Dublin: Wolfhound.

Shiel, Michael (1984) *The Quiet Revolution*, Dublin: O'Brien.

Silke, John J. (1970) *Kinsale: The Spanish Intervention in Ireland at the End of the Elizabethan Wars*, Liverpool: Liverpool University Press.

Skelton, Robin (1969) 'The poetry of Thomas Kinsella', *Éire-Ireland*, 4 (1): 86–108.

Sloan, Robert (2000) *William Smith O'Brien and the Young Ireland Rebellion of 1848*, Dublin: Four Courts.

Smith, Louis P. F. (1961) *The Evolution of Agricultural Co-operation*, Oxford: Blackwell.

Smyth, Gerry (1997) *The Novel and the Nation: Studies in the New Irish Fiction*, London: Pluto.

Smyth, Gerry (1998) *Decolonisation and Criticism: The Construction of Irish Literature*, London: Pluto.

Smythe, Colin and Saddlemeyer, Ann (eds) (1973) *Lady Gregory Fifty Years After*, Gerrards Cross: Colin Smythe.

Stallworthy, Jon (1995) *Louis MacNeice: A Study*, London: Faber.

Stewart, A. T. Q. (1989) *The Narrow Ground: The Roots of Conflict in Ulster*, London: Faber.

Sullivan, Sir Edward (1986) *The Book of Kells*, London: Studio Editions.

Swarbrick, Andrew (ed.) (1984) *Oliver Goldsmith: Critical Essays*, London: Vision Press.

Thornley, David (1964a) *Isaac Butt and Home Rule*, London: MacGibbon and Kee.

Thornley, David (1964b) The end of an era?, *Studies*, vol. LIII, pp. 1–17.

Tóibín, Colm (ed.) (1996) *The Kilfenora Teaboy: A Study of Paul Durcan*, Dublin: New Island Books.

Townend, Paul A. (2002) *Father Mathew, Temperance and Irish Identity*, Dublin: Irish Academic Press.

Tweedy, Hilda (1992) *A Link in the Chain: The Story of the Irish Housewives' Association 1942–1992*, Dublin: Attic.

Vance, Norman (1990) *Irish Literature: A Social History*, Oxford: Blackwell.

Vaughan, W. E. (1984) *Landlords and Tenants in Ireland, 1848–1904*, Dundalk: Studies in Irish Economic and Social History.

Waddell, John (1998) *The Prehistoric Archaeology of Ireland*, Galway: Galway University Press.

Walker, Graham (1985) *The Politics of Frustration: Harry Midgeley and the Failure of Labour in Northern Ireland*, Manchester: Manchester University Press.

Wallis, Geoff and Wilson, Sue (2001) *The Rough Guide to Irish Music*, London: Rough Guides/Penguin.

Walsh, Dermot P. J. (2000) *Bloody Sunday and the Rule of Law in Northern Ireland*, Basingstoke: Macmillan.

Walsh, Micheline Kearney (1996) *Hugh O'Neill, An Exile of Ireland, Prince of Ulster*, Dublin: Four Courts.

Ward, Margaret (1983) *Unmanageable Revolutionaries: Women and Irish Nationalism*, London: Pluto.

Ward, Margaret (1991) *Maud Gonne: Ireland's Joan of Arc*, London: Pandora.

Watson, G. J. (1994) *Irish Identity and the Literary Revival*, Washington, DC: Catholic University of America.

Welch, Robert (1993) *Changing States*, London: Routledge.

Welch, Robert (2003) *The Abbey Theatre, 1899–1999: Form and Pressure*, Oxford: Oxford University Press.

White, Harry (1998) *The Keeper's Recital: Music and Cultural History in Ireland, 1770–1970*, Cork: Cork University Press.

Whyte, John (1996) *Interpreting Northern Ireland*, Oxford: Clarendon Press.

Whyte, Nicholas (1999) 'The Irish astronomical tradition', in *Science, Colonialism and Ireland*, Cork: Cork University Press.

Wills, Clair (1993) *Improprieties: Politics and Sexuality in Northern Irish Poetry*, Oxford: Clarendon Press.

Wills, Clair (1998) *Reading Paul Muldoon*, Newcastle-upon-Tyne: Bloodaxe.

Winstanley, M. J. (1984) *Ireland and the Land Question 1800–1922*, London: Methuen.

Wohlgelernter, Maurice (1977) *Frank O'Connor: An Introduction*, New York: Columbia University Press.

Woodham-Smith, Cecil (1962 repr. 1970) *The Great Hunger: Ireland 184–49*, London: New English Library.

Yeats, W. B. and Kinsella, Thomas (1971) *Davis, Mangan, Ferguson*, Dublin: Dolmen Press.

Younger, Calton (1981) *Arthur Griffith*, Dublin: Gill and Macmillan.

Index

Achill, see art
Adamnán, see Columba
Addison, Joseph, see Berkeley, Swift
Adorno, Theodor, see authenticity
Advent, see Coffey
Aestheticism, see Synge, Yeats (W. B.)
Aghowle, see Finnian
Águila, Don Juan del, see Kinsale
Aherne, Bertie, see Fianna Fáil, Smyth Case
AIDS, see contraception, 'X' Case
Aidan of Dalriada, see Columba
Aiken, Frank, see Civil War
aisling, see Ó Rathaille
algebra, see Hamilton, mathematics
Algeria, see postcolonialism and
    colonialism
Allegiance (Fidelity), Oath of, see Treaty,
    Anglo-Irish (1921)
Allegories for Ulster, see art
allegory, see Spenser, Swift, *Táin*
Allen, William O'Meara, see Manchester
    Martyrs
Allgood, Sara, see Gregory
Alliance Party, see unionism
Altan, see traditional and folk music
America (USA), see emigration, diaspora,
    film, Good Friday Agreement (1998),
    rock and pop music, television and
    radio, Volunteers
Amnesty International, see Troubles
Amongst Women, see McGahern, television
    and radio
An Claidheamh Soluis, see Literary Revival
An Túr Gloine/The Glass Tower Studio, see
    art

Ancient Order of Hibernians, see marches
Andrews, John, see unionism, World War II
Angela's Ashes, see diaspora, film
anglophobia, see Famine
Annaghdown, see Brendan the Navigator
    (St)
Annals of Chile, The, see Muldoon
*Annals of Connacht, Inisfallen, Loch Cé,
    Ulster*, see *Annals of the Four Masters*
Annan Report, see television and radio
Anti-Discrimination (Pay) Act (1974), see
    women
Aoibheal, Queen, see Merriman
Apprentice Boys of Derry; see Paisley,
    Lundy, marches
Aran Islands, see film, Ó Direán,
    O'Flaherty, Synge, Yeats (J. B.)
Áras an Uachtarán, see Robinson, Mary
Ardagh Chalice, see art
Ardmore Studios, see film
Ardnacrusha, see electrification
Ards Peninsula, see colonization
Arena, see literary and cultural journals
Arensberg, see familism
*Argument on Behalf of the Catholics of
    Ireland*, see Tone
Aristotle, see Celts
Arlen House Press, see Boland
Armagh, see astronomy, Patrick (St)
Armagh County, see Ulster Plantation
Armenians, see diaspora
Arminianism, see Presbyterianism, Trinity
    College Dublin (TCD)
Arms Trial, see Haughey, Fianna Fáil,
    republicanism

Undertones, The, see rock and pop music
unemployment, see Dublin, emigration,
    O'Flaherty
United Ireland Party, see Cumann na
    nGaeldeal, Blueshirts, Fine Gael
United Ireland, The, see Land League
United Irish League, see Irish
    Parliamentary Party
United Irishman, The, see Mitchel
United Ulster Unionist Council, see power
    sharing, Ulster Workers' Council Strike
UUP, see Ulster Unionist Party
UVF, see Ulster Volunteer Force
Unlawful Societies Act (1825), see Orange
    Order
Unnameable, The, see Beckett
Untilled Field, The, see Moore (George)

Vallency, Charles, see antiquarianism
Van Dieman's Land, see Mitchel, O'Brien,
    William Smith
van Nost, John, see art
Vanbrugh Quartet, see music
Vaughan Williams, Ralph, see music
Vatican Council, Second (1962–65), see
    Catholicism
Verner, Jane, see Mitchel
Versailles Treaty (1919), see art
Vicar of Wakefield, The, see Goldsmith
Victory, Gerard, see music
Vierpyl, Simon, see art
View of the Present State of Ireland, A, see
    Spenser
Vindicator, The, see Duffy
Virgil (*Aeneid*), see Stanihurst
Virgin Mary, see sex and sexuality
Vocaycion, The, see Reformation and
    Counter-Reformation
Volans, Kevin, see music

Wagner, Richard, see Moore (George),
    Shaw
Waiting for Godot, see Beckett
Wales, see Brendan the Navigator (St),
    Finnian, Gerald of Wales, internment
Walker, Joseph, see music
Wallace, William, see medicine

Walsh, Catherine, see literary and cultural
    journals
War of the Buttons, The, see film
Warbeck, Perkin, see Parliament
Ward, Judith, see Troubles
Warren, Raymond, see music
Waterford, see Vikings
Wayne, John, see film
Week-End of Dermot and Grace, The, see
    Watters
Wejchert, Alexandra, see art
Welfare State, see medicine, Stormont
Wellington, Duke of, see Catholic
    Emancipation
West, the, see art, Corkery, Irish-Ireland,
    Irish language, Irish-language
    literature, Literary Revival, Sayers,
    Synge, Yeats (J. B.),
    Yeats (W. B.)
West Africans, see diaspora
'West Britonism', see Irish-Ireland
West, Harry, see power sharing
Wexford, see Cromwell, Vikings
Whelan, Bill, see television and radio
Whelehan, Harry, see Smyth Case, 'X' Case
Whistle in the Dark, see Murphy (Thomas)
Whistler, James MacNeill, see art
whiskey, see alcohol
Whitaker, T. J., see economic expansion,
    Lemass
White Stag Group, see art
Whitelaw, William, see direct rule, power
    sharing
Whitman, Walt, see MacDonagh
'Whiskey in the Jar', see rock and pop
    music
Who Bombed Birmingham?, see television
    and radio
Wide Street Commission, see Dublin
Widgery Lord, see Bloody Sunday, Kinsella
Winding Stair, The, see Yeats (W. B.)
Windsor, Treaty of (1175), see Norman
    Invasion
Woman Calling, A, see television and radio
Women of Belfast, see art
women's employment, see family, women
Woodenbridge, see Redmond
Woodward, Benjamin, see architecture

LIBRARY, UNIVERSITY COLLEGE CHESTER